Gogol from the
Twentieth Century

Э. Мамонтов
1852. М.

Gogol from the
Twentieth Century

ELEVEN ESSAYS

Selected, Edited, Translated, and Introduced by

ROBERT A. MAGUIRE

PRINCETON UNIVERSITY PRESS
PRINCETON, NEW JERSEY

*Library of Congress Cataloging in Publication data will
be found on the last printed page of this book*

Publication of this book has been aided by a grant from
the Andrew W. Mellon Foundation

Printed in the United States of America
by Princeton University Press, Princeton, New Jersey

First Princeton Paperback printing,
with corrections, 1976

For Leon and Galina Stilman

Preface

FOR nearly a century and a half, Nikolay Vasilievich Gogol has remained consistently popular in Russia, as a reader's companion and a writer's friend. He has also been irresistible to critics of all temperaments, styles, and philosophies; indeed, much of the history of Russian literary criticism could be written around the opinions generated by him. He has been proclaimed a realist and a fantast; a subtle student of the human heart and a creator of cardboard characters; a revolutionary and a reactionary; a monger of the lewd and a hierophant of the sublime; a pathological liar and an honest anatomist of the soul; a self-promoter and a self-immolator; a typical Russian and a typical Ukrainian; a narrow nationalist and a universal genius; a jejune jokester and a tragic poet.

The anthology offered here explores the happy coincidence of perceptive and interesting critics dealing with one of the giants of world literature. Each of the eleven essays has been chosen for intrinsic merit, in the belief that it will help elucidate Gogol's art from an angle generally unfamiliar to readers who know no Russian. At the same time, each essay illustrates one of the major approaches or schools of criticism that have been cultivated by Russians in the twentieth century: the psychological, the religious or theological, the sociological, the historical or comparative, and the formalistic or structural. In my opinion, these essays are among the best representatives of an impressive critical achievement that is only now beginning to come to the notice of non-specialists outside Russia. My introductory essay attempts to sketch out the main lines of development and to account for the nineteenth-century background as well.

Other considerations have also guided the choice of essays. One is availability: with a single exception (Eichenbaum),[1] none has been turned into English before; many are hard to come by even in the original Russian. Another is coverage of Gogol's work. Naturally, *Dead Souls* and *The Inspector General*, being his major

---

[1] As "The Structure of Gogol's 'Overcoat,'" *The Russian Review*, No. 4, 1963. I had at first intended to reprint it here, but it required such substantial revisions that I finally decided to make a new translation.

achievements, tend to figure prominently. "The Overcoat," as his best and most famous short story, seemed to warrant two essays, which offer interesting points of comparison and contrast. Other essays deal specifically with "The Nose" and *Evenings on a Farm Near Dikanka*, and also at least make reference to nearly everything Gogol wrote. Finally, all the essays date from the twentieth century: many of their assumptions and techniques will be familiar to readers of modern British and American criticism.

The fact that this collection is not intended primarily for specialists in Russian literature has persuaded me of the need to annotate the individual articles rather copiously and the general introduction rather sparingly. Annotations have been provided for all important names, places and events. To avoid duplication, I have made each annotation only once; the relevant page is indicated in italics in the index. My own annotations are enclosed in square brackets; all others belong to the author of the article in question.

Two of the essays—Pereverzev's and Yermakov's—are chapters from book-length studies. The others are complete in themselves. My translations, naturally, strive to honor the letter and spirit of the originals, but I have not hesitated to edit for the sake of clarity—dropping some details that are of importance only to specialists, cropping particularly sprawling specimens of prose, rearranging paragraphs, making expansions of otherwise cryptic points. My introductory remarks to each essay characterize the kind of changes (if any) that have been made. I have checked all quotations from Gogol against the originals—as found in the fourteen-volume Soviet Academy of Sciences edition of the complete works—have made corrections where necessary, and have identified the sources when a critic fails to do so. In many cases I have updated the bibliographical references in the articles (e.g., for Chernyshevsky, Herzen, Annenkov and Aksakov).

I am assuming that readers are familiar with the prose fiction and the plays of Gogol. These are readily available in English.[2]

---

[2] The best—and most easily obtained—are *Dead Souls*, translated and with a foreword by Bernard Guilbert Guerney, New York, The Modern Library (revised edition), 1965; *The Collected Tales and Plays of Nikolai Gogol*, edited and with an introduction and notes by Leonard J. Kent, New York, The Modern Library, 1969. Of Gogol's non-fictional writings, *Selected Passages from Correspondence with Friends* is available in English, as is a selection of his letters (see the bibliography). Virtually none of his articles has yet been translated, however. See also the Selected Bibliography, on page 405.

In the interest of consistency, however, I have decided to make my own translations. As any student of Russian knows, this is a perilous undertaking: Gogol is undoubtedly the most eccentric stylist in the language. One of his contemporaries, the famous lexicographer Vladimir Dal, put it this way: "Gogol is an extraordinary person! You are carried away by his narrative, you avidly gulp down absolutely everything, you re-read it again and you don't notice the peculiar language in which he writes. You begin to analyze it minutely, and you see that a person absolutely ought not to write and speak this way. You try to correct it and you spoil it—you can't touch a word. What would happen if he wrote in Russian?"[3] Faced with this problem, most translators choose to flatten Gogol's style into "readable" English. I have tried to resist this temptation and have instead hoped to convey some of the peculiarly piquant flavor of the original, very often at the price of "smooth" English (this is especially true of Gogol's non-fiction). My principle, in short, has been to translate as literally as possible.

Two systems of transliteration of the Cyrillic are in effect here. One applies to proper names, and tries to suggest the pronunciation of the originals. For example, "Ermakov" comes out as "Yermakov," "Alekseevna" as "Alexeyevna." (For a few well-known names, I have used the versions that seem to be most common in English, for example, "Dostoevsky" rather than "Dostoyevsky.") In citing Russian titles in the notes, however, I have used a more "scholarly" system, in this case the British Standard, with some slight modifications, the most significant of which renders ё as e. But even in the notes I have stuck to the less "scholarly" system for the names of authors, in order to avoid double entries in the index.

Much of the reading for this book was done at Oxford University. I am grateful to the staff of the Taylor Institution for courteous and efficient help, and especially to J.S.G. Simmons, now Librarian of All Souls College, for his hospitality, his many kindnesses, and his willingness to put his enormous erudition at my disposal whenever I needed it. The Columbia University Council for Research in the Humanities provided a summer grant which helped me to work in Oxford. A number of colleagues read parts of the manuscript and offered helpful suggestions in matters of

---

[3] Letter of V. F. Dal to M. P. Pogodin, April 1, 1842, as cited in *Literaturnoe nasledstvo*, Vol. 58 (*Pushkin. Lermontov. Gogol'*), Moscow, 1952, p. 617.

translation and annotation: Albert E. Anderson, Nina Berberova, Maurice Friedberg, Richard F. Gustafson, William E. Harkins, Eva Kagan-Kans, Charles A. Moser, Anne Pennington, Rose Raskin, Richard Sheldon, Leon and Galina Stilman, Graeme Tytler, the late Boris Unbegaun, and Mrs. Boris Unbegaun. Edward Braun of Bristol University was kind enough to lend me his microfilm copy of the Ivanov article. F. W. Maguire made helpful editorial suggestions. I am very much indebted to Miss Lalor Cadley, formerly of Princeton University Press, for constant encouragement, and to Mrs. Arthur Sherwood, my editor at Princeton, for friendly and patient counsel throughout. Finally, I owe very special thanks to V., who will understand what I mean.

For foreign readers, Gogol's genius has been harder to appreciate than Dostoevsky's, Tolstoy's, or Chekhov's. But no Russian doubts that it is a genius of the highest order; it is my hope that the essays contained in this anthology will help the English-speaking reader understand why this is so.

New York, 1973   ROBERT A. MAGUIRE

Table of Contents

Abbreviations

1. *PSS*, in the notes, stands for Gogol's complete works in the Academy of Sciences edition: *Polnoe sobranie sochinenii*, 14 vols., Izdatel'stvo Akademii Nauk SSSR, Moscow-Leningrad, 1940-1952. Individual volumes and page numbers are specified in the references.

2. Gogol's letters are contained in Vols. x-xiv of the Academy edition. I identify them by addressee and date, using the new style unless otherwise designated (as o.s., old style). The Julian Calendar (o.s.) was used in Russia until 1918, and then was replaced by the Gregorian calendar. But most of Gogol's letters were written from outside Russia and honor the Gregorian scheme.

3. "The Two Ivans" stands for "The Tale of How Ivan Ivanovich Quarrelled with Ivan Nikiforovich."

4. *Evenings*, or *Evenings on a Farm* stands for *Evenings on a Farm Near Dikanka*.

Gogol from the
Twentieth Century

PACKING SLIP:
Amazon Marketplace Item: Gogol From the Twentieth Century [Paperback] by Maguire,
Robert A.
Listing ID: 0214W248198
SKU:
Quantity: 1

0691013268

Introduction

The Legacy of Criticism

I

"IT ALWAYS seemed to me," Gogol wrote toward the end of his life, "that I would become well known, that a wide area of activities was awaiting me, and that I would even do something for the general good."[1] As a nineteen-year-old graduate of an obscure secondary school in the Ukraine, Nikolay Vasilievich Gogol set out for St. Petersburg in December 1828, to follow up his hunch. He did not know just where it would take him: literature was only one possibility; government service and the theater were others. His debut as a writer would have discouraged anyone with a feebler sense of destiny. In May 1829, he published, at his own expense, a long "idyll in scenes" cast in meters borrowed from Pushkin and entitled *Hanz Küchelgarten.* Only two critics took notice; both consigned it to oblivion. Gogol complied: he bought up all the copies he could find and burned them. That was the end of his career as a poet, and the end of "V. Alov," the pseudonym he had adopted. He then switched to prose fiction, began to publish—now under his own name, and no longer at his own expense—stories of Ukrainian life, and in 1831 and 1832 put out a two-volume collection entitled *Evenings on a Farm Near Dikanka.* With their blend of lyricism, humor, folklore, the supernatural, and the demonic, these stories fed the public appetite for "romantic" treatments of subjects then considered "exotic." Now the critics spoke of a fresh and promising talent, and Gogol was suddenly a celebrity.

Had he died just then, he would have rated a footnote in literary histories as one of the better representatives of a populous breed of local colorists active at the time. It was only with the appearance, in 1835, of two new volumes of stories—*Arabesques*

---

[1] "Avtorskaya ispoved'," *PSS*, VIII, 1952, 438. This work was written in 1847, but published posthumously (1855). Actually, the manuscript bears no title; that was added by S. P. Shevyryov for the publication.

and *Mirgorod*—and the production, a year later, of the play *The Inspector General*, that he was established as a major writer who marked a decisive turn in the direction of Russian literature. Vissarion Belinsky, who was just beginning a career that would make him the most important critic of the time, even ranked him beside Pushkin. The death of Pushkin in 1837 made it seem likely that Gogol was now the greatest living Russian writer; the death of Lermontov and the publication of *Dead Souls* in 1842 made it a certainty.

The appeal of Gogol's works certainly did not depend on their story line, which by and large was rudimentary or—in the case of *The Inspector General* and *Dead Souls*—already familiar to the public in the form of anecdotes. His settings and stylistic mannerisms, though striking, were not entirely strange to readers either. He began to write at a time when a new esthetic was developing in Russian literature, one that set prose fiction above poetry, focused on the lower orders of society, saw man as a communal animal, found dirt and evil prevalent in the world, and mixed an olio of modes and genres within a single work. Most of the devotees of this new style—it would come to be called realism or naturalism—had been hacks, toiling away in the lesser journals but admirably documenting (as mediocrity tends to do) the changes that were in progress. But in Gogol, Russia found a writer capable of turning this style into an artistic achievement of such power as to signal the onset of a new literary age.

As heirs to the German romantic movement, young Russians of the 1830's were intensely concerned with the problem of nationality. There was a strong feeling that a great writer, a "Russian Homer," must arise to give expression to the soul of the restless and burgeoning *narod*, or "people." Neither Vasily Zhukovsky (1783-1852) nor Alexander Pushkin (1799-1837) quite qualified: though acknowledged as great poets, both came out of the eighteenth century, and were therefore considered beholden to the literary values of Western Europe. The point was made graphically and querulously by Belinsky, who stated that, as of 1834, "*we have no literature.*" A year later, however, the appearance of *Arabesques* and *Mirgorod* prompted him to hope that in Gogol Russia had produced a writer who would create a truly national literature, independent of foreign models.[2]

[2] The quotation (Belinsky's italics) comes from "Literaturnye mechtaniya," as in *Polnoe sobranie sochinenii*, I, Moscow, 1953, 23; the opinions

The fact that Gogol began his career when Pushkin was at the height of his powers helped define his originality. In the eyes of contemporaries, no two writers could have been less alike. To be sure, Pushkin had written prose fiction, and had also cultivated many of the mannerisms of the new style, as any reader of *Eugene Onegin* was aware. But in the public mind he was above all an aristocrat and a poet, who represented the "classical" values of balance, clarity, and elegant simplicity, was indifferent to topical social problems, and even seemed vaguely "foreign" in his intimate knowledge of French and English literature. Gogol was regarded as his opposite in every important respect. The contrast at first served merely to define a change in literary generations. But before long it took deep root and branched out to cover the whole of Russian literature. "Pushkin" and "Gogol" came to stand for two "schools" of writing, each thoroughly national, but each very different; and Russians have been classifying their literature accordingly ever since. To the "Pushkin" school are assigned mainly poets, such as Afanasy Fet, Anna Akhmatova, and the later Pasternak, as well as a few prose writers like Tolstoy and Turgenev. To the "Gogol" school belong most of the better novelists, such as Dostoevsky, Saltykov-Shchedrin, Bely, and Nabokov. At issue here is not the validity of the contrast (which is familiar to every schoolchild), but its persistence as a truism in the national mind, and its effect on the ways Russians read their writers, including, of course, Gogol.

---

on *Mirgorod* and *Arabesques* are found in "O russkoi povesti i povestyakh g. Gogolya ('Arabeski' i 'Mirgorod')," *Polnoe sobranie sochinenii*, I, Moscow, 1953, 259-307.

The fact that Gogol was Ukrainian by origin did not bother Belinsky: he regarded this as a variant of Russian nationality. In families of the middle gentry, like Gogol's, Ukrainian was spoken with the peasants. Gogol's father, an amateur writer, turned out comedies in Ukrainian. But the moment anything "serious" arose, Russian was used: business dealings, education, government service, etc. And anyone who aspired to more than local celebrity as an author had to write in Russian, as Gogol always did. Over the decades, there has been much speculation about the influence of the Ukrainian language of Gogol's often peculiar Russian. See, e.g., V. V. Vinogradov, "Yazyk Gogolya," in *N. V. Gogol': Materialy i issledovaniya*, II, ed. V. V. Gippius, Moscow-Leningrad, 1936, 281-376. The literature in Russian on the problem of "nationality" (*narodnost'*) is vast. For an especially interesting discussion as it concerns Gogol, see D. A. Ovsyaniko-Kulikovsky, *Gogol'* (*Sobranie sochinenii*, I), 4th ed., St. Petersburg, 1912, 140-142, 157-163.

Other clusters of themes, just as striking and insistent, soon began to form; they were to recur, in various guises, over the course of a century and a half. They concerned: (1) Gogol's subject matter, and his approach to it; (2) the social and political implications of his works; (3) his own life and personality.

Discussions of the first point turned around Gogol's "realism," or, as it was usually put, around the accuracy of his portraits of Russian life. Since those portraits, from 1835 on, were largely of a gloomy and sordid nature, more than mere theory was at stake. Two opposing views were advanced. One saw Gogol's settings, characters, and language as faithful copies of originals: Russia therefore was a nasty and depressing land. The other insisted that reality cannot be entirely negative: the absence of ennobling elements in Gogol's works therefore robbed them of any claim to realism, and made them "dirty" and "low" caricatures. Somewhere in between stood Belinsky. He thought that literary realism neither mirrors nor caricatures, but rather "reflects [life's] various phenomena from one point of view, as if in a convex glass, selecting those aspects which are needed for the formulation of a full, live, and unified image." The result, in Gogol's work, was a typical picture of Russia.[3]

The next question arose naturally from the first. Did all these scenes of venality, stupidity, filth, fear, and despair serve purely esthetic purposes? A few critics apparently thought so, in their insistence that Gogol's works were nothing more than farces aimed at providing harmless entertainment. A greater number believed that Gogol was trying to convey some serious message of moral uplift, but insisted that it bore on individual vices and not on society as a whole. Most commentators, however, did seem to regard Gogol as a social satirist who was bent on pointing up the discrepancies between the real and the ideal world. His humor, in Pushkin's famous phrase, amounted to "laughter through tears,"[4] and it was supposed to provoke indignation and reform.

It was Gogol's personality, however, which exerted the strongest pull on the minds of his contemporaries. He was one of the most bizarre figures of an age that prized eccentricity. To be sure, his

[3] "O russkoi povesti i povestyakh g. Gogolya ('Arabeski' i 'Mirgorod')," *Polnoe sobranie sochinenii*, I, Moscow, 1953, 267.

[4] Review of second edition of *Evenings on a Farm Near Dikanka*, published in *Sovremennik*, No. 1, 1836. Gogol himself later used the same formulation in *Dead Souls* (Part 1, ch. seven).

external biography was unremarkable. He was born in 1809 into a family of small landowners near Dikanka, in the Ukraine. After a thoroughly indulged childhood, he was sent to the school at Nezhin in 1821. There he remained seven years, and then traveled to St. Petersburg in search of his "mission." He failed as an actor; he failed as a poet; he failed as a civil servant. *Evenings on a Farm Near Dikanka* brought him fame, and connected him with the literary luminaries of the capital, among them Zhukovsky and Pushkin. Between 1832 and 1836 he put in a brief and disastrous stretch as a teacher of history at St. Petersburg University, conceived the ideas for virtually all the works of fiction he would ever write, and completed *Mirgorod*, *Arabesques*, and *The Inspector General*. In 1836, he went abroad, where he remained—mostly in Rome—for twelve years, with only two brief trips back to Russia. During the 1840's he finished off the first volume of *Dead Souls* and worked away at the second; but he was becoming more and more preoccupied with a quest for religious verities and self-perfection, which he documented in obsessive letter-writing and tried to formulate definitively in *Selected Passages from Correspondence with Friends* (1847). A pilgrimage to the Holy Land in 1848 failed to bring the spiritual invigoration he had hoped for; in 1851 he returned to Russia, settled in Moscow, and lived there, increasingly self-critical, for the one year that remained to him. He could not make the continuation of *Dead Souls* say what he wished it to; and, repeating what he had done twice before—with an earlier version of this same work, and with *Hanz Küchelgarten* —he threw the manuscript into the fire. Part of it was rescued; but this was, in effect, his farewell to life. A few weeks later he died, largely from self-willed malnutrition and general debilitation. The date was February 22, 1852; he was just short of forty-three.[5]

Though not exciting in outline, Gogol's life did make a pattern that was suggestive to sensibilities nourished on romanticism. As a Ukrainian, he came from an area that Russians regarded as "romantic." With the city of St. Petersburg he demonstrated a

[5] For fuller accounts in English of Gogol's life, see: David Magarshack, *Gogol*, London, 1957; Vsevolod Setchkarev, *Gogol—His Life and Works*, New York, 1965; Victor Erlich, *Gogol*, New Haven and London, 1969; Henri Troyat, *Divided Soul: The Life of Gogol*, New York, 1973. Gogol's letters also provide much valuable information; an anthology is now available in English (*Letters of Nikolai Gogol*, selected and edited by Carl R. Proffer, Ann Arbor, 1967).

love-hate relationship that was characteristically romantic. He was a rootless man, who never married, never had a love affair, found friendships difficult, and chronically complained of being misunderstood. His wedge-shaped face, his long nose, and his evasive ways all suggested demonic mystery. He exiled himself from Russia and settled into a fashionably impoverished life in Rome—one of the more romantic cities in what was of course the most romantic country in Europe. His death amounted to suicide and was regarded by many as an act of protest against the world.

There was also a political dimension to the reading public's conception of the romantic artist, in Russia as in the West. He was regarded as a champion of man's free spirit and therefore as an opponent (conscious or not) of the established order. The point had particular validity in a country like Russia, which was ruled by an autocrat and had a long history of censorship of the written word—sometimes benevolent, but often draconian: Radishchev had been condemned to death, Pushkin had been exiled to the south, Polezhayev had been conscripted into the army as a common soldier. Minor encounters with the censors were a routine occupational hazard; Gogol knew that from the church scene in "The Nose," which the censor pronounced blasphemous, and from the title of *Dead Souls*, which was taken as an impermissible denial of immortality. Such encounters no doubt encouraged many writers to view themselves as practitioners of a "liberal" profession. They could make no plainly subversive political statements in their works; but readers of a certain inclination—helped by like-minded critics—could always find them there. And when pictures of political corruption and social stagnation were presented in Gogol's vivid manner, it was not hard for younger critics with radical leanings to see them as thinly disguised protests against the political establishment.

The publication, in 1847, of *Selected Passages from Correspondence with Friends* came as a shock to such readers. This book grew out of Gogol's long and intensifying preoccupation with the problem of evil. He hoped to make Russians aware of the maladies of their country, and to prescribe remedies. In the thirty-two articles, most of which were based on actual letters to acquaintances, Gogol ranged over the major areas of life in Russia—religious, political, social, economic, and literary—as well as the state of his own soul. He called for moral regeneration through a scrupulous observance of Christian humility within

the existing structure of "everything our Church and our government have decreed for us by law."[6] He considered *Selected Passages* his most important work, and with it he hoped to "atone
for the uselessness" of all his earlier writings, which had "led almost everyone into error with regard to their true meaning," a
meaning he now insisted was moral, not social.[7]

Late in his life Gogol asserted that his political and social views
had never basically changed. No doubt he was right. Those views
had always been conservative, and, like his spiritual struggles, had
been amply documented in a voluminous correspondence. Why,
then, did *Selected Passages* stir up such a fuss? Even Gogol's conservative friends were shocked by what they took to be arrogance,
spiritual pride, false humility, and plain bad taste: the book read
virtually like a parody of their own preoccupations. Officials of
the church and the government resented Gogol's passion for lectur-
ing them about their own business. Among younger readers of
radical mind, however, it was the ideas that excited the greatest
indignation. Belinsky spoke most eloquently for them in a letter
to Gogol that was an acknowledgment of deep disappointment, if
not virtually heartbreak. "Why, if you had made an attempt on
my life, even then I would not have hated you more than I do
for these shameful lines." For "I loved you with all the passion with
which a man bound to his country by blood ties is capable of loving
that country's hope, honor, glory, and one of its great leaders on
the road of reason, self-awareness, development, and progress."
But now, Belinsky said, Gogol had lost the right to such love. He
had refused to see that Russia was ruled by "huge corporations of
sundry official thieves and robbers," and instead had come forth as
"the advocate of the knout, the apostle of ignorance, the champion
of obscurantism and benightedness, the panegyrist of Tartar morals," who was trying to pass off "lies and immorality as truth and
virtue."[8]

[6] Letter to P. A. Pletnyov, October 20, 1846.

[7] "Predislovie," *Vybrannye mesta iz perepiski s druz'yami, PSS*, VIII, 1952,
215, 216. The first English translation of this book, by Jesse Zeldin, appeared in 1969 (Nashville, Tennessee). It contains many mistakes, but
is useful nonetheless.

[8] "(Pis'mo k N. V. Gogolyu)," *Polnoe sobranie sochinenii*, X, Moscow,
1956, 212, 213, 214. This letter is reproduced in the Academy of Sciences
edition of Gogol's works (*PSS*, VIII), presumably as a kind of antidote to
Selected Passages, which appears in the same volume. Gogol returned a

This letter immediately became radical scripture. For many years it was considered subversive by the government, and existed only in manuscript (finally being published in 1872). One of the charges brought against Dostoevsky at the time of his arrest in 1849 was that he had helped circulate it. But it is perhaps more interesting as evidence of the crumbling of a myth that had been created in defiance of the evidence. *Selected Passages*, in its way, was as revolutionary as anything Belinsky envisaged; but that way was certainly not his.

The question of motives naturally arose at once. Why should Gogol apparently have betrayed all his earlier work? The possibility of sincere religious conversion was allowed only by a few like-minded friends. Some people suggested mental derangement (his letters are a litany of sundry disabilities, emotional and physical). Some suspected that he might be trying to tap a few conservative roubles (the book expressed gratitude to the Emperor for a stipend). But the interpretation put forth by Belinsky was destined to have the longest life and the strongest influence on later critical opinion. Faced with the apparently hopeless contradiction between *Selected Passages* and everything else Gogol had written, Belinsky simply decided that the new book was unimportant: Gogol's place in Russian literature rested on his earlier work, which remained unaffected by this unfortunate and incomprehensible aberration.[9]

This distinction was already implicit in a view of the mind that was widely held in Gogol's time. According to Belinsky's version of it, the mind is made up of two large areas: one contains the creative process and is responsible for art; the other contains the faculties of logical thinking, and produces scholarship, science, and criticism. The main difference lies in the means by which each process operates: "One [the rational] *proves* and the other [the creative] *shows*, and both *convince*—the one, however, by logical arguments, the other by pictures [images]."[10] Ideally, these two sides are in harmony; the great artist should also be a great

---

wounded but relatively gentle reply (August 10, 1847), after tearing up his first version, which was savage and often incoherent.

[9] "Otvet 'Moskvityaninu,'" *Polnoe sobranie sochinenii*, x, Moscow, 1956, 227.

[10] "Vzglyad na russkuyu literaturu 1847 goda," *Polnoe sobranie sochinenii*, x, Moscow, 1956, 311.

thinker. But Gogol's career indicated that this was not necessarily so. He was, in effect, split into two entirely different persons. One, the artist, was a towering genius, and therefore served the highest humanitarian (and political) ideals; the other, the thinker, lacked intelligence, common sense, even decency, and must therefore be ignored. This idea of "two Gogols" had been put forth earlier by other critics; it was implicit in romantic esthetics, which thrived on dualities, such as the real versus the ideal. Belinsky's version, however, has proved to be the most enduring. Many critics have taken exception to it, but exceptions depend, of course, on the recognition of rules. It was the last of the truisms about Gogol to be formulated in his lifetime, and it has been perhaps the hardiest of them all.

These early critics set out all the major themes that future generations would honor: realism, typicality, nationality, humor, satire, the two Gogols, and so on.[11] They regarded good art primarily as the vehicle of good ideas, and emphasized the duties and responsibilities of the artist to society. Along with a tendency to moralize about art went an indifference to style, or, rather, a subsumption of style under moralizing criteria too: hence the discussions of Gogol's language in terms of "high" and "low," or the speculations on how "national" in spirit his odd linguistic usages might be. Most of these critics were keenly aware that Gogol's work did not readily fit into the literary systems of the past; but they found it difficult to throw off the hold of those systems and articulate what was new and unique in Gogol. It is easy, however, to indulge in disparagement more than a century later. We may find much of this criticism shallow and unreadable now, but it ought to be judged in the context of its own time. As a later distinguished critic of Gogol pointed out, the important thing is what Gogol "seemed to be to his *audience*, his contemporaries, his readers."[12] And Gogol's own view of the nature of art virtually coincided with that of the majority of his contemporaries. He had always seen himself as being entrusted with a mission to serve

---

[11] For a useful survey of critical opinions about Gogol in his own time, see Paul Debreczeny, *Nikolay Gogol and His Contemporary Critics*, Philadelphia, *Transactions of the American Philosophical Society*, New Series, Vol. 56, Part 3, 1966.

[12] Vasily Rozanov, "Gogolevskie dni v Moskve," *Sredi khudozhnikov*, St. Petersburg, 1914, p. 261.

Russia and be useful to society. His obsession with self-purification in the 1840's was entirely consistent with this view. Its terms were not Belinsky's, but both men agreed on the principle of service as the artist's highest obligation.

This body of commentary on Gogol could never have acquired the weight of a living tradition if literary criticism, in those years, had not come to occupy a position in Russian culture that in prestige and power was almost the equal of the writer's. For criticism had to do with more than mere "literature." Or better, the conception of literature reached out beyond the text itself to society as a whole, as an entity to be not merely depicted, but guided and instructed as well. The critic saw it as his duty to clarify what he considered implicit in the text, to translate the language of art into the language of usable ideas. This view of the role of criticism is exemplified in the career of Vissarion Belinsky, the first fully professional critic in Russia. His rise to eminence made it plain that, by the 1840's, literary criticism was one of the few "intellectual" occupations outside government service open to young men from the lower reaches of society: he himself was the son of an obscure ship's doctor.

Gogol always took a keen interest in the opinions of his critics, or, at least, he professed to do so. Like most writers, he constantly complained of being misunderstood. In his later years, particularly after the spectacular fiasco of *Selected Passages*, his letters were filled with appeals for *negative* criticism; this, he felt, would help him steer a truer course in his quest for self-perfection, and thereby enable him to bring the troublesome second volume of *Dead Souls* to a "positive" conclusion. The pathological implications of such an attitude aside, the parallel careers of Gogol and Belinsky are striking testimony to the close link that existed between belles-lettres and criticism and brought them together under the larger heading of "literature." The two men achieved prominence at about the same time, wrote all their major works contemporaneously, and climaxed their careers in 1847, with Belinsky's final illness (he died the following year) and Gogol's *Selected Passages*. It is absurd to suggest, as some critics have done, that Gogol was virtually the creation of an intensive publicity campaign waged by Belinsky. But Belinsky did manage to make him the measure of all new Russian literature for decades; to this day, most Russians (whether school children or professional critics) cannot think of one without also thinking of the other.

II

Gogol's death in 1852 opened a new phase of criticism, which lasted until nearly the end of the century. The basic themes established in the earlier period now put down deeper roots. But critics began to approach Gogol with a fundamentally different attitude.

It was Nikolay Chernyshevsky, the most influential critic of the 1860's, who set the tone. He insisted that the "two Gogols" theory was false. *Selected Passages*, however regrettable its ideas—and, as a radical, Chernyshevsky found them repellent—was nonetheless the sincere utterance of "an honest enthusiast" who was only endeavoring to "perform the duty imposed on him by his conscience," and who remained "one of the noblest people of our century."[13] The book represented no deviation from the earlier period (as Belinsky had thought) but grew organically from it. Despite apparent contradictions, all Gogol's life and work formed a pattern, and the job of the critic was to uncover it. He must put moralizing aside and ask *why* Gogol had acted as he did. The answers would be found not in speculation on Gogol's intentions or motivations, but in a close examination of his milieu. All men, in Chernyshevsky's view, were basically the same in their instincts and desires; differences were accountable to environment, which either promoted or hindered (usually the latter) the right use of inborn qualities. Study a society, therefore, and you know the men who lived in it.

Chernyshevsky's Gogol was a representative man in nearly all respects: typical of a society intellectually no more advanced than he; typical of a self-educated man who sees life as merely a series of disconnected, patternless phenomena; typical of any human being in his desire to associate with the rich and the famous. Unique to him was "only a tormenting dissatisfaction with himself and his character . . . an extraordinarily energetic desire to minister to social defects and to his own weaknesses"—and the mysterious spark of genius.[14] Yet, even here, he was a representa-

[13] Review of *Zapiski o zhizni Nikolaya Vasil'evicha Gogolya*, ed. P. A. Kulish, St. Petersburg, 1856, *Sovremennik*, No. 5, 1856 (as in *Polnoe sobranie sochinenii*, III, Moscow, 1947, 535).

[14] Review of *Sochineniya i pis'ma N. V. Gogolya*, ed. P. A. Kulish, 6 vols., St. Petersburg, 1857, *Sovremennik*, No. 8, 1857 (as in *Polnoe sobranie sochinenii*, IV, Moscow, 1948, 610).

tive genius: like Pushkin and Lermontov, his nature was too lofty for the society in which he had to live. Had he been born twenty years later (that is, in Chernyshevsky's own time), he would have been more enlightened, and therefore presumably a better writer.

Chernyshevsky was asserting, then, that the "enigma" of Gogol was only apparent; everything could be explained. From now on, Gogol was placed at one remove from the sort of moralizing criticism that had been practiced by most of his contemporaries. Increasingly he came to be regarded as an object of study. In this second period, vigorous efforts were made to gather information on every conceivable aspect of his life and activity. Memoirs and letters came out in a steady flow until the end of the century. New editions of the works (none of them complete) appeared in the 1850's and the 1890's. Shortly after Gogol's death, P. A. Kulish published two essays in biography, but they were hesitant and fragmentary.[15] The Academy of Sciences commissioned S. P. Shevyryov, a first-rate critic with conservative views, to prepare a full-scale life of Gogol; but he died before he could get under way. Otherwise, no significant attempt was made for the next forty years to synthesize a growing body of material. That was surprising, considering that critics, scholars, and the general public continued to take an intense interest in Gogol's life and work: there was virtually none of the decline in popularity which major writers so often undergo for decades after their death (Pushkin being a case in point). Perhaps his personality was still too puzzling to an age that honored the verities of science and positivism.[16] In any event,

[15] The best memoir was by S. T. Aksakov, *Istoriya moego znakomstva s Gogolem so vklyucheniem vsei perepiski s 1832 po 1852 god*, in *Russkii arkhiv*, 1890, No. 8, pp. 1-206 (and, in an individual volume, Moscow, 1960: it is this edition that I shall quote from throughout).

The editions in question are: *Sochineniya*, 6 vols., ed. N. Trushkovsky, Moscow, 1855-1856; *Sochineniya i pis'ma*, 6 vols., ed. P. A. Kulish, St. Petersburg, 1857: *Sochineniya*, 7 vols., ed. N. Tikhonravov and V. Shenrok, Moscow, 1889-1896.

The two works of P. A. Kulish are: *Opyt biografii N. V. Gogolya, so vklyucheniem do soroka ego pisem*, St. Petersburg, 1854; and *Zapiski o zhizni N. V. Gogolya, sostavlennye iz vospominanii ego druzei i znakomykh i iz ego sobstvennykh pisem*, 2 vols., St. Petersburg, 1856.

[16] A political factor seems to have been at work too. For all his conservatism, Gogol was regarded with suspicion by many officials of the government. Vasily Gippius suggests that the reason for this was the belief, among radicals, that Gogol had contributed to the development of a revolutionary state of mind in Russia. He cites as an example Alexander Herzen's

it was only in 1892 that V. I. Shenrok's *Materials for a Biography of Gogol* began to appear.[17] This four-volume work sets forth, in paraphrase and luxuriant citation, virtually everything that was then known about Gogol. Actually, the title is too modest. Although the book does not represent a finished piece of writing (Shenrok intended to produce that later, but never did), it organizes its materials around a theme, and thereby attains a certain unity.

The approach owes much to Chernyshevsky, and the conclusions are similar to his, although they are buttressed, of course, by far more elaborate detail. Like Chernyshevsky, Shenrok assumes that Gogol's life and work, from start to finish, constitute a unity, which can be discerned through scrupulous attention to all the evidence, especially the letters. The investigator must work from "external biographical facts" to reach an understanding of the "inner intimate life."[18] The picture that takes shape here, as in Chernyshevsky, is one of an essentially passive personality: Gogol wrote by way of involuntary response to an irresistible need; but the forms his writing took were fashioned by upbringing, environment, and the literary tradition. Shenrok offered no really new interpretations; in effect, he was consolidating the findings of four decades. But his book was a landmark. It put an end to a long period of mere data-gathering, and indicated that the time for

---

book *On the Development of Revolutionary Ideas in Russia,* first published in German in Bremen the year before Gogol's death; it circulated illegally in Russia for years thereafter. Gippius says that the government was "even more disturbed" by the "demonstration of popular affection for Gogol," as shown by the huge turnout at his funeral, and that it resorted to "repressive measures"—forbidding the publication of a new edition of Gogol's works, and also forbidding this fact to be mentioned in print for three years. (V. V. Gippius, "N. V. Gogol'," introductory essay to Vol. I of the complete works, *PSS,* 1940, 55, 57.) Ivan Turgenev was also arrested and exiled to his country estate for an obituary notice, which was published in Moscow, where the censor did not know that it had been proscribed in St. Petersburg. The notice is utterly innocuous. Turgenev himself believed that the real reasons for the government's action were the publication of *A Sportsman's Sketches* (widely regarded as a protest against serfdom), and the fact that he had put something over on the censor. For the text of the notice, entitled "Pis'mo iz Peterburga," see "Gogol' . . . ," *Polnoe sobranie sochinenii i pisem,* XIV (*Sochineniya*), Moscow-Leningrad, 1967, 72-73; Turgenev's interpretation of the incident is on pp. 74-75.

[17] *Materialy dlya biografii Gogolya,* 4 vols., Moscow, 1892-97.

[18] *Materialy . . . ,* II (1893), v.

interpretation had now come. In suggesting how such interpretations might run, Shenrok prefigured nearly all the directions that the critics of the twentieth century would follow.

III

In the twentieth century, a number of comprehensive or synthetic studies of Gogol have been produced, the best being those by V. F. Pereverzev (1914), Vasily Gippius (1924), and G. A. Gukovsky (1946-49).[19] The distinguishing mark of criticism in this century, however, has been specialization as against generalization, the diorama as against the panorama. Here the insights and techniques of other disciplines have exerted an enormous pull, the most energetic and spectacular having come from psychology, theology, philosophy, sociology, linguistics, economics, and folklore studies. Along with these, critics have worked out and applied techniques aimed at the intrinsic study of literature.

The movement toward specialization was accompanied by a shift of vantage-point. The venerable problem of Gogol's realism was crucial here. Since the 1830's it had been axiomatic that Gogol, whatever else he could be called, was a realist, even if people were not always sure what the term meant. By the 1860's, however, rumblings of dissatisfaction could be heard. Chernyshevsky, for one, credited Gogol with a keen eye for the data of the visible world, but thought that he could not be a realist in any higher sense because he showed only isolated facts and ignored the great underlying patterns. For example, he had perceived that bribe-taking was rampant in Russian society, and had depicted it with healthy indignation in *The Inspector General*; but he never stopped to wonder why the practice had arisen in the first place and why it continued to flourish.[20] By the end of the century, far stronger objections were being put forth. S. A. Vengerov asserted that Gogol actually knew virtually nothing at first hand about his small-town settings, made mistakes in his descriptions of "reality," and looked on Russia with the eyes of a foreigner.[21]

[19] V. F. Pereverzev, *Tvorchestvo Gogolya*, Moscow, 1914; V. Gippius, *Gogol'*, Leningrad, 1924; G. A. Gukovsky, *Realizm Gogolya*, Moscow-Leningrad, 1959 (but actually written in 1946-49).

[20] Review of *Sochineniya i pis'ma N. V. Gogolya*, ed. P. A. Kulish . . . , *Polnoe sobranie sochinenii*, IV, Moscow, 1948, 628.

[21] "Gogol' sovershenno ne znal real'noi russkoi zhizni," *Sobranie sochinenii*, II, *Pisatel'-grazhdanin. Gogol'*, St. Petersburg, 1912, 123-139.

Vasily Rozanov denied that Gogol was a realist at all. His characters were not living people, but "wax figures," "dolls" created out of a "waxen mass of words," yet so skillfully manipulated by the author that generations of readers had taken them for real.[22]

Rozanov's article gave ample evidence of a new mood that had taken hold of Russian intellectual society: a deepening disillusionment with such staples of nineteenth-century thought as science, progress, reason, and, with them, literary realism, whether the naturalistic or "physiologic" variety of the 1840's, or the kind represented by the serenely ordered worlds of the great novelists who came later. Rozanov not only disbelieved in them, but insisted that Gogol had largely been responsible for creating the mood that led to the disbelief: after him, "everyone began to love and respect only his own dreams, while feeling revulsion for everything real, private, and individual. Everything that is alive no longer attracts us, and therefore our entire life, our characters and ideas have become half-fantastic." How, then, was it possible to talk about Gogol's "realism"?[23] This vision of Gogol was taken over, a few years later, by a group of brilliant young writers who soon moved into the center of literary life: the Symbolists. Though primarily poets and prose writers, most of them were vigorous critics and theorists of literature too. They not only discussed their own work, but also aspired to reinterpret the Russian literary past. And, as one of the most prominent of them said, "the closest to us of all the Russian writers of the nineteenth century is Gogol."[24]

A convenient anthology of Symbolist opinion on Gogol appeared on the one-hundredth anniversary of his birth: the April 1909 issue of the movement's leading journal, *The Scales*, contained a number of commemorative articles. The theme of them all seemed to be, in Bely's words: "We do not yet know what Gogol is."[25] But it was clear that whatever definitions might be essayed, they would refuse to recognize Gogol as a "realist" in any of the senses that had prevailed until that time. Valery Bryusov's "Burnt to Ashes" was typical. Picking up one of Rozanov's points, he defined Gogol as "a dreamer, a fantast," who, essentially, "em-

[22] "Gogol' i Pushkin," *Legenda o Velikom Inkvizitore F. M. Dostoevskogo, s prilozheniem dvukh etyudov o Gogole*, 3d ed., St. Petersburg, 1906, esp. pp. 261-262, 265. This article is a good illustration of the Gogol-Pushkin contrast which I have discussed.

[23] "Gogol' i Pushkin," pp. 263-264.

[24] A. Bely, "Gogol'," *Vesy*, No. 4, 1909, p. 70.

[25] "Gogol'," p. 70.

bodied in his art only the ideal world of his visions." These visions consisted in "a striving for exaggeration or hyperbole," which ruled all he did: his style depended on overstatement or on the amassing of detail; his life was marked by sudden and radical changes of mood; even his final days, when he refused food and medical attention, were "a majestic hyperbole."[26] This article had first been read at a meeting of the Society of Lovers of Russian Literature. It caused a sensation: Bryusov was publicly hissed. Actually, the idea of "hyperbole" repeated a point that had been made by Rozanov nearly fifteen years earlier, and by Apollon Grigoriev some forty years before that. The public reaction to Bryusov's reformulation in 1909 indicated that it now struck a chord, and was regarded as daring and even sacrilegious. But it took root, and has become virtually a cliche among Western critics of Gogol.[27]

The article Bely contributed to this issue of *The Scales* offered some explanations of Gogol's appeal to the Symbolists. One was his obsession with the theme of death as the only earthly reality. Another was his ability to create a world that is simultaneously real and unreal: "the earth suddenly starts slipping out from under your feet . . . people are not really people: a Cossack is dancing and suddenly a tusk protrudes from his mouth." (The reference is to the sorcerer in the story "A Terrible Vengeance.") This confusion of appearances and realities was something that many Symbolists virtually equated with art; Bely regarded his novel *St. Petersburg* as Gogolian in that respect. Finally, Gogol's language appealed to a generation that was trying to destroy what for them was the impersonal and formulaic narrative style of much of nineteenth-century prose fiction: it contained "all those devices which are characteristic of the best stylists of our time"; it was "precultural" in its expression of the deepest human values, yet "in its refinement it surpasses not only Oscar Wilde, Rimbaud, Fyodor Sologub and other decadents, but even Nietzsche at times."[28]

[26] "Ispepelennyi," *Vesy*, No. 4, 1909, pp. 98-120. This article is translated in this collection.

[27] For Rozanov, cf. "Gogol' i Pushkin," *Legenda o Velikom Inkvizitore*, pp. 263-264 (I quote from the third edition of 1906, but the article was first published—under a different title—in 1893); for Grigoriev, cf. "Russkaya literatura v 1851 godu," *Polnoe sobranie sochinenii i pisem*, I, Petrograd, 1918, 110; for a characterization of the reaction to Bryusov's lecture, cf. V. V. Gippius, *Gogol'*, Leningrad, 1924, p. 155.

[28] "Gogol'," pp. 73, 80, 91. Bely wrote a good deal about Gogol. His

INTRODUCTION

With a few notable exceptions, like the Marxists, critics in our century have tended to relocate the source of Gogol's art from the external to the internal world. The artist not only reflects his private visions, as Rozanov said, but also imposes them on the world outside, and transforms it accordingly; in M. H. Abrams's phrase, he is now a "lamp," a self-generating source of energy, and no longer a "mirror."[29] This view, according to Abrams, is characteristically romantic. There had been suggestions of it in the writings of critics from Gogol's own time—in the charge, for instance, that he caricatured reality by showing only its "low" and "negative" aspects—or in Belinsky's idea that any artist passes reality through his creative imagination. But the ultimate referent there, whether visible or (as for Belinsky) ideal, was external to the artist. And Gogol himself shared it. The epigraph to *The Inspector General*—"There's no use grumbling at the mirror if your own mug is crooked"—aphorized his view of the workings of his own mind: he saw the characters in his stories as projections, or mirrors, of bad qualities of his own, and his better self as a reflection of something outside and beyond him. It was not until the neoromantic movement commonly called Symbolism that a radically new focus was achieved.

In their estimates of Gogol, the Symbolists were not so consistently original as they seemed to think: we find them repeating many of the clichés of the critical literature. Furthermore, Symbolist criticism had no technique peculiarly its own: it could be psychological, sociological, religious, philosophical, linguistic. It could be as evanescent as Innokenty Annensky's impressionistic appreciations, or as meticulous as Bely's studies of language-usage. It was unified by certain shared assumptions, which answered to the Symbolist view of the world. The most important of these saw art as essentially a projection of the mind, and as a means of bringing the various aspects of that mind into a unified whole. The Symbolists dramatized the great reversal of viewpoint that marked the onset of twentieth-century criticism of Gogol, and specified it in ways that have impressed themselves on some of the best critical writing ever since. The Formalists, for example, also insisted that

---

best-known study is his last, *Masterstvo Gogolya* (*Gogol's Craftsmanship*), 1934. It does not always reward the considerable effort required to follow it, but it is full of fascinating insights.

[29] *The Mirror and the Lamp. Romantic Theory and the Critical Tradition*, New York, 1958, *passim*.

Gogol was an irrealist, a painter of masks, and a creator of caricatures. Although the opinions of the Symbolists have not been
cordially received by Soviet Marxists, many are still common cur-
rency among Western critics of Gogol, Bryusov's idea of "hyperbole" being a case in point.

IV

The other characteristic feature of the new criticism, as I have
said, was the growth of specialization. This was made possible
by the prodigious amount of material on Gogol that had been
collected during the preceding half-century. But dramatic new
advances in many scholarly and scientific disciplines toward the
end of that century also had their say: medicine and psychiatry,
sociology and political theory (largely the Marxist variety), the
study of history, and the interest in theology that accompanied a
religious revival among many intellectuals.

Of all the new approaches, the one best attuned to the inward-
directed view of Gogol derived from psychology.

No Russian writer before Gogol had so elaborately and publicly documented his moods, his emotions, his moral and spiritual
problems. He was thoroughly "modern" in viewing his art as the
product of "a desire to be delivered of [my bad qualities]," which
he was inspired to "transfer to my heroes"; representing each one
as "a deadly enemy who had offended me in the most painful way.
I would pursue it with anger, with ridicule, with everything else that
came to mind." He assures us that "if anyone had seen the monsters that issued from my pen, at first for my own purposes alone,
he would certainly have shuddered."[30] Indeed, Gogol was perhaps
too modern for the time: as one of his friends said, his personality, with its capricious swings of mood, "eludes not only the
observation but even the comprehension of the people who are
closest to Gogol."[31]

But, as we have seen, by the 1860's critics were beginning to
assert that Gogol's personality, though full of contradictions, posed
no hopeless enigmas or mysteries. It remained only to discover
what Chernyshevsky called the "general idea" or the "structure
of thought" that underlay everything but might be disguised by

[30] "Chetyre pis'ma k raznym litsam po povodu 'Mertvykh dush,' " *Vybrannye mesta iz perepiski s druz'yami, PSS*, VIII, 1952, 294.
[31] S. T. Aksakov, as cited by V. Shenrok, *Materialy*, I (1892), 10.

words. His definitions of this structure echoed the moralistic concerns of the criticism of the past: "passionate nature," "thirst for fame," and "melancholia."[32] But Chernyshevsky's assumption that Gogol's life and work form an unbroken whole is one that any psychological critic must also make. And V. I. Shenrok elaborated on it in ways that foreshadowed many twentieth-century approaches. He saw Gogol as a man irresistibly driven to create not by ambition, but by "an indefinable inner need to embody in palpable forms the images that swarmed tormentingly in his imagination and were struggling to achieve a striking clarity."[33] He emphasized the need for a careful investigation of Gogol's crucial early years, particularly his relationship with his parents, and asserted that small details offered better clues to the pattern of Gogol's personality than did apparently large and dramatic changes. But the first major critic of Gogol to make extensive and specific use of psychology was D. N. Ovsyaniko-Kulikovsky. He had been strongly influenced by A. A. Potebnya (1835-91), a psychologist and linguist who rejected idealistic philosophies and insisted that reality was the perceiving mind and its products. From this it followed that the study of any writer had to begin with a map of his mind.

Ovsyaniko-Kulikovsky believes that the key to Gogol's mind is "egocentrism." This is no moral concept, like "egoism"; rather, it means that the world is perceived and organized according to a psyche, or an "I" that is "a plaything of various more or less antediluvian notions slumbering in the unconscious realm of the spirit." Gogol shrank in horror at the spectacle of these notions within him—he called them "vileness" (*merzost'*)—and tried to rid himself of them by confessing in public, that is, by creating works of art. He thereby succeeded in "pulling together his soul, which was being fragmented by the ordinary, daily life of his psyche."

Ovsyaniko-Kulikovsky tries to show how "egocentrism" determined everything Gogol did, as a writer and as a man. For example, his desire to treat his friends charitably was constantly undermined, for "he unwittingly placed himself in the position of being an investigator of other human souls, just as he always was of his own; his friends turned into objects of these researches, and

---

[32] E.g., review of *Sochineniya i pis'ma N. V. Gogolya*, ed. P. A. Kulish . . . , *Polnoe sobranie sochinenii*, IV, Moscow, 1948, 663.

[33] *Materialy*, I (1892), 242.

simple relationships invariably became complicated and were spoiled."[34]

As an egocentrist, Gogol belongs to a large class of artists whom Ovsyaniko-Kulikovsky calls "experimenters." They stand in contrast to the "observers," who try to make a faithful reproduction of the world outside themselves, thereby creating balanced and proportioned works of art that document not an individual mind but an entire society. The contrast serves to classify all of Russian literature: experimenters include Dostoevsky, Chekhov, Gleb Uspensky, and Saltykov-Shchedrin; observers include Lermontov and Tolstoy. Here, Ovsyaniko-Kulikovsky is actually rephrasing a still older contrast: for Gogol is his prime example of an experimenter, and Pushkin of an observer.

This approach does have a certain neatness to it. But it also illustrates the danger to which any criticism built on non-literary criteria is subject: reductionism. Gogol interests Ovsyaniko-Kulikovsky less as an individual than as an instance of a universal psychological type: *the* egocentric. The writer disappears into a file-drawer organized by dividers marked "martyr and ascetic," "misanthrope," "hypochondriac," and so on.

Ovsyaniko-Kulikovsky was not a great critic. Even by the standards of an age that had not yet recognized psychology as a science, he was an amateur. Often he did no more than rehearse platitudes which had been current for half a century or more. And like most of his predecessors, he was relentlessly indifferent to matters of style and form. His own prose sprawls and meanders. Still, his writings had wide appeal at the time, and did much to establish the "psychology" of Gogol as a legitimate concern of critics.

Other studies of Gogol's mind began to appear around the turn of the century. Some were merely medical, like *Gogol's Sickness and Death*, where N. Bazhenov argued that the patient was suffering from a "circular psychosis," or, in other words, was manic depressive.[35] To the extent that the Symbolists tried to define a particular cast of mind—what Bryusov in the article entitled "Burnt to Ashes" calls the *faculté maîtresse*—and trace its workings throughout Gogol's career, they too were practicing a kind of psychological criticism. The most ambitious attempt to make up

[34] *Gogol'. Sobranie sochinenii*, I, St. Petersburg, 1912, 36-37; III, 55-57, 137, 45-51, 65.

[35] N. Bazhenov, "Bolezn' i smert' Gogolya," *Russkaya mysl'*, Nos. 1-2, 1902.

for Ovsyaniko-Kulikovsky's neglect of literary values was I. E. Mandelshtam's book *On the Nature of Gogol's Style*, which came out in 1902. Like his predecessors, Mandelshtam saw art as an outlet for an irrepressible urge, a way by which the artist "eradicates the power that feeling has over the consciousness."[36] But whereas earlier investigators had based their evidence (such as it was) on "themes" and "ideas," Mandelshtam tried to work with the specifics of style and vocabulary, on the assumption that these were patterned by the urgings of Gogol's unconscious mind, and could, in turn, reveal the workings of that mind. Here, recurrent or obsessive imagery took on special importance. The book is chaotic and innocent of methodology, but it is full of fascinating suggestions, to which many later critics, better read in psychology, owe a large debt.

No significant advance was made in psychological criticism, however, until the 1920's. By then Freud had been imported into Russia; and one of his disciples, I. D. Yermakov, brought his teachings to bear on the riddles of Gogol's mind and art.[37]

Yermakov finds it easy enough to assign Gogol to a general character-type: the anal. He incessantly complained about his intestines, although he could eat with great gusto; he suffered from hemorrhoids; his letters abound in unprintable words, most of them referring to bowel functions; he was stingy and had a passion for collecting and classifying; he was given to radical and sudden changes of mood; he was obsessed with the nose, which is a fecal as well as a phallic symbol (p. 36). But Yermakov hopes, in addition, to define his patient's individuality. Predictably, he looks for it in Gogol's relationship with a domineering mother, a weak father, and various strong father-substitutes. The result was a "repressed aggressiveness," which accounted for the duality of Gogol's character—guilt, fear, and self-deprecation on the one hand, arrogance and self-exaltation on the other—and for the special texture of his art.

As we know, "dualism" was one of the hardiest items in the critical canon. And Yermakov, in seeking to document it, resorts to many familiar distinctions: comic and sad; noble and base; expansive and secretive; rhetorical and naturalistic; positive and

[36] *O kharaktere Gogolevskogo stilya. Glava iz istorii russkogo literaturnogo yazyka*, Helsingfors, 1902, p. 53.

[37] I. D. Yermakov, *Ocherki po analizu tvorchestva Gogolya*, Moscow-Petrograd, 1923. Page references cited in text.

negative, and so on. But he tries to incorporate them into his over-arching theory of Gogol's mind. Thus, the Devil is not the "noumenal being" that D. S. Merezhkovsky proposes in his essay,[38] but a personification of Gogol's own aggressive impulses. "Humor" was Gogol's way of handling these impulses: they sought an outlet, but they could not be baldly expressed, and instead clothed themselves in amusing devices (word-plays or poses of naiveté by the narrator) that both concealed and revealed, and thereby enabled Gogol to belittle the authority of others while asserting his own (pp. 13-36, 67-75).

The first part of Yermakov's book was written in 1915. Much of it is an enthusiastic but ill-digested rehashing of recent readings in Freud, although both Potebnya and Ovsyaniko-Kulikovsky have left their mark too. It suffers from the same faults that Yermakov finds in earlier psychological critics, who "devote[d] too much space to the psychological analysis of the personality of the writer, though very little at that, and completely pass[ed] over the writer's works, especially the artistic form" (p. 5). The second part of the book, written seven years later, was meant to remedy this defect by offering close analyses of five of the stories. It was clear that in the meantime Yermakov had been reading the Formalist critics, for many of his observations about language could have come from their pens. But he regarded their work as hostile to the deeper purposes of literary criticism, for it "fragments the whole living body of the work into individual, lifeless atoms" (pp. 133-34). Each "atom," he insists, is linked with all the others to make up the individual work of art, which in turn functions organically within the corpus of the author's work as a whole, with everything reflecting and refracting the "dominant." Such a point of view is to be expected of a psychologist. Its weakness, as a critical position, is that it tends to make every work of art perfect because every component fits, and it assumes that ineptness or incompetence do not really exist because everything has a meaning.

Yermakov is least interesting when he places equal signs between the stories and the "mind" of their author—seeing the numerous threatening father-figures, for example, as reflections of Gogol's attitude toward his own father; deciding that Chichikov, in *Dead Souls*, is an anal erotic because Gogol was one too; at-

[38] See the discussion of Merezhkovsky farther on in this introduction, and his article "Gogol and the Devil," which is translated in the present anthology.

tributing the many instances of double heroes (the two Ivans, or Kovalyov and Ivan Yakovlevich in "The Nose") to Gogol's own dual nature (pp. 143-44). He does make a conscientious effort, however, to fill in his picture of Gogol's mind with specific images. As a psychological critic, he naturally takes for granted that each image carries one or more meanings that remain fixed regardless of context; but, at his best, he can also show how images are patterned in ways unique to individual stories. We usually know what his conclusions will be, because, having read Freud ourselves, we know what his starting-points are. Along the way, however, he offers many concrete suggestions that often open up new sides of Gogol's art.

The article on "The Overcoat" represents his best work. I have not included it in this collection because that would have meant overdoing a single story. But it does make an interesting contrast with the approaches taken by Eichenbaum and Chizhevsky, and I shall therefore try to summarize its main points.

All three critics take great interest in the small details of language. Of special significance for Yermakov are the personal names. "Akaky" could have been derived from the saints' calendar, as are all the other weird names proposed for the infant. But it also strongly suggests the child's word for feces (*kaka*), and therefore situates the story in the world of scatology; this idea is reinforced by the phonic structure of the sentence that immediately precedes the naming: "vidno *tak*aya ego sud'ba. Uzh esli *tak*, pust' luchshe budet on nazyvat'sya, *kak* i otets ego; otets byl A*kak*y, *tak* pust' i syn budet A*kak*y." Akaky's surname, Bashmachkin, derives from the word for shoe (*bashmak*), which is both a male and a female symbol. And the other names proposed by the godparents and rejected by the mother all have infantile sexual or scatological connotations: Mokky suggests *mokry* (wet); Sossy—*sosyot* (sucks); Khozdazat—*zad* (bottom, buttocks); Varadat and Varukh—the word for "beard" (*boroda*, pronounced *baradá* in standard Russian), which is a male symbol.

The detail that interests Yermakov most of all is the overcoat itself. In the anecdote on which the story is based (an account is given in Chizhevsky's article in this anthology), the clerk acquires and then loses a *gun*. Why was the substitution made? Both a gun and an overcoat, Yermakov explains, are male symbols (though the coat can also be female, as it seems to be in this story). Gogol took no interest in hunting, but he was obsessed with clothes,

25

and therefore chose an object within the same symbol-system as the gun. The loss of the overcoat is a symbolic castration performed in punishment for the erotic feelings the new acquisition arouses in Akaky.

But why was Gogol so struck by the original anecdote? Yermakov thinks it is because the hero was a servant of the state. All his life Gogol regarded himself as just that, even when he had become a full-time writer. Yet he believed that he had not served Russia well. An open confession of his sense of failure, however, would have invited punishment. Instead, Gogol resorted to art—more precisely, to that artistic form of confession known as *skaz*, a first-person narration by a character who is usually from the lower ranks of society, none too intelligent, rather self-deprecatory, and addicted to digressions, jokes, and folksy turns of speech. Basically it is an extended joke; as such, it both conceals and reveals what the narrator, or confessor, wishes to say. Even the maddening insistence of this narrator on dotting every "i" is a symptom, for Yermakov, of the compulsive nature of the confession, which wishes to set the record straight with a supposedly accurate rendering of every detail.

"The Overcoat" is Gogol's best short story, and has created a healthy corpus of critical writing. "The Nose" is comparatively unencumbered with commentary: readers apparently have not known quite what to make of it. Many of Gogol's contemporaries thought that the story was "dirty," even without Freud's help. Belinsky disliked it because it unfolded in the realm of fantasy, which he considered alien to Gogol's true talents. The censors disapproved of its flippant treatment of the police and the bureaucracy, and refused to pass the scene in which the nose turns up in the Kazan Cathedral or even to entertain the proposed substitution of a Roman Catholic church. At various times the story has been read as a mere joke; as a parody on Romanticism; as an imitation of the large European literature of "nosology" that was well known in Russia by Gogol's time; as a commentary on philistine society; as a deliberate exercise in nonsense, like Pushkin's "Little House in Kolomna," which makes the point that art is absolutely free in its choice of themes.

Yermakov rejects all these interpretations. As a Freudian, he regards nonsense and joking as highly significant, and the nose as a suggestively surrogate organ. While acknowledging the story's place in the "nosological" tradition, he thinks that the real question is how Gogol transformed the materials he found within that tradition and within his own mind. Despite large gaps in logic, much inept writing, and a tendency to belabor the obvious (it is hard to imagine that many Russian readers, even in the 1920's, were startled to discover that the nose could be a sex-symbol), this article does reveal an eye for patterns of significant detail, and a certain talent for tracing their reverberations in Gogol's life and in his other writings. Yermakov is one of the few critics who have tried to read this story as a serious work of literature, not merely as a compendium of devices or an elaborate joke. In the main, he makes a convincing case.

The critical literature offers a few other examples of the psychoanalytical approach: Freud's famous essay on Dostoevsky and parricide was translated into Russian; A. L. Bem's essay entitled *Dostoevsky: Psychoanalytical Studies* (*Dostoevskii: psikhoanaliticheskie etyudy*) appeared in Berlin in 1938. Within Russia itself, Yermakov's books on Pushkin and Gogol, both published in the 1920's, are the only solid monuments to this school. For, despite some interesting attempts at reconciliation, Freud was anathema to most Marxists, as an "idealist" who divorced human behavior from the class struggle, disallowed the perfectibility of man, and attempted to "use biology to explain things that are in fact socially conditioned."[39] Eventually his teachings were officially proscribed in the Soviet Union, and Yermakov, along with other Freudians, dropped out of sight.

V

In the 1840's Gogol became obsessed with what he called the "upbringing" (*vospitanie*) of his soul. He was convinced that within him "there lives a deep and irresistible faith that the heavenly power will help me ascend the ladder which stands before me, although I am still standing on its lowest and first rungs. . . . My soul must be purer than the celestial snows and more radiant than the heavens, and only then will I acquire the strength to undertake heroic deeds and a great life work, only then will the riddle of my existence be solved."[40] The pursuit of perfection tormented him for the rest of his life. The reading public was aware of it,

[39] A. Tseitlin, "Metody marksistskogo literaturovedeniya," *Literaturnaya entsiklopediya*, VII, Moscow, 1933, column 270.
[40] Letter to V. A. Zhukovsky, June 26, 1842.

in a general way; close friends followed it through their correspondence with him. And the publication of *Selected Passages* in 1847 made it a literary issue.

Gogol stated in the first article, entitled "Testament," that "the duty of a writer is not only to provide the mind and the taste with a pleasant diversion: he will be held strictly accountable if some benefit to the soul is not propagated by his works and if nothing remains as a precept to people after he is gone."[41] He was convinced that *Selected Passages* was more useful than anything he had ever written, and he commended it to his readers as a "brotherly precept" and a spiritual guide. Most readers of his own time were outraged. And throughout the nineteenth century, people tended both to ignore the book and to assume that Gogol's spiritual struggles mattered only because they had supposedly killed the artist in him, for after 1842 Gogol never completed or published another work of fiction.

It was only in the twentieth century that critics began to take Gogol seriously as a major force in the development of Russian spirituality. By and large, these critics have themselves been strongly religious men, participants in and heirs to the revival of Orthodoxy that began around the turn of the century among a small but influential group of Russian intellectuals. One of them was Konstantin Mochulsky. In the course of a long career, he explored the interrelationships of religion and literature in a number of monographs on Russian writers, of which his *Dostoevsky* is the best known. While emphasizing philosophical and spiritual elements in their work, he also showed a genuine sensitivity to problems of form and style. By contrast, *Gogol's Spiritual Path*, which he published as an émigré in Paris in 1934, was exclusively a spiritual biography, and the best example of its kind in the literature on Gogol up to that time.[42]

Mochulsky proceeds from the premise that "Gogol was not only a great artist; he was also teacher of morals, a Christian zealot, and a mystic" (p. 5). The tragedy was that his concept of spirituality (in order to create beauty, the artist must make himself beautiful)

---

[41] "Zaveshchanie," *Vybrannye mesta iz perepiski s druz'yami, PSS*, VIII, 1952, 221.

[42] *Dukhovnyi put' Gogolya*, Paris, 1934. Page references are cited in the text. Mochulsky's study of Dostoevsky is now available in English under the title *Dostoevsky. His Life and Work*, translated and with an introduction by Michael Minihan, Princeton, 1967.

ruined his art: he was "martyr to an idea." Yet Mochulsky believes that the idea itself was sound, and that Gogol was peculiar only because he tried to put it into practice (pp. 89-90).

The central document of Gogol's spiritual Odyssey is, of course, *Selected Passages*. Mochulsky regards it—in a phrase that echoes Yermakov—as a "public confession" unexampled in Russian literature (p. 88). He disapproves of its theology, which defines evil as perverted goodness and thereby denies original sin. But he defends the book as a "harmonious and complete system of religious and moral ideology," which would be built on a "unified Christian culture" in every area of society (pp. 86, 101). For Mochulsky, this has been one of the great fructifying ideas in Russian thought. But Gogol's ultimate importance, to his mind, runs even deeper, and is defined by the familiar contrast with Pushkin. Gogol "shattered the harmony of classicism and broke the esthetic equilibrium" established by Pushkin. He thereby pointed ahead to all the great Russian literature that followed him, with "its religious and moral system, its sense of civic and social duty, its militant and practical character, its prophetic attitude and its messianism" (p. 86).

There have been a few other investigations of Gogol along similar lines—although not, of course, in the Soviet Union—but none has staked out any territory that is strikingly different from Mochulsky's. His book still stands as the most eloquent and persuasive defense yet made of Gogol as a thinker and as a force in Russian intellectual history. Mochulsky deliberately excluded fiction from his purview. Other religious-minded critics, however, have attempted to account for it. The most ambitious of them has been V. V. Zenkovsky, a historian, literary scholar, and Orthodox priest who in a long and rambling book attempts to demonstrate that all aspects of Gogol's life, work, and thought were hypostases of a single spiritual quest. Yet he treats Gogol's fiction only as the "external envelope behind which the complex theme of the human soul takes shape,"[43] and, like Mochulsky, is most interested in Gogol if not as a representative Christian then as representative of a particular brand of Russian Christianity (a view with which Gogol himself might have agreed).

Probably the most stimulating effort to reconcile spirtuality and fiction remains the comparatively brief article on Gogol and the Devil that Dmitry Merezhkovsky wrote in 1906. In it he makes

[43] *N. V. Gogol'*, Paris, n.d., p. 18. Original italics omitted.

obeisance to many of the established themes in the critical literature on Gogol, among them "banality" (*poshlost'*). And in his concern with the ethical dimensions of fiction, he follows a tradition that had begun in Gogol's own time, although he recasts these preoccupations in a religious, specifically a Christian, context. Dualism becomes the struggle between God and Satan for men's souls, character types are the emblems of good and evil in this contest. The opposition of low and lofty language now stands for the powers of darkness and light respectively. Chichikov and Khlestakov are least interesting as specific personalities and most significant as agents of a universal demonism. All this is very reminiscent of the way Gogol himself attempted to reinterpret his works in the 1840's. The most famous instance concerns *The Inspector General*. The town we see before us on the stage, he asserts, does not exist anywhere in Russia, but rather is the "spiritual town" within each of us. The officials are the "passions" of this town; Khlestakov is our "flighty, worldly, venal, deceiving conscience" which prevents us from seeing the town as it is; the true inspector general is "our awakened conscience, which will compel us, suddenly and all at once, to take a good, hard look at ourselves."[44]

Many of the specific points in Merezhkovsky's interpretation of Gogol foreshadow ideas that were to figure prominently in the Symbolists' view of life and art. One is that externals both conceal and reveal, and that what is concealed is more significant than what is revealed. We might call this an esthetic version of Yermakov's theory of humor; it could serve as a thumbnail definition of Symbolist esthetics as well. Another idea celebrates the power and vitality of the trivial, casual, random, or accidental. Merezhkovsky cites the famous passage from *The Inspector General* in which Bobchinsky and Dobchinsky, agitated by the news that an inspector general is about to arrive, rush in and announce that the young man staying at the inn *is* "the inspector general." Once the fateful words are pronounced, they begin to live a life of their own, and take on flesh in Khlestakov himself. Andrey Bely's *St. Petersburg* —an archetypally Symbolist novel—is built on a similar device, although it is developed with far greater complexity than Gogol brings to his use of it.

Running throughout Merezhkovsky's article is a profound sense of disillusionment in the power of reason and science, which had

[44] "Razvyazka Revizora," *PSS*, IV, 1951, 130-131. See also the discussion by Vyacheslav Ivanov in the article translated in the present anthology.

been so celebrated by the nineteenth century. With this mood went an apocalyptic sense of life. Both attitudes were deep-rooted in Russian Symbolism as well. One form they took was a vision of St. Petersburg as a new Babylon. To be sure, this was an old theme in literature by the time the Symbolists picked it up; but as Merezhkovsky suggests, it originated in recognizably modern form with Gogol. Even stronger and more explicit was the influence on Symbolism of the Gogolian demonology, although it had passed through Dostoevsky. By and large it was a demonology of banality, and thus eminently suited that characteristically modern mode of fiction which has been dubbed "low mimetic" by Northrop Frye.[45] (Fyodor Sologub's novel *The Petty Demon* [1907] explored it most effectively.) Yet it can also be awesome and terrible, as it is in "The Portrait." Merezhkovsky finds both aspects present in Gogol's greatest characters: Chichikov is bourgeois and Antichrist simultaneously.

In seeing Gogol's Devil as a universal phenomenon, Merezhkovsky extrapolates from literature to life, thus reversing the usual procedure. This is a characteristically Symbolist habit, and it may help explain how esthetic positions, for many of these writers, so easily became political. He is also reflecting the ambiguous attitude toward history that tormented his generation. On the one hand, the Devil exists "outside space and time, he is omnipresent and eternal"; "progress" is a mirage, for nothing new exists under the sun; and "movement" consists merely of intensification: "he keeps growing." On the other hand, Merezhkovsky entertains the possibility that the individual man (if not necessarily society) can make progress in the dimension of time: Gogol is important because he turned Russian literature from pure art to religion, from contemplativeness to activism. The point depends on the familiar contrast with Pushkin. And the fact that Merezhkovsky considers this spiritualization of Russian literature a good thing, as do Mochulsky and Zenkovsky, shows that his approach, for all the gloom it casts, is optimistic in the sense that any apocalyptic view of life is.

VI

Russians have long regarded responsiveness to social problems as a distinguishing mark of their literature, and have entrusted criti-

---

[45] Northrop Frye, *Anatomy of Criticism*, Princeton, 1957, esp. pp. 49-52, 58-60.

cism and scholarship with describing and accounting for the inter-relationship. In the case of Gogol, many nineteenth-century observers busied themselves with seeking out influences such as upbringing, political milieu, or intellectual fashions. The evidence of *Selected Passages from Correspondence with Friends* suggested that such influences had been unhealthy: sheer genius had somehow kept them at bay long enough for Gogol to produce the masterpieces of his earlier years. Some critics endeavored to winnow information from Gogol's writings in order to draw profiles of various classes and professions in Russian society. At times the mirror was reversed to show Gogol's impact on society; here the effects were normally deemed beneficial, insofar as Gogol was supposedly pointing up disparities between ideals and actualities.

Marxist criticism grew out of a soil that had been fertilized and watered for many generations. That was a strength, because Marxist critics found that their readers did not need to be persuaded of literature's close ties with society. It was a weakness because it made the vigorous exercise of critical muscle seem unnecessary. And more's the pity, because there is no single version of Marxist criticism, as its Russian practitioners themselves discovered in the early 1920's, with something of a shock. "Marxism" has accommodated a variety of approaches—all basically sociological, of course, but many very different in specific techniques. Two extremes are represented by V. F. Pereverzev, and by so-called "socialist realism."

For Pereverzev, "being" (*bytie*) is "that social and economic process which determines both the life of people and their consciousness and poetic creativity." Explanations of "poetic manifestations" must therefore be sought "not in subjective movement but in objective existence, not in the movement of ideas but in the movement of material reality. . . ." Like all men, the writer is formed by the "being," or social milieu, in which he grows up. He may acquire an education or even change social classes; but he can never fundamentally alter his way of looking at the world, which has been indelibly imprinted on him by his "being." Other "beings" he can depict only by analogy, and at the expense of full competence.[46]

[46] "Neobkhodimye predposylki marksistskogo literaturovedeniya," *Literaturovedenie. Sbornik statei*, ed. V. F. Pereverzev, Moscow, 1928. First quotation on p. 12, second on p. 10.

Gogol's native milieu was that of the small landowner. And his task, as an artist, was to find "the most appropriate esthetic forms" for depicting it.[47] When he did, he wrote well: *The Inspector General* and *Dead Souls* are his greatest works precisely because they deal with what he himself knew at first hand. Even the minor government officials who figure in so many of his stories are really small landowners displaced to the towns. But the Cossacks of the *Dikanka* stories are failures: having no immediate experience of their milieu, Gogol had either to import them from literature and folklore, or to dress up small landowners in Cossack costumes. In both cases, the characters ring false. Only when he began to seek analogies with the small landowners did he create passable, if not full-bodied, Cossacks. In effect, he had to "surmise what a rational, practical and rather apathetic type would become in the conditions of Cossack life. . . ."[48] The result was Taras Bulba, a successfully drawn character. Thus, the old problem of the two Gogols becomes, for Pereverzev, a question of Gogol's fidelity to—or betrayal of—his essential view of life.

For all this, Pereverzev insists that literature is not a mirror image of society. Where, he asks, would one seek equivalents to the fairy-tale world of Pushkin's *Ruslan and Ludmila*?[49] The problem of "being," in literature, is relevant for him only insofar as it is approached through a specific text: otherwise, one is not talking about literature. He believes that most sociological critics lavish far too much attention on externals, such as biography, psychology, and ideology, instead of making a detailed study of "the dependencies and linkages which bring the diverse elements and parts [of the work] together into a single organism."[50]

Pereverzev makes a conscientious effort to follow his own prescription by showing how Gogol's styles, structures, landscapes, and genres all embody the point of view that was fashioned by his "being." Thus, the "low" language reflects the close-knit society of small landowners, where everyone knows everyone else and can converse in familiar and easy terms. The absence of strong central heroes restates a fact of this same society (and shows, for Pereverzev, that Gogol cannot possibly be a satirist; for a satirist must deal with the exceptional). The structure of *Dead Souls* as a

[47] *Tvorchestvo Gogolya*, Moscow, 1914, p. 13.
[48] *Tvorchestvo Gogolya*, p. 327.
[49] "Neobkhodimye predposylki . . . ," pp. 16-17.
[50] "Neobkhodimye predposylki . . . ," p. 9.

disconnected series of scenes that can be reshuffled at random bespeaks the static and discontinuous life of rural society. Gogol's "alogical" technique (of which formalistically inclined critics later made so much)[51] grows out of the alogical nature of the society about which Gogol wrote. But the basic unit of the literary work, Pereverzev thinks, is the "image," which represents the point where the writer's mind meets the outside world. And the image is most fully embodied in the literary character—to which Pereverzev consequently devotes nearly half his book. Each is labelled and classified according to a typology: in *Dead Souls*, for example, there are "sentimental do-nothings" (Manilov), "active do-nothings" (Nozdryov), and "calculating do-nothings" (Sobakevich).[52]

Pereverzev's idea of art has many points of contact with the theory of "organicism" as expounded by Apollon Grigoriev (1822-64), a rather original and still underrated critic. Both see the writer and his milieu (although defining the latter differently) as being organically linked, and in fact both frequently resort to biological terms, such as "anatomy," "trunk," "branches," "leaves," to describe this relationship. If we were asked to guess, we might not immediately be able to say which of the two observes that the second part of *Dead Souls* fails not because Gogol tries to create ideal characters (that was a commonplace), but rather because he takes his models from a European idea of man that is non-Russian and out of date—one, in other words, that is inorganic. (It is Grigoriev.)[53] Both believe, as organicists tend to do, that a writer's outlook is determined once and for all by his milieu. And in this particular, both stand apart from many Marxists. G. V. Plekhanov, for example, thinks that an artist can create great works even when he is not in harmony with his milieu (which is the case most of the time).[54]

Pereverzev does have his faults. His theoretical formulations tend to be murky. In his impatience with muzzy terminology that "keeps on babbling about romanticism and realism," he does not trouble to make his own very precise or sophisticated, as anyone

[51] Cf. the essay by Alexander Slonimsky, translated in the present anthology.

[52] *Tvorchestvo Gogolya*, pp. 90-94, 99-112, 212-299.

[53] "Realizm i idealizm v nashei literature," *Sobranie sochinenii*, IV, ed. V. F. Savodnik, Moscow, 1915, 16.

[54] *Art and Social Life*, Moscow, 1957, *passim*.

who tries to explain his concept of "imagery" soon discovers.[55]
He takes little interest in the details of Gogol's language: the one
chapter he devotes to it in his book is the weakest by far. He
recognizes the need to develop a methodology that is irreducible
to other disciplines, but, like most sociological critics, he tends to
equate what is good with what can be paraphrased. For all his
insistence on respecting the text, he nonetheless proceeds from
the idea that Gogol is a sociological type, who is illustrated by his
writings. His method is therefore not inductive, as he would like to
have us think. But his analyses of specific works are often lucid and
persuasive in ways that his theoretical disquisitions are not. Most
sociological critics split works of literature into "form" and "content," but never manage to pull the two together. Pereverzev is
one of the very few who not only proclaim the division fallacious
but try, with considerable success, to overcome it. He strives to
honor the reality of the text itself, even though he cannot do so
consistently because his ultimate reference-point lies in a world
outside.

"Socialist realism" names the theory of art which has been
officially binding on all writers and critics in the Soviet Union
since the early 1930's. It resists precise definition; for, as an instrument of politics, it reflects frequent shifts in the Party line. (Besides, in literature, as in other areas of Soviet life, practice often
diverges markedly from theory.) But it reveals certain constants;
one of them has been a concern with how far any writer is indelibly
marked by the ideology of the society in which he originates.

This was a matter for lively debate in the 1920's among Marxists who were trying to work out a definition of what it meant to be
a "proletarian." One extreme view held that a proletarian could
only be born, not made. The other insisted that ideology, not blood,
counted and that any rational man could acquire the proletarian
outlook through study and experience. More than mere doctrine
was at issue here. In politics, the "born not made" argument would
have discredited virtually everyone who had led the proletarian
revolution, not the least of them Lenin, who came from the middle-
class intelligentsia. In literature it would have scrapped all the
great writers of the nineteenth century and most of the important
new ones of the 1920's as being irrelevant and even harmful to the
working-class, except perhaps as witnesses to anachronous ideolo-

[55] It should be noted, however, that the word *obraz* can mean *both*
"image" and "character" (personage in a literary work).

gies that might have had a negative educational value. However, the Soviet government, throughout the 1920's, required the services of non-proletarian specialists in all fields. In literature, it was eager to appropriate the riches of the past and to encourage new writers regardless of social origins (most were not proletarians). Such writers would be gradually led to the correct point of view, by gentle persuasion and the inescapable logic of the Marxist argument. For writers whom death had put beyond change, a number of arguments were devised. One rested on something resembling the distinction between artist and thinker that had been applied to Gogol for nearly a century. This distinction now facilitated the acceptance of much of the art—though not the ideas—of Dostoevsky, Turgenev, Tolstoy, and others, as it did for Gogol too. And it opened the door to another argument: that individual works of art may have an "objective value" quite apart from the ideologies that they or their authors profess. Such value enables the reader to derive pleasure and edification from works of art no matter how vile the societies in which they were produced, and it has conferred respectability on virtually all the writers of the past.[56] The source of this objective value is Truth, which shows forth in great universal ideals such as freedom and justice. As history progresses, these ideals disclose more and more of themselves until they are fully realized in Communism. Every genuine artist strives to serve Truth and succeeds in doing so depending on his native talent and the extent to which his class outlook is progressive or backward, that is, close to or distant from the Truth. But such service may be unconscious, and may even contradict his intentions. Reasoning of this sort led one Soviet critic to declare that the ending of *The Inspector General* is wrong because it makes the government responsible for exposing vice. This, he thinks, chimes with Gogol's backward (and consciously held) political views, but does not ruin the play, for Gogol's genius (of which he was presumably less consciously aware) has already created a sense of disparity between the actual and the ideal and has therefore led the reader to draw the right conclusions.[57]

[56] A fuller account of these questions can be found in my book *Red Virgin Soil: Soviet Literature in the 1920's*, Princeton, 1968. For a detailed treatment of socialist realism, cf. Herman Ermolaev, *Soviet Literary Theories, 1917-1934. The Genesis of Socialist Realism*, Berkeley and Los Angeles, 1963. For an example of the distinction between "objective" and "subjective," cf. the article by Gippius in the present anthology.

[57] N. L. Stepanov, *N. V. Gogol'. Tvorcheskii put'*, Moscow, 1955, p. 361.

This view of art clearly could not accommodate Pereverzev's idea of the passive artist who is incapable of altering his class outlook in any significant way without distorting his work. From the late 1920's onward, Pereverzev and his disciples came under increasingly heavy fire. Their writings were branded as "vulgar sociologism" and eventually consigned to virtual oblivion.[58] The Gogol described by the socialist-realist critics of the 1930's and 1940's would have been unrecognizable to Pereverzev. The "reactionary" and "romantic" sides were played down; Gogol, by and large, was now a "progressive" and "realistic" writer who forged his works as weapons to be used against the prevailing order. For example, *Evenings on a Farm Near Dikanka* was read as an outcry against serfdom, "The Nose" served as "a means for the satirical exposé of reality," and *The Inspector General* registered "an angry social protest."[59] The fact that many Russian revolutionaries, including Lenin, peppered their speeches with quotations from Gogol helped buttress such claims; the fact that a revolution did occur often seemed to clinch them.

The major achievement in Soviet scholarship on Gogol during the last three decades has been an edition of his works (designated as "complete"), which was published in fourteen volumes by the Academy of Sciences between 1937 and 1952. The introductory articles, commentaries, and technical apparatus are very uneven in quality; but despite some omissions, this edition represents the fullest collection of Gogol's writings to date. The centenary of Gogol's death, in 1952, stimulated an outpouring of writing on his life and works, most of it undistinguished. Generally speaking, critics since then have trodden the well-worn paths of socialist realism. There have, however, been a few refreshing exceptions.

[58] Cf., e.g., "O literaturovedcheskoi kontseptsii V. F. Pereverzeva: Rezolyutsiya prezidiuma Kommunisticheskoi Akademii," *Pechat' i Revolyutsiya*, No. 4, 1930, p. 4. See also the discussion in Ermolaev, *Soviet Literary Theories*, esp. pp. 95 ff. Pereverzev himself in 1926 had made a slashing attack on all other "approaches" to Gogol, whether Marxist, psychological or Formalistic. It was an interesting, although of course biased, survey of Gogol criticism in Russia between 1916 and 1926. Cf. "Gogolevskaya kritika za poslednee desyatiletie," preface to second edition of *Tvorchestvo Gogolya*, Ivanovo-Voznesensk, 1926, pp. 3-17.

[59] The first opinion belongs to M. Ya. Polyakov, "N. V. Gogol' v otsenke russkoi kritiki," in *N. V. Gogol' v russkoi kritike. Sbornik statei*, ed. N. K. Kotov and M. Ya. Polyakov, Moscow, 1953, p. vi; the second and third opinions come from N. L. Stepanov, *N. V. Gogol'*, pp. 251, 302.

One is the book by G. A. Gukovsky, entitled *Gogol's Realism* (*Realizm Gogolya*). It is an incomplete and unrevised manuscript, the writing of which was interrupted by the arrest and death of the author in 1949, and published only a decade later. Despite the unpromising title (a concession, no doubt, to the official view of Gogol), it is a perceptive attempt at surveying all of Gogol's work from a sociological point of view; unfortunately, it breaks off just as it begins to get into *Dead Souls*. During the past fifteen years, the strictures of socialist realism have loosened, even though it is still official doctrine. One result has been a distinct improvement in the standards of literary scholarship. And Gogol has been a beneficiary. For example, a recent book traces the parallels to *Dead Souls* in the eighteenth- and nineteenth-century novel of Western Europe. Such an approach would have been taboo a generation earlier, when scholars were expected to play up the uniquely Russian qualities of Russian literature.[60]

VII

In Pereverzev's system, works of literature belong to a "superstructure," whose components are shaped by "being" but cannot shape one another. Consequently, there can be no question of literary influences. Most twentieth-century critics, including many Marxists, do not agree: they have taken a lively interest in Gogol's use of and contributions to the work of other writers. Insofar as they have concentrated on defining the nature of such influences, we may call them practitioners of historical criticism.

Naturally, Gogol's contemporaries could not help but measure his achievements against the traditions, and they were well aware of his debts, whether generic, thematic, or stylistic. Nonetheless, they tended to put the greater emphasis on his originality, and to play up his importance as the initiator of what they saw as a totally new direction in Russian literature. Apollon Grigoriev, for example, argued that each literary age is defined by a single commanding genius, who lays out a "new path" which is then "merely widened and kept clean by talents" that come after him. Gogol, he insisted, was the great figure of his age; his followers imitated various aspects of his art—such as farce or naturalism—but could never duplicate his achievement as a whole.[61] The fascination with

[60] A. A. Yelistratova, *Gogol' i problemy zapadno-evropeiskogo romana*, Moscow, 1972.

[61] "Russkaya literatura v 1851 godu," *Sobranie sochinenii*, IX, ed. V. F. Savodnik, Moscow, 1916, 9, 8.

Gogol's legacy has endured. Some critics have located it in certain attitudes or activities such as didacticism, moralizing, a commitment to the betterment of society, satirical exposés of social evils, and the outright advocacy of revolution. Some have pointed up particular traits of style or tone, such as humorous non sequitur, caricature, or the grotesque. Much has been written about the "natural school" that supposedly originated with Gogol's portrayals of city life and the downtrodden "little man."

By and large, however, there has been little systematic investigation of this legacy: scholars have mostly been content with making impressionistic generalizations.[62] In contrast, much first-rate work has been done in the twentieth century in an area that held out little interest to Gogol's contemporaries: his relationship to the literary tradition.

One of the pioneers was Russia's great comparativist Alexander Veselovsky. A brief article dating from 1891 raised the problem of the origins of *Dead Souls*, and proposed a new approach to it. It had always been generally accepted that Pushkin gave Gogol the plot of the novel. But the more interesting and possibly more significant source, for Veselovsky, is suggested by Pushkin's argument that Cervantes would never have achieved real eminence in world literature had he not written *Don Quixote*; Gogol, who until then had produced only short stories and one play, must therefore do the same. "What if one were to depict," Veselovsky speculates, "in complete contrast to the hero of La Mancha, an acquisitive man [i.e., Chichikov] who was striving not to free the persecuted but rather to oppress and bring ruin on them himself; and what if one were to have him move constantly from place to place in just the same way, seeking not so much adventure as the opportunity for perpetrating 'large, middling, and small misdeeds'?" In the second part of Cervantes's novel, Don Quixote, after an interval of ten years, takes on Christian virtues, among them meekness and humility; Gogol planned a similar destiny for Chichikov in the never-completed second and third books of *Dead Souls*.[63]

It is a pity that Veselovsky—one of the most erudite and original

---

[62] One interesting exception can be found in Andrey Bely's *Masterstvo Gogolya* (*Gogol's Craftsmanship*, 1934), where he illustrates Gogol's influence on him through parallel passages from his own novel *St. Petersburg* and various works of Gogol's.

[63] "Mertvye dushi. Glava iz etyuda o Gogole," *Vestnik Evropy*, March, 1891, pp. 69-74. The quotation is on p. 69. We know of Pushkin's argument from Gogol himself: cf. "Avtorskaya ispoved'," *PSS*, VIII, 1952, 439-440.

scholars Russia has produced—never finished his monograph on Gogol, of which this article was to constitute one chapter. It was left to a critic of far more modest endowments to write the first large-scale study of the problem of "influences" on Gogol. N. A. Kotlyarevsky's book has a double focus—Gogol's place in the literature of his own time and of the past. He tries to distinguish between the tradition as it was received and as Gogol reworked it, between borrowings, parallels, and original contributions—an example of the first being Gogol's ideas on esthetics; of the second, the basic similarity in narrative structure of the several versions then current of the "inspector general" anecdote; of the last, the "little man" theme as established in "The Overcoat." Kotlyarevsky concludes that "Gogol was great not only because he conquered new areas of life for the art of the word, but also because he brought old literary devices to artistic perfection."[64]

Kotlyarevsky's writing is diffuse and impressionistic. But his book was responsible for launching "influence" studies on a large scale. Since then, especially good work has been done in exploring the sources of Gogol's themes—Russian, Ukrainian, and foreign.[65] In the 1920's, comparative studies of Gogol's style got under way. Here Laurence Sterne was a favorite point of reference, because of his fondness for making "mosaic assemblages of fragments," and because of "the abruptness of the digressions, which help the author play with the plot at will, the absence of logical motivations or the habit of playing around with them, the manner of breaking the structural line off into infinity"—all of which were supposed to characterize Gogol's style as well.[66] Investigations of the literary "setting" contemporaneous to Gogol have also been pushed deeper

[64] *Nikolai Vasil'evich Gogol'. 1829-1842. Ocherki iz istorii russkoi povesti i dramy*, 3d ed., St. Petersburg, 1911, p. 525.

[65] A good bibliography up to the mid-1920's can be found in V. V. Vinogradov, *Gogol' i natural'naya shkola*, Leningrad, 1925, pp. 31-41. For a virtually complete bibliography covering the period 1916-34, cf.: "Bibliograficheskii ukazatel' sochinenii Gogolya i literatura o nem na russkom yazyke za 1916-1934 gg.," in *N. V. Gogol'. Materialy i issledovaniya*, I, ed. V. V. Gippius, Moscow-Leningrad, 1936, 377-464. For a survey, from a basically socialist-realist viewpoint, of various critical approaches to Gogol, cf. V. A. Desnitsky, "Zadachi izucheniya zhizni i tvorchestva Gogolya," in *N. V. Gogol'. Materialy i issledovaniya*, II, ed. V. V. Gippius, Moscow-Leningrad, 1936, 1-105.

[66] Vinogradov, *Gogol' i natural'naya shkola*, p. 20. Cf. also V. B. Shklovsky, *"Tristram Shendi" Sterna i teoriya romana*, Petrograd, 1921.

during the past half century. Gukovsky, for one, has tried to show that the time-honored problem of Gogol's "realism" was relevant to themes and attitudes current in Russian literature as a whole in the 1830's.[67]

The acknowledgment of influences, whether operating on or proceeding from Gogol, requires a historical perspective. Still, it does not necessarily entail a belief in a purposeful history, as so many nineteenth-century critics thought. Thus, Gukovsky specifically rejects the idea that Gogol's works represent "some moral and philosophical school, in which he keeps on improving himself and overcoming various sins and peccadilloes and finally achieves perfection and victory in death. . . ." On the contrary, he points out that Gogol conceived virtually all his works in one brief span during the 1830's, and his later years represent, if anything, a decline.[68] Marxist criticism of Gogol embodies both views of history. Being teleological, it sets Gogol in a line of "progressive" writers stretching back into the Middle Ages, rising steadily throughout the nineteenth century, and culminating in Soviet times. Yet the idea of "objective value" tends to make the question of the writer's class loyalties irrelevant to his art, and thereby pulls away at what is, after all, the mainstay of the Marxist theory of history and culture. And by emphasizing universal values it tends to detach the writers of the past from the processes of history. Marxist critics hereby move closer to the ahistoricism of other twentieth-century schools of criticism than they care to admit.

Something of the same ambiguous attitude toward history can be detected in the articles by Vyacheslav Ivanov and Vasily Gippius which are included in this anthology. Ivanov's idea of comedy has much in common with that of Northrop Frye. Both distinguish varieties of the comic mode; assume that it can be embodied in any genre and is more or less universal in Western literatures; and insist that a writer, once he undertakes a comedy, is bound by certain conventions, whether or not he is consciously aware of them.[69] Ivanov's statement that *The Inspector General* points to something beyond itself and thus has both a "real" and a "mystical" dimension reminds us that he is a Symbolist. That "something beyond," however, is not merely a metaphysical or spiritual world, but also

---

[67] *Realizm Gogolya*, Moscow-Leningrad, 1959, p. 12.
[68] *Realizm Gogolya*, pp. 23-24.
[69] Frye, *Anatomy of Criticism*, esp. pp. 43-49.

a world of literary conventions, of which Gogol was largely ignorant, specifically the Greek Old Comedy (which Ivanov, as a trained classicist, knew well).

Gogol himself was aware that in *The Inspector General* he had created a new kind of comedy. In one sense, Gippius's article is an extended gloss on the provocative but not always lucid comments on the nature of laughter that are scattered throughout Gogol's writings.[70] He is interested (as Ivanov is not) in the history of the Russian comedy between the 1770's and the 1830's, as a way of defining Gogol's achievement. He takes care to tie the changes that occurred in the drama to changes in society itself: this was *de rigueur* in 1936, when socialist realism had become official doctrine. He also echoes the Soviet insistence on Gogol's "realism." But he brilliantly turns what was perhaps political stricture to literary advantage. First of all, he shows that whatever Gogol's intentions may have been, social commentary is inherent in social comedy: the playwright must follow the conventions of the genre. More important, he demonstrates that the social theme of the play—true and false service—is at the same time an esthetic theme. His emphasis on Gogol as a conscious craftsman recalls the Formalists, but unlike most of them he confronts the political and social aspects of the play and makes a successful case for them as esthetic categories. Ivanov does much the same in demonstrating how the play's esthetic and social functions merge in the chorus: Gippius's "collectivity" and Ivanov's "chorality" are not so very different.

Nearly all sociological criticism measures the art of *The Inspector General* by externals: society as it "actually was" in Russian provincial towns of the early nineteenth century. Gippius —and to a lesser extent Ivanov—demonstrates that a respect for "ideas" in literature need not grate upon an ear that is sensitive to the dynamics of plot and tradition. His essay is a *tour de force* which brings together two very different critical approaches and grounds them firmly on the bedrock of literary history.

VIII

Gogol's contemporaries had remarked certain peculiarities of his style: the mixture, within the same work, of "high" and "low"

---

[70] The most extensive expression of his ideas on "laughter" is to be found in his essay "Peterburgskie zapiski 1836 goda," *PSS*, VIII, 1952, 177-190.

language; the lavish deployment of small details; the Homeric similes; the supposedly eccentric imagery (such as "coal-black clouds"); the violation of orderly structure by digressions. But it was only in the twentieth century that critics began to classify random observations of this sort and work out a description of Gogol's style. Primacy here—if not in chronology, then certainly in importance—belongs to a book I have already mentioned: *On the Nature of Gogol's Style*, by I. E. Mandelshtam.[71]

Mandelshtam posits the existence of "a general poetic style"— a familiar, accepted, and therefore neutral language, deviations from which define individual styles. (Here he foreshadows, by nearly twenty years, the Formalist notion that literary development occurs when innovations become accepted as normal and therefore fail to strike the reader's notice; a truly creative writer is then compelled to make his art "strange.") In Mandelshtam's view, Gogol began with "the absence of any style" and gradually introduced certain "elements" to create a style that was uniquely his. Much of the book is given over to listing and classifying these elements—epithets, Ukrainianisms, vulgarisms, metaphors, and the like.

This is the book's most useful feature. But its most original one is also the least developed. Mandelshtam believes that every "word" (a concept he never defines) contains both objective and subjective elements—that is, an "aggregate of objective signs" (presumably referential or denotative meanings), and connotations introduced by the attitude of the user toward the concept being expressed (pp. 165-67). He is convinced that we must know the writer's psyche in order to distinguish these elements. "To the degree that works bear traces of what a man has experienced, felt, and thought, then more elements from his own soul and personality will enter into the language of these works, the language will be more individual" (p. 53). It is therefore possible to deduce the psyche from imagery, particularly when repetitions occur, and imagery from the psyche. Regrettably, Mandelshtam does not practice what he preaches. As a kind of afterthought, he wonders how far Gogol's style "determines the traits of his character" (p. 345). With this he raises, but again carries no further, a problem that interests workers in the field now known as psycholinguistics: to what extent is our perception

---

[71] *O kharaktere Gogolevskogo stilya. Glava iz istorii russkogo literaturnogo yazyka*, Helsingfors, 1902. Page references in text.

of the universe determined by the way our native language is structured? Can we "see" what our language does not give us to see?[72]

For all its unevenness, Mandelshtam's book has had an enormous influence on the course of style-studies in Russian. One of its close readers was V. V. Vinogradov, a critic and linguist who became famous in the 1920's largely because of his books and articles on the styles of Gogol and Dostoevsky. He lavished praise on Mandelshtam's factual material but grumbled about the excursions into psychology: these, he felt, introduced an extra-literary dimension and required the critic to work with two incompatible methodologies. "Psychology," for Vinogradov, is merely a function of style: it operates as a "mask" within the work itself, as can be seen in the persona of the narrator in Gogol's early stories, or the lyrical digressions in *Dead Souls*. Understandably, he could not approve of Yermakov's book on Gogol, but declined to comment on it "in view of my lack of a sense of humor."[73]

In insisting that literary analysis is properly an analysis of style, in defining style as the language of a specific writer in a specific text, and in calling for a critical methodology independent of all other disciplines, Vinogradov was restating articles of faith that had already been set forth by the Formalists. They had begun to write around the time of the Bolshevik Revolution, and had been producing provocative studies of the language, structure, and devices of Russian and foreign works of literature.[74] Here they

[72] Cf. *Language, Thought, and Reality. Selected Writings of Benjamin Lee Whorf*, ed. and with introduction by John B. Carroll, Cambridge (Massachusetts), 1956.

[73] *Gogol' i natural'naya shkola*, esp. pp. 46-58. The remark about Yermakov is on p. 20.

[74] The standard account of the Formalist movement has been written by Victor Erlich, *Russian Formalism. History—Doctrine*, 2nd ed., The Hague (*Slavistic Printings and Reprintings*, 4), 1969. Cf. also Krystyna Pomorska, *Russian Formalist Theory and Its Poetic Ambiance*, The Hague (*Slavistic Printings and Reprintings*, 82), 1968. A useful brief account, with reference to other Slavic countries as well, can be found in William E. Harkins, "Slavic Formalist Theories in Literary Scholarship," *Word*, VIII, No. 2, August, 1951, pp. 177-185. For a stimulating treatment of Formalist prose-theory, cf. Jurij Striedter, "Zur formalistischen Theorie der Prosa und der literarischen Evolution," *Texte der Russischen Formalisten*, I, Munich, 1969, ix-lxxxiii. A useful anthology of readings in Formalist and Structuralist

had been reacting against what one of them, Boris Eichenbaum, called the "primitive historicism" that prevailed in Russian universities before World War I. Literary scholarship at that time, said Eichenbaum, was mainly devoted to biographical and psychological studies, and, in its treatment of the development of literary history, had not gone beyond the large-scale monographs of the later nineteenth century, in which "the main role was played by general concepts, which were clear to nobody, such as 'realism' and 'romanticism' . . . [literary] evolution was understood as a gradual perfecting, as progress [from romanticism to realism]. . . . Literature as such did not exist—it was replaced by material taken from the history of social movements, from biography, etc." In effect, Eichenbaum was restating objections made twenty years earlier by Symbolist critics in their reappraisals of Russian writers. But he attacked them too, for what he called "impressionistic studies and 'silhouettes,' " and, like his fellow Formalists, insisted that literary studies could be put on a strictly "scientific" basis.[75]

As a writer with especially striking traits of style, Gogol was a favorite of the Formalist critics, and stimulated some of their best work. One of the earliest examples was an article by Eichenbaum himself, entitled "How Gogol's 'Overcoat' Is Made," first published in 1918, and translated in the present collection.

The punning title could stand as a capsule definition of Formalism in its earliest period: the writer is a conscious craftsman, a highly skilled maker of artifacts. His "mind" is of no relevance or interest: we need not even know *who* created a particular work, only *what* that work is. Thus for Eichenbaum, the "personal tone" of the narrator of "The Overcoat" does not represent a "confession" by the author, as it does for Yermakov, but is a technical device that creates *skaz* and makes possible those experiments in sound which are the story's chief aim. Just as irrelevant as "psychology," for Eichenbaum, are literary history, Gogol's other works, and any ideas that can be paraphrased from the text. He

---

theory is now available in English: *Readings in Russian Poetics: Formalist and Structuralist Views*, ed. Ladislav Matejka and Krystyna Pomorska, Cambridge (Massachusetts), 1971.

[75] "Teoriya 'formal'nogo metoda,' " in *Literatura. Teoriya. Kritika. Polemika*, Leningrad, 1926, pp. 142-143. The works of A. M. Pypin and S. A. Vengerov are examples of the kind of "historicism" that displeased the Formalists. For an example of what Eichenbaum would undoubtedly regard as Symbolist "impressionism," cf. Innokenty Annensky, *Kniga otrazhenii*, St. Petersburg, 1906.

fastens his gaze on the workings of language, which are self-contained and self-propelling, and have no meaning or purpose outside the story.

Eichenbaum does owe debts to earlier theorists and critics. The assumption that sound shapes content—indeed, often *is* content—echoes a tenet of Symbolist esthetics. The description of Gogol's characters as "petrified poses" repeats an observation made by Vasily Rozanov. Mandelshtam had already discussed Gogol's puns and his fascination with foreign words. Vinogradov detected the influence of so-called *Ohrenphilologie* on Eichenbaum's treatment of sound, and believed that the narrative techniques of writers like Remizov, Bely and Zamyatin—all of whom critics have tended to include in the "Gogol school"—had shaped his conception of style. But by and large, Eichenbaum's approach is original: Vinogradov aptly defined it as one that emphasizes "articulated sound and acoustics."[76] It recasts many of the stock themes of the critical literature in fresh terms. The duality of "laughter" and "tears," for example, now becomes the alternation of two levels of style—comic and rhetorical—which creates a grotesque texture that motivates the ending. And the fact that Eichenbaum weaned this technique on the best-known of all Gogol's stories, and the one about which Russian critics have had the most to say, gave his article a resonance quite disproportionate to its modest size.

Eichenbaum's article provided one possible model for a Formalist analysis of a work of art. Other Formalists worked in different ways—Viktor Shklovsky, for example, largely with plot in prose-fiction, Yury Tynyanov most impressively with poetic diction.[77] Such variety gave some substance to Eichenbaum's

[76] *Gogol' i natural'naya shkola*, pp. 13-15. Krystyna Pomorska characterizes *Ohrenphilologie* as a "school of phonetics associated with the names of two German scholars, E. Sievers and his disciple B. Saran," which stood in contrast to "the traditional 'Augenphilologie,' " and, when applied to literary analysis, emphasized "oral composition [*skaz*]" (*Russian Formalist Theory*, pp. 17-18).

[77] Cf., e.g., Shklovsky, *"Tristram Shendi" Sterna i teoriya romana*, Petrograd, 1921. In English as "Sterne's *Tristram Shandy*: Stylistic Commentary," in *Russian Formalist Criticism: Four Essays*, translated and with an introduction by Lee T. Lemon and Marion J. Reis, Lincoln, Nebraska, 1965, pp. 25-27; this collection also includes a translation of Shklovsky's important theoretical article "Iskusstvo, kak priem" under the (not entirely accurate) title of "Art as Technique." For an example of Tynyanov's approach, cf.

statement that Formalism was concerned with "a question not of method but of the object of study," that it was an inductive, not a deductive, procedure. Presumably, then, each "object of study" dictates the approach best suited to it: "We do not vouch for our schemes if people try to apply them to facts we do not know."[78] This claim of "scientific" accuracy was typical of early Formalism. But the critical performances themselves rarely demonstrated it. Eichenbaum, in his own article on Gogol, begins with a theory of narrative technique, and brings in material from "The Overcoat" by way of substantiation—hardly an inductive approach. Those parts of the story which do not fit the theory are simply left out of consideration—notably the long stretch of "neutral" narrative in the middle of the story. That is to say, Eichenbaum does not account for the *entire* work, even in terms of style, and he thereby fails to skirt one of the pitfalls into which Formalist analyses tend to tumble.

Alexander Slonimsky makes a specific disclaimer in his *Technique of the Comic in Gogol*: "My method is not 'formalistic,' as it might appear to be at first glance, but rather 'esthetic.' "[79] He obviously is heavily indebted to Formalist techniques and assumptions, but his theoretical apparatus is much more visible than that of most early Formalist studies, and his range far greater. Gogol's work is studied not so much for itself as for what it says of a state of mind, a particular comic vision of the world which pervades everything he wrote and is in turn an instance of a nearly universal concept of the comic. No pure Formalist (assuming that one exists) would tie a discussion of the grotesque to Gogol's religious and moral preoccupations, as Slonimsky does. He also creates a historical underpinning to explain Gogol's version of the comic. In these ways, he forecast the direction that Formalism as a whole ultimately took: it moved outward, from a preoccupation with the work itself, into the *œuvre* of the writer as a whole, and from there into literary history. It was not long before V. V. Vinogradov, among others, was asserting that the scholar must investigate the stylistic traditions a writer appropriates, the methods by which he transforms them, and the

---

"Oda kak oratorskii zhanr," in *Arkhaisty i novatory*, Leningrad, 1929, pp. 48-86.

[78] "Teoriya 'formal'nogo metoda,' " p. 143.

[79] *Tekhnika komicheskogo u Gogolya*, Petrograd, 1923, p. 5. This study is translated in the present collection.

ways in which these transformations are perceived and used by his contemporaries and his followers.[80] And as the 1920's wore on into the 30's, previously "irrelevant" disciplines like sociology and economics began to leave their mark. Even the work of an erstwhile purist like Vinogradov, who had protested against the admixture of different methodologies, underwent change. It is instructive to compare two long studies he wrote on Gogol's style: the first in 1925, the second more than ten years later. In the earlier one, he described the development of Gogol's style as a "struggle" among various elements within a closed literary system. But in 1936, he took care to identify the various social groups out of which the styles in question arose, and concluded that "the breadth and authenticity of the scope of Russian social life was determined by the extent to which Gogol knew the styles and dialects of the Russian language as spoken by various classes, groups and professions."[81]

To some extent, these developments were the result of natural dynamics within Formalism itself. But outside forces were also at work. Most Marxists had long been hostile to Formalism. They granted that it could perform a useful preliminary operation in collecting and classifying literary "facts," but they deemed it incapable of making those grand syntheses that were essential for placing a literary work into the context of history, not only because Formalism disregarded a writer's class outlook, but also because it did not share the correct (Marxist) view of the world.[82] In the relatively permissive climate of the earlier 1920's, these two radically different approaches to literature were allowed to coexist and compete. But such tolerance withered toward the end of the decade, and by 1932 the doctrine of socialist realism was proclaimed as the only true and therefore trusted way of approaching art.

Formalism had in effect come to an end in Russia two years before, when its chief theoretician, Viktor Shklovsky, announced that it was a "scholarly error," allowed it only a limited usefulness for defining the "technical" aspects of literature, and declared that

[80] *Etyudy o stile Gogolya*, Leningrad, 1926, p. 10.

[81] The earlier study is *Gogol' i natural'naya shkola*, Leningrad, 1925. The later one is "Yazyk Gogolya," in *N. V. Gogol'. Materialy i issledovaniya*, ii, ed. V. V. Gippius, Moscow-Leningrad, 1936, 330.

[82] For a discussion of the polemics between Marxists and Formalists, see Erlich, *Russian Formalism*, ch. six.

Marxism was the only true "method."[83] But Formalism continued to develop among Russian critics in emigration. One of its finest achievements can be seen in Dmitry Chizhevsky's article on "The Overcoat," which appeared in 1938 and has been translated for this anthology.

Clearly, Chizhevsky owes a great deal to Formalism, with his emphasis on craftsmanship, his assumption that everything in the text is meaningful, his focus on the word as the basic unit of structure and semantics, his equation of form and content, his interest in word-play, and his attempt to break through the crust of critical clichés by making the story "strange," that is, by applying a technique of slow, careful reading that aims to recapture some of the impact that the story must have had on its first readers. But Chizhevsky ranges far beyond the neat but narrow technique of Eichenbaum's article, and even beyond the much looser Formalism of Slonimsky's approach. Had Eichenbaum discussed the word "even," he would probably have made the point that it functions to stylize speech as *skaz*. Chizhevsky does say this; but he goes on to show how the little word carries the structure and meaning of the story as a whole, by virtue of its capacity to "elevate" what follows it. Both critics believe that the story is built on contrasts. Eichenbaum locates them in two different kinds of style (comic and rhetorical), which do not account for long stretches of narration; Chizhevsky proposes a thematic definition of the styles (petty and big) which is less rigid and therefore covers more of the story.

Although Chizhevsky does not regard literary history as essential to an understanding of "The Overcoat," he devotes some attention to it nonetheless. He approaches some of the more traditional (and non-Formalistic) views of Gogol when he says that "The Overcoat" was written to explore a particular theme that runs throughout Gogol's work and life: "the kindling of the human soul, its rebirth under the influence of love." Unlike most traditionalists, however, he begins with the text itself—indeed, with one of its smallest meaningful units ("even")—and works centrifugally. He can therefore talk about what the story *does* mean, whereas most critics who deal with over-reaching themes begin with a prefabricated "personality" of the author and end up talking about what the story *should* mean. Chizhevsky's talent for

[83] "Pamyatnik nauchnoi oshibke," *Literaturnaya gazeta*, No. 4, January 27, 1930, p. 1.

finding the whole contained in a part may remind some readers of the work of Erich Auerbach.

At the outset, Chizhevsky distinguishes three approaches in critical writings on Gogol: the social, the formalistic, and the moral or ethical. Each he finds wanting: the first and third because they misread the text and cannot account for the ending; the second because it is self-contained and respects neither the story's "basic content" nor its place in Gogol's *œuvre* as a whole. In his concern with a meaning that ultimately involves more than the text itself, Chizhevsky leans toward the first and third; in his belief that meaning must come out of the work itself, he leans toward the second. His method may be taken as an illustration of what some historians of literature, in attempting to define the course taken by Formalism in the 1930's, have labeled "structuralism."[84]

Another offshoot of Formalism studies recurring patterns of plot, theme, or imagery. It has been called *syuzhetologiya* (literally "plotology"), and Leon Stilman's two brief articles, translated here, are good examples of how it works.

Stilman recognizes that recurrent motifs, especially when concealed, may answer to unconscious promptings within the writer's psyche; and in other articles he has shown himself to be an adept practitioner of psychological criticism. Here, however, he is interested only in "the conscious artistic usage" of such motifs, as a Formalist would be too. One of the major Symbolist poets and critics, Innokenty Annensky, has pointed to the predominance of a single anatomical image in two of Gogol's works—the nose in the story of the same name, and the eyes in "The Portrait."[85] Actually, as Stilman shows in his first article, the eyes, or vision, are a basic image in nearly everything Gogol wrote, whether fiction or non-fiction, from his earliest to his last years. But this image is not really organic to the structure of the works: it could be moved around at random; sometimes it is introduced by way of digression. In a sense, the critic has merely to enumerate each instance. But there is a subtler and more interesting sort of recurrent imagery in Gogol too, as Stilman points out. It is organic to the plot—indeed, it builds the plot—and is often so concealed that it can be uncovered only by a careful comparison of different

[84] E.g., Erlich, *Russian Formalism*, pp. 159-161, 198-201.

[85] "Problema Gogolevskogo yumora," *Kniga otrazhenii*, St. Petersburg, 1906, p. 26.

texts. Such is the pattern of man-woman-matchmaker, which forms the subject of Stilman's second article. The play *Marriage* establishes the pattern in an obvious way. From there, Stilman traces its submerged variations through a number of works that are very different in genre, mode, and style. A less disciplined critic might not have resisted the temptation to discourse on Gogol's intentions, or mind, or psychology. Stilman sticks to the text, and makes his points with a precision and clarity that few Russian critics command. His work—which in these two cases dates from the mid-1960's—shows that the legacy of Formalism is still vigorous.

IX

By now the facts of Gogol's life are well established. We know everything about it that we are likely ever to know; any "enigmas" or "contradictions" must simply stand. The same certainly cannot be said about his work. Large problems of interpretation remain. For one thing, no substantial monograph on Gogol's masterpiece, *Dead Souls*, has ever been published. For another, his non-fictional writings are largely unexplored. They have been ransacked to strengthen the flimsy fabric of his biography; otherwise, critics have tended to treat them as aberrations from the "true Gogol" (that is, the writer of fiction) or have tried to read them as more explicit statements of what supposedly is implicit in the fiction. Yet their deeper connections with the fiction have not been really probed—connections that depend not so much on paraphrasable common ideas, but, say, on structure and imagery. What, for example, does Gogol's tendency to devote each letter to a single subject, in the eighteenth-century manner, tell us about the structure of the first part of *Dead Souls*, where each scene is normally devoted to one character or one incident? Can the various and often contradictory personalities that Gogol puts forth in his letters conceivably be poses or masks which he is testing out before incorporating them into his fiction?[86] Some of the better critics have seen possibilities for explorations along such lines. Vasily Gippius, for one, regards *Selected Passages* as a purely literary work, with roots in the sentimental and utopistic tradition. Vinogradov believes that Gogol, in his later years, was preoccupied not

[86] These two problems have been suggestively raised by William Mills Todd, "Gogol's Epistolary Writing," *Columbia Essays in International Affairs*, v, *The Dean's Papers, 1969*, New York, 1970, esp. 72-76.

only with a spiritual Odyssey but also with a struggle to develop a new style. Yet neither Gippius nor Vinogradov pursues these suggestive ideas. Vyacheslav Ivanov, in his article on *The Inspector General*, sees Gogol's moral interpretation of the play as "another artistic transformation" of it; what if this were also true of everything he wrote in the 1840's and 50's?[87]

Entirely fresh approaches are of course conceivable. New scholarly disciplines can leave deep marks on literary studies as well. For example, some of the theories of psycholinguistics might help bridge the gap between linguistics and psychology of which Vinogradov complained. One of the more fruitful and spectacular of modern Western disciplines—mythology—has not been applied systematically to any major Russian writer. Gogol's works teem with promising material, the motifs of incest and cannibalism in "A Terrible Vengeance" being one obvious instance. There are hints throughout the critical literature at insights that could be called proto-mythical. Apollon Grigoriev, for example, presupposes the existence of a "primordial tradition" and a "primordial unity of the human race," which interconnect all art.[88] The familiar notion of characters as types has mythological implications, as we see in Merezhkovsky's interpretation of Chichikov and Khlestakov as manifestations of primordial evil. Vyacheslav Ivanov puts a toe on a part of the territory that early "myth" critics like Gilbert Murray and Jane Harrison have mapped and tracked. Perhaps Yermakov, of all the critics represented in this collection, goes further toward outlining a "mythological" view of Gogol than anyone else so far. He dwells on the content of the unconscious that is shared by all men, dolts and geniuses alike, and points up the meanings of certain universal symbols, such as the cloak, the shoe, and the nose. But no significant work has continued along these lines. This is not surprising in Soviet Russia. Marxism is at bottom hostile to mythology for the same reasons that it is hostile to psychological criticism: both tend to deny the workings of class and of history, and emphasize unchanging values instead.[89]

[87] Gippius, *Gogol'*, Leningrad, 1924, pp. 168-186; Vinogradov, *Gogol' i natural'naya shkola*, p. 63; Ivanov, article in the present collection.

[88] "Kriticheskii vzglyad na osnovy, znachenie i priemy sovremennoi kritiki iskusstv," *Sobranie sochinenii*, II, ed. V. Savodnik, Moscow, 1915, 90.

[89] J. G. Frazer's *The Golden Bough* appeared in a Russian translation in the Soviet Union, as *Zolotaya vetv'*, 1928. But cf. the characterization of Frazer in the authoritative *Great Soviet Encyclopedia*: "Frazer's theory is built on idealistic foundations, inasmuch as it derives magic, and religion in

The old approaches, however, have certainly not been exhausted. No satisfactory sociology of Gogol's work has yet been produced. Historical criticism has so far made no systematic and comprehensive account of Gogol's impact on Russian literature. Of course, formalistic, psychological, and religious approaches cannot at the moment be developed as such in the Soviet Union. But the lines that separate them are not, after all, very precisely drawn. Marxists, for example, share certain biases with critics of a religious orientation. Both take for granted that ideological growth is desirable, and see Gogol's career as a dialectical development marked by crises of faith. An interest in crises marks the psychological critics, even though they regard the personality as more or less fixed from childhood. In addition, psychology and religion emphasize the hidden sides of Gogol and regard his writings as "confessions" aimed at working off, in the one case, compulsive drives, in the other, a sense of original sin. Even Formalism and certain sociological approaches share some common ground, such as indifference to the artist's personality, and an emphasis on the work as an objective fact. Many other points of contact and lines of interaction can be drawn. Their existence suggests the possibility of devising new approaches from various combinations of the old ones. Vasily Gippius's article on *The Inspector General* suggests, for instance, what can be done with an intelligent mating of formalism and sociology.

In the Soviet Union itself, several recent studies suggest that a new generation of critics is finding new things to say about Gogol. And what about other countries? During the past forty years, much excellent work has appeared in Europe, especially in Scandinavia and Germany (which seems to have a special affinity for Gogol and Dostoevsky). And during the past quarter-century, the great upsurge in Slavic studies outside the Soviet Union has stimulated many excellent appreciations of Gogol by professional Slavists.[90] Nearly all of it, however, is on a small scale.

---

general, only from the psychology of the individual," and fails to connect religious phenomena "with the material conditions of the life of society" ("Frezer," *Bol'shaya sovetskaya entsiklopediya*, Vol. 45, 2nd ed., 1956, p. 584).

[90] The bibliography is extensive. For suggested readings in English, cf. the bibliography in the present study. For a much fuller listing of works on Gogol in English, German, French, Italian, and Spanish, cf. *Letters of Nikolai Gogol*, selected and edited by Carl R. Proffer, Ann Arbor, 1967, pp. 237-244.

So far there has been no large monograph that breaks much fresh ground: Gippius's book of 1924 still stands as the best compendious treatment of Gogol. Vladimir Nabokov's *Nikolai Gogol*, first published by New Directions in 1944, is not a particularly profound study; but it has probably done more than any other work of criticism in this country to spark an interest in Gogol among readers who know no Russian. Translations of all the major works of fiction and drama do exist. It is time for our better literary critics—regardless of linguistic equipment—to look more closely at Gogol. Their attention will be richly rewarded, and their readers will discover that Gogol's voice sounds as modern to English ears today as it has to Russian ears for nearly a century and a half.

1

Dmitry Merezhkovsky
(1865-1941)

As a poet and novelist, Merezhkovsky was prolific but not of the first rank. He broke into print in the 1880's, first with poems on social themes, and then with the sort of "decadent" verse that was soon to become modish. His best-known novels, which still enjoy some popularity in English, are represented by the trilogy *Christ and Antichrist: Julian the Apostate* (1896), *Leonardo da Vinci* (1901), and *Peter and Alexis* (1905).

However, it is on his activities as a critic and cultural figure that Merezhkovsky's real importance in Russian literature rests. More than anyone else among his contemporaries, he was responsible for popularizing (largely through his fiction) a knowledge of classical antiquity and the Renaissance. His long article entitled "On the Reasons for the Decline of Contemporary Russian Literature and on the New Currents in It" ("O prichinakh upadka i o novykh techeniyakh sovremennoi russkoi literatury," 1892) propounded an idea of culture which became virtually programmatic for the Symbolist movement that was to follow. His reinterpretations of nineteenth-century Russian writers set a standard for an entire generation. For example, he valued Turgenev not for "realistic" novels like *Fathers and Sons*, but for later works of a "mystical" or "supernatural" cast (like "Klara Milich"), which he considered proto-Symbolist. *Tolstoy and Dostoevsky* (1901) established an antithesis between the "seer of the flesh" and the "seer of the spirit," which critics have honored ever since. The duality is characteristic of Merezhkovsky's thought—Christ and Antichrist, Chichikov and Khlestakov, and so on—although he envisaged the ultimate creation of one vast synthesis.

With his wife Zinaida Gippius—a much finer poet—Merezhkovsky became the leader, in 1903, of the so-called Religious-Philosophical Movement. It opposed positivism and materialism, cultivated spirituality and idealism, and aimed at reconciling the religiously inclined members of the intelligentsia with Russian

Orthodoxy. The Merezhkovskys also gave encouragement to a number of young writers, notably Alexander Blok and Andrey Bely, and for a time, literary life in St. Petersburg more or less revolved around them. In 1920, Merezhkovsky and his wife emigrated from Russia. They spent the rest of their lives in Paris.

"Gogol and the Devil" ("Gogol' i chert") was first published in 1906. I have used the text as reprinted in a later edition of Merezhkovsky's works (*Polnoe sobranie sochinenii*, x, St. Petersburg-Moscow, 1911). Apart from correcting some errors of fact, I have made virtually no changes in Merezhkovsky's text, and I have tried to suggest his highly rhetorical manner of writing.

Gogol and the Devil

by Dmitry Merezhkovsky

One senses something terrible
in the fate of our poets.
Gogol.[1]

I

"HOW TO PRESENT the Devil as a fool"—this, by his own acknowledgment, was the central idea of all of Gogol's life and thought. "My sole concern has long been that after my work people should have a good hearty laugh at the Devil."[2]

In Gogol's religious outlook, the Devil is a mystical essence and a real being, in which eternal evil, a denial of God, has been concentrated. Gogol the artist investigates the nature of the mystical essence in the light of laughter; Gogol the man contends with this real being using laughter as a weapon: Gogol's laughter is man's struggle with the Devil.

God is the infinite, the beginning and end of all being. The Devil is the denial of God and consequently the denial of the infinite as well, the denial of all beginnings and ends. The Devil is something that is begun and is left unfinished, but purports to be without beginning or end. The Devil is the noumenal median of being, the denial of all heights and depths—eternal planarity, eternal *banality*.[3] The sole subject of Gogol's art is the Devil in

---

[1 "V chem zhe nakonets sushchestvo russkoi poezii i v chem ee osobennost'," *Vybrannye mesta iz perepiski s druz'yami* (hereafter abbreviated as *Vyb. mesta*), *PSS*, VIII, 1952, 402.]

[2 Letter to S. P. Shevyryov, April 27, 1847. [Stepan Petrovich Shevyryov (1806-64) was a professor at Moscow University, an important (now undeservedly neglected) literary critic, and one of Gogol's closest friends. "My work" in the passage quoted refers specifically to *Selected Passages from Correspondence with Friends*, but at this stage in Gogol's career, it is likely, as Merezhkovsky suggests, that he meant it to apply to all his work.]

[3 "Banality" renders *poshlost'*, probably the most famous of all the untranslatable Russian words. It indicates ostentatious bad taste, or pretentious vulgarity. "Planarity" renders *ploskost'*: it is rather too "high" a stylistic correspondence, but I chose it in an effort to suggest the rhythm and rhyme of the original *véchnaya plóskost', véchnaya póshlost'*.]

just this sense, that is, the Devil as the manifestation of "man's immortal banality," as seen beneath the specifics of place and time—historical, national, governmental, social; the manifestation of absolute, eternal, universal evil—banality *sub specie aeternitatis*.

"People have had a good deal to say about me, attempting to analyze certain sides of my character, but they have failed to define what is essential about me. Pushkin was the only one who perceived it. He always told me that no other writer to date has possessed this gift of bringing out the banality of life so clearly, of knowing how to delineate the banality of a banal individual with such forcefulness and in such a way that all those *tiny details* which ordinarily escape notice suddenly gleam *large* in everyone's eye. This is my hallmark; it is mine alone, and no other writer seems to possess it."[4]

Everyone can perceive evil in great violations of the moral law, in rare and unusual misdeeds, in the staggering climaxes of tragedies. Gogol was the first to detect invisible evil, most terrible and enduring, not in tragedy, but in the absence of everything tragic; not in power, but in impotence; not in insane extremes, but in all-too-sensible moderation; not in acuity and profundity, but in inanity and planarity, in the banality of all human feelings and thoughts; not in the greatest things, but in the smallest. Gogol did for the moral dimension what Leibnitz had done for the mathematical: he discovered, we might say, the *differential calculus*, the infinitely great significance of infinitely small magnitudes of good and evil. He was the first to understand that it is the Devil who is the smallest thing that exists, and seems big only because we ourselves are small; that he is the weakest thing that exists and seems strong only because we ourselves are weak. "I give things their true names," Gogol says, "in other words I call the Devil 'the Devil,' I don't deck him out in a magnificent costume à la Byron, because I know that he goes around in an ordinary tail-coat. . . . The Devil has already come into the world without a mask; he has appeared in his own true form."[5]

[4] "Chetyre pis'ma k raznym litsam po povodu 'Mertvykh dush,'" *Vyb. mesta, PSS*, VIII, 1952, 292.

[5] Letter to S. T. Aksakov, May 16, 1844. The Aksakov family gave some of the best minds to Russian culture of the nineteenth century. The father, Sergey Timofeyevich (1791-1859), wrote the wonderfully sensitive and poetic *Family Chronicle* (*Semeinaya khronika*, 1852) and *Years of Child-*

The greatest power the Devil possesses is his capacity to look like something he is not. Though a median, he looks like one of the two extremes or infinities of the world—sometimes the Son made Flesh, who has rebelled against the Father and the Holy Spirit, sometimes the Father and the Holy Spirit, who have rebelled against the Son made Flesh. Though a creature, he seems like a creator; though dark, he seems like the dayspring; though inert, he seems winged; though laughable, he seems to be laughing. The laughter of Mephistopheles, the pride of Cain, the strength of Prometheus, the wisdom of Lucifer, the freedom of the superman —these are some of the various "magnificent costumes," the masks which this eternal mime, this parasite, this ape of God has donned, in different ages and among different peoples. Gogol was the first to glimpse the Devil without a mask, the first to glimpse his real self, a self that is terrible not because it is extraordinary, but because it is ordinary and banal. He was the first to realize that the self of the Devil is not remote, alien, strange, fantastic, but is, rather, a very common, familiar, real and "human, all too human" self, the self of the crowd, a self such as everyone has, almost our own self at those times when we dare not be our real selves and consent to be like everyone.

Gogol's two principal heroes—Khlestakov, in *The Inspector General*, and Chichikov, in *Dead Souls*—are two contemporary Russian selves, two hypostases of eternal and universal evil, of man's immortal banality. As Pushkin put it: "Those were the representations of two demons."[6]

The inspired dreamer Khlestakov and the worldly entrepreneur Chichikov: concealed behind these two diametrical opposites is a third self which unites them: the self of the Devil "without a mask," "in a tail-coat," "in his own true form," the self of our eternal alter ego, who shows us our reflection in himself, as in a

---

hood (*Detskie gody Bagrova vnuka*, 1858), both regarded as classics of Russian literature, and *The History of My Friendship with Gogol* (*Istoriya moego znakomstva s Gogolem*, first complete edition 1890), one of the best memoirs of Gogol ever produced. His two sons, Konstantin (1817-60) and Ivan (1823-86), were influential intellectuals and leading figures in the so-called Slavophile movement (see footnote 28).]

[6 "To byli dvukh besov izobrazhen'ya"—a line from the poem "V nachale zhizni shkolu pomnyu ya" (1830). It does not refer to any of Gogol's characters—its date alone makes that impossible—but rather to two statues seen by the poet in a garden. But these statues do have certain traits that may have suggested Chichikov and Khlestakov to Merezhkovsky.]

mirror, and says: "What are you laughing at? You're laughing at yourselves!"[7]

II

Just bash this swine [the Devil] in the snout and don't let it bother you a bit. He's nothing more than an ink-slinger and a double-dealer. He's like a minor civil servant who turns up in some town ostensibly to conduct an investigation. He'll throw dust in everyone's eyes, give everyone a dressing-down, and start shouting his head off. All you have to do is tremble a bit and draw back, and he'll pluck up his courage. But the moment you make a move toward him, he'll tuck his tail between his legs. We're the ones who make a giant out of him; actually, he is the Devil knows what. There's a reason why proverbs exist, and a proverb says: "The Devil bragged about ruling the whole world, but God didn't give him power even over a pig." . . . Scaring, swindling, driving people to despair—that's his business.[8]

It is easy to guess the real identity of this "minor civil servant who turns up in some town ostensibly to conduct an investigation," that is, someone who comes disguised as an inspector general and proceeds to give everyone a dressing-down.

In the draft notes for *Dead Souls*, Gogol writes: "The whole town, with the whole whirlwind of gossip, a prototype of the slothfulness (that is, the banality) of the life of all mankind in the mass. . . . How can a depiction of universal slothfulness in all its varieties be reduced so as to bear some resemblance to the slothfulness of the town? And how can the slothfulness of the town be expanded into a prototype of universal slothfulness?"[9]

Thus, in both of Gogol's greatest works—*The Inspector General* and *Dead Souls*—the scenes of a provincial Russian town of the 1820's, again by his own acknowledgment, have, aside from the obvious meaning, a certain veiled, eternal, universal, prototypical, or, as we would now say, *symbolic* one: for "symbol"

[7 This is the mayor's apostrophe to the audience in the final act of *The Inspector General*.]

[8 Letter to S. T. Aksakov, May 16, 1844. The second sentence actually comes much earlier than the first. Original italics omitted.]

[9 "(Zametki) k 1-oi chasti ('Mertvykh dush')," PSS, VI, 1951, 693. The parenthetical remark is Merezhkovsky's.]

means "prototype." In the "slothfulness," the emptiness, the banality of man's world, it is not man but the Devil himself, the "father of the lie" in the form of Khlestakov or Chichikov, who weaves his eternal, universal "web of gossip." As Gogol wrote in a personal letter on a personal matter:

> I am fully convinced that it is the Devil and not man who weaves the web of gossip. From carelessness and often from stupidity someone will blurt out a meaningless word, a word he might not even have intended to say (isn't this precisely the way that Dobchinsky and Bobchinsky blurted out the word "inspector general")? This word starts making the rounds; apropos of it someone else idly lets some other word drop; and little by little a tale weaves itself, without anyone's being aware of it. It's senseless to try to find its real author, because you can't find him. . . . Don't accuse anyone. . . . Remember that everything in the world is deception, everything appears to us to be something other than it really is. . . . Life is very, very difficult for us, forgetting as we do every minute that our actions will be inspected by the One Who cannot be bought off with anything.[10]

Does this not reveal the design of *The Inspector General* in full—not only the obvious one, which is understandable to all, but also the mystical one, which apparently has not been understood by anyone even to this day?

Khlestakov is not only a real human being, but a "phantom" as well: "he is a phantasmagoric figure," Gogol says, "who, mendacious deception incarnate, was carried off in the troika Heaven knows where."[11] The hero of "The Overcoat," Akaky Akakievich, becomes a phantom, just like Khlestakov, only not in life but after death—a corpse who frightens passers-by at the Kalinkin Bridge and pulls off their overcoats. And Poprishchin, the hero of "Diary of a Madman," becomes a fantastic, phantom figure, "Ferdinand VIII, King of Spain." All three start from the

[10] Letter to A. O. Smirnova, December 6 (o.s.), 1849. [Alexandra Osipovna Smirnova (1809-1882) was a lady-in-waiting to two Russian Empresses, a beautiful and intelligent woman, the friend of many Russian writers and the subject of many poems. She took Gogol very seriously as a spiritual guide, and tried to live up to the ideals he was preaching in the 1840's.]

[11] "Preduvedomlenie dlya tekh, kotorye pozhelali by sygrat' kak sleduet 'Revizora,'" *PSS*, IV, 1951, 118.]

same point: they are minor civil servants in St. Petersburg, de-personalized cells in the vast body of the state, infinitely tiny parts of an infinitely great whole. And from this starting-point—the almost total ingestion of a living human personality by a dead impersonal whole—they thrust out into emptiness, into space, describing three parabolas, each different but all equally monstrous: the first a lie, the second madness, the third a superstitious legend. In all three cases, the personality avenges itself for being negated as a reality; rejecting reality, it takes its vengeance in spectral, phantasmal self-assertion. Man tries to be something other than what he is, because he does not wish to be, he cannot be, he should not be—nothing. In the dead self of Akaky Akakievich, in the insane self of Poprishchin, in the lying self of Khlestakov, something genuine and suprarational glints through mendacity, madness, and death, something that exists within every human personality and from it cries out to mankind and to God: I am unique, there has never been anyone like me anywhere, nor will there ever be. I am everything for myself: "I, I, I," as Khlestakov shouts in his drunken frenzy.

As a real quantity in the state, Khlestakov is a cipher: "one of those people who are dubbed 'rather empty' in government offices." His own servant Osip, a fool and a rogue, despises his master: "it would be okay if he was really someone big, but he's just a plain old registry clerk."[12] However, he is the son of a nobleman, an old-fashioned sort of landowner from the depths of Russia, although he has maintained no ties with his family, his peasants, or his land. He is a landless and kinless St. Petersburg "proletarian" to the marrow of his bones, an artificial man, a homunculus sprung from Peter the Great's Table of Ranks as from an alchemist's retort. In his eyes, the people of the past, such as his father, are barbarians, virtually not people at all: "The yokels, they don't even know what 'at home' means. If some fool of a landowner pays them a visit, he crashes into the parlor

[12 I.e., a collegiate registrar, the lowest grade in the civil service. Osip mispronounces the word *registrator* as *elistratishka*, because it is foreign and he is uneducated. The Table of Ranks (Tabel' o Rangakh) was established by Peter the Great in 1722, as part of his reform of the state bureaucracy, and lasted until the end of the Romanov dynasty in 1917. Three branches of service were distinguished—court, military and civil—and each was divided into fourteen ranks, the fourteenth being the lowest. Promotion, in the military and civil service, depended on years of service or on merit: Khlestakov obviously has neither.]

like a bear." Yet the denial is mutual. As Osip says: "His daddy sends him a bit of money"; but if daddy should ever find out what sort of life his little boy is leading in St. Petersburg—"he don't work at nothing; instead of going to the office, he strolls along the [Nevsky] Prospect and plays cards"—then, "he wouldn't give a hoot that you was working for the government, he'd pull up your shirt and give you such a smacking you'd be rubbing yourself a good four days."

Intellectually and morally, Khlestakov is by no means a complete nonentity. "Khlestakov," as Gogol defines him, "is an adroit person, completely *comme il faut*, intelligent, perhaps even virtuous"—not too intelligent or too virtuous, to be sure, but not too stupid or wicked, either. He has a most ordinary sort of mind, a most ordinary sort of worldly conscience—common and lightweight. He embodies everything that has now become voguish and will later prove vulgar.[13] He is fashionably dressed and he also speaks, thinks, and feels according to fashion. "He belongs to a circle of people who apparently are in no way different from other young people," as Gogol remarks. He is like everyone else; his mind, his soul, his words, his face: all are like everyone else's. Again, according to Gogol's own profound characterization, *nothing should be sharply accentuated* in Khlestakov, that is, accentuated definitively, conclusively, decisively. Khlestakov's essential quality is precisely this lack of definition, this inconclusiveness. "He is incapable of giving sustained attention to any particular thought," incapable of focusing a single one of his thoughts or feelings and developing it fully. He has "lost all his beginnings and his ends," as Ivan Karamazov's Devil expresses it; he is the negation incarnate of all beginnings and ends, a moral and mental *median* incarnate, a mediocrity.

But the main forces that impel and control him reside not in his social, mental or moral self, but rather in his impersonal, unconscious, elemental being—in his instincts. Pre-eminent among them is the blind animal instinct of self-preservation—an unbelievably ravenous hunger. "I've never been so hungry in all my life. . . . Ugh, I even feel sick. . . ." This is not the simple hunger of a peasant who is satisfied with his daily bread, but the hunger of a lord and master. In asserting his right to satisfy this hunger, Khlestakov is very much aware of his social position: "you explain

[13 There is an untranslatable pun here: *V nem est' vse, chto teper' v khod poshlo i chto vposledstvii okazhetsya poshlym.*]

63

to him [the inn-keeper] in all seriousness that I need to eat. . . .
He thinks that just because a peasant like himself can go a whole
day without eating, other people can do the same. That's ridiculous!" "I want to eat, I need to eat"—by now this is something
absolute and infinite in Khlestakov's essential nature. In any event,
it is his natural beginning and end, his primary and ultimate truth.

Nature, having endowed him with this need, has also armed
him with a special power for satisfying it—the power of the lie, of
pretense, of knowing how to appear to be something other than he
is. And this power, once again, resides not in his intellect, not in
his will, but in the innermost recesses of his unconscious instinct.

Certain insects, by the shape and color of their bodies, can
mimic the shape and color of dead twigs, withered leaves, stones,
or other objects so exactly that even the human eye is completely
deceived. They make use of this ability as a weapon in the struggle
for existence, in order to evade enemies and capture prey. Something resembling this primordial, natural lie or mimicry of hypocrisy
has been lodged in Khlestakov by nature. In his mouth a lie is
an eternal "game of nature." His tongue lies as automatically and
uninhibitedly as his heart beats and his lungs breathe. As Gogol
says: "Khlestakov does not lie in a calculating or theatrically
bragging manner—not at all! He lies with feeling; his eyes express
the pleasure he derives from this. All in all, this is the best and
most poetic moment of his life—it is almost a form of inspiration."[14]

Khlestakov's lying has something in common with the artist's
power of invention. He intoxicates himself with his fancies to the
point of utter self-oblivion. Least of all has he any practical goals
or advantages in mind. His is a disinterested lie; it is lying for
lying's sake, art for art's sake. At this moment he asks nothing
of his listeners—only that they should believe him. He lies in-
nocently, guilelessly, and is the first to believe himself, the first
to deceive himself: this is the secret of the spell he casts. He lies
and he feels: this is good, this is true. For him, as for any artist,
what does not exist is more beautiful and therefore more true
than truth itself. He burns and quivers as if in holy ecstasy. There
is a kind of voluptuousness or sensuousness in such lying. If any-

[14 "Otryvok iz pis'ma, pisannogo avtorom vskore posle pervogo predstavleniya 'Revizora' k odnomu literatoru," *PSS*, IV, 1951, 100. Most of
Gogol's characterizations of Khlestakov as cited by Merezhkovsky come
from this article.]

one should try to expose him, he would simply not understand at first; then, with a sense of higher poetic truth and righteousness, he would look with scorn upon such a low and vulgar point of view. He would feel wounded, in a helpless and resentment-free way, like a child who has been wronged, like a poet who has been insulted by the mob. There is good reason why Gogol asserts that one of Khlestakov's chief characteristics is "disingenuousness and simplicity." Like any true genius, this genius of the lie has an almost childlike simplicity and openness. The Khlestakov who with such brazen effrontery takes bribes from the officials he has duped is now an utterly different person. The poet has vanished, inspiration has been extinguished:

> The soul drinks in the dream so cold,
> And he, perhaps, among the world's
> Inconsequential offspring, is
> The most inconsequential of them all.[15]

Another characteristic of his—equally primordial and elemental—is connected with lying. "I have," he acknowledges, "an extraordinary lightness of thought." Not only his thoughts but his feelings too, his actions, his words, even his "slender and delicate physique"—his entire being—manifest an "extraordinary lightness." He seems to have been entirely "spun from air."[16] He barely touches the ground: at any moment he may flutter up and fly away. Nothing difficult, burdensome, or profound exists for him or within him; there are no restraints, no barriers between truth and falsehood, good and evil, the lawful and the criminal; he does not even step across or transgress "all bounds and all limits," but rather flies over them by virtue of his inspiriting lightness. The greatest ideas that have weighed upon man century after century suddenly become lighter than a feather as soon as they enter Khlestakov's head.

Consider, for example, one of the leading ideas of the seven-

[15 These lines are from Pushkin's "The Poet" ("Poet," 1827). The translation is mine.]

[16 Literally, "lined with wind" (*vetrom podbit*). The "lightness" in the preceding sentence has a double meaning, which does not quite come off in translation. Khlestakov says that he has (literally) an "extraordinary lightness in (my) thoughts" (*legkost' v myslyakh*). By this he presumably means a ready wit or a quick mind; but the expression also suggests light-mindedness, frivolity (*legkomyslennost'*), and Merezhkovsky reinforces this with his "lined with wind" image.]

teenth and eighteenth centuries, an idea of Montaigne, Hobbes, and Jean-Jacques Rousseau: that of the "natural condition," of man's return to nature. When Khlestakov declares his love for the mayor's wife, she replies, in diffident bewilderment: "But allow me to observe that I am, in a certain sense—I am married." Khlestakov objects: "That doesn't matter. Love recognizes no distinctions; as Karamzin said: 'Only the laws condemn.' We shall betake ourselves beneath the bosky shade of babbling brooks. . . ."[17] That is to say, the laws of man condemn our free love, but we shall withdraw from mankind into nature, where other laws, eternal laws, hold sway. From the ancient Greek idyll of Daphnis and Chloe, who also found happiness beneath the bosky shade of babbling brooks, to the sentimental novels of the eighteenth century, the pastoral scenes in the style of Watteau and Boucher, and through Karamzin to Khlestakov—see what an incredible route human thought has travelled, and what it has become!

Still another version of this same idea of the opposition of nature and man, of the natural and the civilized state of existence is: "The country, of course, does have its hillsides and its brooks. . . . But then, who could compare it with St. Petersburg! Ah, St. Petersburg! Quite a life, indeed!" His servant Osip has exactly the same view of the blandishments of culture: "a refined and cultured life; theaters, dogs doing a dance for you, anything you want. Everyone talks refined and nice. . . . Everyone treats you real good, damn it all!"

Epicurean free-thinking, regenerated pagan wisdom, the principle of "enjoy life while you are alive"—Khlestakov condenses all this into an aphorism that conveys a new and affirmative wis-

[17 This is as absurd in Russian as in English. Literally it would read: "beneath the shade of streams" (*pod sen' strui*). Khlestakov is trying to imitate the language of sentimental novels, but gets the imagery all mixed up. The quote about the laws comes from Karamzin's story "The Isle of Bornholm" ("Ostrov Borngol'm," 1794). Nikolay Mikhailovich Karamzin (1766-1826) was a man of letters and the leading representative of Russian Sentimentalism. He created the modern Russian literary language, wrote the first recognizable modern short stories, and topped off his career with an immense history of Russia. He was also important as a popularizer of eighteenth-century European literary fashions in Russia. His best-known work is *Letters of a Russian Traveler* (*Pis'ma russkogo puteshestvennika*, 1792), which is available in an abridged English translation (New York, 1957).]

dom: "After all, that's what life is for—to pluck the flowers of pleasure." How simple, how easy for everyone to grasp! Will not this emancipation from all bonds of morality later become the Nietzschean and Karamazovian "There is no good or evil, all is permitted"? In both cases, the origin is the same: the wings of the eagle and the wings of the gnat struggle against the same universal laws of gravity.

This is paganism. But there is Christianity here too, in Khlestakov's longing for a homeland beyond this earth, in the "idealism" that can be seen in the letter he writes to his friend Tryapichkin: "Farewell, Tryapichkin old man. . . . This sort of life is dull, my friend; I crave food for the mind. I see it really is necessary to devote myself to some higher calling."

This, then, is what his mind encompasses. Everything with three dimensions he reduces to one or two—to utter planarity and banality. All this has become so voguish because it is so vulgar. He abbreviates every idea to the ultimate, lightens it to the ultimate, discards the beginning and the end, leaving only an infinitely tiny point in the middle. What once had been the summit of a mountain ridge now becomes a speck of dust swept along the highway by the wind. There is no feeling so noble, no idea so profound that it cannot be reduced to dust by the abrading and weathering action of Khlestakov's genius for making everything small and light.

His spirit is kindred to the spirit of the times. "I exist on literature," he says, and this is no lie but a profound avowal. He is a friend not only of Tryapichkin, of Bulgarin, of Senkovsky, of Marlinsky, but even of Pushkin himself: he can be found embodied in any one of those thoroughly stylish and fashionable fops of the *haut monde* who were among the numberless one-day acquaintances of that gentleman of the bedchamber, Alexander Sergeyevich Pushkin, and would press that "good fellow's" hand at court balls and say to him, with condescending familiarity: "Well, how are things, friend?" And Pushkin would reply: "Everything is fine, friend, just fine." And they would think: "A really original fellow!" And needless to say, the malicious gossip that caused the death of Alexander Sergeyevich could not have circulated unless Ivan Alexandrovich Khlestakov had had a hand in it. Pushkin perished, but Khlestakov continues to flourish.[18]

[18 The "malicious gossip" concerned the supposed infidelity of Pushkin's wife, particularly with Baron Georges d'Anthès, a Frenchman in the Russian

His spirit makes itself felt not only in the "bloody forget-me-nots" of early nineteenth-century Romanticism,[19] but also in the decadent horseplay, the Nietzschean impertinence of our own times. If common sense should find out what is going on, it would not care—like Khlestakov's old father—whether you were a decadent or a Nietzschean but would "pull up your shirt and give you such a smacking you'd be rubbing yourself a good four days." Khlestakov could also say of today's poets that "I used to correct all their verses. . . . Actually, I've written lots of things myself . . . I can't even remember the titles of all of them." We need only lend an ear to Tryapichkin's friend: "Farewell, Tryapichkin old man. . . . This sort of life is dull, my friend; I crave food for the mind. I see it really is necessary to devote myself to some higher calling."

This is what is encompassed by his mind. Everything that has three dimensions he reduces to two. We need only listen to the music of the operetta—that leitmotif of the past century which so persistently drowned out Beethoven and Wagner—in order to detect the presence of the immortal Khlestakov, who was not in the least discouraged from "plucking the flowers of pleasure" by the pessimism of the nineteenth century. He says that he has written "a few light pieces for the stage." And we need only drop into any

service. Pushkin wrote him an insulting letter, was challenged to a duel, and was killed, in January, 1837. A gentleman of the bedchamber (*kammerjunker*) was a very minor court rank.

Faddey Venediktovich Bulgarin (1789-1859) and Osip Ivanovich Senkovsky (1800-58) wrote highly popular pulp fiction (Senkovsky often using the name "Baron Brambeus"), and were important journalists: Bulgarin published the newspaper *The Northern Bee* (*Severnaya pchela*), and Senkovsky the journal *Library for Reading* (*Biblioteka dlya chteniya*). Bulgarin's co-publisher was Nikolay Ivanovich Grech (1787-1867). The three were known as the "triumvirate of journalism," which was synonymous, for "better" writers, with hack fiction, and, especially in Bulgarin's case, with reactionary political views.

Marlinsky is the pseudonym of Alexander Alexandrovich Bestuzhev (1797-1837), a popular writer of romantic tales in the manner of Byron and Walter Scott.]

[19 The expression "bloody forget-me-nots" occurs in a poem written in 1838 by Aibulat, the pseudonym of the minor poet K. M. Rosen: "And until the end of my sad days/ Neither proud experience nor reason/ Will crush with their hand/ The bloody forget-me-nots of life." This is, of course, thoroughly bad poetry by most standards, except for Khlestakov's. There is an amusing reference to this poem in Chapter VIII of Ivan Turgenev's *Rudin*.]

theater to see that managers nowadays are also saying to their good friend Ivan Alexandrovich, "Do write something, my dear fellow." And he thinks: "Well, why not, my dear fellow? And then I sat down and knocked off everything in one evening, I guess."

We need only glance at any of today's newspapers to feel the breath of "an extraordinary lightness of thought" in the opinions expressed there on the benefits of bicycling, freedom of conscience, the charms of Cavalieri and the Venus de Milo, predictions about the weather and about Russia's future. It is here, in the press and publicity of our times, that Khlestakov keeps growing and growing with every passing day. Now more than ever before, he could say without boasting: "I exist on literature, and literature exists on me." A horrified Gogol exclaims: "And the newspaper page . . . is imperceptibly becoming a legislator of human beings, although they have no respect for it. What is the meaning of all these unlawful laws, laws which are evidently being formulated, before everyone's eyes, by an unclean power issuing from below? And the whole world sees this, and dares not make a move, as if it were mesmerized. What a dreadful mockery of mankind!"[20] This unclean power issuing from below is, of course, the power of Khlestakov, who is now dashing off his "light pieces for the stage," and weaving the web of his gossip, not just in literature, but also on the pages of world history, from Paris to Peking, from London to the Transvaal.

And on he goes, growing and growing like a blurry apparition, like a *fata morgana*. Higher, higher—excelsior! This is Khlestakov's battle cry, the cry of contemporary progress.

"Once I even headed a government department." Is this a lie? Hardly. Perhaps in fact he has headed many departments many times since then. Perhaps even in our own times people beg him: "Ivan Alexandrovich, come and head the department." And he replies: "All right, gentlemen, I will take on the job, I will take it on, so be it, but I am very strict, I keep a sharp eye out. I. . . . Even the State Council is afraid of me." Perhaps even in our times there is "simply an earthquake, with everything trembling and shaking like a leaf" whenever the eternally youthful Khlestakov passes through one of the more liberal government departments. And he is still being served, if not by 35,000 messengers, then by express trains, telegraphs, and telephones. Which of us has not

[20 "Svetloe voskresenie," *Vyb. mesta*, *PSS*, VIII, 1952, 415.]

heard his directorial bellow in our ear: "Oh, I don't like to fool around; I'll throw the fear of God in all of you!" But higher, higher, excelsior!

The phantom grows, the soap-bubble swells in a magic play of rainbow colors. "Well, why not? That's the sort I am! I don't let anyone stand in my way. . . . I tell everyone: 'I know my business myself, I know! . . . I am everywhere, everywhere.' " This is the noumenal word; this is now the face of the Devil almost without the mask: he stands outside space and time, he is omnipresent and eternal. "I go to the palace every day. Why, tomorrow I'm being promoted straight to field marsh—." Here the stage directions read: "He slips and almost falls to the floor, but is deferentially supported by the officials."

How far would he have gone if he had not slipped? Would he have proclaimed himself an autocrat, like all the pretenders to power in Russia's history? Or perhaps these days he would not have been content with even a royal title—or for that matter with any human title—but would have gone ahead and dubbed himself a superman, or man-god. Would he have said what Dostoevsky's Devil advises Ivan Karamazov to say: "Where God stands—that is God's place; where I stand will at once be the foremost place— and all is permitted." For that is actually what Khlestakov almost does say—at least what he wishes to say; if he cannot, it is because the words do not as yet exist: "I know my business myself, I myself . . . I, I, I!" It is but one step from this frenzied self-affirmation to the sort of self-deification which, in Poprishchin's sick brain, yields the insane yet comparatively modest conclusion that "I am Ferdinand VIII, King of Spain," and, in the metaphysical brain of Nietzsche and of Kirillov, in Dostoevsky's *The Possessed*, the ultimate and far grander conclusion: "If God does not exist, then I am God!"

The unfortunate officials of the provincial town have good reason to be overwhelmed by what looks to them like the super-human grandeur of Khlestakov. After all, a general in their eyes is practically the equivalent of a superman:

Bobchinsky: What do you think, Pyotr Ivanovich? Who is he, anyway, with respect to rank?
Dobchinsky: I think he might even be a general.
Bobchinsky: And in my opinion, no general could hold a candle to him. If he is some sort of general, then he must be at least a generalissimo!

70

"There's a man for you, Pyotr Ivanovich! That's what a real man looks like!" Bobchinsky concludes. And Artemy Filippovich Zemlyanika, utterly annihilated by Khlestakov's drunken monologue, can only babble, pale and trembling: "It's simply dreadful. But why—I myself don't know." And, indeed, something like a breath of supernatural horror does seem to waft over the stage.

The audience laughs and fails to see that what provokes their laughter conceals something dreadful. They do not realize that they have been duped perhaps even more thoroughly than the stupid officials. No one sees the gigantic phantom rising up behind Khlestakov; it is a phantom to which our own passions lend enduring service and support, as the officials do for the inspector general when he starts to slip and fall, and as the lesser demons do for Satan the Great. Apparently no one has even to this day caught a glimpse of this phantom and recognized him, although he now appears "in his own true form," either wearing no mask at all, or wearing the most transparent of masks; he brazenly mocks people to their faces, shouting: "It's me, no one but me! I am everywhere, everywhere!"

III

Certainly the characters in the play—if not the audience—do have a sense of being enveloped in a stupefying and soporific fog, a fantasy-mirage created by the Devil.

"What marvelous things have been happening to me," Khlestakov writes Tryapichkin, in arch ingenuousness. "What the Devil!" says the mayor in bewilderment, "rubbing his eyes" as if he were waking up. And once he is fully awake, just before the climax, he says: "I still can't get over it. It really is true that if God wants to punish you, He takes away your reason first of all." An astonished Artemy Filippovich says, "spreading out his hands" helplessly: "How this could possibly have happened I can't for the life of me explain. It's as though a fog of some sort had blinded us, as though the Devil had confounded us." The postmaster describes his state of mind as he was opening the letter of the false inspector general: "Some supernatural power pushed me on. . . . I seemed to hear some demon whispering: open it, open it, open it! And as soon as I pressed on the sealing wax, fire shot through my veins, and as I opened it, an icy shiver, I swear, an icy shiver ran through me. My hands trembled and I felt dizzy." The mayor asks about

Khlestakov: "Then what do you think he really is?" And the
postmaster replies: "Neither this nor that: the Devil only knows
what he is!"—thereby unwittingly defining the mystical essence of
the spirit of the Eternal Median.

If Khlestakov had not galloped off in his troika, if he had not
melted away like a phantom in the fog that he himself had generated, the mayor might well have asked him the same thing that
one swindler asks another in Gogol's comedy *The Gamblers*:
"Who are you, anyway? The Devil? Speak up, who are you?" And
Khlestakov would answer the mayor in virtually the same words
which the second swindler uses and which the real Devil, in
Dostoevsky, might well have used to answer Ivan Karamazov:
"All right, who am I? I used to be an honorable man, and willy-
nilly I became a swindler."

"Life's dreadful murk passes by," Gogol writes in one of his
scattered notes, "and there is still a profound secret hidden here.
Is this not a horrible thing? Life, raging and empty—is it not a
dreadfully great phenomenon . . . life."[21]

In this dreadful murk those who have been blinded go wandering about, appearing as phantoms to one another. "I can't see a
thing," moans the mayor, his mind befogged. "I can see what
look like pig's snouts instead of faces and nothing else." In "The
Fears and Terrors of Russia," Gogol explains the Devil's mirage as
follows: "Remember the *Egyptian darkness*. . . . Pitch-black night
suddenly enveloped them amidst broad daylight; dreadful figures
glared at them from all sides; hideous decaying specters with melancholy faces rose up irrepressibly before them; they were fettered
not by chains of iron but by fear, and robbed of everything; all
feeling, all incentive, all strength perished within them; only fear
remained."[22]

And then comes the last scene of the play, not only in the usual
dramaturgical sense, but in a deeper, symbolic sense: the "final
scene," the apparition with which everything ends. The stage-
directions read: "The same characters plus the gendarme." And
the gendarme says: "The official who has arrived from St. Petersburg by imperial command requires your presence at once." These

[21 "(Zametki) k 1-oi chasti ('Mertvykh dush')," *PSS*, VI, 1951, 692.
Merezhkovsky's quotation is not quite accurate; I have corrected it.]
[22 "Strakhi i uzhasy Rossii," *Vyb. mesta, PSS*, VIII, 1952, 344-345.]

words strike everybody like a thunderbolt. And then comes the dreadful "mute scene"—a petrification of horror.[23]

Gogol intends us to believe that this official from St. Petersburg, who appears like a *deus ex machina*, like an angel in the medieval mystery plays, is a bona-fide inspector general, the incarnation of fate, the conscience of mankind, the justice of Heaven. However, we do not see him; for us he remains an even more illusive and ghostly figure than Khlestakov. But if we had caught a glimpse of him, then who knows? Perhaps the two "officials from St. Petersburg," great and small, might have borne a strange resemblance to one another after all. Perhaps the stern countenance of this supposedly genuine inspector general might show a glimmer of the familiar countenance of a man of the world—a cut well above Ivan Alexandrovich Khlestakov, to be sure, but just as adroit, just as "completely *comme il faut*, intelligent, perhaps even virtuous," yet at the same time "in no way different from others," from everyone else. And when from the lofty sphere of his supposedly perfect justice he starts laying into his lesser brethren, the poor provincial officials, will not his authoritarian bellow echo the familiar tirade we have just heard: "I won't put up with any nonsense! I know everything that's going on! . . . Oh, I don't like to fool around; I'll throw the fear of God in all of you!" What if the first Ivan Alexandrovich, who has just driven off, is actually completing one of his eternal circles, and is returning in the person of the second inspector general—as a Khlestakov of a higher cut, in a new, definitive, and final manifestation of himself?

"From St. Petersburg by imperial command": this is what deafens everybody, like a thunderclap—not only the characters in the play, not only the audience, but apparently even Gogol himself. A command from St. Petersburg? From where else indeed but St. Petersburg, that most ghostly, foggy, fantastic of all cities on the globe, would all this issue and spread over Russia: the stupefying fog, "life's dreadful murk," the "Egyptian darkness," the Devil's mirage, in which nothing can be seen except "what look like pigs' snouts instead of faces, and nothing else?" Are not both inspectors general, the first and the second—the simple registry clerk and the real generalissimo—equally legitimate offspring of the same Table

[23 *Okamenenie uzhasa*. In another edition of this article, this expression is reworded as *okamenenie ot uzhasa*: "petrifaction from horror."]

of Ranks, products of the same "St. Petersburg period" of Russian history?

Furthermore, is not this whole monstrosity of a provincial town a part of the great, all-Russian polity and its citizenry, is it not a miniature image of St. Petersburg itself, reversed but absolutely accurate, as in a drop of water? St. Petersburg brought this town into being out of nothingness. By what right, from what superior height can St. Petersburg then pass judgment on it and mete out punishment to it? What had actually happened in the St. Petersburg of Gogol's time that could have burst not in a Khlestakovian but actually in a divine thunderclap over this tiny Sodom of a town? What was there in St. Petersburg that could have appeared in this town, amidst these pigs' snouts, wearing not the face of a gendarme (which after all does bear some resemblance to Derzhimorda's) but actually the human face of divine justice?

No, *The Inspector General* was not completed; it was not fully apprehended by Gogol himself, and it was not understood by the audience. The denouement is merely brought off according to the conventions of the stage; it is not a real, not a religious denouement by any means. One comedy is brought to an end; another one, higher and far more amusing and terrible, begins, or ought to begin. We will never see this particular comedy on the stage; but it is being played off stage, in life, in actuality, to this very day. In fact, Gogol was aware of this to some extent. "*The Inspector General* has no ending,"[24] he said. We might add: *The Inspector General* is endless. Its laughter is not grounded in time and history; rather, it is the endless and enduring laughter of the Russian *conscience* at the Russian polity of its day.

"In the last analysis," as Gogol himself says, through the lips of one of the characters in the piece entitled "The Denouement of *The Inspector General*," "in the last analysis something . . . I can't really explain it to you—something monstrous and gloomy remains, a certain feeling of terror created by the disorder in our lives. The gendarme's appearance in the door, the way everyone is petrified by the words announcing the arrival of the real inspector general, who is to wipe them all off the face of the earth and annihilate them utterly—this is all somehow inexpressibly terrible."[25]

But really, why is it so terrible? Does not this mute scene also

[24 "Razvyazka Revizora," *PSS*, IV, 1951, 128.]
[25 "Razvyazka Revizora," pp. 127-128.]

contain some deep prototypical meaning, like everything else in *The Inspector General*?

"Giddyap, my beauties!" cries the coachman off stage at the end of Act IV. The bell jingles, the troika springs forward, and Khlestakov, that "fantasy-figure, mendacious deception incarnate, is carried off in the troika Heaven knows where." Khlestakov's troika is reminiscent of Poprishchin's, in "Diary of a Madman": "Give me a troika with steeds swift as a whirlwind! Driver, to your seat! Ring out, little bells! Soar upward, my steeds, and carry me out of this world! Gallop far, far away, so that nothing, absolutely nothing can be seen." Likewise, Khlestakov is carried off in the troika into an indeterminate expanse, into emptiness, into the void from which he, void and emptiness incarnate, has emerged—into nothing. And while everything real and existent, past and present, freezes into immobility and stands petrified in mindless horror at the inevitable final appearance of the mystical Derzhimorda, only the phantasmal Khlestakov, endued as he is with "an extraordinary lightness of thought," sweeps off, forever moving, into the immeasurable expanses of the future.

"It would seem that an unknown power has caught you up on its wing and you yourself are flying and everything else is flying too" (*Dead Souls*). Onward, onward—excelsior! What is the meaning—to use Gogol's own words—of this "horror-inspiring motion" on the one hand, and this horror-inspiring lack of motion, on the other? Can it really be that the petrified Russian polity, fettered not in chains of iron but in "Egyptian darkness," is all of Russia, past and present? That Khlestakov, flying off to the Devil's domain somewhere, is the Russia to be? Massive heaviness and diaphanous lightness—the actual banality of what is now and the phantasmal banality of what will be—these are two equally lamentable ends that are being pursued by Russia, two equally dreadful roads that lead to the Devil, to emptiness, to nihilism, to nothingness.

In this sense, Gogol's comparison of Russia to a speeding troika, at the end of *Dead Souls*, has a horribly mocking ring to it that Gogol himself did not anticipate: "Russia! Whither art thou speeding? Give me an answer! She gives no answer. The bells set up a wondrous ringing. (Ring out, little bells! says Poprishchin in his delirium; and in Act IV of *The Inspector General* the bells ring out as Khlestakov drives off.) . . . Everything on earth flies past, and other peoples and nations, eying her askance, stand aside and make

way for her." The demented Poprishchin, the quick-witted Khlestakov, and the commonsensical Chichikov are the ones carried off
by this symbolic Russian troika in its terrible flight into boundless
space or boundless emptiness. "A horizon without end. . . . Russia!
Russia! I behold thee. . . . What does this boundless space portend? Is it not here, in thee, that a boundless idea will come to
birth, since thou thyself are without bounds? Is it not here that a
titan will come to life, where there is space for him to develop his
powers and stride about?" Alas, the answer to this pitiless question
was given by Gogol's prophetic laughter! Only two "heroes of our
time" appeared before his eyes, two titans born of the boundless
expanses of Russia, like gigantic visions, like "hideous decaying
specters with melancholy faces"—Khlestakov and Chichikov.[26]

IV

The principle of motion or progress predominates in Khlestakov;
in Chichikov, the principle of equilibrium or stability. Khlestakov's
strength lies in the lyrical outburst, in intoxication; Chichikov's
strength lies in judicious composure, in sobriety. Khlestakov possesses an "extraordinary lightness," Chichikov an extraordinary
weightiness and solidity of mind. Khlestakov is a contemplative;
Chichikov is an activist. For Khlestakov everything desirable is
real; for Chichikov everything real is desirable. Khlestakov is an
idealist; Chichikov is a realist. Khlestakov is a liberal, Chichikov is
a conservative. Khlestakov is the poetry, Chichikov the prose of
real life in contemporary Russia.

But all these obvious contrasts notwithstanding, their essential
natures are identical. They are the two poles of a single force; they
are twin brothers, offspring of the Russian *middle* class and the
Russian nineteenth century, the most average and bourgeois of all
centuries. The essential nature of each is the eternal median,
"neither this nor that," utter banality. Khlestakov affirms what
does not exist, Chichikov affirms what does exist—and both are
equally banal. Khlestakov conceives projects, Chichikov carries
them out. The illusive Khlestakov proves to be responsible for

[26 The reference is to Mikhail Lermontov's novel *A Hero of Our Time*
(*Geroi nashego vremeni*, 1840), whose hero is Pechorin. "Titan" is not
really an accurate rendering of the Russian *bogatyr'*, the hero of the epic
folk song, but it suggests the spirit of Gogol's remarks. The parenthetical
comment in the quotation above is Merezhkovsky's.]

very real events in Russia, just as the real Chichikov is responsible
for the very illusive Russian legend of "dead souls." These, I repeat, are two contemporary Russian men, two hypostases of eternal and universal evil—of the Devil.

"It would be most accurate," Gogol observes, "to call Chichikov
a proprietor, an acquirer. Acquisitiveness was to blame for everything."

"So that's it! That's how it is, Pavel Ivanovich! So you've
made some acquisitions," says the chairman after the deed for
the purchase of the dead souls has been drawn up.
"Yes, I have," says Chichikov.
"A fine thing, a really fine thing!"
"Yes, I can see myself that I couldn't have undertaken anything better. No matter how things stand, a man's goal remains
vague if he hasn't planted his foot firmly on some solid foundation—not on some liberal chimera of youth."

Is not all nineteenth-century European culture expressing its
really essential nature here, through the mouth of Chichikov?
Life's highest meaning and man's ultimate purpose have not yet
been determined here on earth. The beginning and the end of the
world cannot be known; only what is in between—the world of
phenomena—is accessible to the mind and to sense-experience,
and consequently is real. Only the durability, solidity, or "positiveness" of this sense-experience, that is, of man's ordinary,
"healthy," *average* sense-perceptions provides the definitive cri-
terion for evaluating anything. All the philosophical and religious
expectations of ages past, all their aspirations toward a supra-
sensuous realm, without beginning or end, are, in Comte's formulation, merely metaphysical or theological rantings—or "liberal
chimeras of youth." "But our hero"—the hero of our times, as well
as the times themselves—"was already of middle age, and of a
circumspect and phlegmatic temperament." He sets to thinking
more positively, that is, more positivistically. And Chichikov's
positivistic thinking is devoted largely to considering how to reject
everything that strikes him as being a chimera, a deceptive phantom of the infinite and the absolute, considering how to "plant his
foot firmly on some solid foundation" of the conditional, the finite,
and the relative, which is supposedly the only reality.

"But remarkably enough," Gogol adds, "his words betrayed a
certain lack of assurance, as if he had said to himself at the very

same time: 'Ah, my friend, you're talking nonsense—and then some!' " Yes, the same universal "nonsense" is at the heart of both Chichikov's "positivism" and Khlestakov's "idealism." Chichikov's desire to "plant his foot firmly on some solid foundation" is just what has become voguish and is therefore vulgar. The same thing can be said, incidentally, of Khlestakov's desire to devote himself to some "higher calling." Both only talk and think "like everyone else"; actually, Chichikov cares nothing about solid foundations, and Khlestakov nothing about the higher levels of being. Chichikov's conservative solidity and Khlestakov's liberal "lightness of thought" both veil the same "chimera," the same emptiness, the same nothingness. These are not two antithetical beginnings and ends, not two insane yet honest extremes, but two medians, dishonest because they are too commonsensical, the two identical planarities and banalities of our times.

If man's life lacks any definite meaning beyond this life itself, then man also lacks any definite goal on earth beyond winning a material victory in the material struggle for existence. "I've never been so hungry in all my life"—this instinctive, elemental howl of Khlestakov's, this "voice of nature" becomes, in Chichikov, a conscious idea with a social and cultural dimension, the idea of acquisition, private property, capital.

"Above all keep and save every kopeck; it is the most reliable thing in the world. . . . The kopeck won't·betray you. . . . You can do and acquire anything in the world with the kopeck." This is the legacy of Chichikov's father and of the whole of his spiritual fatherland—the nineteenth century. This is the most positivistic idea of the most positivistic of all centuries, with its bourgeois, industrial-capital system, which has permeated culture through and through. This is supposedly the only solid foundation, discovered if not through abstract contemplation then through the experiences of life, and set in opposition to all the "chimeras" of centuries past. Of course there is no divine truth here, but there is a "human, all too human" truth, perhaps even a partial justification.

For Chichikov, there is nothing vulgar and ostentatious about the power of money; it is an inner power, a power of the spirit, of thought, of will, of a kind of disinterestedness, heroism, and self-sacrifice. In Part 2 of *Dead Souls*, the Prince—who, like the second inspector general, has arrived "from St. Petersburg by imperial command"—berates Chichikov in the presence of two hefty gendarmes: "You will be taken to jail this very instant and there you will await the disposition of your fate, along with the lowest of scoundrels and thieves." Chichikov protests: "I am a human being, Your Excellency!" And then to Murazov: "I had to earn my daily bread with my blood. I earned every kopeck by patience stained with blood, so to speak, through toil and labor—not by fleecing anyone or embezzling public funds, as some people do. . . . Where is the justice of Heaven? Where is the reward for my patience, for my exemplary persistence? . . . I had to overcome so much, I had to endure so much! Every single kopeck was earned, you might say, with all the strength of my soul!" For him, there is something absolute, even, it almost seems, infinite, almost religious, in the idea of money. "My coffer!" he wails in a heart-rending voice as he sits in prison, just before he rips apart his tail-coat of "Navarino smoke-and-flame."[27] "My coffer! All my property is in it. . . . They'll steal everything and carry it off! Oh Lord!" The mysterious coffer is for him a new ark of the covenant.

A knight-errant of money, Chichikov, like Don Quixote, sometimes looks like not only a truly comic hero but a truly tragic one as well, an epic hero of his times. "Your mission is to be a great man," Murazov tells him. And this is partly true: Chichikov, like Khlestakov, keeps growing, and he grows before our eyes. As we diminish in stature and lose all our "beginnings" and our "ends," all our "liberal chimeras," then our commonsensical middle position, our bourgeois "positiveness"—Chichikov—looks ever greater and even infinite.

V

"Why did I try to get some kopecks?" Chichikov asks. "So as to live out the remainder of my days in prosperity, to leave something to the wife and children I intended to acquire for the welfare and service of my country. That's why I wanted to acquire them!" Gogol says:

Strictly speaking, he felt no attraction for money as such, he was not ruled by avarice or stinginess. No, it was not these that motivated him: he envisaged his future life in terms of the great-

[27 Navarino was an important naval battle (October 20, 1827) in the War of Greek Independence. It pitted the English, French, and Russian fleets against the Turks and the Egyptians; the latter lost. "Smoke and flame" refers, of course, to the color of the cloth.]

est possible prosperity, all the good things: carriages, a splendidly appointed house, delicious dinners—these were the things that swirled through his head continually. It was in order that he might without fail enjoy all this eventually, ultimately, in good time, that he was saving each kopeck and stingily denying himself and others for the time being. When a rich man whirled past in an elegant carriage drawn by pacers in ornate harness, he would stop as if rooted to the spot and then, coming to his senses as if awakening from a long sleep, say: "Why, he used to be a clerk and have his hair cut like a peasant's!" And everything that smacked of wealth and prosperity produced an impression on him that he himself did not understand.

So-called *comfort*, that is, the fairest flower of today's industrial-capital, bourgeois system, comfort, which is served by all the forces of nature that science has subdued—sound, light, steam, electricity, every invention, every art—this for Chichikov is the ultimate crown of the earthly paradise. "Above all you want to live in peaceful prosperity—that's what you're concerned with above all"—this is how the servant Smerdyakov defines the real and essential spirituality of his master Ivan Karamazov. Not rapture, or luxury, or intoxication, or the pinnacle of happiness, but merely an average well-being, a modicum of plenty for spirit and body, "peaceful prosperity"—this is the secret ideal which, through Smerdyakov, links Ivan Karamazov, a tragic hero, with Chichikov, a comic hero.

"You are like Fyodor Pavlovich [that is, Karamazov senior]," Smerdyakov says to Ivan, and he might have said with even greater justification: "You are like Pavel Ivanovich [Chichikov]. Of all the children you've turned out to be most like him; you and he have the same soul." Ivan's rebelliousness, the pride of the superman which makes him exclaim: "All is permitted—if God does not exist, then I am God"—all this is still the "liberal chimera of youth," still the Khlestakovian "lightness of thought," that is, still nonsense or self-deception, more or less. But Khlestakov will grow weary of talking nonsense, the storm will abate, the waves will subside, and once again our century will reveal its *median* level, its noumenal averageness, its unbreachable dam, its "solid foundation": "most of all, to live in peaceful prosperity." And even in the dread figure of the Grand Inquisitor there is a glimmer of the familiar figure not only of father Fyodor Pavlovich Karamazov, but of grandfather Pavel Ivanovich Chichikov, too. And the kingdom of the Antichrist, which the Grand Inquisitor sets in opposition to the kingdom of Christ—those "thousands of millions of happy children," a modicum of plenty, "peaceful prosperity" for all mankind in comfortable "aluminum palaces" and in Social Democracy's tower of Babel—all this is nothing more than the kingdom of Chichikov, the universal and everlasting Chichikov *sub specie aeternitatis*; for his kingdom is indeed a kingdom of this world. As Gogol says: Chichikov contained "everything that was necessary for this world."

VI

Instead of felicity, well-being; instead of nobility, propriety—that is to say, an external and relative virtue, because for Chichikov, as a true positivist, there is nothing absolute in either good or evil. Inasmuch as man's only definite goal and his greatest good on earth consists of "peaceful prosperity," and the only way of reaching it is through acquisition, then all morality is subordinate to this goal and this good, for "once the goal is chosen, you have to push on, stopping at nothing." "Onward, onward! Excelsior!" This, the battle cry of modern progress, is the cry both of Khlestakov and of Chichikov.

"I did some twisting and turning, I won't try to hide it, I did. . . . What else could I do?" Chichikov confesses to Murazov on one occasion in a moment of despair. "But actually, I did it only when I saw that the straight road would never get me anywhere, and that the winding road was more direct." Ikharev, the hero of Gogol's play *The Gamblers*, might be speaking for Chichikov when he says: "What do I owe everything to? To what people call cheating. That's nonsense, it's not cheating at all. . . . Well, even supposing it is cheating. But after all, it's a necessary thing—what can you accomplish without it? . . . I look at life from another angle entirely. It's no great achievement to live like a fool, anyone can do that; but to live with subtlety, with art, to cheat others without being cheated yourself—that's the real aim and purpose of life!"

If this had been said not by a wretched little provincial card-sharper but by a Renaissance politician like Machiavelli or a conqueror like Cesare Borgia, *biondo e bello*, then who knows? Perhaps Ivan Karamazov and Nietzsche would have recognized their freedom "beyond good and evil," their supermannish "all is permitted" in this particular freedom from all moral laws. And the Devil, in the guise of Smerdyakov, would once again have exclaimed to Ivan Karamazov: "All that is very nice; but if you had the urge to swindle, then why did you think you also needed the sanction of truth?" When Chichikov says: "As a human being, I can be guilty of anything, but never of baseness," he is sincere. Good and evil, for him, are so relative in comparison with the highest good—acquisition—that at times he would be incapable, by himself, of distinguishing one from the other; he himself does not know where his natural instinct as proprietor and acquirer ends, and where baseness begins: average baseness and average nobility both merge into propriety or decorum.

The first thing people noticed about Chichikov was an "amazing decorum," Gogol says. "The reader should know that Chichikov was the most decorous person who has ever walked the face of the earth." Chichikov's esthetics, like his ethics, is the common property of today's philistine money-culture. "Even though he was obliged at first to push ahead in a low order of society, he nonetheless always preserved a sense of cleanliness in his heart; he liked to see desks of varnished wood in government offices, and he liked everything to be refined . . . he changed his linen every other day and in summer, when it was hot, even every day: any even slightly unpleasant odor was offensive to him. For this reason, whenever Petrushka came to undress him and pull off his boots, he would put a clove up his nose." Usefulness to everyone, convenience, comfort, cleanliness, hygiene—these are a golden mean in the beautiful as well as the good.

For all his deep conservatism, Chichikov is also a Westerner in part.[28] Like Khlestakov, he feels that in the backwoods of pro-

[28 "Westernism" is often dated from Peter the Great and the "St. Petersburg period" of Russian history; his reforms were designed to make Russia a modern nation along Western lines, and supposedly created a chasm between the educated upper classes and the peasantry. As the name of an intellectual movement, it dates from the 1840's. The Westerners insisted that Russia was basically a European nation, whose development had been retarded by the Mongol conquest. They demanded the modernization of the country along European lines—technologically, culturally, socially, and politically. In a certain sense, they carried on the spirit of Peter the Great's reforms (during the "St. Petersburg period" of Russian history). Their leading spokesmen were Vissarion Belinsky and Alexander Herzen. Between the 1840's and the 1860's, they were opposed by the Slavophiles, who played up

vincial Russia he is a representative of European enlightenment and progress. This attests to Chichikov's close ties with the "Petersburg period" of Russian history, with the reforms of Peter the Great. Chichikov is attracted to the West; he seems to sense that his power and his future "kingdom" are located there. "That's what it would be good to get into," he says as he dreams of entering the customs service; "the border is nearby, and so are enlightened people. And what a stock of fine Holland-linen shirts I could get hold of!" Gogol comments: "It must be added that at the same time he was thinking about a special brand of French soap which imparted an unusual whiteness to the skin and freshness to the cheeks." European enlightenment only makes the Russian gentleman even more aware of the age-old gulf that separates him as an "enlightened citizen" from the ignorant common folk. "A handsome fellow, really handsome!" Chichikov exclaims on one occasion when he sees that his servant Petrushka is drunk. "Why, you might say that he's astounded all Europe with his beauty!" So saying, Chichikov stroked his chin and thought: "Indeed, what a difference there is between an enlightened citizen and the coarse physiognomy of a servant!"[29]

Russian culture—and this has been the case ever since Peter the Great—plucks only Khlestakovian "flowers of pleasure" from universal culture, and skims off only the choice cream or foam: the finer fruits of Western European enlightenment enter Russia along with other "fancy goods," on just the same basis as Holland-linen shirts and a "special brand of French soap which imparts an unusual whiteness and freshness" to the Russian nobleman's skin. Chichikov selects what he wishes from world culture, and anything else that is too profound or too exalted he reduces to two dimensions, with the same ease as Khlestakov, he lightens, abridges, and flattens it to the ultimate possible degree. Chichikov's discourse "on the felicity of two souls" and his reading to Sobakevich of Werther's verse epistle to Charlotte are worthy, in their own way, of Khlestakov's "beneath the bosky shade of babbling brooks." Chichikov "had a compassionate heart, and he could never resist

---

the idea of a uniquely Russian national tradition, emphasizing autocracy, Orthodoxy, and the peasantry, as bulwarks against European rationalism, materialism and democracy. Their leading representatives were Alexey Stepanovich Khomyakov (1804-60), Ivan Vasilievich Kireyevsky (1806-56), and the two sons of S. T. Aksakov (see footnote 5).]

[29 Merezhkovsky misquotes the last sentence as "an enlightened nobleman."]

giving a copper coin to a poor man"—such is his Christianity, his love for others. But there is paganism here too, in his love for himself: as he stands before his looking-glass, he "creates a multitude of pleasant surprises for himself, he twitches his eyebrow and his lips, does something even with his tongue. . . . Finally he chucks himself under the chin and exclaims, with tender affection: 'Oh, what a good-looking kisser you've got!' " Christianity, which distributes a copper coin out of charity, and paganism, which ends up in love for your own "kisser," easily meet in a judicious and safe median, in comfortable service to God and Mammon both.

From Confucius to Comte, implicit in any variety of positivism as a guide to the meaning of life is the denial of an end, the affirmation of an endless continuation of the human race and endless "progress": we have it good, our children will have it better, our grandchildren and great-grandchildren even better—and so on, without end. Mankind is not in God; rather, God is in mankind. Mankind itself is God, and no other God exists. There is no personal immortality, only immortality in mankind. Every age "toils away" and "acquires" for the ages yet to come. The endless acquisition and accumulation of *dead* capital, of a treasure of "dead souls" which is never spent: such is the implicit yet absolute nature of progress. From this follows the ancestor-worship of Chinese positivism, and the descendant-worship of European positivism; from this come marriage, procreation, and the family as a religion. "A wife and children"—this is the justification everlastingly put forward for all the monstrous absurdities of the bourgeois system, the objection everlastingly raised against religion, which says: "A man's foes shall be they of his own household." This is the "solid foundation" against which all the winged "chimeras," all the Christian prophecies about the end of the world supposedly smash and break.

"Chichikov," Gogol says, "was very much concerned about his descendants. 'I wanted to acquire money . . . so as to leave something to the wife and children I intended to acquire for the welfare and service of my country! That's why I wanted to acquire them!" Chichikov himself avows. "As God is my witness, I have always wanted to have a wife, to do my duty as a man and as a citizen, so that I might then truly merit the respect of my fellow-citizens and of my superiors." Chichikov's greatest mortal fear is not for his own skin, but for his future kin, his family, his seed. "I would disappear," he thinks in a moment of danger, "like a bubble on the water, without any trace, leaving no descendants." To die without creating new life is as if one had never lived at all, because each individual life is a bubble on the water; the bubble will burst, the person will die—and nothing save vapor will remain. An individual life has meaning only in a family, a clan, a people, a state, in mankind, just as the life of a polyp, a bee, or an ant has meaning only in a polypary, a hive, or an anthill. Any "yellow-faced positivist" disciple of Confucius, and any "white-faced Chinese" disciple of Auguste Comte would concur with this metaphysic, which Chichikov holds to instinctively: here extreme West meets extreme East, Atlantic meets Pacific.

"What am I now?" Chichikov ruminates, after he has been ruined. "What am I good for? How can I now look any respectable father of a family in the face? How can I help but feel the gnawings of conscience, knowing that I am a useless burden on earth? And what will my children say later on? They'll say: 'Father's a real beast: he didn't leave us any property at all.' " Gogol then observes: "Another person would perhaps not have gotten so deeply involved if it had not been for the question which for some reason arose by itself: what will my children say? And so, the future procreator, casting a sidelong glance out of the corner of one eye only, like a wary tomcat . . . hastily snatches up everything within immediate reach." When Chichikov imagines himself as a property-holder, as the possessor of capital and of an estate, he immediately pictures a "fresh, fair-skinned young woman . . . and a younger generation destined to perpetuate the Chichikov name: a lively little boy and a beauty of a little girl, or even two boys, two or even three girls, so that all should know he really had lived and existed, and had not merely passed through the world like a shadow or a phantom, so that he would not feel that he was a disgrace to his native land either."

The Devil says to Ivan Karamazov: "I long to become incarnate, once and for all, irrevocably." This is Chichikov's greatest "positivistic" dream as well: he needs a young woman and little Chichikovs in order to become incarnate once and for all, in order that all should know that he had actually existed (as if his reality were otherwise dubious to everyone else and to himself) and was not merely a shadow or phantom, a bubble on the water. Without descendants, the existence of Chichikov the "positivist" bursts like a soap-bubble, as does the existence of the "idealist" Khlestakov without his fantastic chimeras. Chichikov's longing for a young

woman and little Chichikovs is the same longing that the Devil—
phantom of phantoms—feels for earthly reality. And the "kingdom
of this world," the "millions of happy children" foretold by the
Grand Inquisitor, are nothing more than a "Middle Kingdom,"
made up of countless little positivists—Chinese destined to over-
run the earth (this is the spiritual "pan-mongolism" which so
alarmed Vladimir Solovyov),[30] millions of happy "little Chichikovs": as each droplet of the Pacific reflects and reduplicates the
sun in miniature, so each of these little Chichikovs reflects and
reduplicates the one "procreator" of this kingdom, the immortal
proprietor of dead souls, the noumenal Chichikov.

VII

"I would like to have the dead ones . . . ," Chichikov said to
Manilov.

"What's that? Pardon me, I'm a little hard of hearing, I
thought I heard a most peculiar word. . . ."

"I propose to acquire the dead ones, who would, however,
still be carried on the tax rolls as living," said Chichikov.

(Manilov stands gaping, first in astonishment and then in
fear.)

"Perhaps here . . . in this explanation you have just offered
. . . something else is hidden . . . ," he suggests timidly.

"No," said Chichikov quickly, "no. I mean the matter to be
taken exactly as it is—that is, souls which are actually already
dead."

The phrase "dead souls" was once a stock expression in the
bureaucratic language of serfdom. But nowadays we certainly
need not be sensitive Manilovs for the expression to sound "most
peculiar" to us and even most terrible, like some incredible blasphemy; we need only have a genuine feeling for an understanding
of "the matter exactly as it is." In other words, we need to grasp
not the conventional, bureaucratic, "positivistic" Chichikovian
meaning of these two words—"soul" and "death"—but rather,
their absolute, religious, human, and divine sense. Is it not a pe-

[30 "Panmongolism" is a poem by the philosopher and theologian Vladimir Sergeyevich Solovyov (1853-1900); its theme is the destruction of
decadent Western (including Russian) culture by the primitive yet vital
"yellow" hordes from the East.]

culiar and terrible thing to talk not just of dead souls but of living human souls as inanimate commodities in a marketplace? Does not the language of a very familiar and concrete reality, as it is used here, sound like the language of a most exotic and fantastic fairy tale? It is improbable that dead souls should be listed as living in certain official "fairy-tales," that is, on some tax roll or other. But perhaps the opposite is true: perhaps the living are listed as dead, for ultimately there proves to be no solid, positivistic basis for distinguishing the living from the dead, or being from non-being.

Here there is a monstrous confusion of words arising from a monstrous confusion of concepts. Language expresses concepts; how utterly and cynically banal these concepts must be in order to produce such cynically banal language. And, despite their innate cynicism, Chichikov and his entire culture maintain an "amazing" outward decorum. Of course, it was people of common sense and even of statesmanlike mind who brought the popular term "dead souls" into official usage; yet what a chasm of Khlestakovian "lightness of thought" yawns in this Chichikovian "solidity!" I repeat, it is not necessary to be a Manilov, one need only not be a Chichikov in order to sense that "something else" is hidden in this pairing of words, that some deeper meaning is concealed behind the trivial and obvious one, and feel cold shivers at these two meanings, at this ambiguity.

"I've never sold any dead people before," Korobochka protests. "Lord knows where he came from," she thinks, "and at nighttime too." Chichikov replies: "Listen, my dear woman, they're nothing but dust. You understand? Absolutely nothing but dust. Take any completely worthless object—even a plain old rag, for instance— even a rag has some value; they'll at least buy it for a paper mill. But what I have in mind, after all, is of no use at all. Well now, you tell me yourself, what use is it?"

"Lay up for yourselves treasures in Heaven. For what is a man profited, if he shall gain the whole world, and lose his own soul? Or what shall a man give in exchange for his soul? With God all are living"—so says Christ. But the Devil—otherwise named Chichikov—objects: dead souls are not of this world. They are dust, nothing but dust. A rag in a paper mill has greater value than does a human soul in all eternity. "They're just a dream. . . . They're just—poof!" as Chichikov says to Sobakevich.

To whom then shall we, the children of a positivistic age, give greater credence—to Christ or to Chichikov? This would seem an easy matter to decide, not by what we say and think, but by the way we live and die. In our positivistic Chichikovian "poof" do we not see, instead of a "solid foundation," the same yawning chasm of a Khlestakovian "lightness of thought" and unbounded cynicism? And is it not true that the only sincere word we utter over any dead body is Chichikov's remark that "a dead body's good only for propping up a fence." The ancient Greeks, the Hebrews, the Egyptians would have been horrified at the godless positivism that is expressed in this "Christian" proverb. "Really, a human soul, as far as you're concerned, is worth no more than a boiled turnip," as Sobakevich says to the ever-living buyer of dead souls.[31] We have abolished serfdom, we deal in neither living nor dead souls. But is it not true that in the nations of the present day, with their hideous proletariat and their prostitution, the human soul is also sometimes worth no more than a boiled turnip?

When Chichikov, losing his patience, tells Korobochka to go to the Devil, "the landowner became unusually frightened. 'Oh, don't mention him, leave him be!' she exclaimed, turning deathly pale. 'Just the day before yesterday I dreamed of him all night long, the accursed one. . . . He looked so nasty; he had horns longer than a bull's.' "

It is not only this simple-minded landowner, but we readers too, perhaps no less simple-minded, who do not suspect just how close to us the Devil stands at this very moment—not the old Devil of the fairy tales, who has horns longer than a bull's, but the new one, the real one, who is far more terrible and mysterious, and who roams at large in the world "without a mask, in his own true form, in an ordinary tail-coat."

> "Well, maybe they'll be of some use around the place somehow or other . . ." the old woman replied; but she did not finish speaking, and gazed openmouthed at him almost in fear, waiting to see what he would say to this.
>
> "Dead men being of some use! That's really stretching it! You're going to put them in your garden to scare off the sparrows at night, perhaps?"
>
> "The power of the Cross be with us! What terrible things you're saying!" the old woman exclaimed, crossing herself.

[31 In his text, Merezhkovsky attributes Chichikov's statement to Sobakevich, and vice versa. I have made the necessary correction.]

"What else were you thinking of doing with them, then? Actually, the bones and the graves will stay with you: the transfer is only on paper."

Here the words and the deeds are of this world, yet also not of it: they intermingle and create a comic effect. But the comic also contains something terrible, and the more comic it is, the more terrible. Korobochka's fear is comical to us; but perhaps the reverse is true: perhaps our laughter is terrible, although we are not even aware of it.

When I began to read him the first chapters of *Dead Souls*, Pushkin, who had always laughed while I read (he liked to laugh very much), gradually became more and more somber, and finally grew positively gloomy. And when I finished reading, he said, in an anguished voice: "Lord, how sad our Russia is!" At this point I understood just how horrifying was the aspect in which darkness could be presented to people.

It was the banality of everything taken together that frightened readers. They were frightened by the fact that each of my heroes was more banal than the one before; that there was not a single consoling feature; that there was not even a place where the poor reader could pause or catch his breath; and that after he had finished reading the entire book, he seemed in fact to have come out of some sort of stifling cellar into God's green world."[32]

Dead Souls leaves us with the same impression as *The Inspector General*: that it is "something monstrous and gloomy," that "all this is somehow inexpressibly terrible." Even in Pushkin's luminous and childlike heart this feeling of fear, though at first drowned out by laughter, gradually kindled in an ominous glow. It was not sadness and not tears, but actually fear through laughter.[33]

"There seemed to be no soul at all in this body," Gogol observes of Sobakevich. Sobakevich's living body contains a dead soul. And Manilov, Nozdryov, Korobochka, Plyushkin, the public prose-

[32 "Chetyre pis'ma k raznym litsam po povodu 'Mertvykh dush,'" *Vyb. mesta, PSS*, VIII, 1952, 294, 293.]

[33 This rephrases Pushkin's famous characterization of Gogol's story "Old-Fashioned Landowners" as "laughter through tears." Cf. review of *Evenings on a Farm Near Dikanka*, 2nd ed., in *Sovremennik*, No. 1, 1836, and in standard editions of Pushkin's works. It quickly became one of the clichés of Russian criticism and was applied to Gogol's work as a whole.]

cutor "with the thick eyebrows"—all of them are *dead souls*
within living bodies. That is why they inspire such fear. It is the
fear of death, the fear felt by the living soul on contact with dead
ones. "My soul ached," Gogol acknowledges, "when I saw, right
here, in life itself, how many mute and dead inhabitants there were,
terrible in the cold inertness of their souls."[34] And in *Dead Souls*,
just as in *The Inspector General*, an "Egyptian darkness" descends,
"pitch-black night amidst broad daylight," a "stupefying fog," the
Devil's mirage in which nothing can be seen except pigs' snouts
instead of human faces. And most horrible of all is that these
"hideous decaying specters with melancholy faces" that glare at us,
these "children of non-enlightenment, these Russian freaks," are, in
Gogol's words, "taken from our very own soil," from actual Russian life. For all their illusiveness, they are "of the same body as we
ourselves": they are we, as we are reflected in some demonic yet
undistorted looking-glass.

In one of Gogol's early stories, "A Terrible Vengeance," "the
dead men gnaw at the dead man," they are "pale, very pale, one
taller than another, one bonier than another." Among them is
"another, taller than the rest, more terrible than the rest," a dead
man who has "grown immense in the earth." Likewise, in *Dead
Souls*, Chichikov, an "immense dead man," grows and rises up
amidst the other dead men, and his physical human form, refracted
through the fog of the Devil's mirage, becomes an immense specter.

The same tangle of gossip weaves itself around Chichikov as
around Khlestakov. "All the investigations conducted by the officials revealed only that they probably had absolutely no idea of
who Chichikov was: whether he was the sort of person who should
be seized and detained as being politically unreliable, or whether
he was the sort of person who himself could seize and detain all of
them as being politically unreliable." The postmaster puts forth the
brilliant idea that Pavel Ivanovich Chichikov is none other than a
new Stenka Razin—the celebrated brigand Captain Kopeykin.[35]

The others, however, managed to keep their end up too, and,
inspired by the postmaster's clever surmise, went even further,
if anything. Among the many theories—all ingenious in their

[34 "Teatral'nyi raz"ezd posle predstavleniya novoi komedii," *PSS*, v,
1949, 170.]

[35 Stepan (Stenka) Timofeyevich Razin (died 1671) was a Don Cossack
who led an extensive peasant and Cossack rebellion in South East Russia
between 1667 and 1671. He was captured and publicly executed. He has
become a popular hero in Russian folklore, as a symbol of the free man.]

own way—one finally emerged (which is even strange to mention): that Chichikov must be Napoleon in disguise, that the English had long been envious because Russia was so large and vast. . . . And now perhaps they actually had let Napoleon loose from the isle of St. Helena, and now he was actually making his way into Russia looking like Chichikov but really not Chichikov at all.

Of course, the officials did not exactly believe this, but still they did grow thoughtful, and each one, on considering the matter for himself, decided that Chichikov's face, if he turned and stood sideways, did bear a strong resemblance to a portrait of Napoleon.

The legend percolates from the upper reaches of society to the lower: talk about Chichikov-Napoleon starts up among the merchants drinking tea in the tavern. They have been alarmed by "the prediction of a certain prophet who had been in prison for three years by now. The prophet had turned up—no one knew from where—wearing bast shoes and a coat of undressed sheepskin that reeked horribly of rotten fish, and proclaiming that Napoleon was the Antichrist and was being kept on a chain of stone, behind six walls and beyond seven seas, but that one day he would break the chain and gain possession of the whole world."

Khlestakov is a generalissimo; Chichikov is Napoleon himself, and even the Antichrist himself. And here, just as in *The Inspector General*, and just as everywhere in Russia throughout its history, a very fantastic Russian legend is the instigation for a very real Russian happening:

For some unknown reason, all these discussions, opinions, and rumors affected the public prosecutor more than anyone else, to such an extent that on arriving home, he took to brooding and brooding and suddenly, with no rhyme or reason, as they say, he up and died. Whether it was a stroke or what, the fact is that as he sat brooding, he suddenly pitched forward out of his chair. People threw up their hands and cried out: "Oh, my Lord!," as is usual on such occasions; they sent for the doctor to bleed him, but they saw that the prosecutor had long since become a body without a soul.

Among the common folk, the actual effect of the phantoms is even more terrifying. "The schismatics were getting restive again. Someone had spread the rumor among them that an Antichrist had been born who would not let even the dead rest in peace, buying up, as he was, certain dead souls. They did penance and then sinned, and, under the pretext of trying to catch the Antichrist they did away with some non-Antichrists. . . . The peasants had risen up in rebellion against the landowners and the police chiefs. It became necessary to adopt repressive measures." The positivist Chichikov proves to be the unwitting creator of a highly "liberal chimera," which takes on flesh and blood and becomes a terrifying reality; for, as we know from the history of the Pugachov rebellion, for instance, an uprising of Russian peasants is no "dream" at all, no "poof," even from a positivistic point of view.[36] "This rabble can be subdued only by harshness," as Peter the Great's terrible phrase had it. A few more phantoms of this sort and the earth would begin to groan and the sea would begin to rage, as one of Dostoevsky's terrorists in *The Possessed* puts it. And now it is no longer the poor stupid officials who are given to a Khlestakovian "lightness of thought," but even, it would seem, the wise Prince Khlobuyev, who has come from St. Petersburg, when, in connection with the "earthquake" touched off by Chichikov, he turns to the fear-riveted officials with the fantastic statement that "we must save our native land."

Gogol says:

"But come now, this is absurd! It makes absolutely no sense! It is impossible that officials could throw such a scare into themselves, make up such nonsense, stray so far from the truth, when even a child could have seen what was going on!" This is what many readers will say, and they will accuse the author of writing nonsense. . . . It is easy for readers to sit in judgment, gazing out from their peaceful and lofty vantage-point, from which they can see the whole horizon open before them. . . . And in the universal chronicle of mankind there are many entire centuries which, I suppose, man would delete and eliminate as being unnecessary. Many errors have been committed in the world which nowadays, it seems, even a child would not commit. . . . The present generation sees everything clearly, marvels at the errors of its forebears, laughs at their follies, and does not see that this chronicle has been etched in heavenly fire, that every letter in it

[36] Yemelyan Ivanovich Pugachov (?1742-75) was a Cossack who led the greatest peasant and Cossack uprising in Russian history. Ultimately he was betrayed, captured, and executed. He, too, is prominent in Russian folklore and Russian literature (cf., e.g., Pushkin's novel *The Captain's Daughter*).]

cries out, that from every direction an accusing finger points at it and none other than it, this present generation. But the present generation laughs and with complacency and pride initiates a series of new errors at which its descendants will laugh in turn.

Who knows, perhaps the "unclean spirit" himself is whispering to us, the present generation, through the mouth of Chichikov: "What are you laughing at? You're laughing at yourselves!" Perhaps the tongue-lashing that in our civic-mindedness we administer to Chichikov will prove no less Khlestakovian than the tongue-lashing administered by Prince Khlobuyev in *Dead Souls*, where he comes to conduct an investigation. "What's to be done?" Chichikov could reply to us, as he does to Murazov: "I did not observe moderation, I was not able to stop in time. Satan, the accursed one, tempted me and led me beyond the bounds of reason and human prudence. I have transgressed, I have transgressed"—and with this reply he would make fools of all of us too, because it is his essential characteristic precisely never to reach a point that can be either transgressed or not transgressed, but to observe "moderation," the mean, in everything only too well, never to exceed the bounds of "human prudence," not to be tempted by Satan, for he himself is Satan, and is endeavoring to tempt everyone else.

Perhaps our feelings of Christian charity toward Chichikov also resemble the charity of Murazov, the new Christian millionaire, which is reminiscent of the philanthropical copper coin that Chichikov himself hands out by way of charity. Therefore, in the final analysis, our civic justice and our Christian charity both roll off him like water off a duck's back: having deceived not only the officials and Prince Khlobuyev, but also us and even Gogol himself, Chichikov will again emerge from prison, adjudged not guilty, going on as if nothing had happened, regretting only the coat that he has ripped apart in a fit of despair: "Why did I have to succumb to such distress?" And he will order himself a new coat of the same material, Navarino smoke-and-flame, and the new one will be "just like the old in every particular." And then: "Driver, to your seat! Ring out, little bells! Soar upward, my steeds, and carry me out of this world!" Like Khlestakov, he will fly away on his bird-troika, "like a phantom, mendacious deception incarnate," into the measureless distances of the future. And again "a horizon without end. . . . Russia! Russia! . . . why dost thou look at me thus, why hast thou turned on me eyes full of anticipation? . . . What does this boundless expanse portend? . . . Is it not here that a titan will come to life . . . ?"

Chichikov has vanished. But a Russian titan will indeed emerge from the boundless Russian expanse, the immortal proprietor of dead souls will once more appear, now in a final, terrifying manifestation: Chichikov. And only then will what is now still hidden, not only from us readers but even from the artist himself stand revealed: how terrible is the ludicrous prophecy:

"Chichikov is the Antichrist."

VIII

"Well, friend, you certainly did concoct a Devil!" Gogol might well have said to himself, as the man in his story "The Portrait" says to the artist who has painted the picture of the old moneylender with a face resembling the Devil's. "Paint my portrait," the moneylender asks. "Perhaps I shall die soon. . . . But I don't want to die altogether, I want to live." As the artist goes on painting, "such a strange feeling of revulsion, such an inexplicable feeling of oppression" well up in him that he throws down his brush and refuses to go on. The old man falls at his feet and begs him to finish the portrait, "saying that his fate and his existence in the world depended on it, that the artist had already captured his living features with the brush; that if he should reproduce them faithfully, his [the old man's] life would be preserved in the portrait through some supernatural power, that because of it he would not die completely, that he must remain present in the world."

Does this not recall Chichikov's fear of "disappearing without a trace, like a bubble on the water," and his desire that "all should know he really had lived and existed and had not merely passed through the world like a shadow or a phantom?" Does it not also call to mind the words that the Devil speaks to Ivan Karamazov: "You see, I myself suffer from the fantastic, just as you do, and that's why I like your earthly realism. Here with you everything is circumscribed, formulated, geometrical, whereas with us, everything is a kind of indeterminate equation. . . . I am the 'x' in the indeterminate equation. I am some phantom of life, who has lost all beginnings and ends, and finally has even forgotten his own name. I long to become incarnate, once and for all, irrevocably."

The artist is horrified at the moneylender's words. "They seemed so strange and terrible to him that he threw down his brushes and his palette and rushed out of the room." A radical change took place in him: "He plunged into deep and serious thought, sank into melancholy, and at last became fully convinced that his brush had served as the instrument of the Devil." He renounced his former art, which seemed criminal to him, renounced "earthly realism," abandoned the world, and entered a monastery. "To this day I cannot understand what that strange being was whose likeness I painted," he says in his confession, which is strongly reminiscent of Gogol's own "Author's Confession." "It was surely some diabolical manifestation. I know that the world denies the existence of the Devil and so I will not speak of him; I will only say that I painted him with revulsion: I felt no love for my work at that time. I tried to force myself to be true to nature (here is the 'earthly realism' or 'naturalism' in Gogol that our critics of the 1860's used to wax so enthusiastic about),[37] and I tried to stifle everything within me. It was not a work of art, and therefore the feelings it arouses in everyone who looks at it are restless and agitated feelings, not the feelings of an artist; for an artist creates a feeling of peace even in agitation."

The fate of the hero of this early story seems to portend or "prototype" the fate of Gogol himself.

The impression which the portrait produces on everyone and on the artist himself calls to mind the impression created by *The Inspector General* and by *Dead Souls*: "In the last analysis something monstrous and gloomy remains . . . all this is inexpressibly terrible." Pushkin—the jolliest of men, with an especially great fondness for laughter—suddenly stops laughing and sinks into gloom: "Lord, how sad our Russia is!" The artist, when he is painting the portrait, feels such inexplicable oppression and such strange revulsion that he is compelled to throw down his brush.

"*The Inspector General* has been produced," Gogol said, "and there is such a confused and strange feeling in my heart. . . . My creation struck me as being repulsive and grotesque; it did not seem to belong to me at all. . . . I am tired in both soul and body. I swear, nobody knows of or senses my sufferings. Well, let them

[37 Cf. the introduction to the present collection for a discussion of the nineteenth-century interpretation of Gogol as a "realist." The parenthetical remark is Merezhkovsky's.]

all go their merry way! My play is loathsome to me. . . . What dreadful anguish! I myself don't know why I feel such anguish."[38]

Likewise, Gogol confessed that while he was working on *Dead Souls*, he "could feel no affection for the project. . . . On the contrary, I felt something akin to revulsion. . . . Everything came out strained and forced."[39] The artist in "The Portrait" finally runs away from his creation. Similarly, Gogol ran away from *The Inspector General*: "I would now like to escape Heaven knows where, and only the journey that lies ahead of me—the ship, the sea, and new, far-off skies can refresh me. I yearn for them as I yearn for Heaven knows what."[40] And Gogol tried to run away from *Dead Souls* in just the same way he did from *The Inspector General*—by knocking about from pillar to post, from Paris to Jerusalem. The artist in the story never completed the portrait. And both *Dead Souls* and *The Inspector General* "have no ending" either. The artist entered a monastery. Gogol's dream, throughout the second half of his life, was also a complete renunciation of the world—monasticism.

"Before me stands a man who is laughing at everything we have. . . . No, this is not a mockery of vices; it is a disgusting lampoon of Russia"[41]—perhaps not only of Russia but of all mankind, of all God's creation: that is the charge against which Gogol tried to defend himself and, consequently, that is what he feared. He saw that "laughter cannot be trifled with." "What I was laughing at became sad."[42] One might add: it became terrible. He felt that his very laughter was terrible, that the power of this laughter was lifting some last remaining veils, and baring some ultimate secret of evil. By looking too directly into the face of the "Devil without a mask," Gogol glimpsed something that no human eye should see: "a decaying hideous specter with a melancholy face" glared into his eyes, and he took fright and, beside himself with fear, set up a shout for all Russia to hear: "It is a dreadful thing, fellow countrymen! . . . At the mere presentiment of the grandeur beyond the grave, the soul turns rigid with horror. . . . All my dying organ-

[38] "Otryvok iz pis'ma, pisannogo avtorom vskore posle pervogo predstavleniya 'Revizora' k odnomu literaturu," *PSS*, IV, 1951, 99-104.]

[39] "Avtorskaya ispoved'," *PSS*, VIII, 1952, 441.]

[40] "Otryvok iz pis'ma . . . ," *PSS*, IV, 1951, 104.]

[41] Both quotes are from "Razvyazka Revizora," *PSS*, IV, 1951, 124. 145.]

[42] "Avtorskaya ispoved'," *PSS*, VIII, 1952, 441.]

ism groans in intuition of the gigantic growths and fruits whose seeds we have been sowing in life without discerning or suspecting what horrors would arise out of them."[43]

IX

One of Hans Christian Andersen's fairy tales, "The Snow Queen," tells of a looking-glass made by the Devil. Everything looked distorted, ludicrous, and hideous when reflected in it. The Devil's minions coursed the length and breadth of the earth with this looking-glass, and soon there was not a single country or person left that had not been reflected in it. Finally they set their sights on Heaven itself, so that they might mock the angels and even the Creator. The higher they rose, the more the looking-glass grimaced, twisted, and turned, and they could scarcely hold on to it. Then they rose still higher, and suddenly the glass gave such a heave that it wrenched itself from their hands, fell to earth, and was smashed to pieces. Millions and billions of fragments were scattered over the world. Some were no bigger than a grain of sand; once they got into people's eyes, they remained there. Anybody with one of these fragments in his eye began to see things backwards, or noticed only what was absurd about them; for each fragment retained the properties of the looking-glass as a whole. Some people got fragments in their hearts, which then turned into lumps of ice. One fragment lodged in the heart of the hero of the tale, a young man named Kay. After numerous adventures, Kay found himself in the palace of the Snow Queen. "In the midst of the largest deserted hall of snow was a frozen lake. Its ice had cracked into thousands of pieces, wondrously even and straight, each just like every other. . . . Kay had turned quite blue, indeed almost black, from the cold, but he did not feel it: the kiss of the Snow Queen had made him insensitive to the cold, and besides, his heart was a lump of ice. He fussed with the flat, sharp slivers of ice, arranging them in all kinds of patterns, as in the game known as a 'Chinese puzzle.' He made whole words out of the ice-slivers, but he never could form the one word he particularly wished to—the word 'Eternity.' "

Kay's fate was also Gogol's fate: a fragment of this accursed mirror seemed to have lodged in his eye and in his heart. And

[43 "Zaveshchanie," *Vyb. mesta, PSS,* 1952, 221.]

his endless fussing with his rules of virtue, which in their way were also straight, sharp slivers of ice; his fruitless attempts at putting his soul in order[44]—all this resembled a Chinese puzzle. And sitting atop the ice-coated ruins of the world destroyed by his own laughter, he attempted to make something out of the ice-slivers, something he particularly yearned for yet could not bring off: the words "Eternity" and "Eternal Love." And when he tried to console himself by saying that "in the depths of cold laughter, warm, mighty sparks of eternal love can be found," he nonetheless sensed that these sparks could not thaw his own heart, which had turned into a lump of ice. And when he tried to set his mind at rest by saying that "the person who often weeps tears from the depths of his heart also seems to laugh more than anyone else in the world," he nonetheless felt that he himself would never weep such tears.[45] Poor Gogol, poor Kay! Both would freeze to death, without ever having put together the words "Eternal Love" from the slivers of ice.

In order to tear the fragment of the Devil's looking-glass out of his heart, Gogol was prepared to tear out the heart itself; in order to resurrect the world, he was prepared to put himself to death; in order to serve others, he was prepared to sacrifice himself to his own murderous laughter. "No, you are not laughing at yourselves" —he said, taking back his own words (the words uttered at the end of *The Inspector General*)—"you are laughing only at me."

None of my readers knew that in laughing at my heroes, he was laughing at me. . . . I was a collection of every conceivable abomination . . . and moreover in such numbers as I have never yet found in any one individual. . . . If they had revealed themselves to me all of a sudden and all at one stroke, I would have hanged myself. . . . I began to endow my heroes with my own vile traits, in addition to their own. This is how it was done: taking one bad quality of mine, I would pursue it in some other calling, some other profession; I would try to represent it as a deadly enemy who had offended me in the most painful way. I would pursue it with anger, with ridicule, with everything else that came to mind. If anyone had seen the

[44 The "ordering" or "educating" of his soul is an obsessive theme of Gogol's letters throughout the 1840's.]

[45 Both quotes are from "Teatral'nyi raz"ezd posle predstavleniya novoi komedii," *PSS*, v, 1949, 171.]

monsters that issued from my pen, at first for my own purposes alone, he would certainly have shuddered.[46]

The two greatest "monsters," who were closer to Gogol and more terrible than any others in his eyes, and whom he therefore pursued with all the anger he could muster, were Khlestakov and Chichikov. "My heroes," he said, "have not yet detached themselves from me completely and have therefore not become really independent." It was just these two—Khlestakov and Chichikov—who were least of all detached from him.[47]

In a letter to Zhukovsky, Gogol wrote: "I cut such a Khlestakovian figure in my book [*Selected Passages from Correspondence with Friends*] that I haven't the courage to glance into it. . . . There is indeed something Khlestakovian in me."[48] What terrible significance this avowal assumes if it is juxtaposed to another: that in Khlestakov, Gogol saw the Devil!

In Gogol there was perhaps even more of Chichikov than of Khlestakov. He could have said both to Chichikov and to Khlestakov what Ivan Karamazov says to his Devil: "You are the incarnation of me, myself, though of only one side of me . . . the incarnation of my thoughts and feelings, but only the vilest and most stupid of them. . . . You are myself, me, only with a different face." But Gogol did not say this, he did not perceive, or simply did not wish or dare to perceive, his own Devil in Chichikov, perhaps in fact because Chichikov had detached himself from Gogol and gained real independence to a much lesser degree than had Khlestakov. Here the truth and power of laughter suddenly betrayed Gogol: he took pity on himself in the image of Chichikov. There was something in Chichikov's "earthly realism" that Gogol had not overcome in himself. Sensing, however, that Chichikov in any event was no ordinary individual, he set out to make him a great man. "Your mission, Pavel Ivanovich, is to be a great man,"

[46 "Chetyre pis'ma k raznym litsam po povodu 'Mertvykh dush,' " *Vyb. mesta, PSS*, VIII, 1952, 293-294.]

[47 "Chetyre pis'ma . . . ," p. 295.]

[48 The letter is dated March 6, 1847. Vasily Andreyevich Zhukovsky (1783-1852) wrote much original poetry, some of first-rate quality, but is perhaps most important for his translations from the classics (notably *The Odyssey*) and from the German and English Romantics and pre-Romantics. He was a close friend of Gogol's, and, as tutor to the future Emperor Alexander II, provided a channel into the court, which Gogol sometimes used to secure money and other favors from Emperor Nicholas I.]

Gogol tells him through Murazov, the new Christian. Gogol had to save Chichikov at any cost: for he thought that by saving him he would be saving himself.[49]

But he failed to save him; he only destroyed himself along with his hero. The idea of a great vocation for Chichikov was the last and most cunning of the snares, the last and most alluring of the masks behind which the real proprietor of *Dead Souls*, the Devil, lurked in wait for Gogol.

Just as Ivan Karamazov wrestled with the Devil in his nightmare, so Gogol wrestled with the Devil in his work, which was also a nightmare of sorts. "These nightmares have oppressed my own soul. Only something already present in my soul could have emerged from it."[50] And the important thing in his soul was "a concern that people should have a good, hearty laugh at the Devil." Did he succeed? Ultimately, who was laughing at whom in Gogol's work—man at the Devil, or the Devil at man?

In any event, the challenge was accepted, and Gogol sensed that he could not decline to fight the duel, that it was too late to back out. But this terrible struggle, which had begun in art and in a contemplativeness divorced from life, had to be decided in life itself, in real activity. Before vanquishing eternal evil in the world outside, as an artist, Gogol had to vanquish it within himself, as a human being. This he understood, and he did in fact shift the scene of battle from his work into his life: in this battle he saw not only his vocation as an artist, but also the business of life, the business of the soul.[51]

Nevertheless, Gogol's own contemplativeness already contained the beginning of activity, his very words the beginning of the "business." Here he stands in contrast to Pushkin:

> Not for life's stir and agitation
> Have we been born, nor to make gain
> Or war, but rather for sweet sounds,
> For inspiration, and for prayer.[52]

[49 This refers to Gogol's intention of "rehabilitating" Chichikov in the projected continuation of *Dead Souls*.]

[50 "Chetyre pis'ma k raznym litsam . . . ," *PSS*, VIII, 1952, 297.]

[51 This is a paraphrase of the statement: "My business is the *soul*, and *the solid business of life*," which Merezhkovsky quotes correctly in the next-to-last paragraph of his article. From "Chetyre pis'ma . . . ," p. 299.]

[52 Pushkin, "The Poet and the Mob" ("Poet i tolpa," 1828). The translation is mine.]

Gogol did acknowledge the eternal truth of this Pushkinian precept—the truth of contemplativeness—but at the same time he also saw the other truth, antithetical but equally eternal—the truth of action. And here Gogol embodied the inevitable transition of Russian literature and the Russian mind from art to religion, from great contemplativeness to great activism, from word to deed—a transition that is being completed among us only now, in our own times. "It is impossible to repeat Pushkin," Gogol said. "No, neither Pushkin nor anyone else should serve as a model for us now: different times have come . . . the business of poetry is now different. During the adolescent period of nations, it served to summon them to battle by arousing the martial spirit; now it must summon them to another, higher battle—a battle no longer for our temporal freedom, but for our very soul."[53]

Pushkin summons us away from battle; Gogol summons us into battle. This of course is the battle against eternal evil for eternal good, man's ultimate battle with the Devil. The martial spirit in Gogol is just as ingenerate and genuine as is the spirit of peace in Pushkin; there is no self-betrayal or self-renunciation on Gogol's part here: he is as true to his own nature as is Pushkin to his.

"Day and night I dream of St. Petersburg and of service to the state," Gogol wrote his mother from Nezhin at the age of eighteen.[54] "The thought of rendering service has never left me," he said at the end of his life. "I did not deviate from my path. . . . My subject has always been one and the same: my subject has been life, nothing else. . . . I have pursued life in its actuality, and not just in the visions of my imagination. . . . My mind has always been inclined to essentials and to useful things. . . . I have always felt that I would be an active participant in the business of the general good and that I could not be dispensed with. . . . I conceived a desire to serve my country. . . . I became reconciled to writing as a career only when I felt that I could serve my country in this occupation as well. . . . It has always seemed to me that great self-sacrifice lies ahead of me in this life. In Russia today a person can become a titan at every turn. The qualities of a titan are required in every calling and place." But before entering, like the Russian heroes of old, into the fray with

[53 "V chem zhe nakonets sushchestvo russkoi poezii i v chem ee osobennost'," *Vyb. mesta, PSS,* VIII, 1952, 407-408.]

[54 Letter to mother (M. I. Gogol), February 26 (o.s.), 1827. Nezhin was a small Ukrainian town where Gogol's school was located.]

"specters," Gogol had to vanquish the most terrible specter of all, the one that lived within him. "I love the good, I search for it and am consumed with it; but I do not love my nasty qualities. . . . I am struggling with them and I shall go on struggling, and God will help me in this."[55]

Here too, in this war with himself—as everywhere else—Gogol remained faithful to his own nature, to his true inner nature; yet he could not help but make the transition from "imagination" to "actuality," from word to deed: "my business is the *soul* and the *solid business of life.*"[56] Art he abandoned for test and trial; the Pushkinian attitude of prayer and sacrificial offerings left off; the Gogolian attitude of struggle and self-sacrifice began. The poet disappeared; the prophet emerged.

And at the same time, this marked the beginning of Gogol's tragedy—*incipit tragoedia*; the beginning of this struggle with everlasting evil, with banality, no longer in creative contemplativeness, but in religious activity; the great struggle of man with the Devil.

[55 These quotations are taken from various sources. Nearly all come from "Avtorskaya ispoved'," *PSS*, viii, 1952; the last one is from "Chetyre pis'ma k raznym litsam . . . ," *PSS*, viii, 1952, 291; the one beginning "I always felt that I would be a participant" is from a letter to S. P. Shevyryov, May 25, 1847.]

[56 "Chetyre pis'ma . . . ," p. 299.]

2

Valery Bryusov
(1873-1924)

AT THE BEGINNING of the 1890's, Dmitry Merezhkovsky was rising
to prominence as a "decadent" poet and critic. Among his ad-
mirers was a highly ambitious young man named Valery Bryusov.
With a collection of verse entitled *Russian Symbolists* he made his
debut in 1894, determined to transplant and cultivate on Russian
soil the new poetic techniques being practiced by the French Symbolists. Although he wrote most of the poems himself, he attached
fictitious names to a number of them in the hope of creating the
impression that a new movement was already flourishing. From
that time on, he poured out a steady stream of original verses and
translations that were generally regarded as outrageous by the
prevailing standards. At first he was ridiculed and excluded from
the established literary press. But his sense of timing was keen: a
number of brilliant young poets of similar persuasion—notably
Andrey Bely, Alexander Blok, and Vyacheslav Ivanov—were beginning to appear around the turn of the century. By 1905 they had
firmly established the predominance of Russian Symbolism, and
were creating a body of poetry which would later lead critics to
refer to this entire period as the Silver Age of Russian Literature
(the Golden Age being the nineteenth century).

Although Bryusov was inferior in poetic talent to Bely, Blok,
and Ivanov, he was nonetheless acknowledged as the intellectual
leader of the Moscow Symbolists. This was testimony to his prodigious erudition, energy, and versatility, which were remarkable
even among a group of exceptionally erudite, energetic, and versatile artists. He was not only a poet and a literary entrepreneur,
but a writer of short stories and novels (the best one being *The
Fire Angel*, 1907), a translator (especially from the French), a
theorist and critic of literature, and the editor of the most important literary journal of the time, *The Scales* (*Vesy*, 1904-09).
After the October Revolution, he was one of the very few established men of letters to join the Bolshevik Party, and to work

103

energetically (if not always effectively) in the service of the new government. This made him acceptable to the Soviets at a time when virtually all the other Symbolists were officially despised as "decadents."

The essay translated here was first read at a meeting of the Society of Lovers of Russian Literature in Moscow, on April 27, 1909, in celebration of the centenary of Gogol's birth. It was then published (under the title "Ispepelennyi") in *Vesy*, No. 4, 1909, pp. 100-120. I have made no important changes in the text, and have attempted to suggest the rather hieratic tone of Bryusov's style.

Burnt to Ashes

by Valery Bryusov

I

IF WE WISHED to define the essential characteristic of Gogol's mind, the *faculté maîtresse* that is predominant in both his art and his life, we would have to call it *a striving for exaggeration or hyperbole.* After the critical essays of Vasily Rozanov and Dmitry Merezhkovsky, it is no longer possible to regard Gogol as a consistently realistic writer whose works reflect the life of the Russia of his times in an unusually faithful and accurate manner.[1] Quite the contrary: although Gogol did make a strenuous effort to present an honest picture of the world around him, still, in everything he wrote, he always remained a dreamer, a fantast, and in his art, essentially, he embodied only the ideal world of his visions. Gogol's fantastic tales as well as his realistic works are in like manner the creations of a dreamer who dwells alone within the solitude of his imagination, isolated from the entire outside world by the unbreachable wall of his reverie.

It does not matter where we turn in the pages of Gogol's work—whether he is eulogizing his native Ukraine, whether he is heaping ridicule on the banality of contemporary life, whether he is trying to frighten or terrify us with hair-raising folk-tales or enchant us with some picture of beauty, whether he is endeavoring to teach, exhort, or prophesy—everywhere we find a tone that is highly overwrought, imagery that is exaggerated, incidents that are improbable, and desires that are deliriously intemperate. Nothing average or ordinary exists for Gogol: the boundless and the limitless are all that he knows. If he is painting a scene from nature, he cannot help but insist that we are looking at something exceptional, something divine. If it is a beautiful woman, then she is sure to be without peer. If it is courage, then it is unprecedented, superior to all other instances. If it is something monstrous, then it is more

---

[1] Vasily Rozanov, "Pushkin i Gogol';" "Kak proizoshel tip Akakiya Akakievicha," in *Legenda o Velikom Inkvizitore F. M. Dostoevskogo, s prilozheniem dvukh etyudov o Gogole,* 3d ed., St. Petersburg, 1906; Dmitry Merezhkovsky, *Gogol' i chert,* Moscow, 1906. [Merezhkovsky's essay is translated in the present anthology as "Gogol and the Devil."]

monstrous than anything ever before engendered by human imagination. If it is insignificance and banality, then it is an extreme, drastic, unparalleled instance. Under Gogol's pen, the drab daily life of Russia in the 1830's is transfigured into an apotheosis of banality, the likes of which cannot be found in any other period in the history of the world.

One of Edgar Allan Poe's stories, "King Pest," tells of two sailors who make their way into a deserted, plague-ridden section of London. Entering one of the houses, they come upon a hideous company seated around a banquet-table. What is striking about each of these revelers is that one particular part of his face is developed out of all proportion to the whole. One has a fantastically high forehead that juts above the rest of his head like a crown; another has an incredibly vast mouth that runs from ear to ear, opening and closing like a horrible gaping chasm; another has an incongruously long and thick nose that hangs flabbily below her chin like an elephant's trunk; still another has grotesquely sagging cheeks that droop onto his shoulders like wineskins, and so forth. All Gogol's heroes resemble these specters that presented themselves to Poe's imagination. In all of them, one part of the self or one trait of character has undergone a grotesquely disproportionate development. Gogol's creations are great and terrible caricatures which a great artist has mesmerized decades of readers into taking for mirror-images of Russian reality.

Before us is a provincial town, so remote that "even if you ride for three years you won't come to any other country."[2] The curtain rises, and we see the inhabitants of this town, its officials, sitting around a table in a room in the mayor's house. Have we not opened the wrong door? Have we not—with the two drunken sailors—stumbled into that ghastly banquet-hall in Poe's plague-ridden London? Do we not see before us those same hideous freaks that greeted the eyes of the stunned and frightened sailors? Do not the mayor (Skvoznik-Dmukhanovsky), the judge (Lyapkin-Tyapkin), the welfare director (Zemlyanika) and the others—all so familiar to us from childhood—do not all of them suffer from the same disease that afflicts Poe's grotesque characters? Is it not true that one of them has a monstrously high forehead, another an incredibly vast mouth, another unimaginably flabby cheeks?

Let us listen to what they are saying.

[2 This is said by the mayor in *The Inspector General* (Act I, Scene 1), the work to which the next several paragraphs refer.]

"We don't go in for expensive medicines," says Zemlyanika. "They're just ordinary people: if they're going to die, why then they'll die; if they're going to get well, why then they'll get well."

The mayor complains that the assessor smells as if he had just come out of a distillery. "No, there's no way of getting rid of that now," the judge replies. "He says his nurse bumped him against something when he was a baby, and ever since then he's smelled slightly of vodka."

Khlestakov makes his appearance. "Now what was there in that featherbrain the least like an inspector general?" the mayor wonders at the end of the play. In fact—nothing. A traveler staying in the hotel in a room "behind the staircase," not paying his bills, wheedling dinners out of the management—what sort of inspector general is that? In a provincial town, nobody has a private life; and *during the two weeks* that Khlestakov has been living there, everyone must have at least caught a glimpse of him on the street. Nevertheless, the following conversation takes place between him and the mayor:

Khlestakov: Well, what am I to do? . . . It's not my fault . . . I will certainly pay. . . . They'll send me money from home . . . .

Mayor: Pardon me, it's really not my fault. . . . Permit me to suggest that you accompany me to other quarters.

Khl.: No, I will not! I know what "other quarters" means—it means jail. But what right have you? How dare you? . . .

M.: Have pity on me, don't ruin me! I have a wife and little children. . . .

Then there is the boasting scene in Act III. Khlestakov says: "On the table, for instance, there's a watermelon that costs seven hundred roubles. The soup in the saucepan has come straight from Paris by ship. . . . Before you knew it there were messengers, messengers, and more messengers dashing through the streets . . . just imagine it: 35,000 messengers alone. . . . Why, tomorrow I'm being promoted straight to field marsh—." No matter how drunk a person might be, he could scarcely utter such absurdities unless he had gone out of his head. This is not ordinary lying, but a kind of superlying, immoderate lying, as immoderate as everything else in Gogol.

"It seems to me," Khlestakov says to Zemlyanika, "that you were a little shorter yesterday, isn't that right?" And Zemlyanika replies: "It's entirely possible." Anna Andreyevna, the mayor's wife, asks Khlestakov: "I suppose you must write for the journals too?" And he replies: "Actually, I've written lots of things myself: *The Marriage of Figaro, Robert the Devil, Norma.* I can't even remember the titles of all of them. And it all happened by chance. I didn't intend to do any writing, but the theater-managers kept saying: 'Do write something, my dear fellow.' And I thought to myself: 'Well, why not, my dear fellow?' And then I sat down and knocked off everything in one evening, I guess." Khlestakov makes a play for Anna Andreyevna. She protests: "But allow me to observe that I am, in a certain sense—I am married." Khlestakov replies: "That doesn't matter. Love recognizes no distinctions; as Karamzin said: 'Only the laws condemn.' We shall betake ourselves beneath the bosky shade of babbling brooks . . . I'm asking for your hand, your hand."[3]

"Thirty-five thousand messengers"—"Yesterday you were a little shorter"—"It's entirely possible"—"I sat down and knocked off everything in one evening"—"We shall betake ourselves beneath the bosky shade of babbling brooks"—nothing of the sort can be heard in actual life. Such remarks are inconceivable in the world of reality; they are parodies of reality. The banalities of ordinary conversation are clustered in the dialogues of Gogol's comedies and blown up to enormous dimensions, as if we were observing them through a powerful magnifying glass.

The scene shifts. Before us is another town—the one in Part 1 of *Dead Souls* where there is a shop with the sign "Vasily Fyodorov, Foreigner." A new cast of characters passes before us; yet every one of them has some particular trait of personality that is overdeveloped. The miserliness of Plyushkin, the crudeness of Sobakevich, the simpering sentimentality of Manilov, the obtuseness of Korobochka, the impetuosity of Nozdryov, the laziness of Tentetnikov, the gluttony of Petukh—once again we see the outsized nose, the grotesque mouth, the incredible cheeks of the heroes of Edgar Allan Poe. And all these landowners, everyone in this little world of monomaniacs, who is visited each in turn by the money-grubbing Chichikov and presented with his strange proposition—everyone speaks in a way that nobody in real life speaks, and does things that nobody would be capable of actually doing.

[3 See Merezhkovsky, "Gogol and the Devil," footnote 17, in the present anthology.]

Chichikov proposes that Korobochka should sell him her dead souls. "As a widow, I'm very inexperienced in such matters," she replies. "I'd better hold off for a while, maybe some merchants will come by and I'll see what the going rate is."

Chichikov is bargaining with the miser Plyushkin. "Most honored sir," he says, "I would pay not only forty kopecks for each soul, but five hundred roubles! I would pay it with pleasure because I see an honorable and kind-hearted old man suffering misfortune because of his own good nature." Plyushkin says: "Yes, yes, that's just it, that's true! It's all because of my good nature."

And here are Chichikov and the Manilovs in conversation:

"And what did you think of our governor?" asked Manilov's wife.

"He is a most estimable and amiable man, is he not?" added Manilov.

"Perfectly true," said Chichikov, "a most estimable man. . . ."

"And the vice-governor, he's such a nice man, isn't that so?" said Manilov. . . .

"A very, very worthy man," Chichikov replied.

"And, pray tell, how did the chief of police strike you? A very pleasant man, isn't that so?"

"Extremely pleasant—and such an intelligent and well-read man! . . ."

"And what is your opinion of the chief of police's wife?" Manilov's wife added. "An extremely charming woman, isn't she?"

"Oh, she is one of the worthiest women I know," replied Chichikov.

All these conversations are lampoons in which the ridiculous side of human relationships is egregiously exaggerated, and the absurd side is turned into a kind of cult.

When the townspeople discover that Chichikov has been trying to buy up dead souls, the officials propose this and suppose that about him, and their talk immediately reaches the absolute limit of probability. Some say that Chichikov is a counterfeiter; others, that he wants to abduct the governor's daughter; others, that he is Captain Kopeykin. "Among the many theories—all ingenious in their way—one finally emerged (which is even strange to mention): that Chichikov must be Napoleon in disguise." Gogol adds that "the officials did not exactly believe this, but still, they did grow thoughtful." And the public prosecutor, "on arriving home, took to brooding and brooding and suddenly, with no rhyme or reason, as they say, he up and died."

In still another town—the one in Part 2 of *Dead Souls* where there is a shop bearing the sign: "Foreigner from London and Paris"—the appearance of a Gogolian hero creates confusion on an even greater scale. After Chichikov is arrested, his lawyer begins "working miracles in the civilian area."

> he let the governor know indirectly that the public prosecutor was writing a secret report against him. He let an official in the police know that an official living in the town incognito on a secret mission was writing secret reports against him; he assured the official living in town incognito on a secret mission that there was another official on an even more secret mission who was informing against him. . . . One secret report piled on another, and such things as had never seen the light of day, and such as had never even existed were exposed one after another. . . . Scandals and intrigues and everything else got so mixed up and entangled with Chichikov's case and with the dead souls that there was absolutely no way of determining which of these matters was the most nonsensical. . . . When, at last, the papers began pouring in on the governor-general, the poor prince could not make head nor tail of them. A most intelligent and efficient official who had been assigned the task of making an abstract of the case nearly went out of his mind. . . . In one part of the province there was famine. . . . In another part of the province the schismatics were getting restive again. Someone had spread the rumor among them that an Antichrist had been born who would not let even the dead rest in peace, buying up, as he was, certain dead souls. They did penance and then sinned, and under the pretext of trying to catch the Antichrist they did away with some non-Antichrists. . . . In another place, the peasants had risen up in rebellion.

But is this astonishing revolution, which has been stirred up by the adventures of Chichikov, really any less plausible than the incident in which Major Kovalyov's nose disappears from his face and starts riding around St. Petersburg dressed in a uniform with gold braid ("The Nose")? Gogol, carried away by his own account of the general chaos created by the adroit counsellor-at-law, is almost ready to forget that this is all an exaggeration, is almost ready to believe, himself, that Chichikov is the Antichrist; and, in Part 2, he puts words we certainly do not expect to hear into the mouth of Prince Khlobuyev, who has called the officials together just before he leaves for St. Petersburg: "We must save our native land." Nothing separates the real from the fantastic in Gogol's works; something that is possible can, at any moment, turn into something that is impossible.

And wherever Gogol looks—whatever the town, whatever the country house—he sees the same disorienting absurdity, he encounters the same improbable heroes. Anna Panteleymonovna asks Zhevakin why he is paying them a visit, and he replies: "I too saw an announcement of something in the newspapers. Well, I thought to myself, I'll go. The weather looked good, grass was everywhere along the road" (*Marriage*). When his aunt proposes marrying him off Ivan Fyodorovich objects: "What do you mean, a wife? Oh, no, for heaven's sake, auntie . . . I've never been married before . . . I wouldn't know what to do with her" ("Ivan Fyodorovich Shponka and His Aunt"). Such remarks give the appearance of being "realistic"; but they are all of a piece with the deliberate absurdities in "The Nose": "You have lost your nose?" the policeman asks Kovalyov. "Yes, indeed." "Now it has been found. . . . It was about to start off on a trip when it was seized. It was already boarding the stagecoach, intending to leave for Riga. And its passport had long ago been made out in the name of a certain government official." After all this, how can we fail to give credence to Gogol's own words: "If anyone had seen the monsters that issued from my pen, at first for my own purposes alone—he would certainly have shuddered."[4]

But it is not only Gogol's depictions of the banality and absurdity of life that exceed all normal limits. In themselves, such excesses could be explained as a device consciously employed by a satirist bent on setting up his targets in a particularly ludicrous and deliberately exaggerated way. Actually, Gogol indulges in exactly the same sort of exaggeration even when he wishes to depict beautiful as well as ugly things. He has absolutely no idea how to aim for an effect by bringing parts together into a harmonious whole. All the power of his art is concentrated in one device and one only: an extreme thickening of colors. He depicts not relative but always absolute beauty, not things that are dread-

[4 "Chetyre pis'ma k raznym litsam po povodu 'Mertvykh dush,' " *Vybrannye mesta iz perepiski s druz'yami*, PSS, VIII, 1952, 294.]

ful in certain specific circumstances but, rather, invariably and absolutely so. Here, for example, is a description, from *Taras Bulba*, of the Cossacks doing battle with the Poles at the walls of Dubno:

> Demid Popovich ran his lance through three of the rank-and-file soldiers and knocked the two best noblemen off their horses. . . . And he drove the horses far afield, shouting to the Cossacks standing there to catch them. Then he again fought his way into the center of the fray and again fell upon the noblemen he had unsaddled; one he killed and around the neck of the other he threw a noose, tied him to his saddle and dragged him the length and breadth of the field. . . . Like a stately poplar-tree, he [the Pole] was galloping here and there on his dun-colored steed. . . . He clove two Cossacks in twain. . . . Kukubenko, spurring on his horse, bore straight down on him from behind and let out a mighty shout, so that all who were standing nearby shuddered at the unearthly sound. The Pole tried to wheel his horse around and face him; but the horse would not obey. . . . And Kukubenko caught him with a bullet from his gun. The burning bullet struck between his shoulder blades. . . . Borodaty was tempted by greed: he bent down to strip the costly armor from [the corpse]. . . . And Borodaty failed to hear the red-nosed standard-bearer galloping down on him from behind. . . . Greed brought the Cossack to no good: his mighty head flew off his shoulders, and the headless corpse fell, watering the earth with blood far and wide. And up to the height of heaven flew the stern Cossack soul, frowning and indignant.

In what age do these heroic deeds take place? In the Ukraine of the sixteenth century, or in the mythic times of the Trojan War? Who are these men who cleave their enemies in twain, overcome five adversaries singlehandedly, strike dread into everyone's heart with unearthly shouts—the Zaporozhian Cossacks of Gogol, or the heroes of Homer: god-like Diomedes, Achilles, born of a goddess, Agamemnon, the lord of men?[5]

But what is the epic of *Taras Bulba* if not a series of hyperbolic

---

[5] It is highly probable that the description of the battle of Dubno was not so much based on a careful study of Ukrainian history as it was influenced by Gnedich's translation of *The Iliad*. [Nikolay Ivanovich Gnedich (1784-1833) was a poet and translator, best known for his rendering of *The Iliad*, which appeared in complete form in 1829.]

images, in which scenes of the Ukraine, the dash and boldness of the Cossacks, and the unspoiled simplicity of their life are all depicted in an exaggerated and highly embellished manner? In battle "heads fly off," "Poles are mown down like sheaves," and "sabers flash." Andry kisses "fragrant lips" and is "filled with feelings that cannot be experienced on this earth." The Polish girl feels that Andry's words have "torn her heart asunder." "Neither cry nor groan" is heard from Ostap's lips while he is being so horribly put to death, "even when they began to break the bones in his arms and legs, and when the dreadful cracking could be heard amid the death-like stillness of the crowd." Taras stands unflinchingly on the bonfire, and the poet exclaims: "Are there in the world any fires, any tortures, any strength that could overcome Russian strength?" And so on and so forth. The history of the Ukraine only gave Gogol a pretext for painting scenes of some heroic epoch that existed in his imagination.[6]

There are other heroes of Gogol's who also feel and experience everything hyperbolically. Ivan, in "A Terrible Vengeance," horrifies even God with the intensity of his hatred. "Terrible is the punishment that you have devised, oh man," God says to him. Khoma Brut, in "Viy," falls dead from fear.[7] The hero of "The Portrait" is consumed with envy. "His passions were on too abnormal and colossal a scale for his feeble strength," Gogol says of him. A pretty girl encountered on the street casts a glance at the hero of "Nevsky Prospect" and "his breath caught in his chest, he began to quiver all inside, all his feelings were aflame and everything before him was shrouded in a sort of fog. The sidewalk rushed past beneath him, the carriages with their trotting horses

---

[6] As far back as 1861, P. A. Kulish severely criticized Gogol's Ukrainian tales, from the viewpoint of their historical and ethnographic authenticity. His articles created a lively debate in their time. [Bryusov probably has in mind "Gogol', kak avtor povestei iz ukrainskoi zhizni," *Osnova*, 1861, Nos. 4, 5, 9, 11, 12. Kulish (1819-97) made the first serious attempts at a biography of Gogol, in 1854 and 1856, and in 1857 put out an edition of his works.]

[7 In a note to the story, Gogol explains the name "Viy" as follows: "This is the name that the Ukrainians use to refer to the chief of the gnomes, whose eyelids reach down to the ground." Actually, there is no such creature in Ukrainian folklore; Gogol seems to have invented it himself. See footnote 2 of Stilman's "The 'All-Seeing Eye'" in this collection. "Little Russian" and "Ukrainian" were used more or less interchangeably throughout much of the nineteenth century, with official preference being given to "Little Russian."]

seemed to stand still, the bridge stretched out and broke in the center of its arch, the houses were upside down." And even Kostanzhoglo, in Part 2 of *Dead Souls*, while expounding to Chichikov the joys of being a landowner, "was all aglow, like a Tsar on the day of his solemn coronation," and moreover it looked as if "rays of light were streaming from his face."

Even nature in Gogol is wondrously transformed, and his native Ukraine becomes some strange and luxuriant land, where everything exceeds normal dimensions. In school we all learned by heart the passage from "A Terrible Vengeance" that begins: "Enchanting is the Dnieper in tranquil weather. . . ." But what is there that is faithful and accurate about this description? Does it bear any resemblance at all to the real Dnieper? "And it seems made all of molten crystal, and, like a blue mirror-road, immeasurably broad and endlessly long, it twists and twines its way through the green world . . . rarely does a bird fly to the middle of the Dnieper. It is magnificent! There is no river like it in all the world. . . . No, there is nothing in all the world that could hide the Dnieper. Deep, deep blue, it moves along in an even flow, at midnight as at midday; it can be seen stretching as far away as the human eye can reach." Just what Dnieper is this? It is a fantastic river in a fantastic land! In the same category are the "oaks that reach up to the clouds," the fire that soars "up to the very stars" and is extinguished "under the most distant skies," in the same category are the steppes that stretch out in "measureless waves," and about which Gogol exclaims: "Nothing in nature could be better!"[8]

Was it in this same fantastic land of his imagination that Gogol also gazed upon that night which he called "the Ukrainian night?"

Do you know the Ukrainian night? Oh, you do not know the Ukrainian night! Look at it closely: from the middle of the sky the crescent moon gazes down; the vast dome of heaven has expanded and stretched, more vast than ever. It glows and breathes. The earth is bathed all in a silvery light, and the wonderful air is coolly aromatic and full of languor and it stirs up an ocean of fragrances. A divine night! An enchanting night! The woods stand motionless and inspired. . . . The virginal thickets of cherry, red and black, have timidly reached their roots into the cold spring waters. . . . And up above, everything breathes, everything is marvelous, everything is full of solem-

[8 "The Fair at Sorochintsy"; *Taras Bulba*.]

nity . . . the trill of the Ukrainian nightingale bursts forth in a majestic cascade, and even the moon, in mid-heaven, seems to be listening enraptured . . . ("A May Night").[9]

What intense language, what a theatrically grand scene! Does it correspond to the pleasant but simple and unpretentious landscape of the Ukraine?

But Gogol's penchant for hyperbole comes out most strikingly, perhaps, in his attempts at depicting feminine beauty. In "Nevsky Prospect," the beautiful girl's "lips were sealed with a whole swarm of delightful visions; everything that remains from memories of childhood, everything that induces dreaming and quiet inspiration in the glow of the lamp—all this seemed to be clustered, mingled, and reflected on her graceful lips. . . . Lord, what divine features!" The Polish girl in *Taras Bulba* possesses a "blinding beauty"; the subsequent hardships of the siege cannot "dull her wondrous beauty," and in fact confer something "irresistibly victorious" on it. The daughter of the Cossack captain in "Viy" has a forehead "like snow, like silver," "brows like night amidst a sunny day," "lips like rubies," etc.

Gogol's pen was particularly uninhibited in its portrayal of Annunciata, in "Rome":

> Try to look at the lightning when, cleaving the coal-black clouds, it begins to quiver in an unbearably bright flood of light. Such are the eyes of the Albanian girl Annunciata. . . . No matter how she turns the sparkling snow of her face, her image is firmly imprinted on the heart. . . . When she turns the back of her head to you, with its wonderful upswept hair, showing a gleaming neck and the beauty of shoulders the likes of which

[9] What a difference there is between the hyperbole of Gogol's description and the balance and proportion of Pushkin's lines from *Poltava*: "Quiet is the Ukrainian night./Transparent is the sky, the stars glitter,/The air does not want to overcome/Its drowsiness. The leaves/Of the silvery poplars barely quiver./The moon shines peacefully/Down on Belaya Tserkov." In Pushkin, the night is "quiet"; in Gogol, it is "divine." In Pushkin, the moon "peacefully shines"; in Gogol, it is "in the middle of the sky" (invariably in the middle!) and listens enraptured to the "cascade of the nightingale's trill." In Pushkin, the air "dozes"; in Gogol, it is "full of languor and stirs up an ocean (invariably an ocean!) of fragrances." In Pushkin, the stars "glitter"; in Gogol, "up above, everything is marvelous, everything is full of solemnity." In Pushkin, the leaves of the poplars "barely quiver"; in Gogol, the clumps of cherry trees are "virginal thickets," etc. [The parenthetical remarks are Bryusov's.]

have never been seen on earth—there too she is a miracle. Yet most wonderful of all is when she turns her eyes full on yours, producing a chill and sinking in the heart. . . . No lithe panther can compare with her in swiftness, strength and nobility of movement. Everything about her—from her shoulders to her sculptured, fragrant foot and the last little toe thereon—is the crowning glory of creation. . . .

What is this? A description of a living human being, or an uninhibited flight into a world of the fantastic and the impossible? After Chichikov is arrested, "one secret report piled on another." Are we not justified in saying that in "Rome," "one hyperbole piles on another?"

We know that Gogol worked hard at gathering materials for his stories. Notebooks in which he recorded his observations, various apt expressions, and turns of speech that had struck his attention, etc., have been preserved. We also have the collections of Ukrainian folk songs that he compiled. In his letters, Gogol was continually asking his relatives to give him all the "information about the Little Russians" that they could, and to collect data "on olden times." But it is remarkable that all these materials which were gathered with such care underwent a complete transformation in Gogol's hands: the images that had been taken from the real world swelled and grew in one particular aspect, either becoming something "blindingly beautiful," or revealing "an excess and abundance of baseness." In Gogol's writings, reality underwent a change, as did the sorcerer in "A Terrible Vengeance" when he resorted to witchcraft: "His nose grew longer and hung over his lips; in a trice his mouth stretched from ear to ear, and from it jutted a tooth"; or, like the witch in "Viy," who underwent a metamorphosis as a result of the incantations muttered by Khoma Brut: in place of the old woman "there lay before him a beautiful girl, with luxuriant tresses all tousled, with eyelashes as long as arrows."

Gogol himself suggested that he was always working in just this direction. For example, in the outline for an unwritten play on the Ukraine of old, he says: "Let all of it [the drama] be filled with unendurable brilliance. . . . [It should be invested] in a torrent of unquenchably passionate language . . . in unprecedented, savage and inhumanly magnificent self-sacrifice." Along exactly the same lines, in the notes to *Dead Souls*, he says: "The idea of the town. Emptiness reaching the highest degree. Idle prattle. Gossip exceeding all limits, how all this arose out of idleness and found expression as something comical in the highest degree. How people who are not stupid reach the point of perpetrating utter stupidities . . . how these considerations reach the height of the comical." Yes, Gogol did base his art on observations and on a close study of real life; but he carried everything to the highest degree, to the height of the comical, and turned it into something unprecedented and inhuman.[10]

"Gogol looked upon all phenomena and objects not as they were in reality, but in their extreme"—this is Vasily Rozanov's formulation of the point we are making here.[11] Of course, the Russia of Gogol's time was not populated by the monomaniacs, monsters, and angelic beauties that step from the pages of his stories. The same kinds of people lived then as now, people who combined absurdity and nobility, beauty and ugliness, heroism and paltriness. Pushkin had an eye for such people and depicted them in *Eugene Onegin*, *The Tales of Belkin*, and *The Bronze Horseman*. But Gogol could not see them. He created his own special world and his own special people; and what he found just hinted at in real life, he developed to the ultimate in his art. And such was the power of his talent, the power of his art, that he not only gave life to these fictions, but made them, as it were, more real than reality itself. He compelled generations of readers after him to forget real life and remember only the imaginary world that he had created. For many years we have all looked at the Ukraine and the Russia of Nicholas I through the Gogolian prism.

[10] Gogol had still another way of using the materials he collected: bringing an enormous number of observations together in one place, as if he were trying to deafen the reader with terminology. For example, in his description of Plyushkin's work-yard, in *Dead Souls* (ch. six), he writes of "wood that was fastened together, turned, and joined, as well as wicker-work: barrels, pails, tubs, covered buckets, jugs with spouts and without spouts, ladles, bast-baskets, hampers on which the women keep their fiber for spinning and other odds and ends, wicker baskets of thin aspen wood, boxes of woven birchbark, and a great deal of everything else that is used by rich and poor Russia alike." Likewise, when describing Chichikov's visit to the dog-fancier Nozdryov (ch. four), Gogol mentions "dogs of every kind, shaggy-haired and smooth-haired, of every possible color and breed, reddish-black, black with white spots, white with yellow spots, yellow with black spots, with red spots, with black ears, with gray ears."

[11] Rozanov, "Kak proizoshel tip Akakiya Akakievicha," *Legenda o Velikom Inkvizitore*, p. 276.

II

This urge toward extremes, toward exaggeration, toward hyper-bole, came out not only in Gogol's art, in his writings: this same urge permeated every aspect of his life as well. Everything that went on around him he saw in exaggerated proportions; he had no trouble in taking the phantoms of his inflamed imagination for reality; and all his life he inhabited a world in which one illusion followed another. Not only did he "look upon all phenomena and objects in their extreme"; he also experienced all feelings in their extreme.

"Everything within me is out of kilter," Gogol himself once acknowledged. "For example, if I see someone stumble, my imagi-nation immediately seizes on it and begins elaborating it, always in the form of really terrifying specters. These torment me to such an extent that I cannot sleep, and all my strength is sapped."[12] A great deal in Gogol can be explained by this penchant for "elaborating everything, always in the form of really terrifying specters."

Gogol's letters—from his youth as well as from his adult years— offer striking illustrations of how easily his mind veered off in different directions—extreme despair, then boundless rapture, then pride, then self-depreciation. As a very young man he wrote: "From my earliest years, from almost the time when I could under-stand nothing, I burned with an unquenchable zeal to make my life useful for the good of the state. . . . I swore that I would not let a single moment of my brief life go by without doing some good."[13] This same intensely ecstatic note was struck again ten years later, in a letter to Zhukovsky: "No diversion, no passion had the power of possessing my soul, even for one minute, and distracting me from my duty" (June 28, 1836). After he fled to Europe in 1829, he wrote his mother, in a deeply remorseful letter from Lübeck: "It's a dreadful thing! It's rending my heart. Forgive me, dear, generous mamma, forgive your unhappy son, who desires only one thing at this moment: to throw himself into

[12 As recounted to F. V. Chizhov in 1849; quoted in V. V. Veresayev, *Gogol' v zhizni*, Moscow-Leningrad, 1933, p. 399.]

[13 Bryusov mistakenly identifies this as a letter to Gogol's mother. It is actually to P. P. Kosyarovsky (his mother's first cousin), October 3 (o.s.), 1827.]

your arms and pour out to you his soul, which is uprooted and devastated by tempests" (August 13, 1829).

Going to another extreme, in 1837 Gogol could not find words to express his enthusiasm for Italy: "What a land is Italy!" he wrote. "Everything is beautiful beneath this sky. There is no better fate than to die in Rome." And in another letter: "When at last I set eyes on Rome for the second time, oh, how much better it looked to me than before! It seemed to me that I had caught a glimpse of my native land, which I have not visited for several years. . . . But no, that's not quite it: I saw not my native land, but the native land of my soul, the land in which my soul lived long before me, before I was born into this world." It is doubtful that all this was mere rhetoric: most likely, when Gogol was setting such ideas down he actually did feel that way about them. "My thoughts are a whirlwind," he once said.[14]

In 1837, while in Rome, Gogol received news of Pushkin's death. And this is how he expressed his reaction in a letter to Pletnyov on March 28: "I could not possibly have received any worse news from Russia. All the delight of my life, all my sublime delight, has vanished along with him. I never undertook anything without his advice. I never wrote a single line without imagining him standing before me. What he would say, what he would notice, what he would laugh at, what he would give firm and final approval to—this was all that concerned me, all that inspirited my powers. My soul was embraced in the secret quivering of a pleasure that cannot be experienced on this earth. Lord! The labor I am now engaged in [Dead Souls], which was inspired by him, his creation—I do not have the strength to go on with it. Several times I have taken up my pen, and it has fallen from my hand. . . ." He repeated

[14 The first quotation is from a letter to P. A. Pletnyov, November 2, 1837; the second from a letter to M. P. Balabina, April, 1838; the third from a letter to M. A. Maksimovich, May 28 (o.s.), 1834.

Pyotr Alexandrovich Pletnyov (1792-1862) was Professor of Russian Literature at St. Petersburg University (and later rector), an important critic, and a constant correspondent of Gogol's.

Maria Petrovna Balabina was a private pupil of Gogol's; he was engaged to give her lessons on the recommendation of Pletnyov.

Nikolay Yakovlevich Prokopovich (1810-57) was a classmate of Gogol's at Nezhin, a teacher of Russian language and literature, and a minor poet. He supervised the publication of the first edition of Gogol's collected works (1842), but proved rather incompetent; as a result, he and Gogol had something of a falling out.]

virtually the same sentiments to Pogodin two days later: "My loss is greater than anyone else's. . . . My life, my most sublime delight has perished with him. . . . I undertook nothing, I wrote nothing without his advice. For everything good that is in me, I am indebted to him. . . . What does my life mean now!"[15]

If nothing else, the elevated tone of these lamentations compels us to regard them more as a momentary rush of intense emotion than as an expression of a persistent feeling. It is remarkable that the tone of despair is not sustained even within these same letters. The one to Pletnyov continues as follows: "Send me the money that Smirdin is supposed to deposit for me by early April. Give it to Shtiglits in just the same way, so that he can send it on to one of the bankers in Rome for transmittal to me. It's better if he transfers it to Valentini; they say he's more honest than the other bankers here." This addendum is so unexpected, and is so utterly discrepant in tone from the beginning of the letter, that the editor of the first edition of Gogol's letters did not venture to print it, and included only the lines on Pushkin in his edition.[16] The letter to Pogodin ends as follows: "Do come to Rome. This is where I always live now. . . . The sky is wonderful. I drink in its air and forget the entire world." Does such a conclusion—"I forget the entire world"—go with the words: "All my delight has perished with Pushkin," and with the statement: "What does my life mean now!"?

"Oh Pushkin, Pushkin! What a beautiful dream I dreamed in life!" Gogol exclaimed in a letter to Zhukovsky (October 30, 1847). Indeed, Pushkin was for him a dream, a reverie, a vision. The letters of Gogol to Pushkin and Pushkin to Gogol have been preserved, and we know that no real friendship or intimacy existed between the two men. The three brief letters from Pushkin, though

[15 Mikhail Petrovich Pogodin (1800-1875) was Professor of History at Moscow University, and an important journalist: he published *The Moscow Herald* (*Moskovskii Vestnik*) and *The Moscow Observer* (*Moskovskii Nablyudatel'*). He formed a close friendship with Gogol; it later cooled considerably, but the two men continued to correspond.]

[16 I.e., *Sochineniya i pis'ma N. V. Gogolya*, ed. P. A. Kulish, St. Petersburg, 1857, v, 286-287. Alexander Filippovich Smirdin (1795-1857) is important in the history of Russian literature as the first really successful publisher on a large scale (for those days) of the important contemporary writers in inexpensive editions. Shtiglits was a banker in St. Petersburg, and Valentini a banker in Rome.]

cordial and courteous, are extremely reserved. The letters from
Gogol are carefully worked over, make an effort here and there to
be amusing, and are nearly all full of requests of a business nature.
But in place of the superficial relationship that existed in reality,
Gogol created another relationship in his imagination, where
Pushkin was his close friend, his protector, his mentor. Pushkin
died and Gogol now felt that all the delight of his life had vanished,
he already believed that he "undertook nothing, wrote nothing"
without Pushkin's advice, and that *Dead Souls* was not only
inspired by Pushkin, but was actually Pushkin's own creation.[17]

Actually, there was a great deal in Gogol's life besides Pushkin
that was also a "beautiful dream." As we know, in 1834 Gogol
finally managed (with Zhukovsky's help) to secure an appointment to the chair of medieval history in St. Petersburg University.
He had great enthusiasm for Ukrainian folksongs, read a few
old chronicles and a few history-books, talked things over with
Pogodin—and before he knew it he became convinced that he was
a historian. By then he was certain that if only S. S. Uvarov, the
Minister of Education, were to look at his teaching plan, he "would
single me out from the crowd of mediocre professors that clog the
universities."[18] He wrote Pogodin: "It seems to me that I will do
something out of this world in world history."[19] Even more:
Gogol's imagination promptly inspired him to make the most
grandiose plans, and he envisaged not only a career as a historian,
but the writing of a "history of Little Russia" in six volumes, a

---

[17] P. V. Annenkov says that Pushkin let Gogol have the plot of *Dead
Souls* with great reluctance, and that he remarked in his own family circle:
"You've got to be careful with that Ukrainian; he plucks me clean before I
have a chance to cry out." L. Pavlishchev says the same thing. ["N. V.
Gogol' v Rime letom 1841 goda," *Literaturnye vospominaniya*, Moscow,
1960, p. 71. Bryusov no doubt is referring to Lev Nikolayevich Pavlishchev,
whose memoirs ("Iz semeinoi khroniki") were serialized in *The Historical
Herald* (*Istoricheskii vestnik*) throughout 1888. The reference to Pushkin
is found in the February issue. Pushkin's reaction, as reported here, was
heard by Pavlishchev from his mother, and later from Pushkin's widow:
" 'That crafty, crafty Ukrainian,' Pushkin said to his wife, 'he's stolen my
poem. But it doesn't matter; he's made a good thing of it; I couldn't have
begun to depict "The Adventures of Chichikov" the way he's done.' " Pavel
Vasilievich Annenkov (1812-87) was a critic and translator, noted especially
for his reminiscences of Belinsky and Gogol, and his study of Pushkin.]

[18] Letter to A. S. Pushkin, December 23 (o.s.), 1833.]

[19] Letter to M. P. Pogodin, January 11 (o.s.), 1834.]

"history of the Middle Ages" in nine volumes, and even a "world history."[20] As early as 1833, he wrote to Pushkin: "My projects will really start to bubble in Kiev. . . . There I will complete my history of the Ukraine and the south of Russia, and I will write a world history, which so far unfortunately does not exist in an up-to-date form either in Russia or even in Europe."[21] Actually it is very doubtful that Gogol at that point had written a single line of the history of the Ukraine that he was intending to "complete." Somewhat later he reported: "I am writing the history of Little Russia in its entirety, from the beginnings to the present. It will be in six small volumes or four large ones."[22] Then: "I am writing a history of the Middle Ages, which will consist of some eight if not nine volumes."[23] Not a trace of work on any of these books which Gogol assured his correspondents he was already writing is to be found among his papers. It is possible that the odd outline did exist and was destroyed by Gogol, as was his habit; but it is more likely that in Gogol's enthusiastic mind the projected books actually did exist, and he talked about them as if they were something entirely real.[24]

Gogol was chronically hard up for money, inasmuch as he wrote very little and had no other sources of income besides his literary work. But he carried all his capacity for dreaming over into this area of his life as well. In one letter he offered the following consolation to the painter A. A. Ivanov, who was complaining about the material difficulties of his situation: "Money is like a shadow or a beautiful woman; it runs after us only when we run away from it. . . . Anyone who is truly engrossed in his work cannot be

[20] In a letter to Pogodin, dated February 1 (o.s.), 1833, Gogol also promised to write a "world geography" in three volumes.

[21] December 23 (o.s.), 1833. Gogol was hoping to secure an appointment to the chair of history at Kiev University.]

[22] Letter to M. A. Maksimovich, February 12 (o.s.), 1834. Mikhail Alexandrovich Maksimovich (1804-1873) began his career as Professor of Botany in Moscow University, but then moved to Kiev University as Professor of Russian Literature. He was the author of important collections of Ukrainian folksongs, and of other works on Ukrainian history, culture, and language.]

[23] Letter to M. A. Maksimovich, January 22 (o.s.), 1835.]

[24] This is not accurate. There are numerous surviving sketches on sundry historical topics, including ancient and Ukrainian history: cf. *PSS*, IX. Gogol also wrote *Taras Bulba* and sketched out *Alfred* (i.e., King Alfred) and a "drama from Ukrainian history."]

troubled by the thought of money, although he might not have enough even for the next day. He will borrow it unblushingly from the first acquaintance who happens by."[25] After receiving a stipend from the Emperor, through Zhukovsky's intercession, he wrote to Shevyryov: "Now I am amused when I think about what I was trying to get. It is good that God was merciful and punished me every time: while I was thinking about how I was to live, I never had any money; but when I gave it no thought, then money always came to me."[26] With such an attitude, Gogol did not find it especially embarrassing to accept help from his friends, from the Emperor, and from the Crown Prince. But at the same time, he was concocting fantastic schemes for giving large-scale financial aid to poor students out of the money earned by the sale of his writings. In 1844 he planned to establish one such fund, and entrusted Pletnyov with distributing the money in St. Petersburg, and Shevyryov in Moscow. But nothing came of this fantastic project. Later on, when Pletnyov was trying to secure a grant for Gogol himself, people asked him: "But why does Gogol need any financial support, when he is always setting up a fund to aid students?" Pletnyov replied: "Gogol's fund is a fantasy. Absolutely no money has been collected."[27] A second even more fantastic and equally abortive project was conceived by Gogol in 1846, when he was planning to bring out a new edition of *The Inspector General* for the benefit of the poor: he asked the actor Shchepkin to propose, from the stage, that the audience should purchase the book; he wanted to organize a full-scale committee that would be chaired by Countess A. M. Vielgorskaya, etc.[28]

[25 Letter of January 9, 1845. Alexander Andreyevich Ivanov (1806-1858) was a Russian painter who spent most of his life in Rome. His most famous work is "The Appearance of the Messiah to the People," on which he labored for more than twenty years. He was warmly admired by Gogol as the exemplar of a genuine artist, i.e., one who sacrificed everything to his work and concentrated on religious themes. One of the articles in *Selected Passages from Correspondence with Friends* is devoted to him.]

[26 Letter to S. P. Shevyryov, December 14, 1844.]

[27 The question was asked by Ya. K. Grot (a prominent scholar) in a letter to Pletnyov, February 28 (o.s.), 1845; Pletnyov replied on March 7 (o.s.), 1845. Cited in V. V. Veresayev, *Gogol' v zhizni*, Moscow-Leningrad, 1933, pp. 331-332.]

[28 Cf. Gogol's letter to M. S. Shchepkin, October 24, 1846, and to A. M. Vielgorskaya, November 2, 1846. Mikhail Semyonovich Shchepkin (1788-1863) was a famous comic actor, who often played the part of the

But Gogol did not seek gratification in bright illusions alone; there was also many a dark specter in his world. For example, throughout his life he regarded himself as chronically ill and virtually on the brink of death. Although he did have a weak constitution, this chronic illness was apparently just another one of his innumerable illusions. When he was all of twenty-four, he was already saying: "This frail vessel of mine is often overcome by illness and is becoming extremely decrepit."[29] In letters to his mother and his friends he constantly complained about his health, and his imagination—"elaborating everything always in the form of really terrifying specters"—was already suggesting to him that he would soon die. "I am now cherishing every moment of my life," he wrote Zhukovsky in 1837, "because I do not expect it to be a long one" (April 18). In a letter to Pogodin in 1838, he exclaimed: "Oh, my friend! If only I could be granted four or five years more of health! Is it really possible that that is not destined to be . . . I had intended to accomplish a great deal" (August 14). Gogol gave out widely varying versions of the symptoms of his illness. While still a young man, he had astonished S. T. Aksakov by complaining about his maladies, because to all appearances he enjoyed perfect health. When asked about the nature of his illness, Gogol replied that it was caused by something in his intestines.[30] This, however, did not keep him from enjoying his food. "Gogol was a terrible hypochondriac," wrote one of his friends from Rome in 1840. "Nothing preoccupied him as much as his stomach, yet none of us could tuck away as much macaroni as he sometimes did."[31] When N. M. Yazykov began questioning him about his illness, Gogol explained that it resulted from the peculiar construc-

mayor in *The Inspector General*; Gogol had great respect for his art. The Vielgorskys were a wealthy and prominent aristocratic family who played an important part in Gogol's life. Anna Mikhailovna Vielgorskaya may well have been the only woman Gogol ever loved; the evidence is inconclusive, and in any event nothing came of it. Her sister, Sofia Mikhailovna, was a constant correspondent of Gogol's. Their brother, Iosif Mikhailovich, died of consumption at the age of twenty-three in Gogol's arms in Rome. See also footnote 16 in the article by Yermakov in this anthology.]

[29 Letter to M. A. Maksimovich, July 2 (o.s.), 1833). Bryusov incorrectly gives Gogol's age as twenty-nine; he was only twenty-four at this time.]

[30 S. T. Aksakov, *Istoriya moego znakomstva s Gogolem*, Moscow, 1960, p. 11.]

[31 This seems to be a composite quotation from M. P. Pogodin, "Otryvok iz zapisok," *Russkii Arkhiv*, 1865, p. 894 (cf. Veresayev, *Gogol' v zhizni*, p. 199) and V. A. Panov, letter to S. T. Aksakov: cf. Veresayev, p. 245.]

tion of his head, and from the fact that his stomach was upside down.[32]

Gogol's working methods are extremely significant. We know that Pushkin was a slow and persistent worker, we have seen his manuscripts, which are lined through and covered with countless revisions. But this does not begin to compare with the incredible prodigies of labor that Gogol put in before he acknowledged a piece of writing as being more or less finished. He was utterly incapable of stopping in his work; his mind, with its habit of exaggerating everything, invariably imagined that any new composition was full of defects; and he made strenuous efforts to bring it to a greater and greater state of perfection. Even after a particular work had been published, he would go back to it again and sometimes practically rewrite the whole thing. Examples are the two published versions of *Taras Bulba* and of "The Portrait" (both 1835 and 1842). *The Inspector General* was finished as early as 1834, but then completely rewritten and, in this new version, staged in 1836. However, in 1841 Gogol made changes in a number of scenes for the second published edition, and in 1842 he reworked it once again, for a third edition. Gogol put in six years of assiduous and unremitting labor on the first volume of *Dead Souls*, and almost ten on the second, but he never acknowledged it as being finished.

S. T. Aksakov tells of a reading that Gogol once gave, for the Aksakov family, of the second version of chapter one of *Dead Souls*. Everyone was struck by the skill with which the artist had managed to improve on the first version, and Gogol said, with satisfaction: "Now you see the way it is when a painter has given the final touch to his picture. To all appearances the alterations are very minor: one little word is deleted here, one is added there, one is transposed somewhere else—and everything comes out different." This is precisely the way Gogol worked, taking great care with each word, each small detail, striving for the utmost perfection. According to Aksakov, this method of writing gradually became a "martyrdom" for Gogol, and eventually developed into a "futile torment." And Gogol himself confessed that he carried on his literary work "with painful exertions," and that "every line had been exacted at the price of a shock."[33]

[32 N. M. Yazykov, letter to his brother, Sept. 8, 1841: see Veresayev, p. 271. Nikolay Mikhailovich Yazykov (1803-1846) was a poet much admired by Gogol.]

[33 The first quotation is from a letter of S. T. Aksakov to his sons,

In appraising his own works, Gogol showed the same lack of moderation, the same tendency to go to extremes as in everything else. At times he was ready to deny that they had any significance at all, and he would indulge in extreme self-depreciation. In a letter to Zhukovsky, dated June 28, 1836, he repudiated all his works: "What is everything that I have written to date?" he asks. "It seems to me that I am turning over the pages of an ancient notebook that I kept as a schoolboy, in which carelessness and laziness are evident on one page, impatience and haste on another—the timid, trembling hand of a beginner and the bold scrawl of a young scamp who is drawing little curlicues instead of letters and who gets his hands beaten for it. . . ." The following year he asserted that it was "dreadful" for him to "remember all the scribbling I have done. . . . My soul yearns for oblivion, a long oblivion. And if a moth should appear and suddenly eat up all the copies of *The Inspector General*, and along with them, *Arabesques*, *Evenings on a Farm Near Dikanka*, and all the rest of the nonsense, and if nobody should write or speak a single word about me for a very long time, I would give thanks to fate."[34] In the preface to *Selected Passages from Correspondence with Friends*, he said that he wished "to atone for the uselessness of everything that has been published by me to date," and he called his earlier writing "half-baked and immature."

Yet at the same time Gogol often swung over to an equally boundless pride, an equally immoderate self-assurance. "I always felt," he averred, "that I would be an active participant in the business of the general good and that without me the reconciliation of many things that are at mutual odds would not occur."[35] And in one of these same letters in which he repudiated his past, he said: "How can I fail to give thanks to Him Who has sent me onto this earth! With what lofty, what solemn feelings, invisible and imperceptible to the world, is my life filled! I swear, I shall do something that no ordinary man can do. I feel a lion's strength in my heart," etc.[36] And it was with the serene self-knowledge of the artist that he penned the prophetic words concerning Part 2 of

---

Konstantin and Ivan, February 23 (o.s.), 1852; the second comes from "Chetyre pis'ma k raznym litsam po povodu 'Mertvykh dush,'" *Vybrannye mesta iz perepiski s druz'yami, PSS*, VIII, 1952, 297.]

[34 Letter to N. Ya. Prokopovich, January 25, 1837.]

[35 Letter to S. P. Shevyryov, May 25, 1847.]

[36 Letter to V. A. Zhukovsky, June 28, 1836.]

Dead Souls, words which so enraged the critics of the day: namely, that a time would come "when, in another surge, an awesome storm of inspiration will rise from a head invested in sacred horror and refulgence, and when, trembling and abashed, men will harken to the majestic thunder of other words."[37] When he sent the first part of the manuscript of *Selected Passages from Correspondence With Friends* to Pletnyov for forwarding to the censor, he wrote: "It is necessary, it is only too necessary to everyone." Even after the book had failed, he believed that it would "engender many major works."[38]

All his life Gogol was convinced that he enjoyed the special protection of Providence. In the letters he wrote as a very young man, he often said "God has me in His special care." In 1836 he wrote: "I feel that an unearthly will is guiding my path." He put it even more emphatically the same year: "Someone invisible is writing with a mighty staff before my eyes." In every failure, as in every instance of good fortune, he endeavored to divine the commands and instructions of Providence, and he was "visited by the thought" that even the misunderstandings between himself and his mother came from "God Himself." After *Selected Passages* had been published, he wrote his mother that he would soon begin his "real service to the country, for which I have long been preparing myself, or rather, for which God Himself has been preparing me."[39] This faith in divine guidance was so strong in Gogol that it stifled all the workings of logic and reason within him and obscured his powers of observation and his sense of reality.[40]

[37 *Dead Souls,* Part 1, ch. seven.]

[38 The first quotation is from a letter to P. A. Pletnyov, July 30, 1846; the second is from a letter to V. A. Zhukovsky, March 6, 1847.]

[39 The first quotation in the paragraph is from a letter to his mother (M. I. Gogol), June 3 (o.s.), 1830; the second is from a letter to M. P. Pogodin, May 15 (o.s.), 1836; the third is from a letter to V. A. Zhukovsky, November 12, 1836; the fourth and fifth quotations are from a letter to his mother, August 25, 1829; the sixth is from the first of two letters to his mother, January 25, 1847.]

40 Actually, Gogol always perceived an element of the *miraculous* in the destinies of mankind as a whole and of individual peoples. The Middle Ages struck him as being a series of events that were "miraculous and out of the ordinary." Power "seems to have been deliberately given" to the Popes "so that young states might grow strong and reach maturity during this period. . . . Russia suddenly invested itself in the greatness of a state. . . ." And so on. Many similar examples are brought together in V. Shenrok, *Materialy dlya biografii Gogolya,* IV, Moscow, 1897, 622 ff. [The last

All this left its strongest imprint perhaps on the preparations for the publication of *Selected Passages*. First of all, Gogol was convinced that a special divine miracle had helped him write the book. "Suddenly the most painful afflictions disappeared," he said, "suddenly all the difficulties in my work vanished, and all this persisted until the very last line of the book was written." In sending the manuscript to Pletnyov, Gogol proposed that he should drop all his other business and attend to the publication of this book. "My friend!" he wrote. "I acted resolutely in God's name when I was putting my book together; I took up my pen in praise of His holy name; and that is why all the specters, and everything else that paralyzes powerless man, gave way before me. You act, then, in God's name too, by arranging to have my book printed as if you were hereby doing a deed for the glorification of His name."[41] Gogol was confident that the book would exert a powerful influence on readers and that it would quickly sell out. He charged Pletnyov with laying in a supply of paper for a second edition as well. Alas! The book's being "necessary to everyone" was also one of Gogol's innumerable illusions!

Gogol never had any passionate feeling for a woman; there were none of the usual sort of love affairs in his life. This is not to be attributed, however, to a lack of a passion in his nature, but rather to an excess of passion. In passion, as in everything else he experienced, Gogol could have done nothing but go to extremes. As a young man, he wrote his mother about being in love (perhaps alluding to something that had actually happened, or perhaps simply relating something he had invented), and he couched his account in highly ecstatic language: "An infernal longing, with agonies of every possible kind, seethed in my breast. Oh, what a cruel state. . . . In a fit of madness and in the most dreadful mental torment I thirsted, I seethed with desire to feast my eyes on a single glance, I hungered for but one look. . . . If she had been merely a woman, not with all the power of her charms could she have produced such dreadful, indescribable impressions on me. This was a divinity. . . ." In another letter, addressed to one of his friends who was then in love, Gogol wrote: "I understand and feel the state of your soul very keenly, although I have not had occa-

sentence in quotation marks is from "V chem zhe nakonets sushchestvo russkoi poezii i v chem ee osobennost'," *Vybrannye mesta*; the others are from the article "O srednikh vekakh": both in *PSS*, viii, 1952, 370, 17-18.]

[41 Both quotes are from a letter to P. A. Pletnyov, October 20, 1846.]

sion to experience it myself, thanks be to fate. I say 'thanks be' because this flame would turn me into ashes in an instant . . . it is my salvation that a firm will has twice turned me away from the desire to glance into the abyss."[42]

Everything we know about Gogol permits us to suppose that he encountered the temptation to "glance into the abyss" on roads other than the one leading to sexual love. Every feeling within him threatened to burst into a flame of such intensity as to be capable of reducing him to ashes instantaneously. Did not his love for his native land, for Russia, burn within him, year after year, in a fire ever more consuming? When he was a young man, this love could be satisfied in a simple way, with dreams of doing "service to the state," "important and noble labor for the good of the country"— dreams that caused him to "blaze in a fire of proud self-awareness."[43] But see what this fire has been fanned into in the concluding lines of Part 1 of *Dead Souls*: "Is it not thus that thou too, oh Russia, art whirling along like a spirited troika that cannot be overtaken? . . . The observer comes to a stop, astonished by this divine miracle: is this not lightning hurled down from heaven? What is the meaning of this horror-inspiring motion . . . ? Everything on earth flies past, and other peoples and nations, eyeing her askance, stand aside, and make way for her." And in *Selected Passages*, Gogol asserts, as something that has already become a truism, that there is nothing like Russia, that she is a unique, special, chosen land. "Why do neither France nor England nor Germany . . . but only Russia, make prophecies about themselves?" he asks. "Because she feels, more strongly than the others, the hand of God in everything that befalls her, and she senses the coming of another kingdom."[44]

Similarly, the flame of religious ecstasy that had glowed in Gogol's heart since childhood burst into a consuming fire during the final years of his life. In the preface to *Selected Passages*, he refers to a grave illness that made him turn more eagerly toward God; but no such explanation is really necessary. Gogol in his

[[12] Letter to A. S. Danilevsky, December 20 (o.s.), 1832. The letter to his mother is dated July 24 (o.s.), 1829. Alexander Semyonovich Danilevsky (1809-1888) was a classmate of Gogol's in Nezhin, and remained one of his closest friends throughout his life, despite occasional fallings-out.]

[[13] Letter to mother (M. I. Gogol), March 24 (o.s.), 1827.]

[[14] "O lirizme nashikh poetov," *Vybrannye mesta* . . . , *PSS*, VIII, 1952, 251.]

mystical exaltation was only following to the very end the same road he had walked since childhood, as indeed he followed all the other roads of his life too. He threw himself into asceticism with the same abandon he had brought to his description of the breadth of the Dnieper and the eyes of the Albanian girl Annunciata. Religion was one of the abysses that yawned before him; he looked and leaped into it, as that infinite and limitless state for which his soul had always yearned. "It is a dreadful thing, fellow-countrymen!" he cried, aware himself that at last he was falling into a yawning chasm.[45] But neither the arguments of his friends nor the clear indications of impending doom could stop him. And so, he published *Selected Passages*, wrote "An Author's Confession," journeyed to the Holy Land, tried to burn Part 2 *Dead Souls* one dreadful night, and on one even more dreadful day promised Father Matthew to write no more, to renounce literature.[46]

If Gogol's entire life was a dream, if all his creative work was an exaggeration, then what a fantastic vision, what a majestic hyperbole were his final days! Gogol strove to live to the utmost by the teachings of Christ as he then understood them. He strove to cultivate his humility, his penitence, his zeal for fasting and prayer to the utmost. The accounts by those who observed him during the final weeks of his life create a shattering impression.

"The week of Shrovetide," his doctor wrote, "he began to prepare for Holy Communion and to fast. He took to eating less and less, even though he apparently had no loss of appetite and suffered dreadfully from the lack of food. . . . For several days he ate nothing but the Communion wafer. He did not limit his fasting to food, but also cut down drastically on his sleep. After prolonged sessions of praying during the night, he would get up early and attend matins. Finally he grew so weak that he could scarcely stand. On one occasion he had no desire to take any food all day long, and when later he did eat a Communion wafer, he called himself a gluttonous, ungodly, impatient man, and he

[45 "Zaveshchanie," *Vybrannye mesta* . . . , *PSS*, VIII, 1952, 221.]

[46 Father Matthew was Matvey Konstantinovsky, a very devout, indeed fanatical, priest from Rzhev, who was Gogol's spiritual adviser in the 1840's and 1850's. It was widely believed that he had urged Gogol to renounce Pushkin and give up writing. For an interesting discussion of his role in Gogol's life, cf. Victor Erlich, *Gogol*, New Haven and London, 1969, pp. 203-205.]

was greatly distressed."[47] Gogol's strength began to ebb rapidly and irreparably after this bout of fasting; he was obviously dying, but even this could not shake his determination. His friends tried to coax him to take food and medicine, as did his confessors (at the behest of Filaret, Metropolitan of Moscow), but to no avail. Gogol neither could nor would listen to advice from others, because throughout his life he was accustomed to obeying the powerful impulses of his own soul and mind. Finally he took to his bed; but even then, he countered all the pleas of the doctors, all their attempts to examine him, with an abrupt and firm: "Leave me alone." To the end he kept to the same road on which he had started out.

We know that the doctors decided to treat Gogol as a person who had lost control of himself. They tried to subject him forcibly to treatment, and they made his last hours an agony. But it was not only during those days and hours that Gogol lacked self-control. He was no more in control when he was creating his spectral figures and populating Russia with the visions of his imagination, or when he was turning his work as a writer into a great heroic deed and his struggle over style into a "martyrdom," or when he was setting forth, in letters and in *Selected Passages*, his pitiless demands and austere ideals for himself and for others. The incredible harmony between Gogol's life and art was more evident than ever during his final days. In his life, as in his work, he had no sense of moderation or limitation; herein lay all his originality, all his power, and all his weakness. All Gogol's creations represented the world of his reverie, in which everything grew to incredible dimensions, in which everything appeared in exaggerated form, either grotesquely horrible or dazzlingly beautiful. Gogol's entire life was a road that ran between two chasms, each of which pulled at him: it was the struggle of a resolute will and an awareness of a higher duty that had devolved on him, as against the fire that glowed in the depths of his heart and threatened to consume him in an instant. And when at last he did liberate this force within him and allow it to develop at will, it did, in fact, burn him to ashes.

[47 Bryusov mistakenly attributes this description to S. T. Aksakov. It is actually a condensed and not wholly accurate version of the memoirs of A. Tarasenkov, one of the physicians who attended Gogol in his last illness. Cf. V. Shenrok, *Materialy dlya biografii Gogolya*, IV, Moscow, 1897, 851-852.]

3

Valerian Pereverzev
(1882-1968)

WHILE a student at Kharkov University, Pereverzev became involved in Marxist revolutionary activities. In 1905 he was expelled from the university, arrested, and sentenced to six years of prison and exile. During that time he wrote his first book, *The Art of Dostoevsky (Tvorchestvo Dostoevskogo)*, which was published in 1912 and has been a standard scholarly work ever since. After serving his sentence, he moved to Moscow, where he began a career of scholarship and teaching. In 1921, he was appointed professor at Moscow University. His particular brand of Marxist criticism (see the introduction, above) attracted a number of young disciples, several of whom, such as I. M. Bespalov and G. S. Pospelov, went on to become prominent scholars in their own right. A sampling of their work can be seen in *Literary Criticism (Literaturovedenie, 1928)*, an anthology of articles edited and introduced by Pereverzev himself.

By the end of the 1920's, "Pereverzevism" was coming increasingly under attack from other Marxists as representing a "vulgar sociologism" which denied that a writer could significantly alter the ideology he had absorbed as a child. Pereverzev published an occasional article during the first half of the following decade, but in 1938 he was "illegally repressed," to use the term that Soviet commentators now confer on victims of the Stalinist "cult of personality." He survived, was officially "rehabilitated" in 1956, and published a few articles during his remaining years. His most significant work was devoted to nineteenth-century writers. Besides the study of Dostoevsky, he wrote *The Art of Gogol (Tvorchestvo Gogolya, 1914)* and a study of the sources of the Russian realistic novel (*U istokov russkogo realisticheskogo romana*, 1937; second edition, 1965).

The article entitled "The Evolution of Gogol's Art," which is offered here, is actually a translation of chapters two, three, and four (each entitled "Evolyutsiya tvorchestva") of the 1914 edition of Pereverzev's book on Gogol. I have done substantial editing, mostly by way of pruning prolixities.

133

The Evolution of Gogol's Art

by Valerian Pereverzev

I

In order to amuse myself, I would invent heroes, without any further purpose or plan, and would put them into comical situations—that was the origin of my stories. The passion for observing man, which I had nourished from childhood, lent them a certain naturalness.

(Gogol, Letter to V. A. Zhukovsky, January 10, 1848.)

THERE is no other single work of Gogol's in which all the contradictory elements of his genius come into such violent collision and mingle in such odd ways as they do in *Evenings on a Farm Near Dikanka.* This is something that every reader senses, as a first impression, before he brings any analytical faculties into play. Of course, unless he does undertake an analysis he cannot determine the nature of these contradictory elements. But he certainly can give an accurate characterization of what it is that impresses him: tremendous vitality and at the same time an unreality which is lifeless and oftentimes boring. The reader cannot decide whether these brief stories that are brought together under one title are true or false, real life or implausible invention. What creates this contradictory impression? An objective analysis of the book will unlock the secret.

A close study soon reveals that two very different modes of life coexist here. It is as though two currents, two very different worlds took shape in Gogol's creative imagination, and in turn gave rise to two very different sets of feelings, attitudes, and images. These contrast with one another and give Gogol's work an antithetical character. One of these modes or sets is grounded in ordinary life. This life is festive, vivid, and colorful, yet ever so ludicrous, trivial, and lacking in strong passions, powerful ideas, and heroic impulses. A noisy marketplace, heated squabbles, senseless gossip, inane little flirtations, the play of petty emotions—it is scenes like these that lend color and variety to *Evenings on a Farm Near Dikanka.* And it is in this motley setting, this nonsensical and banal atmosphere, that petty and ludicrous types like

Khivrya and Solokha, Cherevik and Chub—along with their families and paramours—turn their dealings to good account.[1]

But another life unfolds beside this one—a life filled with fears and dangers, yet rich in derring-do, deep-felt joys and noble impulses, meaningful and profound experiences. A quiet, dreamy evening, a dark and mysterious night, the whispers of two lovers, a song poured forth from the heart, secret powers—sometimes dark and unholy, sometimes bright and good—now and again blood, the flash of steel blades, the shouts of a fierce fight: such are the scenes of this tumultuous and dramatic life. And its heroes are different too: the black-eyed and pensive Gannas and Pidorkas, who have hot, pure blood in abundance and give birth to selfless Cossack wives like Katerina; the bold and handsome Petruses and Levkos, who are so much like the dashing Cossack leader Danilo Burulbash, proud and strangers to fear. There is little room for light-heartedness in their lives. Everything here is significant, everything is serious, joys and sorrows both. Sad and tragic endings are common, yet every joy goes straight to the heart. Remember the scene from "A May Night". Under a bright moon, Levko is hastening to tell his beloved that they now may marry: "he approached the hut; the window was open; the moonbeams reached through it and fell upon Ganna as she lay sleeping. Her head rested on her arm; her cheeks were faintly flushed; her lips moved as they murmured his name indistinctly. 'Sleep, my beautiful one! May you dream of everything that is best in the world, but even that will be no better than our awakening!' Making the sign of the cross over her, he closed the window and quietly moved away." This is how Gogol expresses the deep joy that overcomes the lad.

These two antithetical worlds can be seen not only in the con-

[1 Book 1 of *Evenings on a Farm Near Dikanka* was published in 1831. It consists of a preface and four stories: "The Fair at Sorochintsy," "St. John's Eve," "A May Night, or the Drowned Maiden," and "The Lost Letter." Book 2 was published in 1832, and consists of a preface and four stories: "Christmas Eve," "A Terrible Vengeance," "Ivan Fyodorovich Shponka and His Aunt," and "A Bewitched Place." The characters mentioned by Pereverzev throughout the article appear in the following stories: (1) "The Fair at Sorochintsy": Cherevik, Grytsko, Khivrya, Paraska; (2) "St. John's Eve": Ivas, Petrus, Pidorka; (3) "A May Night": Ganna (Galya: a diminutive form), Levko, Makogonenko (the village head); (4) "Christmas Eve": Chub, Oksana, Pereperchikha, Solokha, Vakula, the sister-in-law; (5) "A Terrible Vengeance": Danilo Burulbash, Katerina.]

tents of the book but also in its over-all plan. The author seems
deliberately to have placed each story in such a way that a picture of ordinary life in all its pettiness and comic absurdity is
followed by a picture of heroic exploits and the clash of powerful
passions in all their tragedy and pathos. From "The Fair at
Sorochintsy," which excites merry and easy laughter, the reader
moves on to "St. John's Eve," which is filled with terrors and a
sense of tragedy; from "Christmas Eve," where even the demonic
forces of evil make us laugh despite ourselves, the reader moves
on to "A Terrible Vengeance," with its acts of heroism and its
soul-shattering villainies.

Nearly every one of the stories, then, is structured according to
the principle of antithesis—petty versus profound passions, trivial
versus heroic deeds—as is the book as a whole. This same principle permeates the language as well. There are two styles here
which do not and in fact cannot blend; for each is utterly alien
to the other. We sense that each is also the product of a very
distinct mode or category of life. One is simple and unceremonious:
awkwardly pretentious at times, downright crude at others, it
develops out of a mindless, visceral way of life and is thus eminently suited to people like Khivrya and Chub. The other is a measured and solemn language which reverberates like the tolling
of a cathedral bell and tells of something as lofty as the sky and
as vast as the steppe. This is not the language of prose; it should
be not spoken but sung. And in fact the people Gogol describes
in such language do just that. Do not the bitter words with which
Pidorka sends her brother Ivas to her beloved Petrus sound like a
song? And is not Petrus's reply to her plaints a song as well ("St.
John's Eve")?

But where did Gogol hear this bilingual speech, which combines vulgarity and crudeness with enchantingly beautiful sonori-
ties? Where did he see his heroes? To what milieu and what
period in history do they belong? What mustered and joined the
destinies of people so different in mind and spirit? Any answers we
might find in *Evenings* would be muddled and inconclusive. Gogol
usually designates his heroes as Cossacks. But the conflict of
radically contrasting elements in their lives sometimes seems to
be a conflict between the older and the younger generations, and
sometimes it looks like a confrontation between a heroic past and
a paltry present in the life of the Cossacks. Thus, the stories of a
comic nature are set in the everyday world—such as "The Fair

136

at Sorochintsy" or "Christmas Eve"—whereas those that are preponderantly dramatic are set back in history, like, for example, "A Terrible Vengeance." When comic and dramatic, past and present come together in the same story, the comic role is assigned to the older generation, and the emotional and noble role to the younger generation. Representing the latter are Ganna, Pidorka, Oksana, Grytsko, Petrus, Levko; the former: Khivrya, the sister-in-law, Solokha, Cherevik, the village head, Chub, and so on. We would be happy to believe what Gogol is telling us here. But in the first place, we do not know just what to believe, and in the second place, we feel that there is a certain contradiction in the artist's basic conception that defies resolution. If there was an abundance of vivid, powerful experiences and splendid individuals in times of old, then it is not logical for the older folk to play the comic roles and the younger the heroic ones: in any event, the elders are the custodians of the past to a greater extent than their children. The Cossack society that Gogol is ostensibly describing contains impossible incongruities, and the more we reflect on it, the greater the number of puzzling questions that arise. Let us suppose that the older generation does live such a limited and ludicrous life. Where, in that case, do their children get their spirit and dash, their capacity for lofty feelings and their ability to express those feelings so poetically? Gogol provides no environmental or psychological motivation for these qualities. The young folk inhabit exactly the same world as their elders; they grow up in exactly the same society, and have no knowledge of any other. How is it, then, that people like Khivrya and Solokha manage to bring up people like Ganna and Pidorka? How is it that the Makogonenkos and Chubs bring up people like Petrus and Levko? This simply cannot be. These two categories of characters are so far apart psychologically that it would defy common sense to suppose that they could live together in the same milieu.

It is more likely that these characters belong to different periods of history. In a number of stories, Gogol does attempt to show the heroic natures as existing apart from the Khivrya and Makogonenko types, by placing them in far-off times, as, for example, in "A Terrible Vengeance." But then we cannot understand how it is that people living in very different periods of time can meet in the very same marketplace or in the very same village on a certain beautiful night in May. Regarded from the standpoint of psychology and milieu, all the relationships look impossible, and all the

137

questions we have posed seem to have no answer. But Gogol has
an answer. He simply invites us to take up a different vantage
point, and he replies to all our perplexed queries by saying:
"Miraculous things go on here, my dear sir" ("The Fair at
Sorochintsy"). Here miracles occur; here everything is possible;
here devils and witches do whatever they like with people, muddle
all relationships at their whim and fancy, take individuals from
different periods and different milieus and mix them into one big
batch.

Nowhere in Gogol's art does the element of fantasy play so
important a role as in *Evenings on a Farm Near Dikanka*. This
is a real witches' and devils' sabbath, a world of sorcery and
black magic, a world in which the oddest combinations and associations are possible, a world in which a Makogonenko can beget
a Levko, and a Khivrya a Pidorka, and where flying dumplings can
also exist. All the relationships in the book depend on the intervention of miraculous forces, on the purely fantastic. And it could not
be otherwise. Gogol was striving to express both elements of his
genius in his art, but he had not yet perceived that the two arose
from very different sources and were incompatible. The only
way he had of linking up, in a single work, the very different
images that derived from such drastically different sources was to
resort to the fantastic, inasmuch as the manners, mores, and psychology of real society provided no basis for making such connections.

Gogol's genius, then, developed in response to the workings
of two heterogeneous elements. Each gave him its own special
world of characters, settings, and gestures, its own special language. Gogol had not yet arrived at a clear understanding of himself, and he was unaware of the source of the words and images
that flooded his heart, crowded his imagination, and demanded to
be let out on paper.

And it was Gogol—not witches and devils—who indulged in
carefree disport with these images, following the whims of his
imagination, linking one episode with another in the most fanciful
ways, and taking pleasure in this light-hearted play of creative
powers. But if this is the case, there is no point in trying to find
a substratum in real life itself, no point in trying to arrive at a
psychological explanation of the things the Cossacks do in the book.
This is so simply because no real Cossacks and no real milieu
exist here. Everything in these stories takes place in a far-off fairy-

tale land, into which images and characters from different times and different milieus have been transported by the artist's magic wand. Considered by itself, each character is convincing and life-like; there is no facial feature or gesture or word that detracts from the impression of an integrated and harmonious personality. There are many vivid and full-blooded portraits, and many scenes that are strikingly true to life. But when taken in the aggregate, when regarded as part of a society or as a milieu, the characters immediately lose their realistic quality. And here we have the explanation of that strangely discrepant impression we feel as we read *Evenings on a Farm Near Dikanka*. The author has wrenched different character-types out of those milieus in which they are complete and convincing, and has brought them together to create a new milieu which he calls Cossack society and which is completely untrue to life, impossible, fantastic. One has only to isolate these characters from one another and return them to their original milieus, and they cease to be implausible and fantastic.

As we analyze and compare the two different elements which made up *Evenings on a Farm Near Dikanka*, we can reach yet another conclusion, which is essential to a proper evaluation of Gogol from an esthetic point of view. It is not difficult to observe that Gogol's talent for portraiture falls off as soon as he leaves the world of petty emotions for that of strong and heroic passions. Just let the reader try to picture what Petrus and Levko actually look like! I think he would find that very difficult to do—indeed, it is hardly likely that any two readers would picture them in the same way. On the other hand, how can the reader fail to form a mental picture of what Makogonenko or Chub or the widow Solokha look like, and keep them apart as individuals in their own right? The same point can be made with regard to characterization, settings, and even language. Cherevik, Makogonenko, Chub, and Solokha all have rather well-defined personalities. But with Levko and Petrus, all we can see is that the author is trying to portray something noble and vivid, and that the result is rather pallid. Notice how strikingly Chub's manner of speaking reveals his character—as, for example, in the words he addresses to his beloved Solokha: " 'Good evening, Solokha! . . . Maybe you weren't expecting me, eh? You weren't, isn't that right? Maybe I'm in the way? . . . Maybe you've been having fun with someone else here! Maybe you've got someone hidden here, eh?' And, delighted with these remarks, Chub began laughing . . . ," etc. ("Christmas

Eve"). There is no doubt that these words have the ring of real life to them.

The language in which Levko addresses Ganna is entirely different. It is beautiful and melodious, but somehow abstract and nondescript: " 'Galya! Galya! Are you sleeping, or do you not wish to come out to me? Perhaps you are afraid that someone will see us, or perhaps you do not wish to expose your fair little face to the cool? Do not fear: no one is here; the evening is warm. But if anyone does come by, I will cover you with my jacket, wind my sash around you, hide you in my arms, and no one will see us. And if there is a cool draft, I will press you close to my heart, warm you with kisses, put my cap over your little white feet,' " etc. ("A May Night"). The lad has a pretty way of speaking, but language of this sort cannot be heard anywhere except in songs. Because he is not singing here, his words have a false and lifeless ring.

Not all the stories in *Evenings on a Farm Near Dikanka* can be read with equal interest; some are actually boring. If the reader would take the trouble to look closely, he would notice at once that the more the stories show of the world of petty emotions and of ridiculous people, the greater is their esthetic merit and their vividness. Therefore, Gogol was not equally familiar with the two kinds of life he was portraying; and the two elements that shaped his creative genius did not work upon him with equal force. Why is this so? What is at issue here? We can answer these questions only when we determine just what these elements were, and just what Gogol's relationship to them was. By itself, *Evenings on a Farm Near Dikanka* does not provide enough material for a definitive answer; we must undertake an analysis of Gogol's other works, where the real-life element is not obscured by any elements of the fantastic.

II

Oh times of old, times of old! What joy, what gladness will suffuse the heart when one hears of things done in the world so long ago that the year and month have been forgotten.

(*Gogol, "The Lost Letter,"* Evenings on a Farm Near Dikanka)

I am very fond of the modest way of life of those solitary owners of remote villages, who in Little Russia are usually called "old-fashioned."

(*Gogol, "Old-Fashioned Landowners"*)

Between 1830 and 1832, while Gogol was engaged in writing *Evenings on a Farm Near Dikanka*, he also produced a number of unfinished works, which are ordinarily accorded scant attention by the critics. Their esthetic merit is not great, but they do offer some very interesting materials for an understanding of the evolution of Gogol's art. All were trial efforts, products of Gogol's searchings and gropings for new directions. Evidently his artistic instincts told him that the two very different elements in his work could not possibly blend into an organic and natural whole, so he resolutely separated them and tried to give each an independent artistic existence. Hereby he laid the foundations for two qualitatively different cycles of works. Once each of these elements emerged pure and simple, its source in the world of actuality (the subsoil that produced and nourished Gogol's art) could also be plainly seen. And so, all these unfinished works enable us to observe how Gogol moved from fantasy to reality, how his creative imagination attached itself to a specific, living social milieu.

As early as 1830, Gogol began writing a historical novel, entitled *The Hetman*; it was never completed, and only fragments remain.[2] They are all very similar in theme (the conflict of the Ukrainians with the Poles), in over-all tone and style, and even in some characters, such as Pudko and Glechik. At first glance, it might seem that these fragments have nothing in common with *Evenings on a Farm Near Dikanka*: they have none of its spontaneous laughter, its playful element of fantasy, its vivid scenes, or its barbed comments. But let us not forget that *Evenings* contains more than just laughing and joking: it also has tragedies, and heroes, and a lofty, solemn style. And as soon as we manage to isolate this second element and compare it with the unfinished sections of *The Hetman*, we will see an unmistakable similarity. *The Hetman* is really *Evenings* minus the humor, the banal characters, and the petty emotions. The Khivryas and Chereviks and Chubs and Solokhas have disappeared; only the Gannas and the Levkos remain. To be sure, even they have changed somewhat: over his shoulder Levko now wears a baldric for his sword instead of a bandore, shows his mettle not in merrymaking but in crossing

[2 Pereverzev actually says that in 1830 Gogol made two "sketches," entitled "The Prisoner" and "The Hetman," and in 1831, an untitled sketch "which might be called 'Ostranitsa' after the main hero." This is not quite accurate, and I have made the necessary correction. (Cf. *PSS*, III, 1938, 711-716.)]

swords with the Poles, and is called not Levko, but Taras Ostranitsa. To be sure, Ganna Petrychenkova—a pensive and serious-minded maiden with a tender, warm heart and dark eyes that glow like stars—has become the vigorous and passionate Galya, a companion worthy of Ostranitsa. Yet they are essentially the same people. The only real difference is that in the fragments they are fuller and more sharply delineated. In *Evenings*, the beautiful maidens and handsome lads have a wraith-like, moonlit quality. But in the fragments of *The Hetman* they seem more real. This is because Gogol has transported them into the milieu in which they were born. Everything in the world around them is in complete harmony with their psychological makeup. Bold and active natures, sudden and violent passions (of both love and hatred), heroic deeds and tragic situations are all natural and understandable in the Cossack Ukraine of the sixteenth century, in an atmosphere of unending struggle for freedom, faith and fellow-man.[3] Here Ganna and Levko are in their element; here they make sense. From them come impassioned and stout-hearted Cossack lads like Ostranitsa, gentle yet forceful Cossack maidens like Galya, as well as the temperate, experienced, cautious, yet strong personalities of Cossack elders like Glechik and Pudko. There is no place here for people like Solokha and Chub, Khivrya and Cherevik. In all these unfinished works, Gogol ties his characters to their natural environment. Significantly, the element of fantasy, which plays such an important part in *Evenings*, completely disappears: the specifics of the psychology and the daily life of society are much more in evidence.

It goes without saying that this milieu could exert no direct influence on Gogol. He absorbed it in a purely literary way, through Cossack ballads and songs, through the legends of the Ukraine of old, and through readings in the history of the Ukrainian people. Significantly, the language of the heroes that inhabit this milieu often sounds like an imitation of folk-songs. The images that formed in Gogol's mind were, understandably, very dim and

[3 The Zaporozhian Cossacks, of whom Gogol writes, were the most powerful and influential of several Cossack groups. They settled "below the rapids" (*za porog*) of the Dnieper River in the sixteenth century. Poland at that time was in control of much of the Ukraine, and the Zaporozhian Cossacks resisted Polish efforts to subjugate them politically and religiously (the Cossacks were Orthodox, the Poles Roman Catholic). The struggle went on for decades, and culminated in a great uprising led by Bogdan Khmelnitsky in 1649, which defeated the Poles and led to the absorption of the Ukraine by Russia.]

shadowy, and not wholly accurate. This explains why he never brought off any of his initial attempts to transfer his Levkos and Petruses into their native habitat. In order to do that successfully, he had first of all to acquire a sound knowledge of Cossack history and Cossack life, for he had never experienced or observed them directly. This required much time and much dogged labor of a purely grubbing and uncreative sort. Gogol did put in a good deal of hard work along these lines, but the results did not show until much later. The fragments of 1830 and 1831 were merely trials of the pen, a testing of creative powers, the first steps in the direction of a major work that lay in the future—*Taras Bulba*. Gogol had not yet developed the powers essential for producing a work on this scale. And so he continued with *Evenings* and with his unrealistic treatment of the characters and language that derived from the Ukraine of old.

We have seen how one of the elements in *Evenings* gradually isolated itself and, in a number of unfinished works, crystallized into clear, definite, and more realistic forms. The isolation of one element naturally and inevitably brought about the isolation of the other: the characters and the language of the trivial·and comic element also took on an independent existence. *Evenings*, we might say, was the seed from which the tree of Gogol's art grew. This seed was divided into two lobes, which were so tightly joined and so firmly encapsuled in a covering of fantasy that they could not be seen without the aid of a microscope and a lancet. But the seed grew and put forth two shoots, which immediately revealed the existence of both lobes.

As early as 1831, Gogol wrote two chapters of an unfinished story entitled "The Dread Wild Boar." In its general tone and its characters it bears a strong resemblance to *Evenings*. Katerina reminds us very much of Paraska or Oksana; the cook Onisko is amazingly like the blacksmith Vakula; the shrewish innkeeper Simonikha is a gossip and nag along the lines of Pereperchikha. "The Dread Wild Boar" most closely resembles those stories in *Evenings* where profound experiences, tragic episodes, and heroic characters are least in evidence. But it does offer something entirely new as well, something that is very significant and interesting. The action takes place on a landowner's estate. Laughter, gossip, and wrangling, with appropriately comic heroes, now begin to be specifically associated with this milieu. Vakula has moved from *Evenings* to become the cook in the landowner's house. Solokha has not only moved, but has actually become the owner of the estate, Anna Ivanovna; she has donned a coffee-colored gown and a cap, is no longer forty but sixty, and is even uglier; but she is the same voluptuous widow and clever housewife that she was in *Evenings*.

Thus, "The Dread Wild Boar" represents a first attempt at grounding the humorous scenes and characters of *Evenings* in an everyday world that actually exists. The attempt, however, is timid and halting. Gogol still retains several characters who are bathed in the golden glow of simple yet sincere feelings, and who remind us somewhat of familiar types like the dashing Grytsko and the beautiful Paraska. He keeps on talking about Cossacks, and seems reluctant to make a decisive move into the landowner's house along with his characters. The carefree and banal types had been transported by the author's imagination to a never-never land; after roaming there amidst people who were utterly alien to them, they at last return to their real home, whereas the shades from the fairy-tale world remain outside and disappear, like the morning mist, in peals of pure laughter. This important development finds expression in another story, which was never completed either: "Ivan Fyodorovich Shponka and His Aunt." The story got into *Evenings* quite by accident.[4] To be sure, in over-all style it resembles the other stories there. But it does not show the slightest trace of a double perspective: it is the product of a single element, the one that gave Gogol his humorous scenes and characters. Do not look here for Levko or Ganna or anyone of a deep and serious nature. Do not look for bursts of rapture or dramatic situations. Before you lies a world of petty emotions, impoverished thought, vulgarity and vacuity—a world of insignificant and empty people, like Cherevik, Makogonenko, Khivrya, and Solokha in the other stories. But now the difference is that Gogol has found the setting in real life that corresponds to the psychology of such characters. Makogonenko is no longer the village head or a Cossack, but instead is a landowner of middling means, Grigory Grigorievich Storchenko. And now that Gogol has discovered the reality from which his vacuous

[4 Actually, the story was completed, even though it breaks off. "Unfinished" works were a common device at the time, and Gogol even provides a motivation here. See also Stilman's "Men, Women, and Matchmakers" in the present collection. It is also incorrect to say that "Shponka" was accidentally included in *Evenings*. The other works that Pereverzev mentions as being incomplete really are so, however.]

and ludicrous heroes have emerged, every element of fantasy disappears. Idleness and sloth, a life of satiety and comfort, a semi-vegetative existence devoid of thought and strong feeling, vulgarity and scandal-mongering and squabbling—all this becomes meaningful in the milieu of small land- and serf-owners. When uprooted from the milieu which formed them, such characters lost much of their vividness and distinctness and became unreal Cossacks of the type of Cherevik, Makogonenko, and others. As abstract psychological types they were true, but they lacked the substantiality, vividness, and individuality that are provided by the homely details of the workaday world in which men live. Characters like Cherevik and Makogonenko are so content, idle, lazy, and slothful that they create the strange impression of being true and false at the same time: we feel that the author has made some mistake in not giving each of them a dozen or so serfs. And when Gogol finally did just that, such characters took on flesh and blood, and ceased to be abstractions.

Without any doubt, it was the milieu of small land- and serf-owners which had the greatest influence on Gogol's creative genius. After all, it was the one that was close and familiar to him, the one in which he had been born and brought up, the immediate source of his earliest impressions of the world. Chapter four of *Dead Souls* opens with a reminiscence of these impressions:

Formerly, long ago, in the days of my youth, in the days of my childhood, which has flashed by never to return, I felt happy when I was driving up to an unfamiliar place for the first time. It did not matter whether it was a hamlet, or a poor provincial town, or a village, or some larger settlement—the curious eyes of the child would discover much that was curious there. Every building, everything that bore the mark of some particularly noteworthy feature would arrest and strike my attention. Whether it was a stone government building of a familiar style of architecture, with half its windows false, sticking up all by itself amidst a hewn-log cluster of mean, one-story, shopkeepers' houses; whether it was a well-rounded cupola, all covered with white sheet-iron, rising above a new church that had been whitewashed a snowy white; whether it was a marketplace, or a provincial dandy I happened to see in the town—nothing escaped my fresh and attentive eye; and, poking my nose out of my travelling-cart I would look at the unfamiliar cut of some

frock-coat I had never seen before, and at boxes containing
nails, sulphur that gleamed yellow from afar, raisins, and soap,
of which I caught glimpses through the doors of a vegetable
stall, along with jars of stale candies from Moscow; I would
also look at an infantry officer walking along on one side of the
street, blown by some wind from Heaven knows what province
into the boredom of a provincial town, and at a merchant in
a padded Siberian coat, who whirled by in a racing sulky; and
in my mind I would go off with all of them to share their own
meager lives. A provincial clerk had but to pass by, and I immediately began to wonder: where is he going? To spend an evening
at one of his fellow clerk's or straight on home, there to sit for
half an hour or so on his front porch until darkness falls, then
to have an early supper with his mother, his wife, his sister-in-
law, his whole family? What will they be talking about while the
servant girl, in her coin-necklaces, or the servant boy, in a heavy
jacket, brings in, after the soup is served, a tallow candle in a
candle-holder that has seen long family service? As I drove up to
some landowner's village, I would turn my curious eyes on the
tall, narrow wooden belfry or the wide, dark, old wooden
church. Through the green of the trees I would catch enticing
glimpses of the red roof and white chimneys of the landowner's
distant house, and I would impatiently await the moment when
the orchards screening it would part on either side and it would
appear in its entirety, with an exterior which at that time (alas!)
was by no means vulgar; and from it I would try to deduce what
sort of man the owner himself was, whether he was fat, whether
he had sons or a brood of six daughters, with their ringing girlish
laughter and their games, and the youngest the prettiest, as is
always the case, and whether they had dark eyes, and whether he
himself was good-natured or as gloomy as the last days of Sep-
tember, consulting the calendar and talking about rye and wheat,
subjects which are so boring to young people.

Gogol absorbed these impressions involuntarily and unintention-
ally, and laid up a rich hoard of faces, images, scenes, and words
in the subconscious depths of his mind. They burst forth and
flooded his consciousness when he was in the process of creating.
The characters, scenes, and attitudes that were suffused with these
impressions came easily for him, and they are therefore predominant in his works.

As each of the two elements of Gogol's art underwent separate development, it became quite evident which of them was destined to gain priority. In this connection it is interesting to compare the unfinished stories about Cossacks with the unfinished stories about landowners. From 1830 through 1831, Gogol wrote three stories of Cossack life, all of them fragmentary and unsuccessful.[5] They were not published during his lifetime. Until 1834, he did not succeed in creating anything satisfactory along these lines. But the stories of landowning life reveal an entirely different picture. After his first abortive effort, "The Dread Wild Boar," he immediately wrote "Ivan Fyodorovich Shponka and His Aunt." It also remained unfinished, to be sure; but it had so much vitality that it was published forthwith. And during this same period—i.e., before 1834—Gogol also wrote such major works as "The Tale of How Ivan Ivanovich Quarrelled with Ivan Nikiforovich" and "Old-Fashioned Landowners." And his success here is understandable: he did not have to study the life of landowners from books in order to write about it, because he had already absorbed the elements of this way of life with his mother's milk, down to the most minute details. Among his landowner-heroes he felt like a fish in water. But before he could write on Cossack life, he had to consult many a weighty tome, for he had no other way of knowing about it. Naturally enough, these stories are far inferior to the others.

III

My subject was the world of today and life in its present form, perhaps because my mind was always inclined to essentials and to useful things of a more palpable kind. The more I worked, the stronger grew my desire to be a contemporary writer.

(Gogol, "An Author's Confession")

By now, two elements in Gogol's art have been distinguished. Their function and significance will become even clearer when we see how his work developed subsequently. Eighteen hundred and thirty-four can be regarded as the year in which each of them clearly separated once and for all and took its own course. It was then that *Mirgorod* was written: here, quite consciously and deliberately, the milieu of the contemporary landowner was set in contrast with Cossack

[5 See footnote 2.]

life of olden times. "Old-Fashioned Landowners" is followed by a story about the life of the Zaporozhian Cossacks (*Taras Bulba*); "Viy," the story of the dreadful fate of the Cossack seminary student Khoma Brut, set in the Ukraine of long ago, is followed by the highly humorous tale of the quarrel of two landowners, Ivan Ivanovich and Ivan Nikiforovich, which is set in the early years of the nineteenth century. Of the four stories which make up this book, then, two are about Cossacks and two about landowners, two are steeped in history and antiquity and two are set in the real world contemporary to Gogol. Moreover, a solemn style, profound and vivid experiences, and noble characters are specifically associated with Cossack life, whereas triviality, banality, odd characters, and a comical way of speaking are inseparably associated with the milieu of the landowners.

In short, each element has now taken on a fully and unmistakably independent existence; henceforth, each follows its own predestined route. From 1834 up to the time of his death, in 1852, Gogol wrote nothing new that sprang from the soil of history and Cossack life. All he did along these lines was to keep reworking *Taras Bulba* until he put it into its final and artistically its best form, in 1839. It was as if he sensed intuitively that this particular element would inspire nothing new or better, either in characters or in style, and he therefore wished to put everything it had given him into this one work. Something entirely different happened with the current that flowed out of the landowning milieu: it continued to broaden and deepen, right up to the time of Gogol's death. "The Carriage" appeared in 1835; *The Gamblers* in 1842; and from 1834 to 1842 Gogol was busy composing Part 1 of *Dead Souls*, an account of the life of provincial serf-owners which for sweep and breadth was unparalleled then and has been unequalled ever since.

Gogol continued work on Part 2 of *Dead Souls* to the end of his life. It remained unfinished, although some of the surviving sections are highly polished. At the same time, he enlarged the dimensions of his art by studying and reproducing variant versions of landowning life—specifically, those which arose as a result of moves from country to town. I do not mean moves which were made for the sake of diversion and variety, and which were temporary. In such cases the landowner remained a landowner; he did not sever his ties with his estate; he was only a visitor to town, and had no power there. Sometimes, however, he left his estate for an extended period of time, established his residence in town, and had a say in running things there, just as he had once had back in the country. In this new capacity, he was known no longer as a landowner, but as a civil servant; he was losing his ties with the old world and forming new ones. The transformation of landowner into civil servant was a rather common phenomenon, and it became more widespread as the serf economy continued to decay.

A ruined and impoverished landowner tried to set himself up in the civil service in order to repair his fortunes. As Gogol described it in *Dead Souls*: "The landowners lost at cards, went on wild sprees, and did a thorough job of squandering their fortunes; the whole lot picked up and moved on to St. Petersburg to work for the government." But as he gradually got back on his feet in his new line of work, he once again set his sights on acquiring a small village and returning to the milieu to which he really belonged. The milieus of landowner and civil servant were very closely linked through continual interchange: the landowner could enter the ranks of the civil service and often did; the civil servant could go back to being a landowner, and often did. "Having served God and the Emperor," as Gogol ironically put it in *Dead Souls*, "and having earned the respect of all, he leaves government service, moves out of town, and becomes a landowner, a fine and hospitable Russian country gentleman, and he does not just live, but lives well. And after him his thin little heirs squander the entire paternal fortune at a slap-bang rate, according to the Russian custom"; and naturally they once more became civil servants and eventually succeeded, to varying degrees, in growing bellies and again acquiring villages.

The social and economic kinship between landowners and civil servants inevitably entailed a psychological kinship as well: the two minds were identical in their most distinctive and characteristic features. Gogol himself, as a product of the landowning milieu, came into constant contact with the milieu of the civil servant. In addition, he had some first-hand knowledge of the psychology of official life, having himself been in government service and having therefore experienced the transformation from landowner into civil servant.[6] It is not surprising, then, that in his writings he moved

[6 Gogol came from a fairly well-to-do landowning family, which held some two hundred (male) serfs. He worked at two minor jobs in the into this new area so easily, and depicted it with such power. The history of the comedy *Marriage* provides a graphic example of the point we are making. This play was conceived and actually drafted as early as 1833, under the title of *The Suitors*. In this early version, all the dramatis personae are landowners, and the action takes place in a country house. In 1842 Gogol reworked the comedy for publication and introduced several new characters, but all the old ones remained, without the slightest change of personality. Now, however, they were all civil servants, and the action took place in a town. From 1834 through 1842, Gogol wrote several other works depicting the life of civil servants: "Diary of a Madman" (1834), "The Nose" (1835), *The Inspector General* (1836—the most important of them), and "The Overcoat" (1842).[7]

The landowners abandoned their estates and fled to the towns not just for financial reasons, and not just to become civil servants. With economic disintegration, the once well-ordered psyche of the landowner suffered dislocation too. Money and trading were introduced into the countryside and destroyed the barter economy of serfdom. Along with them came new books and new ideas, which penetrated into the most remote corners of the provinces. In young and even faintly active minds, these books and ideas generated a vague yearning to experience the strange new life described there, awakened a dim urge to break out of the narrow confines of country houses into the new and unfamiliar world from which these ideas came. Urges became actions, and some individuals— exceptions, to be sure—set off in quest of this new world. Usually all such quests led right into the same old miasma of the civil service and ended with the return of these individuals to their estates when they reached the so-called age of common sense. In exceptional cases, these seekers entered the ranks of the professions, of writers and of artists, where they formed a numerically tiny group which of course retained the typical features of the

civil service in St. Petersburg in 1829-30, first in the Department of State Economy and Public Buildings (Ministry of Internal Affairs), and then in the Department of Royal Estates.]

[7 Pereverzev is inconsistent in his dating of these works. The first two were actually published in 1835 and 1836, respectively; Pereverzev refers to their presumed dates of composition and thereby strengthens his argument. For the third and fourth, however, he gives the dates of publication; in fact, Gogol had been working on them earlier.]

landowning mentality but underwent an extremely complex evolution and developed a personality all its own, one that was radically different from that of the landowners. Vigorous mental activity and close contact with intellectuals not from the gentry or, in still rarer cases, with members of high society—all this made a strong impression on the individuals in this particular group.[8] For them, the break with the landed estate was far more fundamental and decisive.

Gogol also tried to capture on paper the characteristics of this particular offshoot of the landowning milieu. Its psychology was very close to his own. For he himself had become a "seeker" by virtue of his enormous creative talent. Significantly, this group was the theme of his very first work, *Hanz Küchelgarten* (1829). The book was a fiasco, and Gogol pulled it out of circulation; but he returned to the theme of the "seekers" in 1835, with "Nevsky Prospect" and "The Portrait," and again in 1842, when he published a fresh version of "The Portrait," which was so extensively reworked as to look like an entirely new story.

But Gogol does not handle this group with anything like the artistry he displays when he portrays the milieus of landowners and civil servants. Generally speaking, he had no understanding of what a vigorous intellectual life was like, obviously because he had never had a really solid education, unlike Pushkin and Lermontov, or, later, Turgenev and Tolstoy. This lack explains why his powers decline whenever he takes the intelligentsia as his subject. But it also explains his particularly perceptive understanding of the psychology of the ordinary "exister" in the world of the landowner and the civil servant;[9] it entitles him to immortality as *the* portrayer of those milieus. Had Gogol been a more cultivated man, he would have risen too far above the average level of landowners and civil servants; his pictures of these milieus would have been no more talented than the ones that even a giant like Pushkin

[8 "Intellectuals not from the gentry" renders *raznochintsy*, another untranslatable Russian word. It means, literally, "people of different ranks" and it applies to those who originated from non-aristocratic or impoverished orders of society, lived on their own incomes, and usually had "progressive" social and political views. They were usually, although not necessarily, members of the intelligentsia. Belinsky, for example, was a *raznochinets* (his father was a ship's doctor); Gogol was not.]

[9 "Exister" renders *sushchestvovatel'*, a word which seems to have been invented by Gogol.]

produced.[10] Fortunately for Russian literature, this did not happen. Gogol bore the full weight of the philistine psychology of the landowner and civil servant and was therefore ill-equipped to portray the psychology of the intelligentsia. His writings on this particular group are therefore few in number and artistically mediocre.

So far I have not drawn the reader's attention to one other factor that is extremely important for an understanding of Gogol's art. In all the works I have mentioned as growing out of the landowning milieu—beginning with the early fragments and ending with Part 1 of *Dead Souls*—Gogol is primarily and perhaps even exclusively concerned with the small landowner, in all his variants. His civil servants also come from the lower reaches of this same society (Chichikov, Poprishchin, Bashmachkin), as do his artists (Piskaryov and Chertkov).[11] He does not deal with the rich and powerful landowners who developed a so-called worldly way of life, which can be defined by the term *comme il faut*. He did, however, sense that these two opposite extremes of the landowning milieu were organically related, in a very distinctive way; his comments on Korobochka, in chapter three of *Dead Souls*, bear specifically on this interrelationship:

> But why spend so much time on Korobochka? Whether it's Korobochka or Manilov, with their well-ordered or disordered households—let us pass them by! For other things in this world are wondrously arranged: merriment can turn into sadness in the twinkling of an eye if only you stare too long at it, and then Lord knows what notions may pop into your head. Perhaps you'll even start thinking: come now, does Korobochka really stand so low on the endless ladder of human perfectibility? Is the gulf really so great that separates her from her sister, who sits inaccessibly sheltered behind the walls of an aristocratic house, with its sweet-smelling wrought-iron staircases, its gleaming copper, its mahogany and its carpets, and yawns over a book

[10] Pereverzev probably has in mind, among others, *Dubrovsky*, an uncompleted novel on landowning life. Pushkin himself came from a down-at-heels landowning family.]

[11] Chichikov is in *Dead Souls*, Poprishchin in "Diary of a Madman," (Akaky Akakievich) Bashmachkin in "The Overcoat," Piskaryov in "Nevsky Prospect," and Chertkov in the first version of "The Portrait" (as published in *Arabesques*, 1835; the name was changed to Chartkov in the second version, 1842, and hereby less obvious reference was made to the Devil—*chert*).]

she cannot finish, as she awaits the hour for a visit to clever and fashionable society, which will provide her with a forum for showing off her intelligence and spouting ideas she has learned by heart—ideas which, according to the dictates of fashion, will engage the interest of the town for an entire week, ideas not about what is going on in her house and her estates, which are in utter confusion and disarray because of her ignorance of how to manage them, but rather about what political upheaval is in the making in France, and what direction has been taken by the latest tendencies of fashionable Catholicism.

Several of Gogol's works from 1836 on proceed from the idea that these two extremes are but a stone's throw apart. But Gogol never completed any of them: "An Official's Morning" (1836), "The Servants' Quarters" (1842), "The Lawsuit" (1842), "Rome" (1842), and Part 2 of *Dead Souls* (most of whose chapters are devoted to a portrayal of the milieu of large landowners). And the more closely we examine these unfinished efforts, the more strongly we feel that in this particular area Gogol would not really have been capable of creating anything serious and profound. Evidently the artist found it no easier to move from the lower to the higher reaches of landowning society than did people in real life. Gogol was not wrong about the similarity between these two levels of society, for it is unmistakable. The underlying psychology remained the same in all essentials; but a *comme il faut* upbringing and an education which, for all its superficiality, did have a certain luster, built an extremely complex superstructure upon this basic foundation. As a result, the whole pattern of the psychology of the wealthier landowner underwent a change, and the resemblance between him and the humble landowner became very remote. Gogol did not know enough about the higher levels of landowning society to be able to portray this superstructure in his works. His Sobakevich (*Dead Souls*) and Tolstoy's Levin (*Anna Karenina*) have the same basic psychology, but culture and education have made Levin's mind so complex that we would never detect a close resemblance between him and Sobakevich. Because Gogol was merely an incidental and superficial observer of these higher levels of society, Levin, in his hands, would have been simplified into a pale and blurred shadow of Tolstoy's Levin— which is precisely what happened with Kostanzhoglo, in Part 2 of *Dead Souls*. It would, however, be unfair to say that even these largely unsuccessful efforts are devoid of any significance whatsoever. For all their flaws, they do adumbrate several completely new characters in Russian literature, which were filled out and brought to life only much later, in the works of Tolstoy and Turgenev.

To sum up, then: the evolution of Gogol's art shows that the element which was grounded in history and which reflected Cossack life underwent no further development and produced no new works after 1834, whereas the one which derived from contemporary society and flowed from deep within the small landowner/civil-servant milieu continued to develop and produce new works. If we should draw a straight line through Gogol's writings, so that those about Cossacks were on one side and those about landowners and civil servants on the other, the latter would constitute the great majority, whereas the former would be a negligible entity.

The difference is qualitative as well. As proof of this, we have only to consider the extreme or high point of the development of each element in Gogol's art. The social, or landowner/civil servant element culminates in *The Inspector General* and *Dead Souls*, two colossal works that will be forever significant, if in fact there is anything that lasts forever in this sublunar world. The historical or Cossack element reaches its height in *Taras Bulba*, a rather mediocre tale which will long continue to be read only because *Dead Souls* will be. You have only to try eliminating *The Inspector General* and *Dead Souls* from the corpus of Gogol's writings, and what remains of Gogol? An ordinary writer no different from dozens of other ordinary writers, who are forgotten by the dozen as well. But if you eliminate *Taras Bulba*, Gogol still remains the same—a powerful and immortal writer.

Gogol owes his reputation among us today to the works which depict the small-landowner/civil servant world that was in his blood and was so familiar to him. This is his own special genre. Here he has no rivals, and we can boldly say that he never will have. For us Russians, he is therefore a unique and immortal artist.

4

Ivan Yermakov
(1875-19??)

OF YERMAKOV'S life I have been able to learn virtually nothing:
he ran afoul of the official ideologists in the Soviet Union late in
the 1920's (see the introduction, above), and has not even been
mentioned in the standard reference books since then. Between
1939 and 1941 he published three articles in a journal in the Gorky
region (on the right bank of the Volga River); this suggests that he
had been exiled. Presumably he is now dead, but outside Russia
nothing is known of the time, the place, or the circumstances.

Yermakov was a practicing psychoanalyst and, like his mentor,
Freud, had strong literary interests. He was the editor of a series
entitled "The Psychological and Psychoanalytical Library," which
published translations of works by such authorities as Freud, Jung,
Reik, and MacDougall. His own books made up the contributions
to literary criticism in this same series: *Studies on the Psychology
of the Art of A. S. Pushkin* (*Etyudy po psikhologii tvorchestva
A. S. Pushkina*, 1923) and *Sketches for an Analysis of the Art of
N. V. Gogol* (*Ocherki po analizu tvorchestva N. V. Gogolya*,
1923), of which the article on "The Nose" ("Nos"), here translated, constitutes one chapter. The first section of the Gogol book
presents a popularization of Freud's views of the creative process,
and attempts to draw a large-scale map of Gogol's psyche. The
second is devoted to closer analyses of individual stories: besides
"The Nose," there are chapters on "A Terrible Vengeance," "The
Two Ivans," "The Overcoat," and "Diary of a Madman." A third
part, on *Dead Souls*, was announced for publication but never
appeared. Neither did a book entitled *Organic Unity and Expressiveness in Painting* (*Organichnost' i vyrazitel'nost' v kartine*).
Both were perhaps casualties of the official campaign against
Freudian psychology (see the introduction).

Unfortunately, Yermakov had none of his teacher's gift for
style. I have found it necessary to make major cuts and rearrange-
ments in this essay, to bring out its real merit, as virtually the only
example we have of a psychoanalytical study of Gogol's story.

155

"The Nose"

by Ivan Yermakov

I

"What are you laughing at?—
You're laughing at yourselves."
Gogol, The Inspector General.

BEFORE undertaking an analysis of Gogol's story "The Nose," I ought to offer some justification for my approach, which readers unfamiliar with psychoanalysis might otherwise find bewildering and objectionable.

Underlying the creative process in art is the vast realm of the unconscious, which is shared by all human beings. It contains not only the instincts, but also all the contents of the psyche which the consciousness finds uncomfortable and intolerable, because of the strictures of civilized society, and therefore represses. Nevertheless, these contents seek an outlet into the consciousness and express themselves, through art or through neurosis, in a great variety of ways (that is, in social and in anti- or asocial manifestations).

Although man cannot really give vent to these repressed psychic contents, he nonetheless does feel an irresistible need to rid himself of them and become as aware of them as he possibly can. The pleasure derived from works of art is a way of gratifying the most primitive drives of the unconscious. However, the experiencing of works of art cannot in itself produce any activity beyond the actual experiencing, even though it is directed not at itself but at new objects; and it leads us to a consideration of hedonism in the esthetic process.

Hedonism in art is the basic yet lowest level on which works of art are apprehended and does not in itself have any great cultural value. Catharsis, or resolution, is another very powerful factor in art, but we must go beyond it too in considering the effect that works of art have on us. For catharsis exists not for its own sake, but for the sake of creating new spiritual values, objective values. Just as the literary artist cannot merely seek self-satisfaction in working on his material, but is "compelled" and obliged to create

156

certain values, so the viewer or listener cannot merely experience works of art but must above all respond actively to them. He must find in them stimuli to action and to the creation of new relationships and new understanding, stimuli to an expansion of the possibilities of contact—intellectual, spiritual and practical—with reality.[1] Art creates its own world; but this world is nothing more than a pale likeness of the world in which we live. The work of art ought to teach us not to retreat from our world, but, on the contrary, to go back into it, in order that we may assert our mastery over it and, with new eyes, see everything of value in it that we would not see without art. Thus, art represents not a retreat from reality, but a thirst for reality and a need to be linked with it.[2]

The creator draws materials for his work from reality. He is strong and perceptive only through contact with reality and with truth. His work is universal only because it is grounded in unconscious drives that all men share and therefore understand. In revealing and contemplating himself, the writer can perceive and reveal to us not only what is individual but also what is typical, what is true not only of him but also of all men. Likewise, the listener or reader, if he is to grasp the real meaning of a work of art, must not merely live and experience esthetic reality, but must also find through it a new opportunity for approaching, understanding, and studying the world in greater depth and with greater awareness. For art is the artist's way of knowing the world, and his opportunity for working out his own attitude toward it. What this attitude is determines what his art will be.

In the dark and teeming realm of the primitive instincts, which supposedly have long ago been overcome by the civilized conscious mind, the artist finds the basis for his communion with mankind. The dark forces seek outlet and expression. Art enables them to take on definite form, and directs them toward the creation of new cultural values and toward a struggle with and condemnation of everything that is egotistical for the sake of everything that mankind has in common, that is, everything that in the final analysis is served by any healthy art. Even if we often detect what sound like sick notes in Gogol's work, we must not be misled: it is not

[1] Cf. my *Etyudy po psikhologii tvorchestva A. S. Pushkina* (*Studies on the Psychology of the Art of A. S. Pushkin*), Moscow-Petrograd, 1923.

[2] A link with reality through art betokens strength and spiritual growth, whereas withdrawal from reality betokens weakness and a sense of groundlessness and purposelessness.

only Gogol's sickness, but the sickness of every cultured person. We must not brush aside something that looks so alien to us at first glance. Rather, we should examine it more closely, and then we will see that what excites our laughter and indignation is nothing more than our own faults: we are more willing to laugh at our faults as they are revealed in others. And this we must understand, if we are not to find ourselves in a ridiculous situation, like Major Kovalyov in "The Nose."

II

"The doctor tried as hard as he could to discover the mysterious connection between the specters he [Chartkov] had seen and the events of his life. . . ."

Gogol, "The Portrait."

Gogol's fantastic tale "The Nose" occupies a special position among those works of his which are linked, if not exactly by the same theme, then by the tormenting questions he put to himself and endeavored to resolve. Included in this group are a number of his best stories, such as "Viy," "The Tale of How Ivan Ivanovich Quarrelled with Ivan Nikiforovich," "The Nose," "The Overcoat," and "Diary of a Madman." To be sure, it is to some extent arbitrary and artificial to lift just a few stories out of the corpus of Gogol's works, all of which are organically interconnected; for, as we shall see, the theme of "The Nose" had long been in the making, in stories where the nose itself had not yet been assigned the role of protagonist. This fact makes it clear that Gogol did not borrow his theme from elsewhere, as literary historians suppose; he was not simply echoing certain literary fashions of the beginning of the nineteenth century; rather, he responded to them, interpreted them, and gave them a particular form, out of an inner need and compulsion to do so.

Pushkin's apt characterization of Gogol as a Russian Laurence Sterne does honor to the great poet's powers of perception. Still, for all the outward resemblances between the two, the Russian Sterne, Gogol, differs radically from his predecessor in the same degree that the Russian mind differs from the English.

The important thing, of course, is not that Gogol, influenced by the "nosological" theme that was rampant in the journals and newspapers of the first quarter of the nineteenth century, might have been fired with enthusiasm for *Tristram Shandy*—which had been translated into Russian—and might well have appropriated something from it. We are, naturally, interested not so much in the fact of borrowings themselves (that is the business of historians of literature) as in what Gogol managed to make of this theme, what new content he introduced into an infinitely varied theme that had been used by many writers, major and minor.

Some of this work has already been done in a preliminary way in an article by V. V. Vinogradov. Here he examines the nose theme: its historical evolution, its various treatments, and its gradual elaboration; and he compiles rather considerable and over-subtle material on the way Gogol's contemporaries viewed the theme and the ways in which various writers worked it up.[3]

Understandably, this problem is of far less interest to us, and we shall not linger over it. Let us merely note one feature characteristic of Gogol's art: for some reason, he tried to avoid devising plots of his own; he always took them ready-made from other people. Some regard this as a negative feature of his work, but such an attitude will not enrich our understanding of the problem.

The reason why this was so, why Gogol was always begging his friends to give him anything they had, is to be found in certain specific characteristics of his art and personality. The chief characteristic of Gogol is what we call anal erotism. It comes out vividly in his character and in his works. Given his repressed aggressiveness, his efforts to avail himself of the works or themes of others have a compulsive quality; he could not know why he was unable to come up with his own. This phenomenon is extremely characteristic of neurotics, and I have observed it in very many patients in psychoanalysis. In his letters and his works of fiction, Gogol betrays an irrepressible need to observe, describe, and castigate the shortcomings of others and of himself as well. In neither case is he free, for he is obeying the command of his unconscious. Gogol torments himself in order to have the right to torment others.

All of a writer's works are nothing more than a confession and self-revelation. Gogol—and he speaks of this specifically in "An Author's Confession"—saw his works as a kind of mirror in which

---

[3] "Naturalisticheskii grotesk. Syuzhet i kompozitsiya povesti Gogolya 'Nos,'" *Evolyutsiya russkogo naturalizma. Gogol' i Dostoevskii*, Leningrad, 1929, pp. 7-88.

he scrutinized and studied himself. This, it seems to me, explains his narrative method, his use of colloquial language and *skaz*,[4] and his habit of putting himself into everything he wrote. The clash of two opposing tendencies in the confession—one revealing, the other concealing—produced a compromise solution to the task that Gogol set himself, and forced him to resort to jests, puns, and unfinished utterances. The attempt to say what cannot be directly expressed in civilized society leads to ambiguity and to witticism. Gogol regarded his works as a confession, an exhibition, for all to see, of something important and significant. In many of his re-marks—for instance, on the life and paintings of A. A. Ivanov—he explicitly advanced the idea that an artist is incapable of creating a positive character-type in his work until it exists in his heart. That is why Ivanov's ascetic way of life seemed to Gogol the only true way to follow in the quest for the ideal through self-purification and self-perfection.[5]

In the complex and interesting course of Gogol's search for his unique, Gogolian self, there is a natural demarcation of two phases, although they are very intimately interconnected. The first is one of open self-ridicule; the second finds him directing his gaze more deeply into the hidden recesses of his own experiences and seeking out "nastiness" there. "The Nose" is one of Gogol's confessions that belongs to this second phase, along with "Viy," "The Over-coat," "Nevsky Prospect," and others.

Two sides of Gogol's personality are revealed in the first phase of the development of his work as a satirist: his attempt to depict both comic and terrible things. Here his tendency to try to discredit other people does not go beneath the surface, and his humor is sometimes not of a very high order. He does hit on some very apt names and situations for his characters; but we also constantly find many awkward and rough-cast attempts, such as Dovgoch-khun, Pupopuz, Krutoryshchenko, and others.[6]

The second phase is marked by greater care in the selection of such names; the dark and terrible side of life, which was localized

[4 For discussions of *skaz*, see the introduction, and the articles by Eichenbaum and Chizhevsky, in the present collection.]

[5 "Istoricheskii zhivopisets Ivanov," *Vybrannye mesta iz perepiski s druz'yami, PSS*, viii, 1952, esp. 330-331.]

[6 The reference is to Gogol's first major work, *Evenings on a Farm Near Dikanka*. These are all "meaningful" names. Dovgochkhun suggests *apchkhi* (ha-choo!); Pupopuz is derived from *pup* (navel) and *puzo* (belly); Krutoryshchenko suggests *krut-* (twist, sharp declivity) and *ryk-* (roar).]

in the countryside in the *Dikanka* stories, is now transformed into universal evil, of which every man is the vehicle.

In the first stage, the writer participates in the stories himself; he consistently does the narrating, as if he were retelling old tales and adapting himself to the people he is talking about, putting himself, as it were, on their level. But in the second stage the situation changes. To be sure, Gogol hews to the same narrative method as before. But fundamentally new is his focus on himself, his desire to reveal and identify in himself the same traits he sees in others. In other words, there comes a time in the development of Gogol's work when, preoccupied with self-purification and self-analysis, he gradually shifts to the confessional form until finally, and with complete consistency, he entitles one of his last works "An Author's Confession." As this inner development proceeds, Gogol begins to take a different view of his early works, which had made him famous overnight. He does not find in them what is now most important to him: the *spiritual* element, which attracts him and fills his life above anything else.

Elsewhere I have shown how "The Overcoat" ties up with the most intimate sides of Gogol's character and life, how it expresses his relationship with his father, and how it reveals the self-flagellation and self-mockery of a writer who has the "praiseworthy habit" of attacking people too weak to defend themselves.[7] This catharsis enables Gogol to take the specifically erotic features present in his works and transform them into higher cultural values. In this intensive self-study, a self-depreciating Gogol uncovers in himself aggressive drives which have been repressed and have seemed dormant, drives which do not manifest themselves in the lives of his heroes, but come out and prove threatening in periods of illness or after death. The disclosure of this other side in Akaky Akakievich—an aggressive side that has been invisible to the people around him—makes him a psychologically full and rounded character-type.

Thus, both "The Overcoat" and "The Nose" are tied to a specific phase in Gogol's psychic development. Our particular ap-

[7 This refers to a sentence toward the beginning of "The Overcoat": "As for rank . . . [Akaky Akakievich] was what people call a permanent titular councilor, at whom, as we know, various writers who have the praiseworthy habit of attacking those who can't bite back have jeered and gibed to their hearts' content." For a discussion of the chapter on "The Overcoat" in Yermakov's book, see the introduction to the present collection.]

proach to these stories is justified, for we can cite Gogol's own statement that his heroes came "from his own soul," and that his aim was to find a way of ridding himself of the vileness that he could see in the depths of his soul.[8] Such self-depreciation and self-struggle are characteristic of the Russian writer, who as a rule regards his literary labor as a kind of martyrdom and as a confession.

As I said, two opposing and endlessly conflicting tendencies underlay Gogol's art: self-depreciation and self-exaltation. The conflict was explicitly reflected not only in what Gogol wrote, but also in the way he wrote, in the style and the imagery he used. Constant inner struggle, withdrawal into himself, into that world where this conflict raged, made Gogol seem strange, capricious, and hopelessly enigmatic even to his close friends.

In his early works Gogol liked to introduce and even elaborate on heroic themes, together with themes drawn from ordinary life. For example, *Taras Bulba*, "Al-Mamun," "Rome," and others contain epic descriptions and characterizations that might well have been taken from Homer. These two styles—the one intense and epic, the other commonplace—intertwine throughout all his writings, for instance in "Diary of a Madman," in *Dead Souls*, and, as we shall see, in "The Nose" as well, even though they are concealed there.

There is something very significant about the ease with which noble and ignoble themes interweave and unfold in tandem. (Gogol's follower, Dostoevsky, brought this tendency to full flower.) Very often such themes develop in unexpected ways; but they grip us, they seem to dull our critical faculties, and we do not notice how outwardly unmotivated and unexpected they are. Among such instances we should include the so-called lyrical digression at the beginning of "The Overcoat" and those in *Dead Souls*—the passage in chapter eleven, for example, where the courier gallops by, shouting imprecations and shattering the reverie into which the writer has fallen.

"There are two natures in me," Gogol confesses.[9] In fact, this is perhaps the chief characteristic of his psyche. In his art he constantly moves between two abysses, falling now into one, now into the other. This is what some critics see as his tendency toward the

[8 "Chetyre pis'ma k raznym litsam po povodu 'Mertvykh dush,'" *Vybrannye mesta iz perepiski s druz'yami, PSS*, VIII, 1952, 293-294.]
[9 Letter to A. O. Smirnova, October 24, 1844.]

extreme, the ultimate.[10] These two natures are the masculine and the feminine, the active and the passive, the holy and the sinful, the pregenital and the genital. Laughter and tears, pleasure and pain are expressed simultaneously in Gogol's works; and the coexistence of these two opposing tendencies is intimately linked with his sexual experiences and is marked both by auto-erotism and by fear or bitter repentance for such self-gratification. Active behavior is repressed and directed against the self. Childhood sadism, which was repressed in Gogol, comes out in the form of masochism, the pangs of conscience occasioned by self-gratification.

III

By the word *Nose*, throughout all this long chapter of noses and in every other part of my book where the word *Nose* occurs, I declare by that word I mean a nose, and nothing more or less.

Laurence Sterne, Tristram Shandy.

In moving toward the extreme, or the ultimate, Gogol, like many fantasts, consistently starts from reality, from some story he has been told, from anecdotes or incidents current in society. He fixes an inquisitive eye on the world around him as he studies man—his words, his gestures, his expressions, and, above all, his nose, to which he attaches a special and very vital significance. One could compile a whole little anthology from the passages in Gogol's works that mention the nose, so tirelessly does he describe the taking of snuff, nose-blowing, and so on. Gogol's advice was to write down everything that characterized a person, to wit: "In appearance he is attractive and presentable; he holds his hand thus, he blows his nose thus, he takes snuff thus: in other words, not omitting anything that is obvious to the eye, from major items to minor ones."[11] Thus, included among the "major items" is the nose and its behavior.

A playful entry that Gogol made in Ye. G. Chertkova's album in 1839 provides abundant material for a characterization of his own nose.

[10 Cf. the article by Bryusov in the present collection.]
[11 Letter to A. O. Rosset, April 15, 1847.]

Our friendship is sacred. It began at the bottom of a snuff-box. There our *noses* met and felt fraternally disposed toward one another, despite the obvious dissimilarity of their natures. In point of fact, yours is attractive and elegant, with a most pleasant curve to it, while mine is absolutely *bird-like*, long and pointed, like *Braun*, and capable of paying a call on the tiniest snuff-boxes all by itself, without the aid of fingers (provided, of course, it's not repulsed by a *flip*). . . . However, despite its funny physiognomy, my nose is a very *kind-hearted beast*: it has never turned itself up in the air or at the ceiling, it has never sneezed in deference to superiors or authorities—in a word, despite its excessive size, it has comported itself very modestly, in consequence of which it has undoubtedly become a liberal. But let's leave noses aside. This is a very fertile subject, and enough has been written and re-written on it: people have always complained about its stupidity and about how it sniffs everything indiscriminately, and about why it scurried off into the middle of the face. They have even said that there's no need for a nose at all, that a snuff-box would be much better than a nose, and then everyone would carry his nose *in his pocket*, in a *handkerchief*. However, this is all nonsense and doesn't lead anywhere. I am very grateful to my nose.

And in a letter to M. P. Balabina he writes: "Perhaps you can imagine my long, bird-like nose just as clearly (oh, sweet hope!). But let us leave the nose in peace. . . ." (The bird is a phallic symbol.)[12]

In these jocular passages, and in many others I will not cite here, we discover one extremely interesting detail which we need for our analysis of "The Nose," and to which we must devote some attention. Of course, every unprejudiced reader will be struck by

[12] Let us note how obvious the double entendres are in the jocular allusions that Gogol makes in his letters, and how restrained and proper he is in his fiction. In his letters and jokes he finds an outlet for what cannot be presented in a raw and unrefined form in his fiction. [The letter to M. P. Balabina was written on March 15, 1838; the italics in the first passage and the parenthetical remarks in the second passage are Yermakov's. I am unable to identify "Braun" in the first passage. It is italicized by Yermakov perhaps because it suggests the color of feces. "Kind-hearted beast" (Yermakov's italics) is what Gogol calls the hero of the first version of "The Overcoat" ("The Tale of a Clerk Who Stole Overcoats"). Yelizaveta Grigorievna Chertkova (1805-58) was a famous and eccentric hostess in Moscow, who specialized in writers and scholars.]

the parallel between the quotation from Chertkova's album and the theme of "The Nose." Particularly worthy of note is the curious statement that the nose could be carried in the pocket, wrapped in a handkerchief. This describes what actually happens with Kovalyov's nose, which is wrapped up in a rag by the barber, Ivan Yakovlevich.

Time and again in Gogol's letters and earlier works we come across images and situations which later passed into "The Nose." For instance, Gogol in his youth expressed a strong dislike for his landlord, a German artisan from Meshchanskaya Street. In "Nevsky Prospect," the nose of Schiller, the frugal German, is bankrupting him with its appetite for snuff, and, while drunk, he tries to have it cut off. The same motif, as V. V. Vinogradov shows,[13] went into "The Nose," in the scene where the clerk in the newspaper office, moved by Kovalyov's misfortune, tries to console him by offering him a pinch of snuff. In the story "Christmas Eve," the snowstorm that nips Chub's nose and lathers his beard and mustache evokes the image of "a barber tyrannically seizing his victim by the nose." The parallel to this in "The Nose" is Ivan Yakovlevich's attitude toward noses: "while he was shaving [his customers], he pulled so vigorously at their noses that they scarcely stayed on." One nose actually did come off. Here, clearly, the nose-pulling conceals an allusion to fears of castration, about which we shall have more to say later on.

We find the same motifs in "Diary of a Madman," in the section where Poprishchin is talking about the moon:

A lame barrel-maker put in a tarred rope and a portion of cheap lamp oil, and that's why there is such a dreadful *stench* all over the world that you have to *stop up your nose*. And that's why the moon is such a soft sphere that people just can't live on it, and *nothing but noses* live there now. And it's for that same reason that we *can't see our own noses*, because they're all located on the moon. And when I imagined that the earth is a heavy body and that *when it falls it can grind our noses into flour*, I suddenly felt such *uneasiness* . . . (fear of castration).[14]

13 Vinogradov, "Naturalisticheskii grotesk . . . ," p. 39.

14 Kovalyov and Poprishchin are preoccupied above all not with what is right under their noses, but rather with what cannot be seen, has no meaning, and is none of their business—Poprishchin, for instance, with the throne of Spain. Both note what the people around them are looking at—

The moon, moonlight, and the inhabitants of the moon are linked with the author's own autoerotic urges. An interest in the moon is closely associated with nocturnal dreams, dreams about the nose, self-gratification—none of which can be disclosed during the day. In "Diary of a Madman," the stench on the moon is directly related to a debasement of the sexual element, and establishes an association between noses and coprophilic pleasures. And at the very end of the story, Gogol returns to this theme. After the words: "Oh, mother! Have pity on your sick child!" there comes: "And did you know that the Dey of Algiers has a lump right under his nose?" Here we see the obsessive nature of the image of the nose, and the double meaning of the lump too: this is a variant of pimple [*pryshch*], which is the root of Po*prishch*in's name and also alludes to the pimple on Major Kovalyov's nose. In speaking of Poprishchin's delusion that he is King of Spain, Gogol has already explained the meaning that the word "Spain" has in the sick man's mind: "I have discovered that every cock has a Spain, and that it's located under his feathers, right by the tail." Here we have clear evidence of the polysemantic meaning of the nose-symbol, as indicating—in witticisms, jokes and ambiguities—both the sex organ and the act of defecation.[15] Gogol can therefore use it wherever propriety forbids open and frank talk about such matters. The same device is constantly found in Sterne.

This penchant for saying things with double meanings was characteristic of Gogol. V. A. Sologub cites two such instances in his memoirs. One is particularly to the point here. In Countess Vielgorskaya's salon, Gogol once told how he and a married friend had looked through the open shutter of a house of ill fame and had seen a prayer-service in progress just before the girls set out for the fair at Nizhny-Novgorod. As far as Sologub was concerned, the fact that Gogol told this story in polite society was an early manifestation of his illness.[16] But an association after the fact is not

---

the nose (they exhibit themselves)—and do not see the fundamental thing, which they need most of all and which is right under their noses. [The italics and the parenthetical remark in the quotation are Yermakov's.]

[15] Cf. Sigmund Freud, *Basic Psychological Theories in Psychoanalysis*, 1909. [Here and elsewhere the titles of Freud's writings are translated according to the Standard Edition, 24 volumes, London, 1953–.]

[16] This incident took place in Moscow, toward the end of Gogol's life. Sologub says: "He was already beginning to suffer from the attacks of melancholy and the loss of memory which were the sad harbingers of his death." (*Vospominaniya*, St. Petersburg, 1887, as quoted in V. V. Veresayev,

enough for us, since we know that Gogol had a definite weakness for stories of this kind—a fact that is corroborated by his letters too. Thus, our conjecture about the double meaning of the nose is substantiated, not only by the strange references to the nose in "Diary of a Madman," but also by our earlier analysis of "The Overcoat," and by numerous other remarks that Gogol made about noses, such as the one in Chertkova's album.

Let us note that besides a nose, there is also a "mantle" in "Diary of a Madman," that is, an overcoat (a phallic symbol).[17]

Bykov tells us something very interesting about Gogol's own nose. While a student in Nezhin, he once spent a month or more trying to touch the tip of his nose to his chin.[18] Among anal erotics we often find evidence of an urge to make the nose longer. This has not only a phallic significance, but a patently coprophilic one as well: that is, the urge to smell, inhale, and arouse oneself with an odor, such as the odor of a stable, and other even more explicit odors present in anal erotism. (Ivan Yakovlevich has held the nose, and his hands give off an odor.) Gogol himself had an especially long nose: it was "bird-like," as he himself described it. The frontispiece-design for "The Nose" was drawn by Gogol himself and consists entirely of noses; what is particularly interesting is that these noses are shown completely surrounding, adhering to,

---

Gogol' v zhizni, Moscow-Leningrad, 1933, p. 416.) [Count Vladimir Alexandrovich Sologub (1814-82) is best known as the author of the novel *The Tarantass* (*Tarantas*, 1844), which has become a Russian classic. He was the husband of Countess Sofia Mikhailovna Vielgorskaya (1820-78), a close friend and constant correspondent of Gogol's, and the daughter of Countess Luiza Karlovna Vielgorskaya, in whose salon Gogol told the story. See also footnote 28 in the article by Bryusov in this collection.]

[17] There is a special body of writing devoted to symbolism in works of literature. The puzzling male symbol of the overcoat can to some extent be understood by consulting Robert Eisler's book *Weltmantel und Himmelszelt. Religionsgeschichtliche Untersuchungen zur Urgeschichte der antiken Weltbilde*, Munich, 1910. Zeus covers Hera with a cloak, which is a male symbol. In the Book of Ruth, Boaz covers Ruth with his cloak, as a symbol of male possession. For the prophet Ezekiel the ritual covering of the woman is symbolic of Jehovah's protection of Israel. To this day, Bedouins cover their wives with an *aba* (cloak), saying: "From this time on, nobody must cover you except me," which has, of course, a symbolic meaning. In Russian [as in English], "to cover" also refers to the mating of animals: cows, mares, etc., are "covered."

[18 This probably refers to Nikolay Vladimirovich Bykov, "K biografii Gogolya," *Russkaya starina*, March, 1888. Bykov was Gogol's nephew by his sister Yelizaveta.]

and sniffing at a stick. (This suggests an association with the coprophilic.) Here again Gogol has pointed to the very close interrelationship of the nose and other phallic symbols, which also include, in Gogol, other rounded parts of the face such as the chin, to which he attempted to touch his own nose.[19]

Gogol attempts to make an organic connection between distinctive physical characteristics of his heroes (such as noses, chins, stature, and shape of the head) and traits of character. He looks for what is most typical in their appearance and in their names (to which he attaches special importance, as we shall see), and finally, he subordinates the very structure of his language to this principle, placing emphasis on the phonic aspect. In other words, he organizes and forges everything into a single organic image. Later we shall see just which drives manifest themselves in this particular way in his works. He describes noses in particular detail, and is almost always mainly interested in the noses of his heroes, or in what is on their noses. For example, Agafia Fedoseyevna has a cap on her head, three warts on her nose, and a coffee-colored dressing-gown decorated with little yellow flowers (coprophilic colors); and it is as hard to see her waist as it is your own nose without a mirror ("The Two Ivans"). A piece of snuff looking like coffee-grounds slips unpicturesquely out of Plyushkin's nose when he is deeply moved; a bit of foreign matter nearly drips from Themistocles' nose into his soup; we see a "tall lean man in a woolen frock-coat with a plaster stuck on his nose" (all in *Dead Souls*). In *The Inspector General* we read that "your master has a cute little nose." In "Viy" Khalyava appears with a broken nose. In "The Two Ivans" Anton Prokofievich gets a crack on the nose. In *Marriage* the first thing Yaichnitsa notices about Agafia is that her nose is too big. In "The Two Ivans" the nose and lips of the judge are described twice and in very great detail. In "Diary of a Madman" "his nose is not made of gold (a coprophilic image), he uses it to smell with and not to eat with (anal erotism), to sneeze and not to cough with." In "The Tale of Captain Kopeykin," from *Dead Souls*, "the nose is still more useless; you can only blow it, and even for that you have to buy a handkerchief." And Gogol's heroes often have nosological surnames: Dovgochkhun, Nozdryov, and so forth. Chichikov's nose "blares like a trumpet."[20]

---

[19] Plyushkin, in *Dead Souls*, looks like a woman and can only *slaver* his chin.

[20] Dovgochkhun, as I have said, suggests *apchkhi* (ha-choo!). Nozdryov

The ritual that accompanies nose-blowing and snuff-taking is so often encountered in Gogol and described in such detail that we cannot possibly even enumerate all such passages in his works without expanding this study considerably.

The very strong anal-erotic element in Gogol comes out in the familiar triad of characteristics described by Freud and somewhat elaborated on by Ernest Jones: capriciousness, stinginess (the collecting of things), and the love of orderliness. For a better understanding of the significance of anal erotism in Gogol, we should note that it is pregenital; and if it does not evolve and is not sublimated, it becomes a kind of surrogate for the mature sex drive. Gogol's story "Old-Fashioned Landowners" describes a typically regressive pregenital erotism: the relationship between husband and wife depends exclusively on the consumption of food, and the disappearance of the ungrateful cat which has been fed by the wife, Pulkheria Ivanovna, portends her death in the near future. (Compare the Assyro-Chaldean prophets.) Gogol's works abound in anal-erotic types: Chichikov, Plyushkin, Korobochka (all from *Dead Souls*), Ivan Ivanovich and Ivan Nikiforovich ("The Two Ivans"), and many others. Particularly noteworthy are Bashmachkin, the hero of "The Overcoat," and Petrushka, Chichikov's servant in *Dead Souls*. Both take a keen interest in words—not in their meaning or purpose, but in their shapes, their length, etc. (Longness or shortness are anal preoccupations.) Long words or nicknames create a comic effect—"Neuvazhay-Koryto," for example. Or, to take a case from my own psychoanalytic practice, the name "Andrea del Sarto," which at first looks beautiful, took on an anal connotation in the mind of a woman who was my patient, because of its length and because its sound suggests the vulgar Russian word for the act of defecation.[21] Gogol's partiality for long words and comic-sounding names was determined by these same traits in his own character. The same phenomenon can be observed in certain other writers as well.

In the pregenital stage, the nose substitutes symbolically not only for the male organ, but also for excrement. Gogol gives graphic

---

is derived from *nozdrya* (nostril), and Chichikov from *chikhat'* (to sneeze). The parenthetical remarks in the quotation from "Diary of a Madman" are Yermakov's.]

[21 Neuvazhay-Koryto is a character in *Dead Souls*. The name means, literally, "don't respect the feeding trough." "Sarto" suggests the verb *srat'*, which is the vulgarism in question.]

emphasis to this in his story, by specifying that the nose was located *between two cheeks* and stating that it was wrapped up in a cloth by Ivan Yakovlevich. The episode with the doctor is significant too: he advises Kovalyov to put the nose in a jar (a pocket, in the entry Gogol made in Chertkova's album) and to wash the spot where the nose is missing as often as possible, and he himself gives the nose a few cracks.

Another version of the nose-symbol, and its association with anal erotism, is the tail, which is frequently referred to in Gogol. In "Diary of a Madman," "Spain," the Spaniard or Spick of Russian jokes and anecdotes, has a specifically phallic connotation. In "The Two Ivans," Ivan Nikiforovich has a tail; so does Solokha, in "Christmas Eve." Khalyava, in "Viy," even knows a way of warding off the witch: you only have to spit on her tail. Gogol drops a transparent enough hint at the real meaning of Ivan Nikiforovich's tail: "Ivan Nikiforovich was born with a tail *in back*. But this invention is so absurd, and, furthermore, so disgusting and indecent (anal erotism) . . . because only witches, and very few at that, have a tail in back. Besides, witches belong rather to the female than to the male sex." (Defecation as parturition is applied to both the male and the female in children's theories of sex.)[22]

Let us note the terms in which the two Ivans are contrasted. "Ivan Ivanovich was rather timid by nature; Ivan Nikiforovich, on the contrary, wore trousers with such ample pleats that if they were to be inflated"—flatus—"an entire farmyard with buildings and outbuildings could fit in them." Fully consistent with this, Ivan Nikiforovich had a "nose that looked like a ripe plum" (the symbolism here is in the color). Gogol then develops the tail-theme further. Once again he gives it what at first looks like a touch of the unexpected, when he asserts that even if there is no tail inside the trousers, they nonetheless can accommodate a whole group of buildings; and the second meaning of these structures is shown by the displacement of the image upward: the "nose like a ripe plum" (again a double meaning). The same theme recurs at the end of his characterization of both heroes: Ivan Ivanovich has a snuff-box whose lid he licks before offering snuff to anyone, while Ivan Nikiforovich keeps his snuff in a horn, which he "puts directly into your hands" (he is also the one who possesses the gun).

This example is very characteristic of Gogol. It reveals the basic

[22] Cf. Freud, "On the Sexual Theories of Children," 1908. [The italics and the parenthetical remark are Yermakov's.]

tendency, which Freud has pointed out, of using a jest or a comic situation or comic juxtaposition to reveal something that cannot be explicitly stated because of the conventions of propriety.

Now we understand why the gun, which provokes the quarrel between these two worthy people, was especially necessary at this point in the story, why it could belong only to Ivan Nikiforovich, and why it was of course the feminine Ivan Ivanovich who especially needed it and had to try to get it. Ivan Ivanovich's head, we recall, resembles a radish with the tail pointing down (i.e., a gun that does not stick up), whereas Ivan Nikiforovich's head resembles a radish with the tail pointing up (the gun sticks up, yet he is not manly). All this, and a great deal more in this story, carries such a definite and unmistakable meaning that one is amazed at its failure to attract attention before now. In contrasting the sexual activity of Ivan Ivanovich (his servant girl Gapka has children), who tries to conceal his masculinity, with the sexual passivity (the tail) of Ivan Nikiforovich, who also tries to conceal it, Gogol employs a large variety of symbols and allusions, and presents two characters that are opposite in significance and meaning.

IV

Gogol uses many other symbols that are associated in some way or other with masculinity. Chichikov, with his feminine ways, must of course have a fully rounded chin. The heads of Ivan Ivanovich and Ivan Nikiforovich present a striking contrast in configuration. Another symbol of the same order is that of the boot, which is extremely characteristic of Gogol. We know that Gogol himself took no small interest in footwear. P. V. Annenkov cites an instance which he thinks indicates that Gogol's habitual severity of manner was just a pose.

> He was very demanding, and you had to see for yourself the important way he would try on a new pair of shoes that had been made for him by a young [Italian] lad with gleaming black eyes and an impish smile. Gogol virtually wore the boy out with his careful examination and then he said to me with a laugh: "There's no other way of dealing with these people: the minute you let your guard down they'll talk you deaf, they'll try to palm off some piece of junk, place a shoe before them, step back and start in: 'Oh, what a marvelous *cosa.*' . . ."[23]

[23 P. V. Annenkov, "N. V. Gogol' v Rime letom 1841 goda," *Literaturnye vospominaniya*, Moscow, 1960, p. 95.]

Annenkov adds: "Gogol was only pretending to find fault." But this is contradicted by what we know about Gogol's great partiality for footwear, and his habit of collecting it in great numbers. One memoir tells how Gogol's curious landlords, peering through the keyhole, observed him sitting for hours on end, the most serious expression on his face, inspecting the heel of his boot. It might seem that Gogol knew he was being watched, but even if that were the case, his choice of this particular form of joke—which seems accidental at first glance—reveals his characteristically keen interest in footwear.

The boot, like the vase, is both a male and a female symbol. Externally it is male; internally it is female, inasmuch as the foot is inserted into it. The heel and spurs are other symbols which emphasize the male or the phallic.[24] In fact, Gogol's literary works are filled with descriptions of boots. Chichikov, in *Dead Souls*, *modestly* covers his boots with a handkerchief, and kisses his boot. Podkolyosin, in *Marriage* (Act I, Scenes 4, 5, and 6), talks incessantly about boots and asks whether getting married amounts to nothing more than shouting "Hey, Stepan, bring my boots!" And there is an interesting passage in "Nevsky Prospect":

> There are a great many such people who, upon meeting you, invariably stare at your boots, and when you have passed, they turn around to have a look at the skirts of your coat. To this day I can't understand the reason for it. At first I thought they must be bootmakers; however, this was by no means the case. . . . (An irresistible urge, dictated by the unconscious.)[25]

And several lines below, there is an enumeration of the items displayed by the public on the Nevsky Prospect: a *frock-coat*, a splendid Greek *nose*, *side-whiskers*, eyes and a hat, a *foot* in a perfectly delightful little *shoe*, *mustaches*—in short, symbols of the same order.

---

[24] The symbolism of the boot and the heel is brought out very vividly in certain poems by Alexey Konstantinovich Tolstoy (1817-75), and in the poem by Alexander Alexandrovich Blok (1880-1921), "Humiliation" ("Unizhenie," 1911), where the last two lines read: "And so, my angel of yesterday [referring to a lady-love], pierce/My heart with your sharp high heel!" (Tak vonzai zhe, moi angel vcherashnii/V serdtse—ostryi frantsuzskii kabluk!) The symbolism of the boot and the heel is very common, as a fetish, among neurotics.

[25 The parenthetical remark is Yermakov's.]

In *Dead Souls*, the foot/boot combination is even more marked:

For all his house-serfs, no matter how many there might be, Plyushkin had only one pair of boots, which always had to be left standing in the hallway. As a rule, everyone summoned to the master's chambers had to dance barefoot across the entire yard; but on entering the hallway, he would put on the boots and, thus shod, appear in the master's room. On going out, he would again leave the boots in the hallway, and once more set off on his own two soles. If anyone had looked out the window in autumn-time, especially when light hoarfrost sets in of a morning, he would have seen all the servants executing leaps such as the most agile dancer in the ballet would scarcely have been capable of managing.

If in this connection we recall the abusive nickname bestowed on Plyushkin by the peasant whom Chichikov encounters on the road—"The patched ―――――,"[26]—then we shall see that Gogol was using this meager supply of boots to give even greater emphasis to the sexual impotence of Plyushkin, a miser and an anal erotic.

V

Weil sie Sünde sind,
Verlassen uns die heimlichsten
    Träume nie;
Wie zuckende Flammen flackern sie
Um unsere Schläfe, die hämmert und spinnt.[27]

After these extensive observations, we will now proceed to an analysis of the story itself. It was written between 1832 and 1836. At first it bore another title: "The Dream." In a letter to his mother, Gogol describes the story as "nothing more than disconnected meaningless fragments of what we have been thinking, which are then stuck together and made into a salad."[28] In the initial ver-

[26 The noun is missing in the original Russian text as well.]

[27 "Because they are sins,/Our most secret dreams never leave us;/Like darting flames they flicker around/Our temples, which throb and reel." Yermakov identifies one "Urich" as the author; there seems to be no such German poet in modern times, and I am unable to determine whom he has in mind.]

[28 Letter to M. I. Gogol, November 10 (o.s.), 1835. Actually, Gogol is not talking about his story here, but is giving a definition of a dream.]

sion, Gogol attributes everything that happens in the story to a dream. "However, everything described here was a dream of Major Kovalyov's. And when he woke up, he felt such joy. . . ."

Gogol discarded the original title and renamed the story "The Nose." In the process, the dream-theme remained, but now it was masked and concealed. The nose is the equivalent of the dream and vice-versa; the nose is nothing more than a dream.[29] By way of confirmation, see the excerpt from "Diary of a Madman" that I have cited: the nose cannot be seen, the nose is a dream, noses are located on the moon, they are in danger of being crushed by the earth. The possibility that a nose can exist independent of its possessor is also suggested here, and I shall have something to say about it later on.

Thus, *nose* and *dream* mean the same thing; and Gogol, while discarding the dream, as it were, nonetheless affirms in the final version of the story that the nose and the dream are the same thing. Likewise, in "The Overcoat" he dropped the epithet of "kind-hearted beast" that he had applied to Akaky Akakievich Bashmachkin in the first variant, yet he carried this theme throughout the entire story in its final version. This phenomenon is very characteristic of symbolic thinking, and I shall have occasion to speak of it again.

Two heroes figure in this "unusually strange incident" which begins and ends the story—a story steeped in fantastic, dream-like elements that utterly baffle the author. At the beginning of the first and second chapters, Gogol both reveals and conceals the state of his heroes. He has each wake up "rather early." This early awakening, for which no motivation is given in either case, leaves room for doubt as to whether the barber and the major have fully awakened, whether both are still in a state of partial consciousness, or even whether they simply go on sleeping. This last possibility is suggested when the major "pinched himself to see whether he was asleep; apparently he was not." The two characters are as different in appearance, social position, and temperament as are Ivan Ivanovich and Ivan Nikiforovich, or Akaky Akakievich before and after his death. One is Ivan Yakovlevich, a barber who has lost his surname—an insignificant, pitiable creature who is hen-

[29 In Russian, "dream" is *son*, and if this word is read backward—*nos*— we have the word for "nose."]

pecked by his wife.[30] The other is the collegiate assessor Platon Kuzmich Kovalyov, who calls himself a major—a foppish, arrogant young man who is in love with himself and is dangling after (but only *par amour*) the daughter of Podtochina, the widow of an army officer. He is an autoeroticist.

Ivan Yakovlevich is the silent target of his wife's abuse; Kovalyov is unmarried, and knows and exaggerates his value as a catch. Ivan Yakovlevich has no surname, but by some miracle, Kovalyov's nose has turned up in the bread baked by his wife. Kovalyov has a splendid surname, the rank of major, and a brilliant future; but he has no nose, he is "neither fish nor fowl, man nor beast."

Ivan Yakovlevich, a defenseless, dirty, unkempt individual, suddenly and to his complete surprise finds the major's nose in his bread, and blames himself, even though he cannot imagine how this could have happened. Submissively taking the nose and wrapping it in a rag, he can think of nothing else but how to get rid of it (there is a penis in the bread, cf. H. Sperber).[31] In contrast, Kovalyov (Major Kovalyov), a clean individual with a fresh collar, suddenly and to his complete surprise loses his nose. At first he does not know whom to blame; then he decides on Podtochina; then he goes to the chief of police, to the newspaper office— in short, he kicks up a fuss. Ivan Yakovlevich, on the other hand, would like nothing better than to hide and efface himself (ambivalence).

The dream makes each hero's sex organ (in this case the nose)

---

[30] The significance of the dimensions of the nose as an indication of the dimensions of the sex organ was familiar to Gogol from the proverb "What's displayed on the signboard is also inside the shop," which has a double meaning. Since the barber's surname has been lost from the signboard, then what could be expected of him? In fact, not a word is said about Ivan Yakovlevich's nose throughout the entire story. He is really an alter ego of Kovalyov himself. He indulges in masturbation, and is punished by being deprived of his independence, his masculinity, and even his surname (he pulls at noses).

[31] The nose is associated with eating. It is in the bread. The flat spot that remains after its disappearance is like a "pancake." In "Diary of a Madman" we read that "he likes to eat with his nose." Innokenty Annensky hints at such an interpretation when he says that the effeminate Ivan Yakovlevich can do nothing else but eat the nose ("Problema Gogolevskogo yumora," *Kniga otrazhenii*, St. Petersburg, 1906, p. 6). [Innokenty Fyodorovich Annensky (1856-1909) is one of the finest Russian lyric poets.]

his most essential characteristic, and gives it the capacity to act independently (cf. Freud).[32]

These two completely different heroes are in fact one and the same person, or, to put it better, two sides of one and the same person—one repressed and faceless, the other aggressive—whether he is facing the policeman on the bridge or his wife at home (as does Ivan Yakovlevich), or whether he is standing in the newspaper office or strolling down the Nevsky Prospect (as is Kovalyov). The same holds true of Akaky Akakievich in "The Overcoat." But let us try to examine the events of the story in the order in which Gogol wrote them.

The story begins: "On March 25th."[33] Notice the way this locution is constructed with respect to pure sound. "March 25th" is not the same as "the 25th of March." In the first, the sounds immediately take on a menacing quality, because of the rolling "r," and this is reinforced by a succession of "r's" in the same sentence: Petersburg, strange [stranno], occurred [proisshestvie]. This is what is meant by sound-structure. Knowing, as we do, the great importance that Gogol attached to it in his works, we are all the more justified in insisting on its significance here.[34]

[32] The size of an object in this story is determined not by its actual size, but rather by the significance it has in the eyes of someone like Kovalyov. The nose is the thing that interests Kovalyov most. (His is not large, and what if it should suddenly vanish from his face?) His concern about the nose betrays other interests, which he does not have the courage to admit to.

Does not Gogol himself, in his letter to M. P. Balabina (April 1838), give us sufficient grounds for drawing such a conclusion? He says there that he would like to turn into a nose [because the Roman spring is so fragrant]. This surely means that his nose and his sense of smell have monopolized all his interests. Is this not true of the hero of "The Nose" as well? The same phenomenon can be observed in drawings by children, where details of interest are exaggerated in size (mustaches, a horn, a sword, spurs, etc.). Eyewitnesses have reported the same phenomenon during the Spanish conquest of Mexico: the native artists, terrified by the muskets of the whites, depicted their conquerors as carrying guns of an enormous size.

[33] In one of his notebooks, Gogol sketches the following beginning for "The Nose": "On the twenty-third in 1832, there occurred in St. Petersburg. . . ." Note the following reversals: consonant plus r in (twenty-) three in the initial version, as against r plus consonant in March in the final version. Thirty-two (1832) is of course 23 reversed (23rd of March). And, as we have shown, the final title Nos (Nose) is a reversal of the initial title Son (Dream).

[34] The second chapter, quite in keeping with the first, begins with two rolling "r's" that have a menacing quality: "Kovalyov prosnulsya (awoke)"

But there is more to it than this. Why did Gogol choose March specifically, and why the 25th? As we know, March is the most unpredictable of all the months. It is also associated with raw, instinctual sex.[35] At the same time, one of the most glorious feasts of the Orthodox Church falls on March 25th: the Feast of the Annunciation.

All this is relevant to an interesting phenomenon in primitive language, to which Abel pointed and for which Freud provided a psychological explanation: the way in which a single word can have two entirely different meanings at the same time.[36] This has been demonstrated for many words; it is true of the title of Gogol's story ("Nose" and "Dream"); and it is true of "March 25th" as well. Phenomena of this kind are characteristic of primitive language and primitive thought, and they remain vital to this day in the literary art.

In the first draft of the story (although not in the final version), Kovalyov meets the nose in the Kazan Cathedral and says: "You ought to know your proper place; I suddenly find you—and in church, of all places! You really must admit. . . ." This incident establishes a link with "March 25th" and its veiled allusion to the Annunciation. It also reminds us of the passage from Sologub's memoirs I have cited, about the prayer service in the house of ill fame. Finally, it is connected with a sentence that appears in the first draft of the story: "There are many majors in the world who do not have even their underwear in decent condition and who hang around all sorts of indecent places."

In "The Nose," the most degrading and disgusting things are associated with animalistic sex, which is appropriate to the spring season, and which contrasts with the pure and lofty Annunciation. Yet both are really the same thing—the sexual—albeit on different levels. Something that in everyday life is usually concealed as being

---

and then made the sound *brrr*, "although he himself could not explain the reason for it." The significance of this *r* cannot be proven in any logical way. It belongs to the area of symbolic thinking and expressive phonic gestures [see Eichenbaum's article in the present collection]. Cf. the month of Martober in "Diary of a Madman." [Yermakov's point is somewhat reinforced by the fact that the "r" in Russian is made with a flip of the tongue.]

[35 Yermakov's expression is *mesyats koshach'ikh svadeb*, "the month of cats' weddings."]

[36 The reference is probably to K. Abel, *Über den Gegensinn der Urworte*, Leipzig, 1884. Freud wrote an essay with the same title: "The Antithetical Meaning of Primal Words" (1910).]

indecent and inadmissible in conversation—sex, impregnation—is openly recognized, celebrated, and talked about as a great event on the feast of the Annunciation. The fabric of Gogol's art and indeed his very mind is woven from this tendency toward contrast and contradiction.

"The Nose" is also built on such contrasts.

After the opening, we come to the barber who lives on Voznesensky Prospect, and we learn that his surname has been lost: he has been deprived of his fair share. The words "Also Lets Blood" on his sign are, as it were, a leitmotif of all his unreal, dream-like activity and of everything that is to happen in the story.

Ivan Yakovlevich has been awakened by the smell (nose) of hot bread. Throughout the first chapter he is tormented by this smell, and by the desire to eat the bread—more precisely, the nose. And he is punished for his desire. Kovalyov wakes up and wants to have a look at the pimple that has popped out on his nose the night before; he is likewise frightened and tormented when he fails to find not only the pimple, but the nose itself (he has discovered the pimple on his "nose," i.e., his organ, on Annunciation Eve).

Ivan Yakovlevich is married and endures humiliation from his wife, despite the fact that, according to his sign, he "also lets blood." Major Kovalyov is a bachelor who loses his nose, he supposes, because of the intrigues of Podtochina, and her desire to humiliate him. In "The Overcoat" and in many of Gogol's earlier works, with very few exceptions, the motif of marriage and relationships with women entails fear, vengeance, and terror. Examples can be seen in "Ivan Fyodorovich Shponka and His Aunt" and in the husband-wife relationship in "Old-Fashioned Landowners." Also, symptoms of sickness and death in connection with sex—the fear of contracting syphilis, of getting an infection (first Kovalyov has a pimple, then he loses the nose entirely)—can readily be traced in many of Gogol's stories. Both motifs are found in "The Nose."

If fear of the sexual is, as we know, nothing more than repressed sexual desire and punishment for this desire, then a great many things in "The Nose" become readily understandable.

Kovalyov has no nose because he is all nose himself. That is, he exists entirely in and of his exhibitionistic sexual activity. His life is devoted exclusively to sex: he runs after women and displays himself.

The identification of the nose with the sex organ is brought out very well in Gogol's opening description of his two heroes. Both Ivan Yakovlevich and Kovalyov are still only half dressed when they first become aware of what has happened to the nose. The barber has thrown a jacket over his shirt for decency's sake. That is, his clothes are open at the front: no mention is made of trousers or underpants. Kovalyov, on the other hand, has not yet even started getting dressed. In the first version of the story, the major, convinced that all this has been only a dream, "began dancing around the room dressed only in his shirt" (again, without underpants). Naturally, Gogol attaches great significance to this fact and retains it in the final version of the story as well.

The nose becomes an object of terror for Ivan Yakovlevich; its loss degrades Kovalyov and makes him look ridiculous. This is not merely a repetition of the situation that Sterne had used in *Tristram Shandy*, where the Widow Wadman wants to find out how badly Toby has been wounded at Namur and whether he is fit for conjugal life. Gogol has carefully concealed the significance of the nose as the sex-organ; his story may well be a parody of the Annunciation, in sexual terms. If so, it is a faint echo of Pushkin's mock-epic *The Gabrielade* (*Gavriliada*). This poem created a tremendous scandal in its time; if we stop to consider that Gogol was familiar with it, we should not be surprised that he would tackle the same theme as well. But he carefully veiled everything that was blasphemous and presented it as a simple anecdote tinged with fantasy.

With this interpretation of "The Nose" in mind, we will have an entirely new understanding of the scene in which Ivan Yakovlevich's wife throws the baked bread onto the table and says: "Here, eat it and choke, you idiot!" This bread contains a particle of strength—a phallic symbol. And so the image of the nose expands and reaches the very brink of blasphemy; later, Dostoevsky went even further (though using different specifics) in his story of the man who intended to commit a "daring and unprecedented act": firing a pistol at the Eucharistic wafer.[37] Here we see an anal concept of food, which is very characteristic of hysterical neurotics.

In Pushkin's poem, the emancipated phallic symbol takes the form of the snake, the Angel Gabriel, and the dove. In Gogol's story, it appears as a nose, in keeping with the workaday-world setting. The nose becomes an individual, an official in a particular

[37 Cf. *Diary of a Writer*, the entry entitled "Vlas."]

government office, and he has so many phallic features that we can only marvel that they have gone unnoticed. They are all the more significant by virtue of the fact that the road to great religiosity, in Gogol, Dostoevsky, and Pushkin, leads through great blasphemy.[38]

The description of this official, Mr. Nose—or Kovalyov himself —is so significant that I will quote it in full: "The door [of the carriage] opened, and out jumped a gentleman in *uniform*, bending over, and he ran up the steps" (compare the chestnut that lodges in the open flap of the trousers, in *Tristram Shandy*). "He was wearing a gold-braided *uniform* with a large *stand-up collar*, *buckskin trousers*, and a *sword* at his side. From his *plumed* hat it could be inferred that he held the rank of *state councilor*." It is interesting to note that nothing further is said about the nose's *face*. "The nose kept his face completely *hidden* in the *large stand-up collar*."[39] Everything that can be associated with tension and with standing applies equally to the official and to the sex organ: hence the jests and the suggestive allusions. Such fantasies of turning completely into a phallus are extremely common among neurotics.

The arguments which Kovalyov advances in hopes of persuading his nose to resume its position on his face are particularly significant. "Some tradeswoman selling peeled oranges on the Voskresensky Bridge can sit there without a nose, but having prospects of receiving . . . and, moreover, being acquainted with ladies in many houses. . . ." Or: "If you regard the matter in accordance with the principles of duty and honor . . . you yourself can understand. . . ." Somewhat later: "But the nose was no longer there: he had managed to drive off, probably to pay a visit to someone else."

In this jerky speech, the word "receive" veils some allusion or other—perhaps to a fear of contracting a sexual disease or of getting married. In any case, the "*peeled* orange" suggests certain things, which perhaps will be confirmed by future students of Gogol. Kovalyov then goes to the police inspector. ("Police" suggests "pollution," the term for a nocturnal emission.) This makes us wonder whether Kovalyov's alter ego might not have had certain suspicions just then that he was sick—that he might lose

[38] Cf. my *Etyudy po psikhologii tvorchestva A. S. Pushkina*, Moscow-Petrograd, 1923.

[39] The italics and the parenthetical comments are Yermakov's.]

his "nose" (phallus). Not finding the inspector at home, Kovalyov proceeds to the newspaper office, where the notices being submitted for publication are chosen with Gogol's customary mastery. The first is about a runaway dog, for which the servant says he would not give four kopecks (again a reference to the runaway nose). Then there is a notice about a coachman of sober habits (perhaps Kovalyov himself is really drunk), a carriage, a drozhky, a spirited young horse (which refers both to Mr. Nose and to Kovalyov), turnip and radish seeds (reminiscent of the radish-comparison between Ivan Ivanovich and Ivan Nikiforovich), a summer house with stalls for horses, and old soles (like Kovalyov without his nose).

The clerk who is taking the notices asks Kovalyov's last name, to which the latter replies that he cannot say: "Suppose they should find out, God forbid!" and then: "Judge for yourself, what really is to become of me without such a *conspicuous part of the body?* (an ambiguous locution instead of the word *face*). It isn't a trifling thing like my little toe (an invisible member: again a downward shift);[40] I could hide the loss of that in my boot (even clearer) and nobody would notice whether it was there or not (the phallus)." A few lines later, the clerk makes a transparent reference to the situation: "If it's lost, that's a matter for the doctor; they say there are people who can fit you with any sort of nose you like." Then, convinced that Kovalyov really does not have a nose, he suggests "publishing a little article in *The Northern Bee*—here he took another pinch of snuff—for the benefit of young people—here

[40 Here the Russian has *mizinets na noge*, which would mean, in modern Russian, "little finger on the foot" (although *mizinets* can refer to the toe as well). Yermakov finds this significant: "The little finger is on the hand, not the foot. This business of the hand, of illness, of something people might, God forbid, *find out about*, hints at masturbation." The anatomical displacement (assuming that Yermakov is right) is not so improbable in Russian. The generic word *palets* means both "finger" and "toe." To specify which is which, the speaker may add "on the hand" (*na ruke*) or "on the foot" (*na noge*). Instead of *palets*, Kovalyov uses the more specialized word *mizinets*, which normally refers only to the little finger. Since, however, it *does* concern the finger, it could presumably be pulled, unconsciously, into the same pattern as *palets*, and thus transferred to the foot. The italics and the parenthetical comments throughout this paragraph are Yermakov's.]

he wiped his nose (could this perhaps be an article on the harm-
fulness of masturbation?)—or just as a matter of general interest."[41] The remark about being of benefit to young people is an
especially transparent allusion to the possibility of losing the nose
as the result of an evil disease. Oil has already been poured on
the fire by the police inspector on whom Kovalyov has called at an
inconvenient time: he remarks sententiously that "a respectable
person doesn't get his nose pulled off." Interesting too is Gogol's
subtle psychological observation that Kovalyov's lodgings "struck
him as being melancholy or rather utterly disgusting after all
these unsuccessful quests. Going into the hall, he saw his servant
Ivan lying on his back on the dirty leather sofa, spitting at the
ceiling and hitting the same spot rather successfully. The non-
chalance of his servant infuriated him." We are most infuriated
by what we conceive ourselves to be; and this scene gives a remarkably vivid characterization of the state of Kovalyov's soul—
as something nasty, dirty, and stupid (he did not hit his target).

Kovalyov abandons himself to lamentations: "Why should
such a misfortune have befallen me? If I had lost an arm or a
leg—even that would have been better. But a man without a nose
is the devil knows what: he's neither fish nor fowl, man nor beast;
he's just something to be taken and thrown out the window! If
only it had been cut off in a battle (an echo of *Tristram Shandy*),
or in a duel, or if I myself had been the cause of it—but no, it is
lost for no cause or reason, it is lost for nothing, for absolutely
nothing!"[42]

The narrator goes on to say: "If a button, or a silver spoon, or a
watch, or something like that had been lost—but to lose *this*, and
in his own lodgings too." The objects enumerated here are significant as the first things that come to Kovalyov's mind. (People
twist a button, eat with a spoon, look at a watch in the privacy of
their lodgings. Compare the structures that could be concealed
in the trousers of Ivan Nikiforovich.) Then, trying to imagine who
might be to blame for the loss of the nose, Kovalyov settles on

[41 *The Northern Bee* (*Severnaya pchela*) was a weekly journal in
newspaper format, published between 1825 and 1865, and edited, during
most of its existence, by Faddey Bulgarin. The serious writers of the time
made it synonymous with hack journalism, and despised it accordingly.
It was also extremely conservative and pro-government—attitudes which
appealed to few of the better writers.]

[42 The parenthetical remark is Yermakov's.]

182

Podtochina, whose daughter he has been dangling after.[43] "She had made up her mind to ruin him, probably out of revenge, and for that purpose had hired some old women skilled in witchcraft—because it was absolutely impossible to suppose that the nose had been cut off." Ivan Yakovlevich had shaved him on Wednesday; on Thursday the nose was still there, and moreover he had felt no pain. His calculations as to who could have been the cause of his sickness are interesting: of course it was a woman, a female; Ivan Yakovlevich is the very last person who would enter his mind.

At the beginning of the story, Kovalyov's nose unexpectedly turns up in Ivan Yakovlevich's bread; now, at the end, it is unexpectedly found by a police officer and brought to Kovalyov. The officer says: "I'm near-sighted, and if you stand in front of me I can see only that you have a face, but I won't notice your nose or beard or anything else. My mother-in-law, that is, my wife's mother, can't see anything either." In the course of this brief conversation, the police officer twice mentions his "mother-in-law, that is, my wife's mother."[44] When read in the context of his near-sightedness and his life (which is difficult enough as it is even without a mother-in-law), this respectful yet indecent expression effectively characterizes the policeman as a weak and downtrodden man.

At last the nose is in Kovalyov's hands: "That's it, that's it! There's the pimple that popped out on the left side yesterday!" But the nose would not stick to its proper place and "fell onto the table with a strange sound, as if it were a cork." The doctor is summoned but refuses to attach the nose, assuring Kovalyov that things will only be worse for him. At the end of his consultation he proposes placing the nose in "a jar of spirits or better still, pour in two tablespoons of nitric acid and warmed-up vinegar and then you can get a pretty fair price for it." This reminds us of Gogol's

[43 There is an untranslatable pun here, which Yermakov spells out in the text. Podtochina suggests the verb *podtochit'*, which means "to eat away, gnaw at"—actions directed, in Kovalyov's mind, at his nose.]

44 The twice-repeated explanation that the mother-in-law is the *mother* of his wife carries a double meaning, which indicates a particular attitude toward the wife. [Yermakov presumably means that it suggests the obscene expression "—your mother!"] Let us recall Gogol's attitude toward women and marriage, which I have already mentioned. [Yermakov unaccountably does not observe that this police officer is the same one whom Ivan Yakovlevich encounters on the bridge after he has thrown the rag-wrapped nose into the river.]

argument that it is better to carry the nose in the pocket and to have a snuff-box instead of a nose.[45]

Kovalyov's exchange of letters with Podtochina makes it clear that she has absolutely nothing to do with the disappearance of the nose. In the meantime, rumors have begun to spread: people are saying "that the nose of the collegiate assessor Kovalyov was strolling down the Nevsky Prospect at precisely three o'clock," and that it was then seen in Junker's shop. "Just for this purpose [to catch a glimpse of the nose] a certain worthy colonel left his house earlier than usual and made his way through the crowd with much difficulty; but to his great indignation he saw in the shop window, instead of a nose, the usual woollen jersey and a lithograph depicting a girl adjusting her stocking, while a dandy in a cutaway waistcoat and a small beard was peeping at her from behind a tree." Gogol, we may remember, used this same picture in "The Overcoat": Akaky Akakievich stood staring at it while he was on his way to the lodgings of a fellow clerk to celebrate his new acquisition, the overcoat. In both stories, the emphasis falls on the erotic element. Here, people see not a nose (something masculine) but a suggestive scene, a girl and a dandy. Then the nose is spotted in the Tauride Gardens "while Khozrev Mirza was still in residence there." Khozrev Mirza, who was called the Indian nabob in St. Petersburg, had come to the capital to make an official apology for the barbaric murder of the playwright Griboyedov in Teheran.[46] Here too, then, there is still another veiled allusion to the theme of "bloodletting," cutting off the nose, murder.

People in high society began to talk about the incident, and one gentleman expressed surprise that "the government had not taken notice."[47] "But once again this whole incident was shrouded in fog, and what happened thereafter is completely unknown." This fog, or the impossibility of providing a logical explanation and motivation for the story, shows us the resistance to rationality which Gogol, with extraordinary skill, introduces as an active element in the story.

[45] The two meanings of the nose intermingle here and create a particularly amusing situation, inasmuch as the advice comes from a doctor who is a typical anal erotic. Cf. Freud, *Introductory Lectures to Psychoanalysis*.

[[46] Alexander Sergeyevich Griboyedov (1795-1829), author of the classic comedy *Woe from Wit* (1825), was in the Russian diplomatic service, and while serving as Minister to Persia was killed by a mob in Teheran.]

[47] In order to catch a glimpse of the nose, it was necessary to climb on a bench (ch. two), whereas to see the sex organ, it is necessary to bend over (note that the nose walks with a stoop).

The nose "again turned up in its proper place, that is, precisely between the two cheeks of Major Kovalyov, as if nothing had happened. This occurred on April 7th." The nose disappeared the morning of the 25th, on a Friday, and exactly two weeks later, on April 7th, *again on a Friday*, it appeared in its proper place.[48] Kovalyov is having great doubts about his good fortune, as he had earlier about his misfortune. In this two-week span, the pimple on the nose has cleared up, the sickness has run its course, and therefore, the first question Kovalyov asks of the barber, now that his own nose is no longer dirty (diseased), is, naturally, whether or not the barber's hands are clean.

Kovalyov says nothing to Ivan Yakovlevich about what has happened to him; but the barber comes into the lodgings "as timidly as a cat who has just been beaten for stealing suet." When the major cries out during the shaving session, Ivan Yakovlevich "let his hands drop, and was more flustered and disconcerted than he had ever been." His shave over, Kovalyov looks with a sarcastic expression "at two military men, one of whom had a nose no bigger than a waistcoat button."

After making sure that his nose is actually in place, and after paying a visit to a friend, Kovalyov runs into Podtochina and her daughter. He has a very long conversation with them, and, taking out his snuff-box, he deliberately puts a pinch "in each entrance," muttering to himself: "That's what I think of you females! A bunch of hens! And I'm certainly not going to marry the daughter. It's just going to be *par amour*, if you please—nothing more!"

VI

In his summary of the story, the author admits that there is a great deal in it that seems implausible. "Not to speak of the fact that it is

---

[48] The two-week difference corresponds to the difference between the old and new style [that is, between the Julian calendar, which was used in Russia until 1918, and the Gregorian calendar]. So the whole episode took place in one day—or one night—between March 25th and 26th. The new style is infinitely more appropriate to the way the whole story ends. The new French disease, news from abroad about plastic surgery on the nose, etc., are linked associatively with this new style. Included in the dream is the residue from the previous day—the impressions of the Feast of the Annunciation (see Section VII of the article), in the form of the church interior itself, and the various visits made by Kovalyov. The one-day error in reckoning can be ignored, especially if we bear in mind that 25, that is, 2 plus 5 equals 7, stands for both these dates (this is characteristic of dream-logic), and also that 7 is a masculine number.

a strange and unnatural thing for a nose to come off by itself and turn up in various places in the guise of a state councilor." This sentence returns us to the beginning of the story, to the nose's mishaps and its riding around in a carriage (perhaps a truss?).[49] It also introduces a passage which bears directly on the author himself and is then developed by him: "How did Kovalyov fail to realize that he could not advertise about his nose in a newspaper office?" Here we should read: how was it possible to use the press to disseminate such ambiguous information? And, assuming a simpleton's pose (which was in Gogol's nature), he adds: "I'm not saying that I think it's expensive to advertise: that's nonsense, and I'm certainly not one of those mercenary people."[50] The jocular tone conceals the large and important problem of Gogol's stinginess, not only in the monetary sense, but most of all as far as sexual obligations were concerned. To Gogol, as an autoeroticist, sexual love seemed terrifying. It threatened him with countless misfortunes of every kind. It walled him up within himself and made him stingy and self-centered. But this is something I cannot enlarge on here.

Hence the logical conclusion: to declare this sort of thing "indecent, awkward, not nice"; to allude, in a joking manner, to something that cannot be said entirely openly. "And the same thing again (i.e., indecent, awkward, not nice): how did the nose get into the loaf of bread, and how did Ivan Yakovlevich himself. . . ."[51] Again there is an unfinished sentence: did he cut the nose off, did he bring himself to throw it away, didn't he understand the meaning of all this, etc.? In short, just what was Ivan Yakovlevich's role here? "No, I can't understand this at all, I simply can't understand it!" It is easy to see that a father-complex is concealed in the person of Ivan Yakovlevich—a punishing father brought down to the level of a barber who has lost his surname.

Then, aware of how very strange his position is as the author of the story, Gogol poses a question for himself: "But what is strangest and hardest of all to understand is that authors can

[49] The nose consistently pays his visits in a carriage; he is carried. This can apply equally well to coprophilic fantasies. Furthermore, the nature of the nose's activity—the incessant paying of visits without any rhyme or reason—is very characteristic of anal erotism, and is associated with the feast-day that has just passed.

[50] See Freud on the connection between money, excrement, stinginess, and other manifestations of anal erotism ("On the Transformation of Instinct as Exemplified in Anal Erotism," 1917).

[51] The parenthetical remark is Yermakov's.]

choose such subjects. I admit this is utterly beyond my comprehension, indeed it is . . . no, no! I simply can't understand it." Even the hint of a possible explanation forces him to interrupt the flow of thought with a vehement "no, no." But what after all can be said at this point, when everything has already been told in such detail that any attentive reader has managed to figure what is going on? It is only the author who must refrain from offering any explanations, in order not to reveal more than he already has, out of considerations of propriety. Therefore, the question he raises here about the story's usefulness to society and to the country is entirely appropriate. It exemplifies the other tendency in the confession: seemingly to discredit the author and expose absurdities on his part by trying to establish, point by point, that such stories are totally unnecessary. "In the first place, it is of absolutely no benefit to the country. In the second place . . . but in the second place too it is of no benefit."[52] This passage echoes the ending of the second chapter, and is prepared by it: there the author speaks of a gentleman who "was obviously one of those who would like to involve the government in everything, even in their daily quarrels with their wives."

Here Gogol may be making a barbed allusion to his own penchant, in other works such as *Dead Souls*, for launching into lyrical digressions and bringing both his country and mankind as a whole into the orbit of his personal experiences. This motif of self-flagellation is readily evident at the very beginning of "The Overcoat," where Gogol laughs at writers "who have the praiseworthy habit of attacking those who can't bite back."

But then, having reached what looks like a definite conclusion about the implausibility of the entire story, Gogol ends by puzzling the reader once more: "No matter what anyone says, such things do happen in this world—not often, but they do happen." The circle is closed. And these concluding words bring the beginning of the story back to mind: "On March 25th, an unusually strange incident occurred in St. Petersburg."

With the sounding of this final chord, the entire story, which has

---

[52] The autoerotic, the egocentric, the person living within and for himself alone, the sterile snuff-sniffer, Kovalyov is, of course, of no benefit to the country from any viewpoint at all, since he cannot be a father or an active member of society. The whole threatening dream also turns out to be useless: everything that has happened is only an episode in Kovalyov's generally empty and untroubled existence.

187

seemed to be a pastiche of disparate elements, somehow suddenly pulls together into a unified whole, in which each part takes on a definite and essential meaning. Life is made up of parts, of episodes: it is a process into which some amusing incident, utterly unexpected and stupid from the viewpoint of the average man, intrudes itself from time to time.

However, inasmuch as Gogol himself at the end raises several questions about the verisimilitude of various episodes in the story, let us address ourselves to them now—the first one being the theme of the "strange and unnatural" disappearance of the nose and its appearance "in various places in the guise of a state councilor."

VII

> Yet which of you, filled with Christian humility, not aloud but in silence, while alone, in moments of solitary converse with yourself, will direct this difficult question into the very depths of your own soul: "And isn't there a bit of Chichikov in me too?"
>
> *Gogol*, Dead Souls

Gogol attaches great importance to finding the right surnames for his characters. He devises those which highlight one particular trait of physiognomy or character and give it a life of its own. From then on, this trait or name-symbol is inseparably attached to a character, who may be complex but may also amount to nothing more than that one trait, which then becomes a surrogate or substitute for him.[53] (For example, the public prosecutor in *Dead Souls* consists exclusively of thick black eyebrows.) The same device is used to make things strange and terrifying, as, for example, the visions in "Viy," or the "display" made by the pedestrians in "Nevsky Prospect." Both tendencies—toward the fantastic and toward the symbolic—are present and interwoven in "The Nose."

Gogol frequently employs this same device in his letters. He writes that Danilevsky will "turn completely into eyes" when he stands before Raphael. And he tells Balabina: "An amazing spring. All of Rome is now bestrewn with roses; but things smell even sweeter to me because of the flowers that have now come into bloom. Would you believe that I often have the wild desire to turn

[53] On the significance of names, see Freud, *Totem and Taboo*, and the works of Karl Abraham and Wilhelm Stekel.

completely into a nose, so that there would be nothing else—no eyes or arms or legs, nothing but one tremendous nose, with nostrils as big as good-sized buckets, so that it could inhale as much fragrance and spring as possible."[54]

The protagonist of the story we are analyzing is not of course Kovalyov, and certainly not Ivan Yakovlevich, but only a certain Mr. Nose. Naturally, therefore, he becomes an individual in his own right, detaches himself from his owner, and becomes an independent being. The desire that Gogol had expressed in his letter to Balabina was realized: this is the nose into which he hoped to be transformed, and it is, of course, his own nose as well.

With this in mind, an analysis of the name "Kovalyov" is of some interest. In its sound-structure, the name is close to Gogolyev on the one hand (the russified version of the Ukrainian "Gogol"); on the other hand, it contains Gogol's first name—Nikolay, the nickname for which is Kolya. It is therefore in effect a composite of Kolya and Gogol, which are artfully concealed by the russified ending -yov (a variant of -yev).[55] And it may also contain Gogol's patronymic, Vasilyevich: the syllable -va occurs in Kovalayov; and the -yev in the patronymic may have suggested the -yov in Kovalyov. At the same time, the sounds in the name Kovalyov echo the word kobel [male dog]; and this is a perfect characterization of the major, who lifts his nose to sniff out opportunity and withdraws into olfactory pleasures. Other associations are: koval, kovach [both meaning blacksmith], podkovali [deceived]. Kovalyov has deceived himself [Kovalyov podkoval sebya].

Kovalyov's first name is Platon, which, besides being the Russian for the philosopher Plato, also means tray, or flat and level space (i.e., plateau). His patronymic Kuzmich suggests the verb podkuzmili [he has been put in an awkward situation]. The name Ivan Yakovlevich is chosen with the same care. Ivan, being the commonest of Russian names, is very impersonal. Yakov—whence the patronymic Yakovlevich—is the proverbial name for vacuous and stupid people: "The magpie chatters about Yakov: you ask her about anyone else and she goes right on chattering about Yakov"—

[54 Letter to A. S. Danilevsky, April 15, 1837; letter to M. P. Balabina, April, 1838.]

[55 Kovalyov is actually spelled Kovalyev in Russian (hence the parallel Kovalyev/Gogolyev). When the stress falls upon the ending, as it does here, yev is pronounced yov, although this is not reflected in the spelling. My transliteration here (as with names throughout the anthology) has honored the pronunciation. The endings -yev or -yov are typical for Russian (but not Ukrainian) surnames.]

that is, speaking nonsense, saying the same thing over and over again.[56]

Once the nose (that is, Kovalyov himself) has been given a surname, then naturally, no such name can be found for Ivan Yakovlevich or for the organ that detaches itself from Kovalyov's face (it is consistently referred to simply as "the nose"). Clearly, the process by which the name Kovalyov was derived can be attributed to so-called symbolic thinking, which is of enormous importance in the creative process.

Another example can be seen in the dialogue between Kovalyov and the clerk in the newspaper office. "A civil servant came in," this particular clerk says, "with an advertisement. It came to two roubles seventy-three kopecks, and all it said was that a poodle with a black coat had run away. You wouldn't think there was anything more to it than that, would you? Yet it turned out to be libelous: this particular poodle was the treasurer of some institution or other, I don't recall which." Kovalyov objects: "But look, I'm not asking you to run an ad about a poodle, but about my own nose: in other words, it's almost the same as an ad about myself" (Kovalyov *is* the nose). (In fact, when he was in school, Gogol was teased by the other boys for his big nose and was even called a *nose*. He and his nose, in other words, were one and the same.)

And so, motifs from a number of sources are interwoven in this story. They attest to Gogol's inability to devise any theme of his own. He always availed himself of an incident from real life, or incidents which he was able to fuse into some unified whole, into the living organism of a work of art. This he could do, in "The Nose," not because of any logical affinity or interrelationship among the various components, but rather because of the intensely personal act of confession which underlies the entire story. It is consistently kept in the background and out of the view of the reader, who is disoriented and bewildered by the elements of fantasy and the sudden shifts in the story.

To speak the truth with a smile, to laugh when the heart is suffused with bitter tears, to conceal while revealing, to expose the ambiguous nature of one's urges, to understand, as fully and honestly as possible, everything that is going on inside—this is the task that Gogol set himself in the works of his last period. And it led him, with complete consistency, to "An Author's Confession," which was written in 1847, but published only after his death.

[56 *Soroka pro Yakova, ty ei pro vsyakogo, a ona vse pro Yakova.*]

VIII

How is one to know? Perhaps these griefs and sufferings which
are visited upon you from on high, are visited upon you precisely in order to draw a cry from your soul which would never
cry out otherwise. . . .

Gogol, Selected Passages from
Correspondence with Friends

We must now study "The Nose" from the viewpoint of that most
unusual work of Gogol's, "An Author's Confession." A confession
is a serious act; Gogol cannot therefore make and exploit the kind
of allusions that are scattered throughout the pages of Sterne's
Tristram Shandy. He is faced with the equally important task of
neither revealing nor concealing anything completely. These two
opposing drives give rise to conflicting needs. They very often
cross and produce so-called compromise solutions, which end up
as puns and double entendres; and these in turn, as Eichenbaum
has shown in his article "How Gogol's 'Overcoat' is Made," become even more complex as double plays on words, metaphors,
and so on, which can no longer be readily grasped and require
closer analysis.

Feeling absolutely unrestricted, and burning with a desire to
repent, Gogol sought an opportunity to bare everything that
lay in the depths of his soul, and to make a confession as
a great sinner. The most blasphemous scenes, the most un-
forgivable similes, the most cynical images and possibilities pass
before his mind's eye; it is his tremendous capacity for self-
analysis which allows him to accept them and to regard their exposure as a heroic deed. To discern these conflicting drives within
himself, to bring them out for himself and even for all to see, to
invite laughter and ridicule and to know that he is "laughing at
himself"—this is what makes it possible for Gogol to confess and
reveal himself to the ultimate. It is at this ultimate—this realm of
our basic, archaic self, this primitive fabric on which the patterns
of our life are later embroidered, this dark, unknown, nether-world
of the mind into which man is usually so ready to cast everything
he finds cumbersome in his conscious life—it is here that the most
contradictory drives come into collision and prove to be identical.
Here the same word, the same symbol takes on two completely
different meanings at the same time. Here religious fervor is blas-

191

phemy, things of the greatest value are valueless, good deeds are evil and sinful. Only after he has reached this ultimate, only after he has brought forth the essence of this basic self can a writer free himself from everything accidental and temporary, touch and understand the innermost secrets of the soul, and then forge a truthful and genuine image of man, and thereby a work of art.

But perhaps there is something dubious about this approach. Perhaps "The Nose" is simply a joke, a trifle, with none of the serious purposes that we have indicated here. Freud in his lectures pointed out that when the celebrated wit Lichtenberg made a joke it concealed not only a problem, but its solution as well. This is precisely the significance of the joke that Gogol has told us in the form of his story. There is a problem posed here, and its solution is given; we have only to open it up and show how Gogol solves it.

By now we are in a position to state the problem in a different way. (This of course does not mean that we are substituting another problem for this one.)

As we have seen, the problem posed in "The Nose" is a sexual one. It throws light on the question of the autonomy of man's sexual activity as symbolized by the separate existence of the nose. (The same thing can be seen in the quarrel between the two Ivans.) Sexual activity asserts its rights, which run counter to the urgings of the ego and the norms of society. The thing that cannot be displayed or talked about without shame and embarrassment— "the nose"—itself evokes a feeling of shame and embarrassment if it is not in its proper place, between the two cheeks. The result is an insoluble problem: it is uncomfortable to have a nose but just as uncomfortable not to have one: the two situations are equally discrediting and disgraceful.

These considerations bring us back to our discussion of the derivation of the name Kovalyov from the nickname or child's name Kolya, and suggest a new hypothesis. Feelings of sexual shame first arise in the early years of life, when the child discovers that there are no decent or commonly accepted names for certain acts and organs, and that it is embarrassing and indecent to talk about them. But everyday experience convinces the child that such things are the most important and most interesting topic of adult conversation and that they excite laughter and approval. He therefore learns to talk about them in such a way as to reveal his adult knowledge and to understand these interesting conversations

192

without explicitly violating the norms of decency. Characteristically, the great majority of children ask meaningless questions without expecting answers. They have a need to find out about this one extremely important question, but they never ask about it, at least not during the period when they have already become aware that such questions are dirty and impermissible. Up to this point in their development, dirtiness has been associated with bowel functions; it is therefore not surprising that from this point on, sex is very closely associated with the excretory functions on the one hand, and with eating on the other. That is, we see in the child those same associations and that same inability to differentiate which we find in Gogol's story "The Nose."

Gogol's own childhood could provide us with much material along such lines, but I will not develop this topic in any great detail. We know, for example, that he was very enthusiastic about the theater, took part in amateur productions, and, according to his schoolmates, sometimes behaved very indecently: for instance, in playing the role of an old man, he groaned and made a noise that is unacceptable in polite society. But another way of getting at Gogol's early years is through the structure of works like "The Nose" and "The Overcoat." They are confessions. And in confessing, a person feels himself to be little once again, and can therefore use a diminutive name in referring to himself (Kolya instead of Nikolay: whence, as we have seen, Kovalyov). Furthermore, insofar as the form of the dream and of the work of art compels Gogol to adhere to the forms of dream-thinking as well, that is, to so-called archaic or symbolic thinking, he returns to the state from which such thinking arises—that is, to childhood, which at the same time embodies the primitive thinking that all men share.

In fact, not a single character in "The Nose" shows any surprise at the improbable happenings; on the contrary, everybody remains interested and curious (as does the reader) right to the very end. Of course, it is not the nose that excites curiosity, as Gogol very subtly indicates in two places: a seller of peeled oranges can lose her nose and no one is surprised or interested; the same is true of the old women whose faces are wrapped up leaving only two openings for the eyes: old women without noses are funny but not out of the ordinary. What is curious is that a man has lost his nose— and not some shabby individual but a major. Gogol was the older

193

son—the "major" son, one might say; and in Russian slang, the term *na mayora* [lit.: for the major] means indulging in masturbation.

In trying as best we can to decipher "The Nose," we must say that two things underlie the story: the fear of castration, which goes along with the repressed wish to possess an enormous sexorgan; and the desire for unlimited erotic pleasures.[57] These desires lead to aggressive acts directed against social life and cultural values, and must be repressed. However, a frivolous individual like Kovalyov is not guided by anything except his own egotistic interests. His activities run counter to the demands of civilized life. They create a feeling of guilt in him which he does not wish to recognize, but which reveals itself to him in the form of an extremely oppressive dream (the dream of castration). But it has been only a dream; on awakening, Kovalyov tries to ignore his painful experiences, and he resumes his interrupted activities. We find him making fun of a military man whose nose is the size of a waistcoat button; he is even buying the ribbon of some order, but it is not known why, since he has not been so honored. In other words, life has once again fallen into its old rut. The mysterious disappearance of the "nose" remains as mysterious as ever to Kovalyov. After everything that has happened in the course of this fantastic tale, after all the agitation and the torment, after the opportunity that Kovalyov has had of perceiving and understanding his weakest sides, after his inability to see and understand his own weakness and guilt, which in the story are represented imagistically as vengeance for the profanation of virgins—one of them the Virgin Mary of Annunciation Day, the other the widow Podtochina's daughter—after all this, Kovalyov's self-satisfaction comes out once again in his cynical gesture, still associated with the nose, of taking snuff "in both entrances" while muttering to himself: "That's what I think of you females! A bunch of hens! And I'm certainly not going to marry the daughter. It's just going to be *par amour*, if you please—nothing more!" All Kovalyov's life, all his interests are concentrated on the sexual, the examination of others and of himself (*Schaulust*), on displaying himself to women and regarding them cynically.

[57] The fantasy-wish to possess the father's very large phallus (it seems so large because of the interest the child takes in it and the importance he attaches to it), envy of the father, the fantasy-wish to castrate him (so that his name might be lost)—these are common symptoms among neurotics.

Something that could have brought about catharsis, awareness, purification, further growth and development, a turning point in life (an "annunciation"), has been lost beyond recall. The laughter in the story is suffused with tears, the bitter tears of the author: no, man will not become aware of all his vileness, he will not understand what he is really like. Even in the case of a "learned" collegiate assessor such as Kovalyov, the unconscious attempt to reveal his essential inner self in the form of images and actions has passed without leaving a trace.

In keeping with the structural requirements of the humorous story, Gogol is obliged to bring off a happy ending. But somehow, we feel like saying, as he himself does at the end of "The Two Ivans": "It's a dreary world, my dear sirs!"

All these surprisingly perceptive discoveries are the result of the same process we observe at work in psychoanalysis: one must be honest and courageous when faced with oneself. Gogol possessed a sufficiency of honesty and therefore succeeded in bringing out a great many things in his own mind and the minds of others, things which need much more extensive elucidation and analysis.

For the present, however, we can draw two conclusions from our analysis of "The Nose." First of all, what strikes the reader as being mere chance, "nonsense," a dream yet not quite a dream; what makes Ivan Yakovlevich and Kovalyov constantly test themselves to see whether they are asleep or losing their minds—all this has its own logic and has been skilfully prepared by the author.[58] From here it is only a step to the assertion that sleeping and dreaming are not such nonsense after all. The statement that the nose was found by a near-sighted police officer with a mother-in-law who could not see anything either is fraught with significance. Does it not say that the real meaning of the loss of the nose can be discovered and revealed only when a person is near-sighted, when he can see nothing but his own nose, or, in other words, nothing but a dream?

Second, as certain critics such as Vasily Rozanov have noted, Gogol's characters frequently carry on meaningless conversations

---

[58] The chance happening is of interest, but it is legitimate in a work of art only when the writer puts it there *not by chance*. In a work of art, what may look like a chance happening on the surface is actually subject to the inner laws of the work.

that would hardly be conceivable for normal people.[59] Evidently
they do not understand what they are saying or why. But it is just
such utterances which best characterize individuals; in psychoanalysis they are called free associations, and they reveal that area
of the mind that contains drives which man cannot understand
but which nonetheless determine his actions.[60] The further development of this penetrating insight of Gogol's is found in
Dostoevsky, who declares, in *The Raw Youth*: How could I dream
such things if they were not already in my waking thoughts? Thus,
the intuitions of the writer anticipate the discoveries of the
scientist.

IX

From that position or level in society on which he is placed by
his employment, his rank, and his training, every person has a
chance to view the same object from an angle that nobody but
himself commands.

Gogol, Selected Passages from
Correspondence with Friends

How far are we justified in approaching a work of Gogol's from
this particular standpoint? What can it teach us? What problems
does it solve? Is it not conceivable that an analysis of this kind may
perhaps create a situation where any possibility of reaching a
proper understanding of Gogol's work—perhaps any understanding at all—will be forever closed to us and lost? Should we not,
rather, put our trust in the author who, in making his act of confession, naturally knew much better than we just what ought to be
revealed and to what extent, and how to make the various allusions
and symbols comprehensible? Does not our approach kill all taste
for art? And can we so immodestly reveal things that the author
considered it necessary to conceal out of a sense of propriety?

If a writer's job consists of trying to show something without
revealing absolutely everything about it, in the hope of stimulating
the reader to undertake some *activity* of cultural significance, then
the job of analysis is to point out the primitive drives and the
symbolic material from which the work is constructed. It is en-

[59] "Pushkin i Gogol'," *Legenda o Velikom Inkvizitore, s prilozheniem
dvukh etyudov o Gogole*, 3d. ed., St. Petersburg, 1906, p. 259.]

[60] Is not Gogol, like other writers, a forerunner of behavioral psychology?

tirely understandable that an author would never venture to write his work in such a way as to give all his primitive drives a crude and egotistic outlet that would offend other people. The purpose of a work of art is to provide another, not so primitive, outlet for these very simple needs. Insofar as the author is tormented and made ill by these urges, insofar as he finds indications in himself of things unsublimated and wishes to free himself of them by bringing them out, he teaches us to perceive, in ourselves as well, the same things from which he suffers. A writer who is able to see his own weaknesses and defects (his "vileness," as Gogol would say) as honestly and courageously as Gogol, is to be honored all the more.

Gogol of course formulated his statements not in the dispassionate language of scientific propositions but in the language of imagery. The story makes it clear that Gogol grasped the significance of the dream as a phenomenon that threatens us and compels us to give serious thought to ourselves. He discerned the possibility of crisis in Kovalyov's petty and intimidated soul—in his useless running around and in his cynical attitude toward women. He created a tragedy, a tragicomedy, and thereby posed the question: what is more important, the sexual or Kovalyov? Is the sexual subordinate to Kovalyov, or Kovalyov to the sexual? The nose comes off by itself and declares its independence of Kovalyov; so far as it is concerned, Kovalyov is nothing more than a carriage for it to ride in. Kovalyov laughs at himself for being foolish enough to take a dream for reality. He does not notice that it is precisely his predicament in the dream which perhaps does more than anything else to expose the emptiness of his life and the humiliation of being utterly dependent on his own nose. Whenever it seems as if the meaning of these events is about to be revealed, everything is shrouded in fog. Kovalyov is not allowed to see; he does not want to see the person who is to blame for everything: himself.[61]

Gogol says that although such cases are rare, they do happen: this is a subtly ironic commentary on people who do not under-

---

[61] Such dreams are by no means rare. I will mention, by way of example, the case of a twelve-year-old boy who dreamed that his nose had been cut off by a streetcar, and of a five-year-old boy who dreamed that he caught a scampering mouse, which he identified with his sex organ, after actually grasping his organ. For the symbolism of the organ, as a bird, a mouse, etc., see Part 2 of Freud's lectures.

stand the significance of dreams, and who consider outer reality truer than inner. But Gogol understands. He takes the fashionable "nosological" theme which intrigued so many writers before him, and does something more with it than simply reshuffle its familiar components. And he is able to make us understand what every person is tormented by, and what must be resolved and grasped so that man can free himself from the power of the dark forces of primitive instinct. He seems to be refusing to give a solution; he leaves the reader baffled; but any attentive eye can see that Gogol knows something about why such dreams occur; and he prods us into "action," into making an effort to see our own dreams in Kovalyov's dream and hearken to the voices that challenge us to evaluate the life and activity of such an individual.

Granting that this is only one aspect of Gogol's story, it is nonetheless of great importance. One of the timeless "accursed questions" is posed here in a magnificently crafted and structured form; and simply by posing it, Gogol really answers it. He stopped at the point where our analysis picked up. We have tried to understand what his answer is, to make additional inquiries of the story, and to reflect on the material it offers.

5

Vyacheslav Ivanov
(1866-1949)

IT WAS NOT until Ivanov was nearly forty years old that his first book of verse, *Pilot Stars* (*Kormchie zvezdy*), came out. With it he immediately won recognition as a major poet, and was set firmly within the rising Symbolist movement. He had other talents as well, which established him as the intellectual leader of the St. Petersburg Symbolists: thorough training as a classicist, historical studies in Berlin with Mommsen, and a vast knowledge of Western literatures. In 1913, he moved to Moscow, where he remained throughout the terrible years of revolution and civil war until his appointment, in 1921, to the professorship of Greek at the University of Baku. Three years later he left the Soviet Union on an official mission to Italy, where he remained for the rest of his life, writing, translating, and teaching.

Ivanov's ideas about art and culture were strongly influenced by the ancients, by Nietzsche, and by Vladimir Solovyov, the Russian religious philosopher. He called for the creation of an organic or collective culture, a new Middle Ages, but with Byzantium, not the West, as the model. Art, he believed, should be myth-making, and should recognize no boundaries between creator and consumer.[1] His most important works of theory and criticism are *Furrows and Boundaries* (*Borozdy i mezhi*, 1916) and *Dostoevsky* (1932).

The article translated here was written in Rome in 1925, and appeared in 1927, in Vsevolod Meyerhold's journal *Teatral'nyi Oktyabr'*, under the title " 'Revizor' Gogolya i komediya Aristofana." I have tried to convey a sense of Ivanov's penchant for rhetoric and archaisms.

[1] Recently a useful study of Ivanov's thought has appeared: James West, *Russian Symbolism: A Study of Vyacheslav Ivanov and the Russian Symbolist Aesthetic*, London, 1970.

Gogol's *Inspector General* and The Comedy of Aristophanes

by Vyacheslav Ivanov

To Vsevolod Meyerhold, in
commemoration of twenty years
of friendship.[1]

I

THE COMEDIC TOWN

IN THE FOURTH century B.C., a new type of comedy arose on the ruins of the Greek democracies and out of the decay of the popular, political "old" comedy of the Aristophanic type, which had been as whimsical, winged, and predatory as Chimera herself. It reflected a municipal slant of mind, dealt with the mundane and the commonplace, and was as wingless and tame as ordinary life itself; it was this new comedy which, owing to the vitality of classical forms, was destined to reign on the boards from those ancient times down to our own.

[1 This article is introduced by a comment from the editors of the journal in which it was published (*Teatral'ny Oktyabr'*): "The editors, while disagreeing with the author on a great many matters (especially his mystical and abstract treatment of the idea of the chorus and the rise of the tragedy), are nevertheless alloting space to his article because of its extremely interesting factual observations, and its value as a focus for discussion."

Vsevolod Emilievich Meyerhold (1874-1940) was one of the greatest producers and directors of the Russian theater. He began as an actor in Penza, and then appeared with the Moscow Art Theater (1898-1902); but he soon branched out on his own as both actor and director, developing his ideas about the "esthetic," non-realistic theater. It was between 1908 and 1917, when he was the director of the famed Alexandrinsky Theater in St. Petersburg, that he won renown with a series of brilliantly experimental productions of classical and modern plays, both Russian and European. He continued working well into the Soviet period (even joining the Communist Party), as head of his own "Meyerhold Theater" (founded in 1920). But in the 1930's—a time when technical innovation in all the arts was officially frowned upon—Meyerhold came under heavy fire as a "formalist." His theater was closed in 1938, and he was arrested in 1939. For years he was ignored in the Soviet Union as a "non-person," but recently he has been "rehabilitated," and his work is again being studied.]

The chief distinction between Gogol's *Inspector General* and this ancient comedy of the workaday world and—with the differences accounted for—its similarity to the Old Comedy of the fifth century, is that its action is not limited to a circle of personal relationships, but, rather, presents these relationships as components of a collective life and embraces a whole social microcosm, self-contained and self-sufficient, which stands symbolically for any social confederation, and of course reflects, as in a mirror, just that social confederation to whose entertainment and edification the comic action is directed. (As the epigraph to *The Inspector General* has it: "There's no use grumbling at the mirror if your own mug is crooked.")

In point of fact, the unnamed town of Gogol's mayor is, as it were, the comedic town (be it Athens or Cloud-Cuckooland) of old Aristophanes; its oafish citizenry, in a certain sense and within certain limits, corresponds to the Aristophanic Demos, now grown senile, just as Gogol's mayor, Anton Antonovich Skvoznik-Dmukhanovsky, corresponds to Aristophanes' leather-monger, that inveterately brazen, wilful and swindling Paphlagonian who manages the estates of Demos. It is the representation of an entire town rather than the elaboration of a personal or domestic intrigue that constitutes the root idea of this immortal comedy, an idea of Pushkin's, who was, significantly, the chronicler of the village of Goryukhino.[2]

In accordance with this brilliantly bold and new idea, all the mundane and commonplace elements of the play are shown in the light of their social significance and are subordinated to the historical principle which rules the destinies of this grotesque state: all the litigations and squabbles, the calumnies and slanders move out of the realm of civil law into the sphere of public law. *The Inspector General* is intrinsically and Aristophanically comic in that the triviality, inanity, and depravity of a way of life based on a generally accepted and unshakable hierarchy of rights that sanctions swindling, fleecing, tyrannizing, coercing, and repressing, are presented as constituting a certain harmonious and foreordained social cosmos. And suddenly this cosmos is shaken to its very

[2 Pushkin wrote "The History of the Village of Goryukhino" ("Istoriya sela Goryukhina") in 1830. It is a fictional chronicle in prose, ostensibly based on old documents, of the life of the narrator's native village. Gogol insisted that Pushkin had given him the plot of *The Inspector General* and of *Dead Souls*: see footnote 4 of the article by Gippius in the present collection.]

201

foundations, and doubt is cast upon the very principle of hierarchy that insures its existence: now we no longer have the squabbles and squalls of families or neighbors, but rather an antheap disturbed at its very bottom.

The integral image of an upturned human antheap should, it seems to me, be set in bold relief before the audience in a truly new future stage production of our *Inspector General*, a play that is old but has as yet not been exhausted either by critical commentary or the art of the theater. This is its fundamental and, as regards style, its most distinctive characteristic.

II

AN ADAPTATION OF *The Inspector General* IN A MEDIEVAL MODE

Gogol himself proclaimed that his comedy presents neither individual, isolated characters nor their private domestic affairs, but rather, the "town" as a collective persona. But this perfectly correct premise yielded consequences that proved troublesome to the author.

Racked with anxiety that his play was being interpreted, perversely and dangerously, as a sweeping condemnation of the whole existing order and structure of society (for the target of ridicule is not details of the general scheme of things, not particulars of the daily round, but the town itself); seeking to clarify for himself the positive inner meaning which the play was certainly supposed to contain (for in creating it, he wished to defame nothing but vice itself), Gogol wrote "The Denouement of *The Inspector General*" with an end to giving public opinion the "key" to a sound understanding of the author's idea, which was not destructive but purely instructive. "I'm glad to oblige, I'll give you a key," he says through the mouth of the first comic actor in "The Denouement." "Go ahead and take a long, close look at the town that is depicted in the play. . . . Yes, we are laughing at ourselves!" But what else is this rotting town of ours—a town of which we ourselves are the constituent element—if not Russia in the totality of its being? In order to evade the fateful conclusion, the author turns artful: "All to a man are agreed that no such town exists in all Russia." He does not notice that his obstinate "in a word, there is no such town" makes for a comedy devoid of truth to life and consequently devoid of substance. However, the slyboots has the "key" up his sleeve: it turns out that the "town" which lives on the stage but has no existence in the outside world of reality is every man's "spiritual town": that the "rascally officials" are the "passions" of this town; that Khlestakov is the "flighty, worldly, venal, deceiving conscience"; and that the real inspector general is our true, "awakened" conscience.[3]

For this attempt to reduce an objective act of social consciousness to naught, to a soul-saving parable, people have expressed their annoyance at Gogol for a hundred years or so. Now that the comedy has accomplished its historical mission, we can take a dispassionate view of this convoluted interpretation. Such a contrivance, so alien to poetry, is no doubt an excogitation not of Gogol the artist but of Gogol the ward of the artist, the conjecture of an outside observer who has put himself to the test and has been staggered and stunned by the spectacle he has seen: a conjecture about the evil spirits grown rank in the subterranean depths of his own soul, the gloomy and repellent secret of a multifarious world he carries deep within himself. But if a work of genuine art is as rich in substance as life itself and, while remaining self-consistent, speaks to different people about different things, then this reflection on an analogy between the structure of society and the structure of the individual mind is in itself ingenious and profound, so long as it is not coercive and does no more than draw a parallel. Without erasing a jot of the text, it does not annul the literal meaning of the play nor blunt its immediate effect. Finally, from the viewpoint of stylistic analysis, it is curious and instructive in that once more, and in a fresh way, it betrays the unconscious attraction which Gogol felt for the large forms of universal art: just as in the original design of the play we have detected something in common with the Old Comedy of antiquity, so too, through the prism of the later reinterpretation, this metamorphic play betrays the characteristic traits of a medieval dramatic action.

[3 "The Denouement of *The Inspector General*" ("Razvyazka Revizora") was written in 1846, ten years after the first performance of the play. The quotations are from "Razvyazka Revizora," *PSS*, IV, 1951, 129-130. Gogol was then deep into his personal and religious crisis, one of whose symptoms was a rejection or radical reinterpretation of his earlier work. See *Selected Passages From Correspondence With Friends*, especially "Preface" ("Predislovie") and "Testament" ("Zaveshchanie")—Gogol was working on this book in 1846, and published it the following year—and "An Author's Confession" ("Avtorskaya ispoved' "), which was written in 1847 but published in 1855, three years after Gogol's death.]

In point of fact, that other Gogol whom we have just called the ward of the artist was in turn an artist, and the justification that he contrived for his work represented a new artistic transfiguration of it. On the ideal stage of his imagination, he now saw *The Inspector General* in a different way, as an edifying parable in dramatic form, and the superstitious vision of his later years is striking in its medieval naiveté and power. One cannot gainsay a distinctively primitive beauty in this visible transformation of a town of scoundrels into a town of devils. For it is not in Khlestakov alone that we are supposed to glimpse demons, more and more distinctly as the play progresses, but also in the other characters, who represent human passions. "The Denouement of *The Inspector General*" specifically makes the point that the words "What are you laughing at? You're laughing at yourselves!" issue not merely from "a certain angry mayor" but from "the unclean spirit itself." Our chief concern, however, is not with this morbid dream that visited the poet after he had completed *The Inspector General*, but with *The Inspector General* itself as seen in full wakefulness.

Whatever kind of town this may be—whether of the external world or of the soul, whether palpable or immaterial (perhaps even both at the same time)—before us, in keeping with Gogol's design, is a town, in various senses. And if the artist, in looking long and hard into the image he has created, gradually discerns in it a "town of the soul" (the latter as a psychic unity of the multiform forces active in man), does this not mean that from the very beginning his formative idea was focused not on discrete comic masks, but rather on the collective persona of a social whole, united in the plurality of its individual manifestations?

III

THE THEORY OF UNIVERSAL LAUGHTER

Another theory devised by the apprehensive Gogol in an effort to justify his ambiguous gift of "comic power" (*vis comica*) was the magnificent theory of "universal laughter"; this new interpretation of *The Inspector General*, to which everyone lent an approving ear but whose music no one caught, again must be recognized as the idea of a great artist.

The laughter which Gogol makes his ally is not the heedless, unmindful laughter with which a pleasure-bent crowd accompanies the *peripetaeias* and witty sallies of the tame comedy. Such laughter does not, in a single harmonious eruption, coalesce people who are isolated one from the other and, however synchronous, it does not thunder with the triumphant affirmation of some positive principle that unites one and all. Gogol requires that the stage create an effect so powerful that "everything be shaken from bottom to top, turning into one feeling, one instant, one individual, that all people should meet, in one movement, as brothers" ("Leaving the Theater"). "Having flown on swans' wings across the dual boundary of space and the ages," our poet's imagination, hyperbolic as ever, bears him, unbeknownst to himself, into far-off times and far-off lands, where once there sparkled and sang another comedy with which a free people tested itself and forged its will.

For the poet, this laughter is a real character. "It is a strange thing," he wrote, "and I regret that nobody has noticed the one honest character in my play. Yes, there was one honest, noble character who was on stage from beginning to end. This honest, noble character was laughter" ("Leaving the Theater"). Of course it is a character: the collective character of a people conjoined in mind and spirit. One day the bright demon of laughter will rise to its full height, and great comedy will be reborn. "Laughter has been created for the purpose of laughing at everything that defiles man's true beauty. Let us restore to laughter its true significance!" ("The Denouement of *The Inspector General*").

Universal laughter is the salubrious, cathartic power of the Old Comedy: Gogol could have put his postulation in the language of the ancient estheticians. Aristotle came too late to experience this comedy psychologically, and he therefore knew the "cleansing" effect of only the tragic muse. "Only that which is gloomy can fill one with indignation; but laughter is bright. Much would fill man with indignation were it to be presented in all its starkness, but illumined by the power of laughter, it restores harmony to the soul" ("Leaving the Theater").

At whom, then, are the collectively laughing people laughing? At no one but themselves, upon seeing themselves as they are in the squalor of their wretched daily lives. "Let us laugh generously at our own vileness! . . . But let us grow indignant in spirit if any irate mayor, or, more accurately, if the unclean spirit himself should whisper through a mayor's lips: 'What are you laughing at? You're laughing at yourselves!' Let us say to him proudly:

'Yes, we are laughing at ourselves . . . because we hear a higher commandment that bids us be better than others' " ("The Denouement of *The Inspector General*").[4]

Let us acknowledge that in these eloquent paeans to the cleansing power of laughter not everything rings true and convincing to our ear; on the contrary, there is something false here, something sentimental, abstract, artificial. In discussing a question relating to the esthetic category of the forms of collective self-awareness, one cannot with impunity be merely a moralist. Gogol's ecstasy is always musical, his intellect moralistic. The Old Comedy of antiquity, which entertained no moralizing, was musical in form as well as in spirit. With this qualification made, let us endeavor to show that the Gogolian ideal of universal laughter comes very close to the objectives which the comedy of the fifth century B.C. set for itself and solved as simply as it did successfully.

IV

The Parabasis in *The Inspector General*

The Attic comedy developed out of a carnival-time custom, sanctioned and regularized by the laws of the republic in the form of public competitions set by the state, of humorous singing and declamation in the presence of the people assembled in the theater, with broad jokes and mocking, sometimes scoffing raillery directed at them as a collective persona, at their politics and their ways, their elected rulers and party leaders, their eminent, influential, or otherwise prominent figures.

This direct address to the people, which was given the name "parabasis," constituted the historically original nucleus of the comedy. Only very gradually did the parabasis come to be fleshed out by poetic fancy, personation, and a plot derived from the farce, which was topical in reference, fantastic in story-line, unrestrained and indecent in tone and manner. It is noteworthy that an essential and apparently indigenous peculiarity of the farce as performed on the stage (indicating its autonomous origin, independent of the parabasis) was a quarrel, a litigation, a fight, abuse on the part of two fiercely contending parties. The entire dramatic action was guided and segmented architectonically into scenes by a fantas-

[4 "Teatral'nyi raz"ezd posle predstavleniya novoi komedii," *PSS*, v, 1949, 169-170; "Razvyazka Revizora," *PSS*, iv, 1951, 132.]

tically or grotesquely garbed chorus—the chief participant in the improbable happening that was being depicted—which, at regular intervals, made utterances from the orchestra that were directly linked with the stages in the development of the story-line.

But at a fixed moment the comic action was suddenly broken off without having reached completion, the actors unexpectedly threw off the comic masks correspondent to their roles, and together with the chorus, which had reformed its ranks, began, to the sound of flutes, an aggressive advance upon the first few rows of spectators. Marching in military cadence, they moved hard upon them, and flung in their faces the searing verses of the abusive parabasis. They were answered, if not by whistling intermingled with oaths, then by the Homeric laughter of a sovereign people making sport of itself.

However, the citizens of Athens did not relish seeing these sometimes too open and explicit domestic scenes played out before alien eyes, before observers from the world outside; and the comic poet was well advised to move tactfully and to moderate his mockery, particularly at large festivals which brought an influx of foreigners. Generally speaking, a bold utterance and even success itself often cost the poet great unpleasantness: a fine, a political trial, or direct and dangerous retribution by the injured party. There was good reason why the young Aristophanes, at the outset of his career as a dramatist, should have hidden behind the well-known name of a fellow playwright, who was respected and therefore spared, and why he first appeared before the people under his own name only after securing the reliable protection of a powerful political corporation.

It suffices to recall these facts to see that Gogol's vision of universal laughter acting in judgment was not something utterly divorced from reality, albeit the reality of a world that is alien to us. More than that: it is not the incorporeal vision of the poet as such which is important to us, but rather his creation incarnate. And here, with a certain sense of surprise, we find in *The Inspector General* a remarkable rudiment of that very parabasis which was the distinguishing characteristic, the hallmark, as it were, of the Old Comedy of antiquity. For what else is that frenzied outburst of the mayor's, directed not so much at the characters around him on the stage as at the auditorium: "I can't see a thing. I can see what look like pig-snouts instead of faces, and nothing else. . . . Now look, just look, all the world, all good Christians: see what a fool they've made of the mayor. . . . And everybody will grin and clap their hands. . . . What are you laughing at? You're laughing at yourselves! Oh, you. . . ."

The impression that is deliberately created by this outburst corresponds, albeit in weaker measure, to the irritation aroused by the parabasis. For, after a new comedy had been performed, ancient Athens would of course hear the same sort of grumbling that issues from Semyon Semyonovich in "The Denouement of *The Inspector General*": "What disrespect! What cheek! I simply can't understand how anyone would dare say this to everyone's face . . . ," and the concurrence of Pyotr Petrovich: "These words did indeed produce a strange effect, and more than one member of the audience very likely had the impression that the author was directing these words at him personally."[5]

V

THE CHORAL PRINCIPLE IN *The Inspector General*

(The Old Comedy, in serving the needs of the community of citizens, required a chorus as an artistic expression of a social idea, as a symbol of the people themselves, who were regarding their own reflection in the glass of comedy; and it therefore rested wholly upon a choral underpinning.) In the fourth-century comedy, which had outlived the age of Greece's independence and had ceased to serve as the voice of a free democracy, the chorus systematically and rapidly degenerated into an ornamental appendage which uselessly retarded the movement of the play; ultimately it not only atrophied as an architectonic principle of form, but also died out as the vital nerve of the action.

When we evaluate *The Inspector General* as one of the links in the genealogical chain of literary history, we observe a powerfully rising wave of choral energy. This choral wave had long since passed from hearing, but now we can distinctly hear its urgent booming as it breaks. The entire town already stirs and buzzes in watchful waiting while the mayor is in consultation with the officials about the fateful visitor. The crowd gives insistent notice of itself, beginning with the third act: with a rumble it approaches the shoreline of the stage; at the end of the play it seems to loom directly before us; the indignant mayor addresses his accusatory

[5 "Razvyazka Revizora," *PSS*, IV, 1951, 124.]

monologue at this silently exultant crowd, and, through it, at us, as we indulge in carefree laughter.

Thus, *The Inspector General* constitutes an extremely rare exception in the modern drama by virtue of its forceful expression of the choral principle which, from time immemorial, has been lodged in and organically (though latently and passively) present in the dramatic action. It is redundant to insist that, in any stage-realization of the play which is artistically adequate to the creative design, this choral principle should be brought out accordingly.

Essentially, in speaking about the choral power of *The Inspector General* we are confirming, for the category of form, what has already been preindicated by our analysis of content. If the comedy is a portrayal of the town as a collective persona, then obviously its action rests—whether overtly or implicitly, but certainly wholly —upon a choral underpinning, as we have remarked about the comedy of Aristophanes.

The nature of the relationship between the chorus and the assembly of spectators is identical in the comedy of Gogol and of Aristophanes. The people of the comedic town, and we, the people who have gathered to watch the spectacle, are one and the same; for, in accord with the poet's intent, we are looking at ourselves in a mirror, and holding ourselves up to ridicule. Those masks on the stage are we ourselves, mummers representative of the groups to which we belong. Yet at the same time, we are different: we, the audience, overpass and transcend our masks, insofar as we recognize them as ourselves, and laugh at ourselves in them. But if we should forget, the actors will, at any moment, throw off their masks and appear before us as ourselves, and they will remind us, in a jeering parabasis, that they are we.

VI

The Chorus and the Hero

"Every work of art," we have written, "is the result of the inter-action, based on a mutual quest, of two principles: a material element, which is subject to transformation, and an effective (active) form, as an ideal image which works the transformation by putting its stamp upon the material element, insofar as the latter can accept it."[6]

[6] The pattern of relationships between the chorus and the hero, which is

In the art of the stage, the first principle—that is, the element that is to be fashioned—is not inert material, like the marble in sculpture, but a living human multitude. Therefore, in the art of the stage—as distinct from the other arts—the fashioning process can only be a free self-fashioning on the part of the collective. Inasmuch as the art of the stage, like music, is realized in time, the self-fashioning of the collective takes place before our eyes in the form of action. In order that this fashioning process be free, the initiative for it must arise spontaneously within the self-fashioning collective itself. The agent of this initiative is an individual who is singled out by the multitude. The name of the multitude, as a corporate, collective persona, is the chorus; the name of the significant individual is the hero.

"Heroism in the drama is the energy which the significant individual expends in effecting the reconstruction and inward change of a milieu which is in a steady state of equilibrium. He embodies the effective form, which acts upon the element that is to be transformed. The acceptance of or resistance to this activity on the part of the element constitutes the substance of dramatic action. Thus, the art of the stage is defined, with reference to the element that is to be transformed, as a mass, social, choric or collective dramatic action, whereas with reference to the form that effects the transformation, it is defined as an heroic dramatic action."[7]

The choric element is the flesh of the drama, the source of its inner health, the condition of its stability and vitality. When the choric element is strong, the drama has no need of a complicated plot (*The Inspector General*, for example, needs none), and gains instead in simplicity and power. As the choric element weakens, the tragedy becomes pathological (*Hamlet*) and the comedy anecdotal. Insofar as the chorus singles out the significant individual from its midst, the pattern of the drama is: as with the chorus, so with the hero.[8] The deeper and purer the shared consciousness, the nobler the collective persona of the chorus, then

---

only hastily sketched in the present article, is developed with the fulness it deserves in my article "The Norm of the Theater" ("Norma teatra," *Borozdy i mezhi*, Moscow, 1916, pp. 260-278).

[7] "Norma teatra," p. 262.

[8 The Russian here has, literally: "Insofar as the significant individual singles out the chorus from his midst," but this makes no sense in the context of Ivanov's argument, and I am assuming that there is a misprint. Just two letters in Russian make the difference.]

the loftier and more tragic is the hero in the daring of his lonely initiative. With a comic chorus, the tragic hero inevitably becomes comic himself, to a greater or lesser degree (e.g., Don Quixote).

"In the drama or comedy of everyday life, the concept of (choric) commonality coincides with the concept of everyday surroundings. The distinguishing feature of heroism and the distinguishing feature of commonality, respectively, are furthest apart, like height and depth, wherever the hero is exalted to the greatest possible degree; in proportion as the hero's personal initiative is lessened, they approach one another until they enter the realm of normal humanity and finally, of ordinary life. The point beyond which neither can approach any closer to the other is the interstitial or medial point between spiritual height and depth, the level of superficiality and mediocrity on which even the hero himself is merely the most insignificant of all the insignificant people in the world, the medium for some petty demon who is bent on aping an act of creative daring. . . ."[9] And behold: before us stands Khlestakov.

Such is the norm of the relationship between the hero and the chorus, which is inherent in the very nature of the drama and therefore shows forth in starkest colors in its early phase; its relative obscuration in the later theater is simply the consequence of this theater's original sin: betrayal of the chorus. When the foundations of the well-defined philosophy of life and the firm moral convictions of earlier times began to shake and totter in the minds of the Athenian people, and when their thoughts, bedimmed by the rantings of the Sophists, became like the clouds, then Aristophanes depicted a chorus of clouds and made their elected one the hero of his comedy: the arch-Sophist Socrates, the living emanation of empty, flatulent bombast which, being abstract and formless, could be shaped into any form of cloudiness.

Turning to *The Inspector General*, we see that the norm we have described above stands out in high relief in the play. We have before us a milieu which is in a steady state of equilibrium—a stagnant, lifeless swamp. Suddenly it is all set in motion by a significant, heroic individual. And everything therein undergoes change and reconstitution: there is a swampish doomsday and last judgment, even a swampish future life. In any event, the collective that appears in the epilogue of the play is not the same as the one that appears at the beginning.

[9] "Norma teatra," p. 266.

"But Ivan Alexandrovich Khlestakov," people will object, "is not 'singled out' by the town from its midst, but rather arrives in the town from the open spaces beyond. Like some deus ex machina he descends from the clouds and plops into a fetid swamp, splashing the turbid waters and churning up filth and impurities of every sort from the bottom." We will reply: Oedipus too came to Thebes as a wandering stranger, but he came—though unaware of it himself—because he was a Theban. Granting that Khlestakov falls from the clouds in order to stir up the swamp, these clouds are the miasma rising from the quagmire that is his home. No, he is no deus ex machina, but the very flesh and bone of the town, which has not only awaited him, but has even magically summoned him into being, breathing its mind and will into him. For he himself does not know who he is; the town, in an act of miracle-working faith, instills in him the idea that he is the "unknown emissary." It is significant that he has been staying at the inn behind the staircase "for about two weeks now," having arrived there on the feast-day of St. Basil the Egyptian (i.e., on February 28); and even in his wildest dreams he does not contemplate any "significant activity," but merely peers into other people's plates out of sheer hunger. He settles into the town easily, and almost puts down roots there, because he has always lived if not in this particular town, then in some other just like it. Although a stranger by passport, he is in his heart a native son. So far he offers only the potential and the raw material for creation; the actual work of creation is undertaken by the town itself, which before our very eyes fashions from him its significant individual, its hero, its "inspector general."

VII

A Possible Production of *The Inspector General*

In conclusion, a few hints at the possibilities of the kind of production of *The Inspector General* which would highlight the essential features that link the play with the great universal art of ages past, and not obscure those features, as has necessarily been (and still is) the case until now, given the usual practices of the stage, which were the only ones known even to Gogol himself.

But inasmuch as the production we have in mind is of a symbolic nature, as we have agreed here, and has absolutely nothing to do with what is called the realism of the stage, we must eliminate

212

one fundamental doubt. According to numerous directions given by Gogol, particularly in his letters, the actors, in performing *The Inspector General*, were to take scrupulous pains to avoid the conventions of comedy, in the style of playing as well as in the costumes and the makeup. The author forbids them the slightest exaggeration and demands complete verisimilitude. He would like a simple, thoughtful, and natural style of acting, and he seems to value fidelity to reality above everything else. That is all very well as regards the technique of acting; as regards the style of the production as a whole, Gogol's own manner of writing challenges these sober precepts. The rules urged upon the actors were apparently not binding up the poet. One thing that strikes us upon close study of *The Inspector General* is precisely the conventional comedy-device of the letter (which is superbly handled in its own right); and the artificial illumination from the footlights cannot conceal those brush-strokes that are intentionally farcical. Did Gogol think that it was incumbent on the actors to tone down rather than heighten those devices he permitted himself by way of comic caricature, buffoonery, and the violation of all measure of realism to the point of outright implausibility (and beyond)? Be that as it may, we in our time can no longer delude ourselves by giving the name of realism to something in· Gogol which, until very recently, was considered just that. And this unties our hands in the observations we are about to make.

Is it possible not to conceal (as is being done to this day) the collective persona, which is the sole subject of the play, not to hide it behind the masks of the individual characters, but rather to display the town itself, all of it, for everyone to see? It is possible, provided the wings and partitions are removed and the drama is reduplicated by representing, in a mystical way, everything that is happening off stage and is mentioned or implied in the dialogue. All this would take place on a large stage-area, where various structures would be situated in various places and would serve to focus the action of each scene, as was the case in medieval dramas. At stage center we would see the mayor's house, opening out to reveal a reception room, with a mezzanine which would serve as an observation-post for inquisitive ladies. Next to it, as a kind of wing to the house, would be the chamber reserved for the honored guest. Further off to one side we would see the colorful spectacle of the inn, and our eye would be able to penetrate into the cubbyhole behind the staircase. On the other side there would be a gloomy row of official buildings, the welfare institution with the patients in nightcaps, the post office, the school, the courthouse, and the jail.

At the edge of the stage, the merchants would be vending their wares, there would be a throng of common folk and peasants in from the countryside, and Derzhimorda would be looking after law and order. The stage would be framed by the houses of the gentry, with streets debouching from between them where Bobchinsky and Dobchinsky would dash out and disappear in search of news. Everything would be alive and in motion, at first according to the established order of things, and then slowly changing as the feeling of anxiety grew. And as everyone became more and more agitated, the molecular movements of the antheap would naturally merge into the mass actions of the mystical chorus.

It seems to us that we have made enough suggestions so that a detailed scenario could be created from them—or, rather, from what is in the actual text of the play. The reader who knows *The Inspector General* well, and who does not lack imagination, will not require any such scenario from us.

6

Vasily Gippius
(1890-1942)

ALTHOUGH he wrote verse in his early years and transfated a number of foreign poets (among them Horace, Novalis, Molière, and Heine), Gippius was primarily a scholar and critic of Russian literature. He took his degree at St. Petersburg University, taught at Perm, and later moved back to Leningrad, where he worked at the Institute of Russian Literature (Pushkin House) of the Academy of Sciences. He died during the German blockade of the city in World War II.

Gippius wrote extensively on nineteenth-century topics. But he was primarily interested in Gogol; and his book, entitled simply *Gogol* (1924), remains the single best monograph on the writer in any language. The essay translated here[1] is taken from a two-volume collection of original source materials and scholarly essays published in 1936 and edited by Gippius (*N. V. Gogol'. Materialy i issledovaniya*, Moscow-Leningrad).

In this article, Gippius, more than any other critic represented here, exploits one quality which the Russian language shares with German (but not with English or French): the capacity to form an abstract noun from practically any substantive, and often, through an array of suffixes, to carry it to higher and higher levels of abstraction. This sometimes makes it difficult to know exactly what Gippius is saying. Such imprecision no doubt had certain advantages for a Russian writing in the Stalin period who touched on matters of Marxist ideology. In most such cases I have tried (often through paraphrase) to set Gippius firmly on the bedrock of the more concrete, English-language way of thinking. Yet I have hoped to preserve some of the flavor of this curiously abstract style, which is characteristic of much critical writing in Russia during the 1930's, 1940's and early 1950's. I have also made considerable revisions in the first few pages for the benefit of non-specialists.

[1] The Russian title is "Problematika i kompozitsiya 'Revizora.' "

215

The Inspector General: Structure and Problems

by Vasily Gippius

I

IN "An Author's Confession" (1847), Gogol looked back over his career and identified 1836 as a major turning-point. Up to that time, he said, he had tried to combine two antithetical elements in his art: the lyrical and the comic. But then he began to feel the need of moving on to something new: comedy of a *serious* nature. Everything written according to the old method he now saw as the expression of a purely psychological process within himself—an alternation between "melancholy" and "merriment"—whereas this new shift toward "serious comedy" was bound up, in his mind, with a sense of social mission. As he put it: "I was assailed by attacks of melancholy. In order to amuse myself, I would invent all the funny things I possibly could. . . . But Pushkin made me take a serious look at the matter. . . . I perceived that in my works I had been laughing to no purpose, in vain, without knowing why myself. If you must laugh, then it is better to have a good hearty laugh at something that is really worthy of general derision. In *The Inspector General* I decided to take everything bad that I knew about Russia at that time and bring it all together into one heap."[1]

But alternation of another sort can be found in Gogol's earlier works too—between "innocent, carefree scenes," as he put it, and satire. Gogol was not aware that this alternation reflected the contradiction inherent in a specific social group—the one which, after the failure of the Decembrist revolt of 1825, occupied an intermediate position between the conservative and apolitical majority of the patriarchal gentry, on the one hand, and the free-thinking

[1 The first version of *The Inspector General* was completed and staged in 1836. Gogol's account of the "change" in outlook which supposedly induced him to write the play is contained in "An Author's Confession," written more than ten years later (1847) and published after his death. The words and phrases in quotation marks are from this "confession." Cf. "Avtorskaya ispoved'," *PSS*, VIII, 1952, 439-440.]

elements of the radicalized gentry and bourgeoisie on the other.[2]

This same point (or one very much like it) can be made with regard to many individuals who were active in literature in the 1830's. Some of them, like Gogol himself, were affiliated with Pushkin's journal *The Contemporary*, and some with *The Moscow Observer*. In general terms, the same thing holds true for Pushkin as well (during the later period of his life); at one point he and Gogol were very close to one another ideologically (despite their many undoubted differences as individuals). The particulars of this closeness cannot be successfully explained (as some critics attempt to do) by blindly and arbitrarily assigning each of them to diametrically opposed groups of the gentry (Pushkin to the aristocrats and Gogol to the small landowners), or by making an equally over-simplified contrast between Pushkin as a member of the "liberal gentry" and Gogol as a member of the "reactionary gentry" (without taking account of the way Gogol's ideology developed).[3]

Significantly, it was Pushkin with whom Gogol associated the new direction taken by his art: "But Pushkin made me take a serious look at the matter." However, the statements contained in "An Author's Confession" require elaboration. The "shift"

[2 The Decembrists were the first of many revolutionary groups in nineteenth-century Russia. They were composed largely of officers from the gentry; their program included the abolition of serfdom and the introduction of a constitution. An attempted uprising in St. Petersburg, in December 1825, was a disastrous failure. Gippius's jargon here honors the Marxist view of the Decembrists as "the first page of the bourgeois revolution in Russia" ("Dekabristy," *Bol'shaya sovetskaya entsiklopediya*, Vol. 21, Moscow, 1931, p. 54).]

[3 *The Contemporary* (*Sovremennik*), one of the most distinguished Russian journals of the nineteenth century, was founded by Pushkin in 1836, and edited by him until his death the following year; it was then taken over by P. A. Pletnyov, one of Gogol's closer friends. It continued publication until 1866, when it was closed down by the censor. *The Moscow Observer* (*Moskovskii nablyudatel'*) came out twice a month between 1835 and 1839. V. P. Androsov was the editor until 1837; S. P. Shevyryov was the leading critic; as Gippius makes clear farther on, the two had very different views of the merits of Gogol at this time.

The "aristocrat"/"petty landowner" distinction may be regarded as an "ideological" version of the Pushkin/Gogol contrast (see the introduction). It was rather a commonplace in nineteenth-century criticism. By his last remark Gippius presumably means that as Gogol grew older he became increasingly conservative and finally ended up a reactionary although he had been more "liberal" in his youth, i.e., while Pushkin was still alive (before 1837).]

cannot be pinpointed so precisely and unequivocally as it is by Gogol in his attempt (conscious or not) to reorder the facts of the past. *Dead Souls* was begun in 1835, at Pushkin's urging; but in that same year, both *Mirgorod* and *Arabesques* (containing the so-called Petersburg stories) appeared; and Gogol's statement about laughter intended purely to amuse himself is clearly inapplicable to these two books. In fact, Pushkin's famous characterization of Gogol's art as laughter "through ·tears of sadness and tender emotion" referred specifically to the story "Old-Fashioned Landowners" (in *Mirgorod*), and Belinsky made his even more apt and accurate characterization—"laughter diluted with bitterness" ("you smile so bitterly and sigh so sadly when you come to the tragi-comic denouement")—mainly with reference to "Diary of a Madman" (*Arabesques*) and "The Two Ivans" (*Mirgorod*). These formulations were made before *The Inspector General* appeared; they did in fact correspond to the realities of Gogol's art as well as to the image he had of himself at the time. In a letter written in 1833, Gogol made the following comment on his play *The Order of Vladimir, Third Class*, which he had begun the previous year—i.e., three years *before* he wrote *The Inspector General*: "And how much anger there is! Laughter! Pungency! . . . But what is a comedy without truth and anger!"[4]

[4 "Petersburg stories" is not actually a title. It is a term used by critics to refer to those stories by Gogol that are set in St. Petersburg: "Nevsky Prospect," "The Nose," "Diary of a Madman," "The Portrait," and "The Overcoat."]

Letter to M. Pogodin, February 20 (o.s.), 1833. [Pushkin's remark is found in his review of the second edition of *Evenings on a Farm Near Dikanka*, in *Sovremennik*, No. 1, 1836; Belinsky's are in "O russkoi povesti i povestyakh g. Gogolya ('Arabeski' i 'Mirgorod')," *Polnoe sobranie sochinenii*, I, Moscow, 1953, 297-298. The quotation in parentheses actually refers to "The Two Ivans."]

[Gogol's account of Pushkin's "urging" him to write *Dead Souls* is found in "An Author's Confession," and runs as follows: "For a long time he had even been trying to persuade me to undertake a large work, and finally, on one occasion, after I had read him a small description of a small scene, but one which, nonetheless, struck him more than anything I had read to him before that, he said to me: 'With this gift for seeing into people and depicting them fully and completely in just a few strokes—with this gift it is simply a sin not to undertake a large work!' Then he began to talk about my weak constitution, my illnesses which might cut my life short early, and he cited Cervantes as an example: although he certainly had written very remarkable and good stories, if he had not produced *Don Quixote* he would never have occupied the place he now does among writers;

And so, the service that Chernyshevsky thought Gogol had performed for Russian literature—"bringing the satirical, or, as it is more accurately termed, the critical tendency unequivocally into Russian literature"—certainly does not date from *The Inspector General*, but, at the very latest, from Gogol's two books of the preceding year.[5] However, even if we confine "inoffensive laughter" to the period when Gogol was writing *Evenings on a Farm Near Dikanka*, we must also make some qualifications. Evidence of a critical attitude toward the world is not wholly absent from these stories either, no matter how far their lyrical and fairy-tale atmosphere may remove them from reality. Examples are: the disapproval shown toward the older generation, which is contrasted with an active and intelligent younger generation; the hostile attitude toward the power of "gold" as destructive of the old patriarchal mores ("St. John's Eve"); the theme of nationalistic political opposition to the central government (the scene where Catherine the Great meets with the Zaporozhian Cossacks, in "Christmas Eve"); and anti-Polish sentiments—very much alive and to the point in 1831—in "A Terrible Vengeance."[6] In other words, the contradictions in Gogol's class ideology, as we have described them, are evident as early as his first book.

These remarks do not invalidate but rather amplify the statements about laughter that Gogol made much later in "An Author's Confession." He was describing the general *direction* taken by his work, as he remembered it: the withering of comedy for comedy's sake, and the development of comedy with a serious purpose.[7]

---

and in conclusion, he gave me a plot of his own, from which he himself had wanted to make a kind of long poem, and which, in his words, he would not have given to anyone else. This was the plot of *Dead Souls*. (The idea of *The Inspector General* was also his.)" ("Avtorskaya ispoved'," *PSS*, VIII, 1952, 439-440.)]

[5 "Ocherki Gogolevskogo perioda russkoi literatury," *Polnoe sobranie sochinenii*, III, Moscow, 1947, 18.

[6 The issue was alive because of the Polish Insurrection of 1830, against the Russians: in the eighteenth century Poland had been partitioned among Prussia, Austria, and Russia.]

7 In the variant of "An Author's Confession" entitled "Art Is a Reconciliation With Life," Gogol stated this matter in a different way: not a word is said here about Pushkin; the shift (which is dated from *The Inspector General* here as well) is attributed to the impressions created by reviews of his earlier works. "My laughter was at first good-natured; I had no intention of ridiculing anything with any purpose in mind; and when I heard that entire groups and classes were offended and even angry with

Without trying in any way to belittle Pushkin's advice that Gogol should "take a serious look at things," we must say that it virtually coincided with the direction which Gogol himself was following and which was being urged on him by his critics. In any event, Gogol's later appraisal of his art—"I perceived that in my works I was laughing to no purpose, in vain"—fundamentally tallies with the opinion that Nikolay Polevoy expressed in 1832 about the second part of *Evenings on a Farm Near Dikanka*: "His jokes pass by quickly; the comparisons, the contrivances, the main ideas leave no trace in the reader's mind."[8]

The literary tradition was also relevant to Gogol's attitude toward his comedies. He aimed at extricating Russian comedy from a cul-de-sac and bringing about its renewal. That this was a task he *deliberately* set for himself is attested to by S. T. Aksakov's memoirs (*History of My Friendship with Gogol*), by Gogol's letter to Pogodin concerning *The Order of Vladimir, Third Class*, which we have just mentioned, by his articles "The St. Petersburg Stage" and "St. Petersburg Notes," and, even much later, by the essay "On the Theater," in *Selected Passages from Correspondence with Friends*. Gogol was not the only one who had a low opinion of the comedy of his day—and of the drama in general—and who saw the need for decisive change. *The Moscow Telegraph* wrote in 1831 that: "Our dramatic literature is in great decline. . . . None of the young writers for the stage shows any outstanding gifts, and the old ones seem to have grown weary."[9] Two years later the same journal wrote, with regard to Griboyedov's *Woe from Wit* (which in its opinion had no successors): "It is time to revive the splendid

---

me, I was so astonished that at last I began to ponder the matter. 'If the power of laughter is so great that people are afraid of it, then it should not be expended to no purpose.' I made up my mind to bring together everything bad that I was familiar with, and to ridicule everything at one fell swoop—this was the origin of *The Inspector General*." Of course, this statement is not entirely accurate either. Belinsky's formulation can serve as a corrective to Gogol's statement that "my laughter was at first good-natured": "a humor that is quiet in its very indignation and good-natured in its very slyness" ["O russkoi povesti . . . ," p. 299]. [Gogol's statements are actually contained in a letter to V. A. Zhukovsky, January 10, 1848. But at the end, Gogol says that if Zhukovsky finds that the letter has merit, he should keep it and include it in the second edition of *Selected Passages from Correspondence with Friends*, in place of "A Testament," entitling it "Art Is a Reconciliation With Life." This was not done.]

[8] *Moskovskii telegraf*, No. 6, 1832.

[9] *Moskovskii telegraf*, No. 10, 1831, p. 259.

art of the drama."[10] Belinsky raised the question in the same terms in his article "Literary Reveries" (1834): "Where is our dramatic literature, where are our dramatic talents? Where are the writers of tragedies, of comedies? There are many, a great many; their names are familiar to everyone, and I will therefore not enumerate them"—following which come ironic compliments to these many and then a discussion of Griboyedov.[11]

After abandoning *The Order of Vladimir, Third Class*, a comedy full of "truth and anger," after working for a long time on the comparatively "innocent" theme of *Marriage*, but failing to bring the play to completion, Gogol moved on to *The Inspector General*, where his originality as a dramatist revealed itself in full measure.[12]

II

The distinctive features of the complex of social problems treated in *The Inspector General* can be seen only when the play is set against its immediate predecessors in the Russian drama. Certain genres which made up much of the comic repertoire of Gogol's time could not, by their very nature, accommodate social problems. These were the so-called vaudevilles and vaudeville comedies. Individual variants aside, all such plays aimed at stimulating "light laughter" (to use Gogol's expression), paid a minimum of attention to character (which was usually reduced to a single comic attribute), and honored the principle that no political or social inferences needed to be or should be drawn from the contents of the play (which in any event were always very meager). This "negative" ideology gave something in common to otherwise very different kinds of comedies, such as Nikolay Khmelnitsky's "high-society" vaudevilles (deriving from Collin d'Harleville), and the "bourgeois-realistic" vaudevilles of the Russian translators and imitators of Scribe. It must be remembered that for several years before the appearance of *The Inspector General*, original Russian comedies amounted to nothing more than vaudevilles. The Russian vaudeville, in the two basic variants we have mentioned, catered to

[10] *Moskovskii telegraf*, No. 18, 1833, p. 247.

[11] "Literaturnye mechtaniya," *Polnoe sobranie sochinenii*, I, Moscow, 1953, 81.]

[12] In fact, *Marriage* was originally entitled *The Suitors* (*Zhenikhi*); the play was abandoned, and later revised and completed under the title *Marriage* (*Zhenit'ba*).]

aristocratic society, which deliberately averted its eyes from social problems, and also to the culturally backward elements of the bourgeoisie and the gentry, which had not yet developed to the point where they could perceive such problems. Gogol himself defined the poetics of the vaudeville in an article entitled "The St. Petersburg Stage in the 1835-36 Season." There is no question that the examples of "light" and "banal" laughter that he cites disapprovingly apply to both basic varieties of vaudeville: "not the laughter which is generated by the quick witticism and the fleeting pun and makes only faint impressions on our minds; (2) not the banal laughter which can be produced only by convulsions and distortions of nature and which moves the vulgar mass of society."[13] These opinions did not stop him from using certain features of vaudeville technique for his own purposes; but he did consider that the specifically social element of the drama was something quite contrary to the vaudeville tradition.

At the same time, another kind of comedy appeared and developed quite naturally along with the comedy of light laughter which distracted people from the realities of their times. It affirmed the moral values of the conservative landowning class, had at its basis the idealization of the large landed estate and the good old patriarchal way of life, and condemned spendthrifts, prodigals, and "infection" from abroad (especially such consequences as harebrained innovations of one sort or another that tinkered dangerously with the status quo). Examples were the comedies of Shakhovskoy and Zagoskin—*A Parvenu's Fancies, Mr. and Mrs. Emptyhouse*, and *Mr. Richman*.[14] Here the Molière type of bour-

[13 The titles may be confusing. Originally Gogol wrote two articles, "St. Petersburg and Moscow" ("Peterburg i Moskva") and "The St. Petersburg Stage in the 1835-36 Season" (Peterburgskaya stsena 1835/36 gg."), but then he brought them together and published them under the title "St. Petersburg Notes of 1836" ("Peterburgskie zapiski 1836 goda"). See also footnote 21. Gippius quotes here from the manuscript version of "The St. Petersburg Stage. . . ."]

[14 Mikhail Nikolayevich Zagoskin (1789-1852) was a writer of comedies, as Gippius indicates, but was most famous for his historical novel in the manner of Sir Walter Scott, *Yury Miloslavsky* (1829), which concerns the Polish occupation of Moscow in 1812. His plays, *A Parvenu's Fancies* and *Mr. and Mrs. Emptyhouse*, are entitled in Russian, respectively, *Polubarskie zatei* and *Pustodomy*. Alexander Alexandrovich Shakhovskoy (1777-1846) was a prolific playwright and a dedicated anti-Romantic. There are actually two "Richman" ("Bogatonov") plays: *Richman, or A Provincial in the Capital (Bogatonov, ili provintsial v stolitse*, 1817) and *Richman in the Country, or A Surprise for Himself (Bogatonov v derevne, ili syurpriz*

geois was moved into the ranks of the gentry and accordingly was transformed into a parvenu trying to climb his way into high society or into the lofty spheres of intellectual life. It is worth noting, however, that the authors invariably took a lenient attitude toward their errant class-brethren. The virtuous characters, who are also exemplary proprietors—for example, Squire Miroslavsky (in *Mr. Richman*) or General Radimov (in *Mr. and Mrs. Empty-house*)—are introduced not only as dei ex machinis, but also for the purpose of bringing about a moral reformation of the heroes by taking them away from the temptations of the capital and high society and returning them "to the soil," where they can do their duty as landowners. Later, in *Dead Souls* and *Selected Passages from Correspondence with Friends*, Gogol showed that he was very much aware of this particular category of social and moral problems, which were rather common in those years. But in the mid-1830's, they evidently held absolutely no interest for him. He remained relentlessly indifferent to the work of Shakhovskoy and Zagoskin, the leading practitioners of Russian comedy from around 1810 to the 1830's—so much so that he makes no mention at all of them in his articles on "The St. Petersburg Stage" and in "St. Petersburg Notes." S. T. Aksakov, in his memoirs, makes a direct connection between Gogol's intention of renewing Russian comedy and his desire to move away from Zagoskin ("Gogol praised him for the merry quality of his work, but said that he did not write what was needed, especially for the theater. . . . From what he said subsequently I observed that he was very much interested in the Russian comedy and had his own original views on it").[15] Gogol's later essay on poetry, in *Selected Passages*, tends to be dispassionate in its opinions; but even here he limits

---

samomu sebe, 1821). Nikolay Ivanovich Khmelnitsky, mentioned in the preceding paragraph, lived between 1789 and 1846, and was well known as a writer of comedies and vaudevilles, most of them translated from the French.]

[15 *Istoriya moego znakomstva s Gogolem*, Moscow, 1960, pp. 11-12.] The draft of Gogol's review of Zagoskin's play *The Dissatisfied Ones* (*Nedovol'nye*)—a comedy which, incidentally, is not very characteristic of him and which was clearly a failure—reproaches the author for a weak "plan," a lack of action, a lack of comicality and of natural characters. [*PSS*, VIII, 1952, 200.] Pushkin disapproved of the play for exactly the same reasons ["Komediya Zagoskina 'Nedovol'nye'," as in *Polnoe sobranie sochinenii v desyati tomakh*, VII, Moscow, 1958, 324-325]. For a comparison of the two reviews, see my article "Literaturnoe obshchenie Gogolya s Pushkinym," *Uchenye zapiski Permskogo Gosudarstevennogo Universiteta*, No. 2, 1931.

himself to a glancing mention of Zagoskin and Shakhovskoy, as two among several writers of comedies, and sets all of them radically apart from Fonvizin and Griboyedov.[16]

This attempt to move away from Zagoskin, and thereby from Shakhovskoy as well, gave Gogol something in common with the progressive literary critics of his time. A reviewer in *The Moscow Telegraph* ironically tied Zagoskin and Shakhovskoy together in the monogram SHZ. "I would buy Diderot's *Memoirs* or a new comedy by Griboyedov without so much as glancing at them, and, if need be, I'd pay a ransom in order to avoid buying the memoirs of Mr. X. or the latest comedy by SHZ."[17]

Griboyedov's *Woe from Wit* was still a thoroughly live issue at the beginning of the 1830's, when it was being performed and published for the first time. It stirred up a controversy; its basic ideas were subject to varying interpretations, often contradictory and blatantly partisan. Nikolay Nadezhdin, writing in 1831, attempted to dispose of the play's satirical element as amounting to nothing more than a picture of "good old Moscow, with its eccentricities, quirks, and caprices."[18] But progressive bourgeois criticism—which in those years was represented by Polevoy's journal *The Moscow Telegraph*—emphasized that Griboyedov's characters were contemporaries, described them as "members of high society," and, a few lines later, defined them as "ignoramuses and scoundrels." To put it another way: by distorting the meaning of *Woe from Wit*, Nadezhdin tried to place Griboyedov on the same footing with Shakhovskoy and Zagoskin, whereas Polevoy—or his collaborators—tried to bring out the real import of the play as a satire and exposé. But the breadth, acuity and unprecedented originality of Griboyedov's comedy became evident precisely when it was set against the "norm" of the "gentry" comedies of Shakhovskoy and Nadezhdin. Griboyedov used a two-pronged device—the authorial voice as represented in Chatsky's speeches, and the actions and sentiments of the other characters—to expose and pass sentence on the phenomena typical not only of social life, but of the social and political views of the dominant elements

[16] "V chem zhe nakonets sushchestvo russkoi poezii i v chem ee osobennost'," *Vybrannye mesta iz perepiski s druz'yami*, PSS, VIII, 1952, 396.]

[17] *Moskovskii telegraf*, No. 12, 1832, review of Ushakov, *Dosugi invalida*.

[18] Nikolay Ivanovich Nadezhdin (1804-1856) was editor of a major journal, *The Telescope* (*Teleskop*), and an important critic and theorist, who believed that literature must be "national" and must convey ideas. Hereby he anticipated Belinsky.]

of the gentry as well. The only possible source of such an attitude could have been the ideology of the revolutionary-minded gentry of the pre-Decembrist period.

Gogol's attitudes were quite different from Griboyedov's, and in general, he made only a feeble response in those years to the problems that were of such concern to Griboyedov and the Decembrists—problems that bore on the relationships between landowners and serfs, the caste-stratification of the gentry, the role of those groups within the gentry which belonged to the court and the military establishment, and the attitude which culturally advanced groups took toward each of these social castes. Characteristically, in his account of *Woe from Wit* (which to be sure was made in his later years), Gogol saw the play as nothing more than a satire on the so-called Demi-Enlightenment, and admitted that he did not understand the positive idea it was advancing ("the audience is still bewildered as to what a Russian should be").[19] But, no less characteristically, his objections to *Woe from Wit* never became objections to the genre, as such, of the comedy of social satire. On the contrary: in this same article, and on the same grounds, he emphasized the significance of a comedy that exposes "the wounds and ailments of our society, its grave internal abuses." The statement he made in "An Author's Confession" about his own work as a writer of comedy was fully in accord with this: "In *The Inspector General* I decided to take everything bad that I knew about Russia at that time and bring it all together into one heap—all the injustices that are perpetrated in those situations and circumstances where justice, above all, is required of men— and to laugh at all of them at once."[20]

And this was not just an afterthought (even though it dates from 1847). The article entitled "The St. Petersburg Stage in the 1835-36 Season" was written immediately after the premiere of *The Inspector General* and served in large measure as a commentary on the play. Here Gogol makes it incumbent on the theater to "note the general elements of our society, its moving springs,"

[19 The article in question is "V chem zhe nakonets sushchestvo russkoi poezii i v chem ee osobennost'," *Vybrannye mesta iz perepiski s druz'yami, PSS*, VIII, 1952, 396-402. "Demi-Enlightenment" renders *Poluprosveshchenie*. The usual term is *poluintelligent* ("demi-intellectual"), or *poluintelligentsia*. In any event, the reference is to people who have only superficial knowledge and polish.]

[20 "Avtorskaya ispoved'," *PSS*, VIII, 1952, 440.]

225

to bring onto the stage the "weeds" which "make it impossible for decent people to live and which no law can watch after," to "expose low vice and unworthy weaknesses and habits in the various strata of our society." The enumeration of these particular objectives gives greater precision to the definition of the genre of high comedy with which the article opens ("there is high comedy, a true copy of the society that is in motion before our eyes, a comedy that stimulates laughter by the depth of its irony," etc.).[21] This definition fully coincided with the concept of the "comedy of civilization" ("in which family man yields to social man") put forth (specifically with reference to *The Inspector General*) by V. P. Androsov, who was sympathetically disposed toward Gogol.[22]

Gogol's retrospective view of his literary career, as well as the plays he actually wrote, indicates that for him social problems occupied a position midway, as it were, between Shakhovskoy and Zagoskin on the one hand, and Griboyedov on the other. "The wounds and ailments of society," "weeds," "low vice," etc.— such concepts, as Gogol thought of them, amounted to much more than merely an aggregation of shortcomings of the kind exemplified by the landowners in Shakhovskoy and Zagoskin; yet they did not lead to the fundamental re-evaluations, the free-thinking on matters of principle, which were embedded in *Woe from Wit*.

III

It was not the theme of the Russian landowner (the landholding proprietor) that was central to Gogol's view of contemporary life

---

[21] In the published version of "St. Petersburg Notes," which also included material from the article on the St. Petersburg stage, there is a considerable toning-down of these agitated statements, which were written while the impressions of the polemics concerning *The Inspector General* were still fresh in Gogol's mind. This also explains the appeals to the monarch (which are omitted in the published text) and the general tone of self-defensiveness against attacks from the right. In "St. Petersburg Notes" only the basic conclusions about the significance of laughter and the significance of the theater as a school are preserved; but the words in quotation marks, which define the social mission of the theater more precisely, either disappeared or (as, for example, the last one) were reworked. The epithet "*high* comedy," for one, disappeared. This must be explained by the fact that Gogol's intense interest in matters of the theater and drama cooled as his preoccupation with his own personal problems drastically increased during his "emigration" [i.e., during his years abroad, largely in Rome].

[22] *Moskovskii Nablyudatel'*, May, 1836, Part 7, p. 122. A little farther on we also find the term "social comedy" (used in connection with *Tartuffe*).

in the mid-1830's, but rather the theme of the Russian official, as either a potentially positive or potentially negative force, as one who either fulfils or neglects his social duty. This theme was meant to run throughout *The Order of Vladimir, Third Class*, a play Gogol never finished. It was also touched upon in individual motifs in *Marriage*, and especially in the so-called Petersburg stories ("Diary of a Madman," "The Nose").[23] In equating the concept of service to the state with the concept of social duty, Gogol was attempting to make a great social problem out of the theme of the machinery of government (which was represented by local government in his works, but which referred by extension to the central government as well).[24] This problem could have been formulated in exactly the same terms that Belinsky used in his 1847 letter on *Selected Passages* (the so-called Salzbrunn letter), where he called for "the strictest possible observance of those laws that already exist" as one of the three points of his minimal program for a decent Russian government.[25] The natural inference to be drawn from this particular demand was that the whole existing machinery of government needed to be reformed. In Belinsky's program of 1847, this was the most modest of the three points put forward; in Gogol's program of 1836, it was perhaps the boldest; but as a corrective to the customary practice of radically dissociating the author of *The Inspector General* from his audience, we should remember the statement that Gogol made in a letter to Pogodin: "Or perhaps I don't know what councilors are, from titular to actual privy ones?"[26]

[23 See footnote 4.]

[24] Cf. A. V. Nikitenko's comment on *The Inspector General*: "Gogol has really accomplished something important. The impression created by his comedy adds a great deal to the impressions that are being built up in people's minds by the prevailing order of things here" (*Zapiski*, Part 1, 2nd ed., p. 274). [Alexander Vasilievich Nikitenko (1804-1877) was a serf by origin, who got a university education and became prominent as a journalist, editor, and especially a censor (working on Gogol's manuscripts, among others). He is now best remembered for his *Diary* (*Dnevnik*, 3 vols.).]

[25 Letter to Gogol, as in Gogol, *PSS*, VIII, 1952, 502.]

[26 March 30, 1837.]

As a counterweight to the widespread tendency to make Gogol's ideology all of a piece, let us cite a well-known statement (although forgotten in the critical literature on Gogol) by P. V. Annenkov (a very reliable witness) concerning Gogol during the first half of the 1830's: "For him, Walter Scott was not the representative of protectionist principles and of affectionate attachment to the past that he was made out to be in European literary criticism; such ideas did not stir the slightest response in Gogol at that

Gogol's negative attitudes were fed not only by the relatively small transitional group of the moderately liberal gentry, but also by the broader circles of the cultivated bourgeoisie and petty bourgeoisie. It is important to understand Gogol's attitude toward this socially heterogeneous group, particularly because it was from them (along with an element of the déclassé gentry) that the ranks of the civil service were filled, primarily on the lower levels. It is important to determine whether Gogol saw the problem of the civil-servant group merely as one component of the problem of the gentry in general; whether his satire, on the one hand, was purely didactic with respect to those elements of the bureaucracy who came from the gentry, and whether, on the other hand, it was motivated by a feeling of class antagonism toward the humbler civil servants who were not of gentle birth. But this would be an oversimplified and essentially mechanistic interpretation of Gogol's position: it would not correspond with what he actually was doing in his writings, or with his own explicit statements on the matter. In the 1830's, Gogol not only was objectively at one with the progressive democratic bourgeoisie, but subjectively, too, he revealed that his outlook on society was comparatively broad. It was only in the 1840's that he became firmly committed to his feudalistic system, according to which society (actual and ideal) is depicted as a dual organism: landowner, on the one hand, and peasant, on the other.[27]

It is not legitimate to attribute this system to Gogol in the 1830's. At that time, neither the peasantry nor the landowning gentry, as classes, held any attraction for him either as an artist or as a thinker. Gogol had as yet developed no well-ordered general sociological system. Rather, he viewed society as a kind

---

time. . . . During this period Gogol was more inclined toward justifying a break with the past and toward making innovations . . . than toward explaining the old or trying to revive it artificially. . . . The only things that came out constantly in his conversation during those years was his striving for originality, for building knowledge and art on different foundations from the existing ones, *for creating ideals of life by means of abstract logical thought, etc.*" (*Literaturnye vospominaniya*, Leningrad, 1928, p. 59; italics supplied).

[27 In Marxist jargon "objective" refers to things as they really are (i.e., as determined by history) and "subjective" to things as an individual thinks they are. Often the two coincide, as Gippius insists they do here. The word "mechanistic" means "undialectical," i.e., un-Marxist. One example of Gogol's "system" can be seen in the letter entitled "The Russian Landowner," in *Selected Passages from Correspondence with Friends* ("Russkii pomeshchik," *Vybrannye mesta* . . . , *PSS*, VIII, 1952, 321-328).]

of loose conglomeration of various "estates" or "classes," and his sympathies lay somewhere between the two extremes (cf. a letter of February 1 [o.s.], 1833, to Pogodin: "The higher and more noble a class, the more stupid it is"). Of great importance is the defense of the "middle estate" which is chronologically and even thematically connected with *The Inspector General*, inasmuch as it was introduced into his article on "The St. Petersburg Stage in the 1835-36 Season": "If we take, for example, our middle estate as a whole—that is, the estate which has little money or lives on a salary and is therefore the most numerous and most purely Russian estate—then we see that it has many remarkable features (never mind that here and there we find a clerk who is absolutely like the document he is copying): the resoluteness of the Russian gentry and, at the same time, patience, sense, and pungency—in a word, the elements of a new character."[28] Very significantly, it is not the two basic classes of serf-society (landowners and peasants) that Gogol endows with purely Russian characteristics, but rather, the "middle estate"; significantly, too, he equates its desirable qualities with those of the "gentry."

In trying to define the social physiognomy of the groups to which Gogol actually belonged and those toward which he gravitated, and in trying to bring out the main features of their critical attitude toward their times, we must remember that no social and political ideology of a *positive* nature had been adequately formulated in the minds of the majority of even the advanced representatives of the groups in question. The same thing holds true for Gogol himself: his ideology expressed itself in the general truths of his art, which were *negative*. However, even these negative truths provide a basis for determining Gogol's class attitude toward his subject-matter.

IV

A rough general formulation of the concept of life that is reflected in Gogol's writings of the 1830's would be: "confusion." What

[28 "Estate" renders the Russian *soslovie*. The estate system developed over a long period, but was finally codified under Catherine the Great. There were basically four divisions: the gentry, the clergy, the peasantry, and the town-dwellers (subdivided into merchants and lower middle class—*meshchane.*) Membership in an estate was determined largely by inheritance and sometimes by a special legal act, and entailed certain privileges (mainly for the gentry) and duties (mainly for the others).]

gives Gogol's stories their impact as exposés is precisely their portrayal of reality as a tangled web of misunderstandings, in which nothing is located where it should be. Self-satisfied vulgarians and "kind-hearted beasts," who contribute, all unsuspectingly, to this general confusion, are the butts of Gogol's laughter.[29] Those who are endowed with somewhat greater awareness lose their minds, like Poprishchin ("Diary of a Madman"), or perish, like Piskaryov ("Nevsky Prospect"); it is the philistines like Pirogov (also "Nevsky Prospect") who flourish. This persistent return to the theme of confusion (which is carried to a grotesque extreme in "The Nose") constitutes both Gogol's strength and his weakness. It is a strength because his realistic method enabled him to reflect the actual contradictions in the society of his time. It is a weakness because even though he reached the point where he could observe "confusion" and understand its tragi-comic nature, he could not explain why it existed. The remark that Chernyshevsky made about the Gogol of this period remains valid: "He was struck by the ugly disorder of things and expressed his indignation about them; but he did not give much thought to the sources of those things, or to the connection between that area of life which contained those things and other areas of intellectual, moral, civic, and governmental life."[30] In attempting to account for the "confusion" of life, Gogol confined himself to metaphysical explanations and an appeal to mysterious, other-worldly powers. An example can be seen in the closing words of the narrator of "Nevsky Prospect," which are comical on the surface: "How wondrously our world is arranged! . . . How strange and incomprehensible are the games that fate plays with us! . . . Everything happens the other way around. . . ."

The Inspector General offers a new variation on this same theme of confusion. The basic situation, as set forth in the first act, shows people who are occupying positions for which they are not suited—self-satisfied philistines on whom the destinies and the very lives of people depend ("injustices that are perpetrated in places and situations where justice, above all, is required of men"). Then a new, and this time intentional, "confusion" appears and

[29 "Kind-hearted beast" is what Gogol calls his hero (later Akaky Akakievich) in the first draft of "The Overcoat."]

[30 Review of *Sochineniya i pis'ma N. V. Gogolya*, ed. P. A. Kulish, 6 vols., St. Petersburg, 1857-58, *Polnoe sobranie sochinenii*, IV, Moscow, 1948, 632.]

grows apace: the "whippersnapper" Khlestakov finds himself in the position of a person of consequence, and the mayor daydreams his way up to a general's rank in St. Petersburg. All these mis-understandings—real and apparent—are dealt a blow at the very end of the play, and Gogol, with great artistic tact, does not reveal its full implications.

Gogol intended not only that "Khlestakovism" should be a gen-eralized and typical phenomenon, but that it should also serve as a commentary on the "confusion" of life. Khlestakov's philosophy is that of vulgar epicureanism; it is translated, with the utmost accuracy, into the language of basic physiology when he says: "I like to eat. After all, that's what life is for—to pluck the flowers of pleasure." (This formulation is one of the great achievements of the final version of the play.) Meanwhile, the "power of general fear" creates a person of consequence out of this nonentity (see Gogol's "Advance Notice" to the actors).[31] This is possible be-cause of his particular traits of character ("he is rather dim-witted, and, as the saying goes, there's no Tsar in his head"). He is ready to enter into any situation and adjust to any: for him the boundaries between the real and the imaginary are easily obliter-ated. He is therefore capable of skimming over the waves of life's confusion, while unwittingly playing the leading role in it.

Khlestakov's inner vacuity and passivity are precisely the quali-ties which ensure that an appropriately negative evaluation of confusion will be made. If he were a deliberate cheat, as is Pus-tolobov in Kvitka's play *A Visitor from the Capital* (in a similar situation), or if he were in general an actively negative character, then the point of the exposé would be blunted.[32] Instead of con-fusion arising from society itself and being therefore *typical*, there would be just an artifical muddle created by the malevolence of a particular individual: it would be an *exceptional* phenomenon, not a typical one. That is why, in Gogol's words, "nothing should be sharply accentuated in Khlestakov," and why he should not be

[31 I.e., "Preduvedomlenie dlya tekh, kotorye pozhelali by sygrat' kak sleduet 'Revizora,'" *PSS*, IV, 1951, 116. The following quotation is from the stage-directions.]

[32 The Russian title is *Priezzhii iz stolitsy*. Pustolobov means "empty forehead." Grigory Fyodorovich Kvitka-Osnovyanenko (1778-1843) was a major Ukrainian writer in several different genres, but is probably best known for the play just mentioned. It was published only in 1840, but Gogol was familiar with it before that. It too is built on an "inspector gen-eral" theme. See also footnote 42.]

equated with the "braggarts and rakes," the fops, the Lovelaces, let alone the "theatrical" cheats of old, even though he does share some of their characteristics.[33] In other words, Khlestakov should not be equated with the stereotypes of the traditional theater and comedy, where the hero is defined by a single schematized trait of character. That is why Gogol, in the process of developing Khlestakov through the several versions of the play, takes great care to eliminate any traits that suggest such stereotypes.[34]

As a social being and as an individual, Khlestakov is typical, not exceptional. He is a minor St. Petersburg civil servant from a landowning family of modest means. But as the other characters in the play see him, he belongs to high society. Indirectly, this case of mistaken identity makes possible a criticism (although muffled) of that society as it is refracted through its unwitting representative. The hostile reaction of the censor Khrapovitsky to *The Inspector General*—"an intolerable abuse of the gentry, civil servants, and merchants"—was undoubtedly determined, to some extent, by the impression the figure of Khlestakov created. And there can be no doubt that the following remarks in Osip's monologue (Act II) must have sounded especially provocative in light of the "decorous" high-society comedy that prevailed on the stage at the time: "Oh, if only the old master found out about that! He wouldn't give a hoot that you was working for the government, he'd pull up your shirt and give you such a smacking you'd be rubbing yourself a good four days. If you're going to work, then go ahead and work."

As regards the central group of characters—the "six provincial civil servants"—there is nothing in Gogol's basic conception that would emphasize their belonging specifically to the *gentry*. They are completely detached from the economic and social relations that are characteristic of owners of land and serfs. Conversely, Bobchinsky and Dobchinsky have no official position but are

[33] "Otryvok iz pis'ma, pisannogo avtorom vskore posle pervogo predstavleniya 'Revizora' k odnomu literatoru," *PSS*, IV, 1951, 100.]

[34] On the prototypes of Khlestakov and other characters in *The Inspector General* in the comedy before Gogol, cf. my article "Kompozitsiya Revizora v istoriko-literaturnoi perspektive" (in the Ukrainian language in the anthology *Lyteratura*, 1928). Some ideas in this article are included in the present essay in reworked form. About Gogol's work on the characters of *The Inspector General*, cf. my note in the journal *Rabochii i teatr*, No. 1, 1935.

fully integrated into the general *civil-servant* type (cf., e.g., Dobchinsky's remark: "When an important person speaks, you feel afraid"). The theme of duty to the state, implicit in the play, is never treated specifically as a problem of duty on the part of the *gentry*. Likewise, there is nothing about Khlopov that identifies him specifically as not of gentle birth; nothing distinguishes him from the collective that is headed by the mayor. All this is quite in keeping with the particular stage in the development of Gogol's own ideology that we have already outlined.

The mayor has a complex function, which becomes clear only within the over-all pattern of comic roles in the play. In the first place, he brings together and heads the collective that is made up of the provincial officials, and establishes relations with Khlestakov in the name of this collective. In the second place, as a provincial dictator he is the antagonist of another collective: that of the ordinary folk who hold no official positions—the merchants and the townspeople.[35]

The impression of solidarity (or, as it were, of "chorality") created by the collective consisting of the officials (and other members of the gentry who are part of the system) is reinforced by the *mise-en-scène* of each act (except the second), by the polyphonic structure of the dialogue, and to an even greater extent by the fact that a more or less independent function is assigned to those characters who are the least individualized: the postmaster, who is described as "simple-hearted," and Bobchinsky and Dobchinsky, who are the "two town chatterboxes" (cf. the two female

[35] Gogol argued with the censor over a sentence spoken by the mayor that was particularly important for the play's satirical intent: "I admit I've really clipped the local merchants and townspeople too much" [first acting version: cf. *PSS*, IV, 1951, 249]. After the original text was proscribed, Gogol still tried to introduce the sentence into the toned-down version: "Now you couldn't even find any barber who could clip anything off them." But this sentence was also deleted by the censor. The only acceptable version was: "I admit I've been pretty hard on them. They'll swoop down on me like vultures and will pull me apart so that all you'll see are feathers flying in every which direction." Later on even this sentence, which was altered to satisfy the demands of the censor, was changed for the sake of toning down the general situation and giving the mayor the traits of a man who is half a hypocrite and half a sincerely simple soul: "They say I've been hard on them, but I swear that if I took anything from anyone, I did it without any malice."

chatterboxes in Lukin's play *The Windbag*).[36] Conversely, those who are more individualized and are created by a more or less complex combination of traditional traits have no independent function in the play. Such are the judge, Lyapkin-Tyapkin, a hunting enthusiast and sententious free-thinker; and Zemlyanika, a cheat, flatterer, and gossip. Neither one exerts any direct influence on the development of the plot: Zemlyanika's attempts to muddy the waters and set Khlestakov against the other officials come to naught. There are two characters who represent both these possibilities: they lack individuality and also have no independent function in the plot, and are therefore perceived only as members of the collective: Khlopov, who is "nothing more than just a frightened man," frightened almost to the point of speechlessness[37] (Zemlyanika accuses him of Jacobinism, but nobody takes that seriously in any sense of the word), and Gibner, who actually cannot utter a word—a pantomime-mask of the foreign doctor who knows no Russian. All these devices serve Gogol's basic artistic purpose of "bringing everything bad all together into one heap" and showing that this is not merely the aggregate of negative personalities, but rather an integral phenomenon of a socially negative nature.

In the cast of characters, another social group is set in opposition to the group of officials: the oppressed citizenry, the merchants and townspeople. Gogol shows his originality here as well, in the ability to use individual characters in such a way as to create the impression of a collective united by shared attitudes and functioning as a unit in the play. At first, this collective offers only passive resistance to the collective of bigwigs headed by the mayor ("The merchants and the ordinary folk are saying terrible things about me"). Then this collective tries to take on the mayor directly. Nothing comes of it, of course, and this only heightens the general confusion. In itself, the creation of a collective agent in this play was an important achievement on Gogol's part; but he makes it considerably more complex. As the plot develops, we see that the ordinary folk, though a collective, are not an integral

[36 Vladimir Ignatievich Lukin (1734-94) was one of the first playwrights who tried to develop a truly native Russian comedy. The Russian title of *The Windbag* is *Pustomelya*.]

37 In the early versions—up to the first one that was published—the superintendent of schools lacks even this much individuality: there are no comments on him in the stage directions.

whole. To Gogol's mind as well, the merchants and the towns-people are two different categories. The merchants occupy an intermediate position: they are oppressed by the powers that be (the gentry) and are prepared to make open (and collective) pro-test; but as soon as conditions change, they strike a bargain with the civil-servant/gentry group, that is, with the head of this group, the mayor. The townspeople are shown as being utterly defense-less. The author's attitude toward each of these groups is hereby clearly indicated. For the townspeople his sympathy is unqualified. For the merchants, it is qualified; it stops at the point where (to his mind) these two groups begin to be differentiated within the one big "chorus" of oppressed and protesting citizens. The mer-chant-group is singled out of the "chorus" at large, and becomes itself an object of exposé and satire from two directions: (1) as allies of the mayor's group and as collaborators in his shady deal-ings, they are censured along with the gentry and the officials (let us again recall Khrapovitsky's reaction to *The Inspector General*: "an intolerable abuse of the gentry, officials, and merchants"); (2) the strong censure of the merchants is made even more pointed by the fact that the author himself maintains the class attitude of a member of the gentry and regards the merchants as a group that is alien and inferior, both socially and culturally. From this point of view, the abusive remarks that the mayor directs at the merchants not only contain elements of satire on the part of the mayor himself, but also coincide to some extent with the author's own opinions of the merchants. (The mayor says: "And he [a merchant] sticks his big belly out; he's a merchant; don't you dare lay a finger on him. 'We're just as good as the gentry,' he says. A fine gentleman! . . . Oh, you ugly mugs! A gentleman studies to get knowledge; even though he's thrashed in school, it's for a good reason, so that he should learn something useful. But what are you? . . .") Despite the double angle of vision, Gogol's portrayal of merchant types was not particularly original: basical-ly, they differ from the traditional comic stereotype of the mer-chant-swindler only by virtue of Gogol's careful attention to the nuances of typical merchant's language. Even here, however, he had predecessors, such as Plavilshchikov and Chernyavsky.[38]

---

[38] It is interesting that the scene with the merchants at the beginning of Act V underwent practically no revisions from the first to the final version. The most important difference in the final version is the omission of a sentence that is found in all the preceding versions: "Now I'm going to

The representatives of the townspeople—i.e., the sergeant's widow and the locksmith's wife, who was added ·in the second draft variant of the play—are developed in a much more original way. They have absolutely no connection with the stereotypes of comedy.[39] V. V. Danilov was mistaken in regarding these episodic roles as highly comical.[40] They have more local color than comicality as such, particularly by comparison with the other pair in the play, Bobchinsky and Dobchinsky. Certain elements of buffoonery that were present in the earlier versions of the play were eliminated in the process of revision.

By implication, an entire collective is behind these two individualized female characters. There are only hints of this in the play itself: beginning with the second draft variant, the following stage direction is given after the appearance of the locksmith's wife: "Hands holding petitions are thrust through the window"; then, despite the warnings shouted by Khlestakov and Osip, "the door opens and a figure in a frieze coat, with an unshaven chin, a swollen lip, and a bandage around his face comes forward." Beginning with the acting version, a sentence is added here: "Behind him several other figures are seen." Moreover, the mayor's remarks amplify the impression we have of the townspeople as a group.

V

We see that the grouping of characters according to social identities does not aim at preaching any specific messages about society

twist all of you so that not a single hair will be left in any of your beards" (again this is undoubtedly in keeping with Gogol's reevaluation of the mayor's character). The other variations from draft to draft consist of minor changes in style.

[Pyotr Alekseyevich Plavilshchikov (1760-1812) was a professional actor and a spare-time playwright. O. Chernyavsky is so obscure that he warrants only slight mention in the standard reference-books.]

[39] The censor removed the sergeant's widow as a character from the acting text of the play and from the first published version (although the reference to the flogging remained). A scene featuring an ordinary townswoman loudly complaining of having been beaten must have struck the censor as offensive to decorum and politically risky as well. In addition, a misunderstanding seems to have figured here: the censor, Oldekop, took the sergeant's wife for an officer's wife (cf. N. Drizen, *Dramaticheskaya tsenzura dvukh epokh*, St. Petersburg, n.d., p. 43).

[40] V. Danilov, " 'Revizor' so storony ideologii Gogolya," *Rodnoi yazyk v shkole*, No. 10, 1926.

or describing manners and mores as such. It is subordinate to the one theme that organizes the entire play: that of official abuses, and the related (though contrasting) potential theme of *true service to the state*.

Gogol's predecessors here are Sokolov (*A Judge's Birthday*, 1781), Kapnist (*Chicanery*, 1798), and Sudovshchikov (*Wonder of Wonders, or an Honest Secretary*, 1801).[41] But the parallels are more by way of contrast than of similarity: these comedies were written decades before *The Inspector General* and are associated with a different historical reality and more elemental social relationships; they are therefore of a different ideological cast. Gogol's own contemporaries are more to the point. N. Kotlyarevsky has already identified them, and has to some extent discussed their relevance to *The Inspector General*: N. A. Polevoy (*Inspectors-General, or The Grass Is Always Greener On The Other Side*), and Kvitka (the two parts of *Elections to the Assembly of the Gentry*, entitled *Shelmenko the District Clerk* and *A Visitor from the Capital*, which was published later).[42]

The appearance of Polevoy's play went unnoticed; but Kvitka's *Elections to the Assembly of The Gentry* was a significant event in its time. A review in *The Moscow Telegraph* characterized both parts of the comedy as follows: "Here we see Russia as she really is, drawn from nature and not fabricated." The same journal's review of *Shelmenko the District Clerk* indicates that the "Teniers-like qualities" of Kvitka's comedies stirred up a controversy which was very much like the one that later raged around Gogol's play. ("It is a living picture *in the Flemish style*, with coarse figures; but these figures are natural to the highest degree.")[43] Unlike the dramatists at the end of the eighteenth century, who portrayed the self-enclosed little world of the judiciary, these immediate predecessors of Gogol present a broader picture: the social activity of

[41 Gippius has in mind Ivan Sokolov and Nikolay Sudovshchikov. The only important playwright in this group is Vasily Vasilievich Kapnist (1757-1823). The Russian titles of the plays are, respectively: *Sudeiskie imeniny, Yabeda, Neslykhannoe divo, ili chestnyi sekretar'*.]

[42 The reference is to N. A. Kotlyarevsky's book *Nikolai Vasil'evich Gogol', 1829-1842. Ocherki iz istorii russkoi povesti i dramy*, 3d ed., St. Petersburg, 1911. The Russian titles are: Polevoy, *Revizory, ili slavny bubny za gorami*; Kvitka, *Dvoryanskie vybory*, in two parts: *Shel'menko—volostnoi pisar'* and *Priezzhii iz stolitsy*.]

43 *Moskovskii telegraf*, No. 19, 1831.

the gentry on the scale of an entire town, or even an administrative district.

Reactionary critics attempted to take issue with the theme of official abuses and the sort of play that dealt with "administrative and judicial" matters. Their reasons, though ostensibly literary, were in fact wholly political. Here Bulgarin and Senkovsky were as one in attacking Gogol. Bulgarin wrote: "True comedy cannot be based on administrative abuses. There must be contrasts and a *plot*, there must be *verisimilitude, truth to nature*—but *The Inspector General* has *none of that*."[44] Senkovsky repeated these sentiments literally, while taking a somewhat different esthetic line of argument: "It is utterly impossible to make a comedy out of abuses, because these are not the manners and mores of the people, nor are they characteristic of society as a whole. Rather, they are the transgressions of a few individuals, and they should inspire not laughter but the indignation of honest citizens."[45] This objection had a semblance of logic to it, but it rested upon a patently reactionary presupposition—that the "manners and mores of the people" allow no room for abuses—and on the arbitrary esthetic premise that indignation is incompatible with laughter.

In effect, Senkovsky was merely canonizing these same norms of comedy which Gogol was endeavoring to transcend in taking issue with the "light laughter" and "innocent plots" of plays written by and for the gentry. These norms required either the depiction of individual foibles (where the offender could be funny provided he was surrounded by virtuous types—who were the mouthpieces for the presumed "manners and mores of the people," which were also virtuous, of course), or the depiction of weaknesses "common to all men," innocent yet amusing, and not incompatible with the ideal image of the "manners and mores of the people," and a picture of "society as a whole." Gogol broke with these stereotypes in all respects—with the idea that the manners and mores of the people exclude the possibility of abuses, with the requirement that all the characters should fall into one of two moral categories (good or bad), and, finally, with the practice of taking the comic devices of the play from traditional and prescribed materials. It was in this last area that Gogol was to show the greatest initiative.

Any concept of "the comic" that is not viewed in historical and

[44] *Severnaya pchela*, No. 98, 1836. Italics in original.
[45] *Biblioteka dlya chteniya*, XVI, 1836, Section v, 43; V. Zelinsky, *Russkaya kriticheskaya literatura o proizvedeniyakh Gogolya*, Part 1, p. 163.

ideological perspective lacks substance. In theory, Senkovsky was setting forth norms for the comedy that were binding on everyone; in fact, he was proceeding from the practices of playwrights who had been active during the reigns of Catherine the Great and Paul I, and by his time these practices were anachronistic. In the comedies of Kapnist and his contemporaries, the problem of how to make official abuses comic was never actually solved. These comedies were based on esthetic principles that set "satire" in sharp contrast to "humor"; but inasmuch as they were specifically intended as satires on the violators of norms (who were not members of the gentry, however, or at least not "true" members of the gentry), they did in fact resemble portrayals of "the transgressions of a few individuals," as Senkovsky put it. At the same time, the satire lost some of its pungency because of the deliberate introduction of extraneous, uncomic material, in keeping with the canons of the sentimental comedy (which featured a group of virtuous individuals and the sentimental love-situations in which they became involved).

It is enough to call to mind one comedy replete with material on official abuses: Kapnist's *Chicanery*. It can rightfully be called a comedy only because of its happy ending (happy for the virtuous characters, that is). But this ending is the result of a purely mechanical removal of obstacles (the arrest of the chief antagonist in the litigation and in the love-intrigue, and the arraignment of those responsible for the official abuses). There is nothing intrinsically comic in the plot itself. The comic element is limited to a few details: certain scenes that make use of standard props (bottles are hidden "under the cloth," i.e., under the table, so that a "Bacchanalian gang" can be turned into a court—Act V, Scene 1), and certain standard remarks and gestures that bear largely on the extorting and taking of bribes. The author also uses an effect that comes straight out of the comic opera—the singing of couplets which recapitulate the play's satirical element in condensed form.

Gogol proceeded from different premises—both social and esthetic—than did his predecessors. The social premise, in his art, was that of the different "estates" of society working peaceably together as members of a single governmental organism to eliminate incongruities (which were regarded as misunderstandings that could be cleared up with comparative ease), and also to heal "wounds and ailments" which were recognized as attributes not merely of individuals, but specifically of society. The esthetic

239

premises were tied to the social ones. In their way they were realistic inferences drawn from romantic theories of the comic. Satire and humor were no longer thought to be incompatible; transitional and mixed forms were now admitted.[46] Jokes made at the expense of isolated phenomena ("electric and enlivening humor," in Gogol's words),[47] turn into something new—satire— as soon as there is an awareness of what connects these phenomena: the social and political function of individual characters and of events that appear to be merely fortuitous at first glance.

Obviously, Gogol had to go beyond his predecessors, and not merely imitate them. First of all, the material he chose answered more specifically to his purposes: instead of the judiciary, he concentrated on administrators—the doings and misdoings of the authorities on the scale of at least a district town. This scale was the minimum required for a social comedy; at the same time, it was large enough to enable generalizations to be made as broadly as anyone wished. As the subsequent history of the play's reception indicated, even on this scale people could make associations that Gogol himself had not foreseen—between administrative arbitrariness on a provincial level and on the level of the state as a whole.

Gogol was also faced with the task of learning how to use this particular kind of material in a comic way. The first essential was to discard the dead weight of moralizing and sentimentalizing—the virtuous lovers, the wise elders, the servant-confidants, and the tradition-encrusted plot-motifs that went along with them and drew off the dramatic energy. This "purgation" had another and much greater significance which will be made clear later. But a purgation in itself was inadequate: Gogol also had to subject the basic plot-material to scrutiny in the light of his particular views of comedy. Murder and arson, which are alluded to in Kapnist's play (Act II, Scene 1, the conversation between Pravolov and Naumych), and in Polevoy and Kvitka, are nowhere to be found in *The Inspector General*, even as details of characterization extrane-

---

[46] Indications of this possibility, though with some qualifications, can be found, e.g., in Jean-Paul Richter, *Vorschule der Aesthetik*, VI Programm, 29, Unterschied der Satire und des Komischen: "Leicht ist indes der Übergang und die Vermischung. . . . Die Persiflage des Welttons, eine rechte Mittlerin zwischen Satire und Schmerz, ist das Kind unserer Zeit," etc. [Difference between satire and the comic: "In any event the transition and blending is easy. . . . High society badinage, which is really a kind of bridge between satire and suffering, is a characteristic of our age."]

[47 "Peterburgskie zapiski 1836 goda," *PSS*, VIII, 1952, 181.]

ous to the plot. As Pyotr Vyazemsky, a contemporary of Gogol's, remarked: "The story of *The Inspector General* is not built on any revolting or criminal act, there is no violation of innocence by the forces of vice, there is no corruption of justice as there is, for instance, in Kapnist's *Chicanery*."[48] To be sure, everything bad is supposed to be brought together in the town that is the scene of the action; but this does not mean everything that is *worst*, just everything that is *merely* bad.[49] An allusion to outright graft on the part of the mayor is found only in variant versions of the preliminary draft ("I admit that I did dip my hand in here and there"). In addition, beginning with the second manuscript draft, there is a remark hinting that the mayor, and perhaps others as well, is guilty of several major crimes: "You don't say! Up till now God has spared us. It's true that we've seen from the papers that in such-and-such a town so-and-so has been locked up for taking bribes, so-and-so has been brought to trial for being an accessory and for larceny or forgery; but all this has happened somewhere else, thank God, and no inspections or inspectors have come our way as yet." In the final version (1842), no administrative transgressions are specified in this speech. "That's the hand of fate, obviously! (*He sighs.*) Up till now, thank God, they've been skulking around other towns, but now our turn has come."

Stylistic considerations aside, this change in the text can be linked with a tendency evident in Gogol by the beginning of the 1840's: to rehabilitate his heroes in part. If this in fact was the case here, then *The Inspector General* did not lose much of its satirical coloration as a result. The vague and deliberately soft-pedaled remarks that the mayor makes by way of self-exposé in the final version ("failings . . . you don't like to let things slip through your fingers. . . . I've been hard on them. . . .") allow us to supply any specific context we wish; and the device of the cryptic allusion keeps both the *satirical* and the specifically *comic* effect intact. Only once is an official wrongdoing spelled out in the play: the mayor's reference to the chapel that has never been built

[48] *Sochineniya P. A. Vyazemskogo*, II, 268. [Pyotr Andreyevich Vyazemskii (1792-1878) was a poet and critic, and a close friend of Pushkin.]

[49] In the initial draft of "Leaving the Theater" there are direct references to this; their meaning, incidentally, is entirely in keeping with the rest of Gogol's comments. Cf. the following exchange: "The mayor is a splendid fellow!"—"What's so splendid about this mayor? Things are a bit cleaner in our town." ["Teatral'nyi raz"ezd posle predstavleniya novoi komedii," *PSS*, v, 1949, 384.]

indicates a misappropriation of official funds (in the first draft this is put somewhat differently: the poorhouse has been under construction for some twelve years). Of course, this much specification is essential as a key to understanding the mayor's remarks about "failings." But it is curious that in every draft of the play, the mention of the chapel or the poorhouse is immediately preceded by a scene of pure farce: the mayor puts a box on his head instead of a hat. This episode casts a comic light, as it were, on the self-exposé that follows.

The main target of the satire is "ordinary sorts" of abuses of power. But to a large extent, these abuses are kept off-stage: they are touched upon in remarks made by the characters, and only now and then are they specifically associated with episodic characters (the merchants, the locksmith's wife, the sergeant's widow). The removal of a motif off-stage makes the exposé more comical, or at least does not prevent it from being comical.

The central motif in this chain of motifs is that of the bribe. Its comic potentialities are very extensive, particularly as the author delves into the psychology of the bribetaker and his victim, and into the various species of garden-variety graft, which are not necessarily associated only with the tyrannical actions or evil motives of an individual wrongdoer. But Gogol sets this more innocuous form of abuse within a distinctive system of devices, wherein the contradiction between the satirical and the comic disappears. First of all, the bribe-motif functions not so much in the plot as in the characterization. The bribes in themselves have no effect on the course of the action, for they are not real bribes, but are merely regarded as such by one particular group of characters. Even the celebrated reversal of circumstances in Act II, Scene 8, is not brought about by the introduction of the bribe-motif as such into the plot, but rather by the mayor's view of Khlestakov. This is even more true of the bank-notes that find their way into Khlestakov's pocket in Act IV: like the sugar, the bag, the tray, and the string in Scene 10, they are merely the material manifestations of the various points of view on which the plot is built. Consequently, there is no *specification* of bribery and extortion in *The Inspector General* as there is in the pre-Gogolian comedies we have mentioned. In Kapnist's *Chicanery* people lend money and lose at cards and make "contributions" of various goods and products and slip five-rouble notes "as a reminder" into the hand of a secretary whose memory of some new development in an official proceeding has "failed him." In Sudovshchikov's *Wonder of Wonders*, the bribetaker drops a hint and the petitioner figures out what he must do. In Polevoy's *Inspectors-General*, the people under investigation learn about the weaknesses of each of the investigators: they entangle one of them in female wiles and even bring off an actual marriage; another (a gourmet) is put on a "fast," not allowed to buy anything good to eat, and then enticed with puddings and pasties and promises that he will be given the recipes; the third—a collector of antiques named Bessrebrenni-kov[50]—is tempted with "rarities" for which, however, he himself has to pay. By comparison with such material—which is elaborated in even greater detail in the satirical literature of the 1850's[51]—the material in *The Inspector General* looks meager: "loans" are made in response to outright requests; lunch is served with wine and smoked codfish; there is a fleeting reference to "wolfhound puppies"—but there is no system or technique of bribery! We can understand the moralizing reproaches made by Bulgarin and echoed by "the angry but evidently experienced civil servant" in Gogol's "Leaving the Theater": "And this isn't the way bribes are taken, if you come right down to it."

The contrasting esthetic categories of satirical and comic were presented by Gogol as a *unity*. Here he is more consistent than any of his predecessors, even Fonvizin and Griboyedov, who achieved such a unity only in *isolated* scenes in their satirical comedies: the over-all structure of *The Minor* and *Woe from Wit* violated this unity in favor of *satire*. (Cf. Vyazemsky's view, cited by Gogol, of these two plays as contemporary tragedies.)[52] So far, I have been trying to point up those devices which insured that the materials used satirically in Gogol's play would be perceived as *comic*. Gogol himself was particularly hopeful that they would have a psychological and, so to speak, didactic effect on society ("Oh, laughter is a great thing!" etc.).[53] But even more important is the other aspect of this unity: the *satirical* resonance of the comic elements.

[50 The name means something like "silverless."]

[51] Cf. V. Gippius, "Literaturnoe okruzhenie Saltykova-Shchedrina," *Rodnoi yazyk v shkole*, No. 2, 1927.

[52 "V chem zhe nakonets sushchestvo russkoi poezii i v chem ee osobennost'," *Vybrannye mesta iz perepiski s druz'yami*, *PSS*, VIII, 1952, 396.]

[53 "Peterburgskie zapiski 1836 goda," *PSS*, VIII, 1952, 186.]

VI

Among the reactionary critics of the time, one faction, represented by Bulgarin and Senkovsky, openly took issue with *The Inspector General* as a satire. But another faction, operating in a different way, endeavored to represent the whole play as being *pure comedy* and nothing more, and either reproached or praised the author (it made no real difference) for it.

Earlier, the censor Oldekop had summed up *The Inspector General* in his report in such a way as to suggest that he was deliberately playing down its social significance. According to him, the play amounted to nothing more than the adventures of Khlestakov; and it therefore followed that "the play does not contain anything reprehensible."[54] The defense of the play made by Nicholas I and, on his orders, by the censors as well, is apparently to be explained by fears that the work would be used for clandestine purposes, and by the ill-founded hope that it would be taken as a harmless farce. Herzen recalled sarcastically that the Emperor roared with laughter at the premiere.[55] But it is a dubious business to assume that the ruling circles naively underestimated the play (the most likely explanation of the statement attributed to Nicholas at the premiere—"everyone got raked over the coals, myself above all"—if in fact he did say it, is that it was a demagogic gesture, which itself was anything but naive). It is also difficult to assume that the critics who at the time seemed to be naively interpreting the play as just an amusing comedy were in fact being naive. Such an interpretation, at its baldest, was made by Pyotr Serebreny, the critic of *Literary Supplements to the Russian Veteran*. His account of the play bears a close resemblance to Oldekop's: "The plot of the new play is very simple. A young St. Petersburg civil servant is taken for an inspector-general in a provincial town (somewhere

[54] N. V. Drizen, *Dramaticheskaya tsenzura dvukh epokh*, St. Petersburg, n.d., pp. 41-42.

[55] *Du développement des idées révolutionnaires en Russie* (*O razvitii revolyutsionnykh idei v Rossii*), *Sobranie sochinenii v tridtsati tomakh*, VII, Moscow, 1956, 98 (French text), 229 (Russian text). Alexander Ivanovich Herzen (Gertsen) (1812-70) was, among other things, one of Russia's most important philosophers of revolution. He lived in Europe after the Revolution of 1848, longest in England, where he edited a newspaper *The Bell* (*Kolokol*), which was regularly smuggled into Russia. His best-known works, both available in English translation, are *From the Other Shore* (*S togo berega*), and *My Past and Thoughts* (*Byloe i dumy*).]

between Penza and Saratov). He does a bit of bragging to the provincials, collects a bit of cash from them, flirts with the mayor's wife and daughter, gets engaged to the latter, and then leaves. The deception is exposed; the mayor and all the rest raise their hands to heaven and the curtain falls!" This account (like the censor's report) does not make the slightest allusion to "everything bad" being brought together "into one heap," that is, to the satirical aspect of the play. Gogol comes out as just a jolly and naive fellow and nothing more—which is the way he portrayed himself, in "An Author's Confession," as being before he wrote *The Inspector General.* "A person with weak nerves might be afraid of having convulsions," the same critic writes in another section of his review; "anyone who is out of sorts or worried ought to run to the theater whenever *The Inspector General* is being given. This comedy will heal many sorrows and dispel much spleen."[56]

Grech regarded *The Inspector General* "not as a comedy, but as a caricature in dialogue."[57] To a large extent, his remarks echo the attacks made on the play by Bulgarin and Senkovsky: "Its plot is not new, and besides, it is not feasible and not plausible. From beginning to end it does not contain a single noble or lofty impulse, not only of thought," etc. But Grech departed from his confederates in recognizing the "liveliness, vividness, and naturalness" of the characters, and he was inclined to excuse the play's shortcomings on the grounds that it contained "so much wit, merriment, laughter, so much that has been successfully captured." It is curious that Serebreny and Grech, while both representing Gogol as a purely comic writer, offered him completely contradictory advice. Serebreny advised him to stick to provincial settings ("he is incomparable at depicting provincial scenes, and people of a middle and lower order of life; but the moment he moves up to higher levels of society, we find ourselves wishing with all our hearts that he would go back to his former area of activity. Small provincial towns are his kingdom!"). Grech advised him to give up the theme of provincial life, as had S. P. Shevyryov, in his comments on *Mirgorod*: "Are minor provincial quill-drivers and other reprobates of like ilk really worth the sustained attention of a man of intelligence and talent? Far more interesting individuals and characters, who are amusing and depraved for other things

[56] *Literaturnye pribavleniya k Russkomu Invalidu*, No. 36, July 22, 1836.
[57] N. Grech, *Chteniya o russkom yazyke*, Part 2, St. Petersburg, 1840, Chtenie desyatoe.

than just bribetaking and gossip, await the playwright in our country."[58]

These two pieces of advice seem to contradict each other, but actually they coincide in that both critics are *afraid* of the satirical aspect of the play. The difference is merely that Serebreny was willing to offer the provincial setting as a sacrifice to Gogol's satire in order to ensure the inviolability of higher society, whereas Grech (like Shevyryov) would have liked to rule out all themes of a socially satirical nature and instead have Gogol shift his sights to themes "common to all mankind," which, to Grech's mind, could be found only on the higher levels of society.

Pyotr Vyazemsky took a middle position in the discussion of *The Inspector General*. His first reaction (even before the premiere) was expressed in a letter he wrote to A. I. Turgenev, on January 19, 1836. It was basically no different from the opinions held by Oldekop and Serebreny: "A good-for-nothing who works in a government office in St. Petersburg happens into a provincial town and cannot leave because he has no money. Meanwhile, the local mayor is awaiting an inspector general from St. Petersburg. In his terror he takes this person, who is just passing through, for the inspector general, lends him money thinking that he's buying him off with bribes, etc. This whole way of life has been described very amusingly, and general speaking the merriment is inexhaustible. But there is little action, as is the case with all his works."[59] Later, Vyazemsky took a more serious view of the play, as we see from a letter he wrote to the same Turgenev on May 8, 1836,[60] and from an article published in the second issue of *The Contemporary*. However, both versions of his defense of the play amount basically to the same thing: a rejection of the attacks made on Gogol by reactionaries, and a defense of the artist's right to exercise a free choice of theme and material. He did not characterize the contents of the play. He wrote that Gogol's heroes "are more funny than odious; there is more benightedness and ignorance in them than there is depravity." Taken by itself, this observation is correct; but in the general context of the article, it in effect apologized to

[58 The reference is to S. P. Shevyryov's article on *Mirgorod* in *Moskovskii Nablyudatel'*, March, 1835, Part 1, Book 2, pp. 396-411.]

[59 *Ostaf'evskii arkhiv*, III, 285. [Alexander Ivanovich Turgenev (1784-1845), was a friend of virtually all the prominent writers of his time, and the author of interesting collections of letters and diaries.]

[60 *Ostaf'evskii arkhiv*, III, 317-318.]

Gogol's enemies for him and hereby put a narrow construction on the social import of the play. Vyazemsky did not understand that the play was progressive precisely because it did not depict "odious heroes"—in other words, because it did not treat negative characters as individual personalities in their own right.

With the sole exception of Griboyedov, Gogol's predecessors and immediate contemporaries thought of the negative element in their plays as the sum total of malevolent attitudes on the part of individual characters, and the plots as the result of the activities of such individuals. Consequently, even comedies that were entirely social in content—such as *Chicanery* and *Elections to the Assembly of the Gentry*—never developed into real satirical comedies, despite their wealth of satirical detail, because they lacked a single social focus. In this respect, Gogol followed neither Kvitka nor Kapnist, but Griboyedov. That is, he appropriated the technique of the comedy of social satire that had been worked out on the basis of the revolutionary-minded gentry's satirical attitude toward society. To these ends—again following Griboyedov—(1) he denied his negative types any sharply defined individual vices; (2) he attributed their negative qualities, in social terms, to "mores" of long standing, to widely accepted "worldly wisdom," to habits, etc.; (3) without robbing his heroes of characteristics that identify them as individuals, he assigned them characteristics that give all of them something in common.

In his article on Griboyedov's *Woe from Wit* (which, as we know, Gogol read with approval), Belinsky offers a superb interpretation of Gogol's character-types. He concludes his characterization of the mayor with the following general remarks: "But note that this is not depravity on his part, but rather the stage that he has reached in his moral evolution, his highest concept of his duties as prescribed by law. . . . He tries to vindicate himself by quoting the simple maxim that all banal people do: 'I'm not the first and I won't be the last; everyone does the same thing.'" Despite his negative attitude in those years toward *Woe from Wit* as a work of art, Belinsky did grasp the elements common to both Griboyedov and Gogol in their method of creating characters: "Famusov [in *Woe from Wit*] is a typical character who is artistically created. . . . He is a Gogolian mayor of this particular level of society. His philosophy is the same."[61] Later, Gogol

[61 Review of second edition of *Woe from Wit*, as in *Polnoe sobranie sochinenii*, III, Moscow, 1953, 482.]

himself made a rather precise formulation of his own method (it referred to *Dead Souls*, to be sure, but was equally applicable to *The Inspector General*): "My heroes are by no means villains: if I should add even one good feature to any of them, the reader would accept all of them. But it was the banality of everything taken together that frightened readers."[62]

Even during the period when he was writing *Selected Passages from Correspondence with Friends*, Gogol continued to think of social life as a connected chain, whose negative aspects could not be reduced to the misdeeds of malevolent individuals. He addresses the following admonition to "one who occupies an important position": "You will not prosecute any one individual by himself for committing an injustice until you have a clear picture of the whole chain, in which the official who has come to your notice forms a necessary link. You already know that guilt has so spread to all that it is absolutely impossible to say at first who is more to blame than the others: there are the guiltlessly guilty and the guiltily innocent."[63] This comes very close to the meaning of *The Inspector General* and to the ideas that Belinsky expresses in his article on *Woe from Wit*. But with characteristic inconsistency, Gogol relied on the efforts of *benevolent* individuals to carry on the struggle with the "whole chain": "cutting evil off at the root and not at the branches" now (in 1847) meant annihilating it in the heart of each individual. But in 1836 there was still no evidence that Gogol was treating political problems in terms of psychology: the official who has arrived from St. Petersburg, at the end of the play, certainly does not come with the purpose of exerting a psychological influence on guiltlessly guilty people.

Gogol developed his method in yet another way which was already specifically characteristic of him and which grew directly out of his concern with showing "the banality of everything taken together." This was the complete elimination of positive character-types. It therefore had a more serious function than merely ridding the plot of non-comic material: it aimed at doing away with the traditional dichotomy in the system of characterization. Once the

[62 "Chetyre pis'ma k raznym litsam po povodu 'Mertvykh dush,'" *Vybrannye mesta . . . , PSS*, VIII, 1952, 293.] Cf. also the conversation between "two members of the audience" in "Leaving the Theater" ("Teatral'nyi raz"ezd," *PSS*, v, 1949, 159-160).

[63 "Zanimayushchemu vazhnoe mesto," *Vybrannye mesta . . . , PSS*, VIII, 1952, 351. *Selected Passages* was published in 1847.]

old category of *vice* had been deprived of its antithesis, *virtue*, it could be replaced more easily with the category of *banality*, which was represented as both an individual and a social category, even when it was applied to individual characters.

The absence of positive character-types gave the play even greater specific identity as a social comedy, and thereby greater significance as a satire too. In the old "administrative" comedy, the group of positive characters gave the play a reassuringly "loyalist" tone, even if they were not themselves officials and did not therefore weaken the force of the exposé. And if we now move from these a priori considerations to what was actually being written in Gogol's own day, we shall see that in other plays the "positive" heroes were in fact becoming vehicles for an unqualified veneration of the government, and their speeches were turning into outright exhortations on its behalf. Thus, in the most satirical of Kvitka's comedies, *Elections to the Assembly of the Gentry*, Blagosudov makes the following reply to Tvyordov's indignant statement about those members of the gentry "who, having trampled on the law, oppress the weak": "The source of this evil is the deep-rooted reluctance to provide children with an education. But thanks to the wise measures taken by our beneficent government, this evil is beginning to be eradicated. We see a great many young noblemen in schools. Military service, which fortunately is so beloved of our gentry, is forming many young people," etc.[64]

Thus, any explicit expression of support for the government was impossible in *The Inspector General*, because of the way the play was structured.

In 1835-36, S. P. Shevyryov had taken exception to what Gogol was trying to do satirically, but subsequently he tried to adapt Gogol's brand of satire to his own ideological purposes; and in the last interpretation of *The Inspector General* that he made (1851), he pointed out, quite correctly, that Gogol had "raised the solution of the problem of moral characters in the comedy to the level of a theoretical proposition."[65] Gogol's method of plot-making depended on the fundamental elimination of positive character types. Three things disappeared in *The Inspector General*: (1) the stereo-

[64 Blagosudov and Tvyordov are "meaningful" names, as was common practice in eighteenth-century plays. The first is formed from the words for "good judgment," the second from the word meaning "firm," "resolute."]

65 "O teorii smeshnogo," Stat'ya 2, *Moskvityanin*, No. 3, 1851, p. 383.

types of plot and theme that were routine in the comedy immediately preceding Gogol (for example, the "rivalry" of good and bad characters, or the "unsuccessful undertaking"); (2) the unsophisticated social didacticism; and (3) the division of the dramatis personae into exemplars of virtue and vice. The "successful blackmail" stereotype that was characteristic of the comedy which had no moral aim but was designed purely to amuse could not be used by Gogol either, in view of the definite social and moral aims of his play and its general ideological orientation. A member of the audience who had been brought up on such stereotypes might have formed the impression that since Gogol's play lacked them, it also lacked plot development. (Cf. the remarks of the first lover of the arts in "Leaving the Theater": "I am speaking about the fact that the play has absolutely no plot"; and the remarks of the fourth lover of the arts: "Somehow we see neither a plot nor a denouement." Cf. also Senkovsky: "It [the play] has neither plot nor denouement, because it tells of something that is already known, and is not an artistic creation; you do not even need a plot when you know how everything is going to come out from the very first scenes.")[66]

The second lover of the arts takes exception to the remarks of the first.[67] He does not spell out the stereotypes that were prevalent in the comedy of the time, but lumps them all together under the general term of "the love-intrigue"; and to it he contrasts a new kind of intrigue, based on more complex motivations which reflect changes that have taken place in history and in the mind of society. ("Everything in the world has long since changed.") The thesis that he advances about the "magnetism of rank, of accumulated money," etc., is familiar to everyone. But less attention has been paid to the way his ideas develop from there. He demands that the "personal plot" should be replaced by a general plot which would include "all the characters, not just one or two," and would be based on "what interests more or less all the characters." This paves the way for a direct transition to the concept of social comedy.

[66] *Biblioteka dlya chteniya*, XVI, 1836, Section V, 43.

[67] The remarks of the first lover of the arts in "Leaving the Theater" make use of Vyazemsky's sympathetic comments (his defense of the play against accusations of "bad taste"), and of the attacks made by Senkovsky. [For the quotations from "Leaving the Theater," cf. "Teatral'nyi raz"ezd posle predstavleniya novoi komedii," *PSS*, V, 1949, 142-144.]

All this very much resembles the ideas of Androsov—the one critic of the time whose views, both social and esthetic, came closest to Gogol's.[68] His esthetics could be defined in the same terms we used earlier for Gogol's—as realistic inferences drawn from romantic principles ("the truth of the possible," an expression of "the basic nature of those people who make up the motley totality of our provincial mores").[69] However, Gogol gave much greater depth to these ideas. The most important point that the second lover of the arts makes—a definition of the new principles of plot—has no direct parallel in Androsov's article. Moreover, neither Androsov nor the second lover of the arts offers a theoretical solution to the problem of the unity of the satirical and the comic. Androsov contrasts the "bitterness of satire" to the "benevolent merriment of comedy," and only vaguely hints that this contradiction can be eliminated as one moves from "external truth" to the "truth of an idea, internal truth." Likewise, the second lover of the arts merely hints, in one of his remarks, that in "a social comedy . . . everything that constitutes the specifically comic aspect" must not "lose its color." (And in keeping with this point of view, he cautions against elaborating the love-intrigue in too much detail.) Meanwhile, in abandoning the "springs" that had long moved both the satirical and the light comedy, Gogol had to find new principles which would enable him to bring about this unity of the satirical and the comic not only in the general tenor of the play and in the delineation of individual characters, but also in the development of the plot itself, in the very dynamics of the comedy. And Gogol found fruitful principles in the vaudeville and the vaudeville comedy: the dynamics of misunderstanding, and exposés based on a false point of view.

In itself, the device of "point of view" easily acquires a comic

[68] Concerning V. P. Androsov, cf. the article by N. I. Mordovchenko, "Gogol' i zhurnalistika 1835-1836 gg.," in *N. V. Gogol', Materialy i issledovaniya*, ed. V. V. Gippius, II, Moscow-Leningrad, 1936, 106-150.

[69] Cf. the following ideas of Androsov's with those of the second lover of the arts, in "Leaving the Theater": "What merit is there in attacking a petty and personal weakness, some obscure shortcoming, some insignificant vice—all this can be very amusing, but to whom is it important? . . . But there is another comedy—or one is in the making—a comedy of civilization, in which the family man gives way to social man, in which personal relationships are replaced by social ones. . . . Do not depict a slice of the life of a certain few individuals . . . but rather a slice of those mores which more or less constitute the physiognomy of contemporary society."

function: it refracts the entire play through a double angle of vision, and forces us to combine things that cannot be combined, thereby creating a comic effect. Because of this, contradictory elements can coexist on the stage: contradictory as to situation (an inspector general and a man who is passing through town just by chance), as to social level (a bigwig and a simple registry clerk), and as to psychology (a "fine fellow" who is at the same time a "good-for-nothing"). They coexist because the viewpoint held by some of the characters, on the one hand, and the viewpoint held by the audience, on the other, are antithetical. This puts the entire plot on two planes, at the very least. These two planes, however, form a unity within a duality, inasmuch as the audience holds the key to the interplay of these points of view, and establishes the necessary correlations between the "real" and the apparent.

Thus, the basic plot, which the audience perceives as the true one, is paralleled by another plot, an internal one, which is false by virtue of the false viewpoint held by the characters who open the play—the officials. This false plot has its own internal system of roles: (1) the principal agents, that is, the mayor and his group; (2) their enemies, the ordinary townsfolk; (3) the inspector general, whose potential actions in any given situation are not immediately apparent, but who, as a potential defender of the ordinary townsfolk, is presumably one of the "enemies." This false plot develops out of the rivalry between the "virtuous" group of zealous officials and the "negative" group of ordinary townsfolk, in other words, out of a situation that was typical of the pre-Gogolian sentimental comedy. But, while making his negative heroes play out a sentimental comedy, Gogol at the same time makes the reader perceive everything that goes on as a light comedy. Gogol himself hinted at this double purpose in his "Advance Notice" to the actors: "The audience, being at a remove, sees the vanity of their efforts. But they themselves are by no means joking, and they do not have the slightest idea that anyone is laughing at them."[70]

The audience identifies the false plot and evaluates it accordingly. The conflict between the two groups that are antagonistic as to class is maintained in the true plot as well, but the positive and negative viewpoints are interchanged, just as Gogol intends.

[70 "Preduvedomlenie dlya tekh, kotorye pozhelali by sygrat' kak sleduet 'Revizora,' " *PSS*, iv, 1951, 116.]

Of primary concern now is the exposé of Khlestakov, that zero entity who in the false plot functions sometimes as a potential enemy and sometimes as a reliable ally.

The problem of the comedy's satirical function is also resolved in this way. It is only in the most primitive types of comedy (which are, however, very common in the vaudeville) that the misunderstanding is either fully motivated by specific attributes of the psychologies of individual characters (absent-mindedness, gullibility, or outright stupidity), or is not psychologically motivated at all (it is just a convergence of chance happenings). Naturally, the way the misunderstanding develops makes it impossible to attribute what happens to malevolent individuals and to draw the appropriate moralistic conclusions. But this very fact opens the way for sociopsychological motivations, especially in cases where the falseness of the viewpoint depends (as it does in *The Inspector General*) on a difference in social levels, which in turn depends not on the personal qualities of errant individuals, but rather on "confusion" of a social nature. Vyazemsky proposed that misunderstandings could be explained by the proverb: "Fear has big eyes"; but from the viewpoint of the author's basic conception, this can be done only if we have in mind not the cowardice of the mayor and the other officials as individuals, but rather cowardice as seen in the context of social satire.

At the same time, the rivalry, which is parodied in the false plot, shows its truly satirical side to the audience. Even when seen from the mayor's false point of view, this rivalry does not become nothing but a contest between "malevolent" and "benevolent" individuals; rather, it is interpreted as a social conflict. This makes it all the more necessary to create a corresponding impression in the true plot, i.e., from the point of view held by the audience. The motif of the rivalry is preserved when it is interpreted as it should be by the audience, although it is not this that determines the development of the plot. On the other hand, because it is interpreted by the audience, and because it has a satirical function, it does to some extent lose its comic function as such. However, in the fabric of the play as a whole, this loss is imperceptible, since the true and false points of view do not exist separately, but form a unity. Thus, the device of the *unity of contradictory points of view* is fundamental and decisive for Gogol's whole system of comedy. For it brings about *the unity of the satirical and the comic* in a concrete way. As the play is structured,

253

the usual obstacle to such a unity (the possibility that bitter or indignant comments may be expressed by the author, directly or indirectly) naturally disappears.

VII

The first act of *The Inspector General* creates the original false point of view; the second builds situations on it; the third and the beginning of the fourth provide a certain respite in the forward movement of the plot, and are concerned, on the one hand, with putting the final touches on the characterizations and, on the other, with consolidating the false point of view even further. And here Gogol departs from the practice of the writers of vaudevilles, who had no need to make consolidations of this sort, for the rapid tempo and the small dimensions of the vaudeville required rapid denouements as well. The middle one-and-a-half acts are structured as a comedy of character, with its sudden disruptions and restorations of point of view. This is possible because the main character, Khlestakov, is more passive than active, and has no point of view of his own ("He has never in his life had occasion to do anything that would attract anyone's attention. But the power of universal fear made him a remarkable comic character," Gogol wrote).[71] Therefore, the lie he tells, so far as its function in the plot goes, is basically different from the lies that are deliberately and consciously told by Corneille's Dorant, Goldoni's Lelio (and Leon, in the Russian reworking of his play *The Liar*, 1786), Semyon in Krylov's *A Lesson for the Daughters*, Zarnitskin in Shakhovskoy's *If You Don't Feel Like It, Don't Listen*, Pustolobov in Kvitka's *A Visitor from the Capital*, and others.[72] In these plays, the lies from which the characters must extricate themselves have a function in the plot. In Act III of Gogol's play there is perhaps an echo of the device of "extrication" in Khlestakov's remark about "another *Yury Miloslavsky*." He is enumerating the works of literature (all of them popular or pulp productions well known at the time) that supposedly have come from his pen.

> *Anna Andreyevna*: So I suppose you wrote *Yury Miloslavsky* too?
> *Khlestakov*: Yes, I did.

[71 "Preduvedomlenie . . . ," p. 116.]

72 The Russian titles are as follows: Krylov, *Urok dochkam*; Shakhovskoy, *Ne lyubo ne slushai, a lgat' ne meshai*; Kvitka, *Priezzhii iz stolitsy*.

Anna Andreyevna: I guessed it right away.

Maria Antonovna: But mamma, it says in the book that Mr. Zagoskin wrote it.

Anna Andreyevna: Oh, I just knew you'd start an argument even here.

Khlestakov: Ah, yes, that's right: it really was written by Zagoskin, but there's another *Yury Miloslavsky*, and that's the one I wrote.

Anna Andreyevna: Well, yours is the one I read, I'm sure. It's so well written!

In general, however, the extrication device is eliminated very explicitly in Gogol's play, inasmuch as the contradictions in Khlestakov's statements do not disconcert any of the other characters and are obvious only to the audience.

The dialogues in Act IV serve not only to delineate character but also to prepare for the climax. The false plot is now concerned not only with the characterization of Khlestakov (Act III had been devoted to that), but also with the apparent success of the other characters, which brings the false inspection-motif to an end. At the same time, the false plot becomes considerably more complex than before. In the first three acts, it developed entirely from the point of view of the mayor and his group; but here it depends on the intersection of two very different false points of view: (1) that of the officials; (2) that of the merchants and townspeople. (In this particular case, the merchants and townspeople are united by a commonly held false point of view.) Taken by itself, each of these false points of view has both a satirical and a comic function—satirical because each motif rests on a contradiction that is seen by the author for what it really is; comic because each motif is paralyzed by the false point of view. The intersection of contradictory points of view strengthens the unity of the comic and satirical function even more.

The role of Khlestakov as the false inspector general really ends here; the love "vaudeville" at the end of Act IV merely adds some details. The introduction of this vaudeville into the fabric of the play deserves attention if only because Gogol, in his theories of the drama, regarded the love-intrigue as being incompatible with the aims of high social comedy, and insisted that it must be abandoned. But it is quite obvious that the love episode in Act IV has absolutely nothing in common with the traditional love-intrigue; on the contrary, it eliminates the intrigue by parodying it.

The mayor's entrance and his ensuing comments (Act IV) return us to the basic satirical theme. The purposes of this satire require that the inspection-theme be broken off by a love-vaudeville, which develops uncontrollably and which, from the point of view of the mayor and his group, completely eliminates this theme. Up to now, the points of view held by the characters and the point of view held by the audience have been moving in a parallel direction, except that the audience has been taking the satirical and comic element into account. But now these points of view intersect and henceforth diverge radically. The result is an absurd juxtaposition of motifs and even of *mise-en-scènes*: Khlestakov simultaneously gets engaged and departs, yet both actions have the same psychological motivation, and the audience is expected to believe in it. The maximum divergence of viewpoints means that the denouement of the comedy is carried out in two diametrically opposed directions: maximum success and maximum failure on the part of the mayor, the first being determined by the daughter's marriage to Khlestakov, the second by Khlestakov's departure. They can coexist because they depend on different points of view. In order to motivate their continued coexistence, Gogol hastily fastens them together by saying that "he [Khlestakov] has gone to ask his uncle's blessing," which lies within the viewpoint of the mayor and his family. The only thing Khlestakov says is "[I'm going] to visit my uncle for a day . . . he's a rich old man." At first the following detail was added: "to let the old man know," but this disappeared as early as the second manuscript version.

From the point of view of the mayor's group, the comedy is brought to an end in keeping with the stock formula of the triumph of the virtuous—i.e., of his excellency the inspector general and "such a fine person" as Maria Antonovna, the daughter of the selfless and zealous governor of the town. At the same time, everything happens "in a most respectable and refined way"; and whenever the patent discrepancy between the sentimental motifs of the false plot and the vaudeville motifs of the true plot becomes obvious, it is promptly eliminated by Anna Andreyevna's remarks, just as easily as is the discrepancy between Khlestakov's engagement and his departure. In Act V, Scene 7, Anna Andreyevna is explaining how the engagement came about:

Anna Andreyevna: In the most respectful and refined way. He expressed himself extremely well. He said: "It is only out of respect for your worthy qualities, Anna Andreyevna." Such a splendid, well-bred man, a person of the most noble principles! "My life—believe me, Anna Andreyevna, my life isn't worth a kopeck: it is only because I respect your rare qualities that I am speaking in this manner."

Maria Antonovna: Oh, mamma! That's what he was saying to *me*!

Anna Andreyevna: Be quiet, you know nothing about it, and don't meddle in what doesn't concern you! . . . And when I tried to say: "We dare not hope for such an honor," he suddenly fell on his knees and said in the most noble manner: "Anna Andreyevna! Do not make me the unhappiest of men. Consent to reciprocate my feelings, otherwise I shall put an end to my life with death!"

Maria Antonovna: Really, mamma, he was saying that about me.

Anna Andreyevna: Yes, of course . . . it was about you too, I'm not denying that.

The denouement has already occurred in the false plot, and there remains only the "punishment of vice," as represented by the ungrateful merchants, or, even better, the mayor's magnanimous forgiveness of their ingratitude and the final "triumph" of the mayor and his family, as a forecast of the still greater triumph that awaits them in St. Petersburg. It is obvious that the stereotypes of the sentimental comedy have been subjected to parody here as well—a parody all the more forceful in that they have been associated with the point of view of a manifestly hostile group (hostile to the author and to the people who presumably share his views—the audience).

From the true point of view (the audience's), Khlestakov's engagement and departure represent not a denouement but a culmination. If from the mayor's point of view the movement of the comedy has depended on the way the rivalry develops (with a group of enemies in all four acts, and with the inspector general in the first two), then from the point of view of the audience it develops out of the way the misunderstanding and unmasking are brought off, with the motifs of the rivalry being interpreted satirically at the same time.

The satirical function of the misunderstanding is now basically at an end. The misunderstanding has helped point up the things that were to be satirized: in the speeches ("interpolated novellas," in their own way) made by the characters from the lower level of society, in the emotionally agitated orders and reminiscences of the mayor, and in the information that is communicated in the remarks made by the mayor's colleagues. The audience perceives the comic duality of the departure/engagement only, of course, as a departure, and hereby as the removal of the direct source of the misunderstanding and the indirect source of the satirical exposés. Because the misunderstanding continues by inertia until the middle of Act V, it can provide a certain amount of additional material for satire (the scene with the merchants); but by now these episodes lie on the falling curve of the plot line.

There remain only the final merging of the different points of view and the final elimination of the misunderstanding, which depends on a new and last appearance of the figure of Khlestakov (this is predestined in the climax, Act IV).[73] The first seven scenes of Act V, with their slow pace and their generally "epic" quality have, from the audience's point of view (in addition to everything else), the obvious function of providing a structural contrast with the sudden unmasking that is inevitably going to come.

Gogol's particular version of this final unmasking may appear to be rather ineffectual. But it is entirely in keeping with the purposes of a social comedy as Gogol conceived of them. A graphic "shaming of the guilty party" might have been necessary in plots of the *Tartuffe* or *Visitor from the Capital* type, which depended on points of view that were not clearly established and on sudden reversals in the roles of accuser and defender. But in *The Inspector General* there is no need for this sort of thing. The audience has long since established its point of view (negative and satirical) toward the mayor and his group and toward Khlestakov—although far less satirical energy has been expended on the latter, precisely because he is an individual *character*, and, moreover, a character who is assigned only a weak social function. But in order to realize the satirical idea to the fullest, it is important that the provincial powers that be (the primary object of the satire) should be brought together, both at the very beginning and at the very end of the play. Gogol does even more, by putting an even larger collective into the final scenes—the "milieu" which has existed only by implication throughout the play but which has in fact deter-

[73 Gippius has in mind the appearance of the "true" inspector general at the end of the play.]

mined the way the mayor and his group have behaved. Once again, this illustrates—and in a most convincing way—that the town is a collective unity, and that the behavior of the officials is determined not by the evil intentions of individuals, but by a community of "manners and habits of common-sense philosophy." (Similar tendencies can be seen in other works that Gogol wrote at about the same time—the play *Marriage*, and the stories "The Two Ivans," "The Nose," and "The Carriage"; later, in *Dead Souls*, the contradiction between individual and social attributes is brilliantly eliminated.) There is a very significant detail here: the merchants are included in this collective, although class antagonism toward them on the part of the others is inevitably emphasized.

Finally, the ending of *The Inspector General* gives us a glimpse of the third point of view that is operative in the comedy: that of the author. As it turns out, then, the comedy exists not just on one plane—as it does from the point of view of the characters (which is why the denouement does not coincide with the engagement of Khlestakov and the mayor's daughter); not just on two planes, as it does for a certain time within the point of view of the audience (which is why the denouement does not coincide with the postmaster's reading of Khlestakov's letter to Tryapichkin), but on three planes.

Within the comedy as a whole—a mock sentimental comedy and a genuine light comedy—there are hints of a tragedy of retribution. This was pointed out by Gogol himself, and by his critics.[74]

There was good reason why Gogol, in "Leaving the Theater," drew a seemingly casual parallel with the ancient tragedy: the "first lover of the arts" expresses surprise that "our writers of comedies absolutely cannot get along without the government. None of our comedies can ever end otherwise. The government appears without fail, like inevitable fate in the tragedies of the ancients." The second lover of the arts seriously proposes that one should have

[74] "This is no longer a joke, and the position of many of the characters is almost tragic. The position of the mayor is the most striking of all." Just before this, the following words were crossed out: "The mayor becomes tragic" ["Preduvedomlenie . . . ," *PSS*, IV, 1951, 118]. Cf. Belinsky: "The appearance of the gendarme with the news about the arrival of the genuine inspector general interrupts this comic scene and, like a thunderclap bursting at their feet, petrifies them with fear and thereby brings the whole play to a splendid close" [review of second edition of Griboyedov, *Woe from Wit*, as in *Polnoe sobranie sochinenii*, III, Moscow, 1953, 469].

faith in the government "as the ancients had faith that fate would overtake wrongdoing."[75]

This interpretation of the play dates from 1842. There is no doubt that it shows signs that Gogol was already beginning to re-evaluate his original conception (this led him to write "The Denouement of *The Inspector General*" in 1846). However, his basic idea—that the play ends on a tragic note—does not contradict the play's objective meaning, both ideological and artistic—provided that we make the essential qualification that the idea of the government in the play was a general and abstract one, and not only did not have to be but could not be given tangible form.

Significantly, the motif of governmental authority is moved off-stage and cannot therefore be shown in any concrete way. Gogol did not follow Fonvizin, Kapnist, and Kvitka, who represented the triumph of law over lawlessness within the play itself. In contrast to the realistically drawn representatives of local authority, who are endowed with various historical, social, national, environmental, and personal characteristics, Gogol presented the abstract, unembellished idea of power at the very end of the play; this idea suggested, implicitly, an even greater abstraction: *the idea of retribution*. As an abstraction, the idea proved entirely acceptable to the groups in society which opposed the status quo. Conversely, Vyazemsky tried to emphasize that the play was making outright propaganda in favor of the government (in the ending and even in the title): he called the government the one honest character in the play.[76] Whether Gogol was aware of Vyazemsky's interpretation or not, we do not know (Vyazemsky did not reiterate this idea in the article he later published). In any event, in the author's monologue which ends "Leaving the Theater," Gogol called *laughter* the only honest and noble character in the play—or in other words, the comic and satirical viewpoint that the author takes toward patently negative characters and phenomena. The contradiction which underlay Gogol's criticism of real life and which impelled him to depict it as a "misunderstanding," as "confusion," also influenced the way he structured the ending of his play. The idea behind the ending was *too* vague to make his criticism consistent and uncompromising, yet vague *enough* to set him apart from the reactionaries who insisted that it contained no

[75] "Teatral'nyi raz"ezd . . . ," *PSS*, v, 1949, 144.]
[76] Letter to A. I. Turgenev, May 8, 1836, *Ostaf'evskii arkhiv*, III, 317-318.

criticism of real life whatsoever. And this vagueness insured that the play could be used as a weapon by progressive opinion.

VIII

The appearance of *The Inspector General* was the signal for a public controversy. The indignant attitude on the part of the reactionary elements of the gentry was expressed, in baldest terms, by F. F. Vigel, in a letter he wrote to Zagoskin on May 31, 1836. (It is very significant that Vigel was seeking sympathy from a writer of popular comedies which had a moral that was acceptable to the conservative landowners.) "I . . . have heard enough about it to be able to say that I could smell its stink from quite a distance. The author has invented some Russia or other, and, within it, some town or other, into which he's tossed all the abominations that can occasionally be found on the surface of the real Russia. . . . I know who the author is: young Russia in all its insolence and cynicism."[77] The same charges of slandering Russia were brought by Bulgarin's group and by Senkovsky, who sympathized with it: attempts to vindicate the play in reactionary circles could be made, as was shown above, only by praising its innocuous merriment (and conversely: Gogol's enemies exploited the view that the play was a farce in order to discredit it even more).

Speaking from an extremely reactionary position, Vigel pinned the label "young Russia" on the politically moderate group that was associated with the journal *The Contemporary*: Vyazemsky, Odoyevsky, Pushkin (who was supposedly "more attached" to Russia than were the others), and even Zhukovsky (who had supposedly changed). We have seen that this group gave *The Inspector General* a sympathetic reception, but failed fully to

[77] *Russkaya starina*, No. 7, 1902 (cf. also Vigel's *Zapiski*). It is curious that both Vigel and Gogol, independent of one another and with diametrically opposite criteria of evaluation, used exactly the same image to characterize the satirical method of *The Inspector General*. Vigel says: "the town into which he has tossed all the abominations"; Gogol says: "to bring everything bad together into one heap." Later, during the period when *Selected Passages* was being written and published, these recent ideological opponents showed a unanimity of thought. [Filipp Filippovich Vigel (1786-1856) was a professional civil servant, a member, in the 1820's, of the famous literary society "Arzamas" (to which Pushkin also belonged), and the author of valuable memoirs.]

acknowledge the social satire in the play.[78] This was what Androsov attempted to do: his ideas, in many respects, came closer to what Gogol had in mind (and helped Gogol formulate his own ideas in the future), but the general conclusions he drew were necessarily limited. The only reaction to the premiere of *The Inspector General* in 1836 on the part of democratic-minded critics was an article by A.B.C., the critic of *Talk* (Belinsky is thought perhaps to be the real author). A.B.C. asserted that the public "is divided into two large categories" and that "the so-called better public" could only take a hostile attitude toward *The Inspector General*. And he gave a brief but graphic and pithy definition of *The Inspector General* as "this Russian, essentially Russian, play which was created not by imitation but out of the author's personal and perhaps bitter feelings. Those who think that this comedy is just funny and nothing more than that are mistaken. Yes, it is funny externally, so to speak; but internally it is all bitter misery, sown with misfortune and dripping with tears. And could the public that was represented in the play—could they, should they see this inner lining, this inner side of the comedy? . . ."[79]

[78] Concerning Vyazemsky's article in *The Contemporary*, No. 2, 1836, see above. Writing in this same issue, Vladimir Odoyevsky made sympathic mention of *The Inspector General*, calling Gogol "the best talent in Russia" ("O vrazhde k prosveshcheniyu"). Pushkin made glancing reference to the play in the first volume of this same journal, in his review of the second edition of *Evenings on a Farm Near Dikanka*. See also his letter to his wife, May 5, 1836. ["Even" Zhukovsky because he was conserva tive politically, being, among other things, tutor to the future Emperor Alexander II. Vladimir Fyodorovich Odoyevsky (1803-69) was an important philosophical writer. His most famous work was *Russian Nights* (*Russkie nochi*, 1844), which criticized Western European culture and called for the creation of a new Russian spirituality.]

[79] [The Russian equivalent of "A.B.C." is "A.B.V."] *Molva*, No. 9, 1836, reprinted in the book *Revizor*, ed. N. L. Brodsky, in the series "Russkie i mirovye klassiki," Moscow, 1927; an excerpt in my book *Gogol' v pis'makh i vospominaniyakh*, Moscow, 1931. Undoubtedly it was this article that Gogol had in mind when he said the following about *The Inspector General* in "An Author's Confession": "Through the laughter, which had never appeared with such force in my works before then, the reader could detect a note of sadness." ["Avtorskaya ispoved'," *PSS*, VIII, 1952, 440.] Unfortunately, Belinsky's actual reactions to the play, in the 1830's, have not been preserved—except the most cursory ones; his later (1840) analysis of it, which he made in his article on Griboyedov's *Woe from Wit*, is important, but it bears traces of the idea of "reconciliation with reality." This came close to the ideas of the *later* Gogol,

The article by A.B.C. was the first symptom of the revolutionary effect created by *The Inspector General*. This effect was later described even more powerfully by Herzen in his book *On the Development of Revolutionary Ideas in Russia*: "Before him [Gogol] nobody had ever given such a complete course of lectures on the pathological anatomy of the Russian civil servant. With an ironic smile on his lips, he penetrated the most hidden twists and turns of this unclean and spiteful soul. Gogol's comedy *The Inspector General* and his novel *Dead Souls* are a horrible confession on the part of contemporary Russia, like the exposés made by Kotoshikhin in the seventeenth century."[80]

Let us sum up the characteristic features of *The Inspector General* which, seen in the perspective of literary history, made the play politically progressive and, objectively, anti-governmental:

1) The elaboration of the traditional "official abuses" plot but the elimination of malevolent individuals; in this way, the plot was opened up to broader social problems which could not be solved by either reforming or removing individual wrongdoers.

2) The complete absence of positive character-types, and hence the elimination of any possibility of introducing not only explicitly "loyalist" motifs, but also motifs which would in any way weaken the potency and thrust of the satire.

3) The assignment of an oppositional role—and hence, to some extent, of the author's positive point of view as well—to a group of episodic characters from the lower levels of society who are oppressed by the powers that be.

4) Structuring the play so as to exclude the possibility not only of making eulogistic or even merely sympathetic statements about

---

but it is not the Gogol of 1836. [Cf. Belinsky, *Polnoe sobranie sochinenii*, III, Moscow, 1953, esp. 452-470. "Reconciliation with reality" refers to the early phase of Belinsky's career when, under the influence of the Hegelian idea that "all that exists is rational" he accepted the status quo in Russia. For Gogol's idea of art as a reconciliation with reality, see his letter to V. A. Zhukovsky, January 10, 1848.]

[80 *Du développement des idées révolutionnaires en Russie* (*O razvitii revolyutsionnykh idei v Rossii*), *Sobranie sochinenii v tridtsati tomakh*, VII, Moscow, 1956, French text on 98, Russian text on 228-229. Grigory Karpovich Kotoshikhin (ca. 1630-67) was an official of the foreign office who turned over secret documents to Sweden, fled there and become a subject, and was later executed for murder. He wrote an interesting account of Russian life.]

the government, but also of soft-pedaling the satirical and realistic tone in any way.

5) The incorporation into the play's fabric of the motif of power as the abstract idea of retribution, without developing it in any tangible way.

Besides this system of devices, which made the play a progressive phenomenon, both in a literary and a social sense, the realistic and typifying devices, taken as a whole, enabled associations of the boldest possible sort to be made, up to and including explicitly revolutionary ones.

These associations went beyond the limits of Gogol's artistic teleology. Only two circumstances made them possible. One was negative: the *absence* from the play of a politically reactionary element, which would have prevented such associations from being made. The other was positive: the *presence* in the play of a general tendency which was socially progressive and which reinforced these associations. Both these conditions are met in *The Inspector General*.

As regards Gogol's later emphasis on reforming the government, his patriotic appeals to the "benevolent eye of the monarch," and his interpretation of the play along these lines: there is no reason why such ideas could not have developed while Gogol was writing the play, as a result of theories which were either imperfectly thought through and formulated, or which were formulated in contradiction to the play's general spirit. But when we take account of the facts of Gogol's development as an artist and of the actual text of the play, we are compelled to introduce qualifying details into this proposed explanation. The patriotic motifs appeared later, chronologically (in the article "The St. Petersburg Stage" and in the draft version of "Leaving the Theater"). The context makes it clear that the relevant pages were written after *The Inspector General* had been performed and, to some extent, when Gogol was already abroad. Gogol's social and political views at that time had already undergone a fundamental change—in connection with the "chaotic chorus of comments" about *The Inspector General*.[81] Unable to find his bearings in this welter of opinion, unable to discern the powerful social organisms that were behind the individuals who thought as he did, he formed the impression that "all the estates" had risen up against him, whereas this was in fact the case only

[81 "Teatral'nyi raz"ezd," *PSS*, v, 1949, 168.]

264

with the militant reactionaries, who could not tolerate any subversion of their idyllic picture of the well-being of all the Russias. So far, Gogol's biography has provided no real justification for his impression; it must have come not so much from published as from spoken opinions, which we can no longer always reconstruct.[82] In some way or other, Gogol came to feel that he was alienated from "all the estates," and this inspired his efforts (naive, to say the very least) to find support in the Tsar, whom he regarded as belonging to no estate at all. This is the mood reflected in the letters he wrote to his friends from abroad in 1836 and 1837, as well as the earliest fragment of the extant drafts of *Dead Souls*. This was his mood when he was finishing up his article on the St. Petersburg stage, and jotting down the first agitated draft of "Leaving the Theater."

Thus, in those years there were already signs of the process which was so fateful for Gogol's life as an artist, the process which led the author of a satirical comedy of genius to carry on a lengthy and painful struggle with himself and to delimit his own satirical realism and his own progressive role in the history of Russian literature and Russian social thought.

---

[82] The summary account made by Gogol in a letter to Shchepkin on April 29 (o.s.), 1836, was undoubtedly based on some concrete facts: "Elderly and respected officials shout that nothing is sacred to me, since I have dared to speak in such a way about people who serve the state; the police officials are against me; the merchants are against me; the men of letters are against me."

7

Boris Eichenbaum
(1886-1959)

EICHENBAUM began his career as a medical student but switched to literature, studying and later teaching at St. Petersburg University. His earliest essays were rather conventional efforts in the historical and biographical criticism then prevalent among Russian academics; but he soon became a champion of the new Formalist movement, and applied its principles in the article "How Gogol's 'Overcoat' is Made." His surgical approach, his "factual" and "scientific" tone, and his interest in the physiology of sound all betrayed the doctor still living within the critic. Later, his views of literature and of criticism broadened to take in history, biography, and society.

His best work dates from the 1920's: *The Melodic Features of Russian Verse* (*Melodika russkogo stikha*, 1922); *The Young Tolstoy* (*Molodoi Tolstoi*, 1923); *Lermontov* (1924); and *Through Literature* (*Skvoz' literaturu*, 1924). But he maintained a steady output of first-rate scholarly writing throughout a long career, most of it spent in Leningrad at the Institute of Russian Literature (Pushkin House) of the Academy of Sciences. Nearly everything he produced is original and provocative.

This article first appeared in 1918, but I have used the text as reprinted in *Skvoz' literaturu* (Leningrad, 1924). The Russian title is "Kak sdelana 'Shinel'' Gogolya." There are many difficulties involved in translating Eichenbaum, indeed most of the Formalists. Few of them were stylists; in fact they often seem to be deliberately cultivating clumsiness, perhaps in the interest of a less "esthetic" and more "scientific" tone. In addition, they were concerned with creating a new critical terminology, for which there is often no real equivalent in English. I have tried to convey both the clumsiness and the innovativeness in my own translation, but by and large I have resisted the temptation to footnote every specimen of Formalist jargon that crops up here. The context should make such instances clear.

I would, however, like to comment on four terms that occur frequently in Eichenbaum's article. One is *igra*, which can mean either "game" or "performance." Both meanings are relevant to the Formalists' idea of the nature of a work of art. I have usually stuck with "performance," which seems better attuned to Eichenbaum's idea of the narrator as a kind of actor. The other three are: *kompozitsiya*, *struktura*, and *postroenie*. All can mean "structure," but they are really not synonymous. *Kompozitsiya* I render as "texture" (see the first sentence of the article), by way of suggesting, in the words of Webster's Second International Dictionary, "the characteristic disposition or connection of threads in a woven fabric," or "the structural quality resulting from the artist's blending of elements": the English "composition" is vague, and does not (to me, at least) convey the idea of both process and component elements, as does the Russian *kompozitsiya*. (On the other hand, for the title of Gippius's article in this collection, "structure" does seem to me a better way of rendering *kompozitsiya*.) "Texture" also goes with Eichenbaum's image of "interweaving" (*spletenie*), in the first and second paragraphs. "Structure" renders *struktura*, and suggests the finished work as a whole. "Construct" renders *postroenie*, and indicates the process of putting the work together. "Motif" (*motif*) and "motivation" (*motivirovka*) are also key Formalist concepts. A motif is the basic narrative unit (e.g., the duel-motif); each work may contain many motifs; and the factor or factors determining the way in which they are brought together is the motivation (e.g., the journey is the motivation for *Don Quixote*). It is the interrelationship of motifs and motivation that especially interests Formalist writers on prose-fiction, as we see from the first two paragraphs of Eichenbaum's article.

How Gogol's "Overcoat" is Made

by Boris Eichenbaum

I

THE TEXTURE of a story depends in large part on the role played by the author's *personal tone*, i.e., on whether this tone is an organizing principle and creates more or less the illusion of *skaz*,[1] or whether it has the purely formal function of linking events and is therefore of secondary importance. The primitive story, as well as the adventure-novel, has no *skaz* and needs none, because its dynamics and its intrinsic interest are wholly determined by the rapid succession of events and situations of various kinds. Its organizing principle is the interweaving of motifs and their motivation. The same is true of the comic story as well: it is based on an anecdote that is rich in comic situations in and of itself, quite apart from *skaz*.

An entirely different kind of structure results if the plot as such (the interweaving of motifs by means of their motivation) ceases to play an organizing role, i.e., if the narrator, in one way or another, puts himself in the foreground and seems to be using the plot merely to interweave individual stylistic devices. The center of gravity is shifted from the plot (which is now reduced to a minimum) to the devices of *skaz*; and the most important comic role is assigned to plays on words, which sometimes amount to nothing more than simple puns, and sometimes develop into small anecdotes. Comic effects are achieved by the *manner* in which the *skaz* is presented. Therefore, for a study of this type of structure, it is precisely these apparently trivial details scattered throughout the narrative which prove to be important—so much so that if they are removed, the structure of the story falls apart. Here two kinds of comic *skaz* can be distinguished: (1) that which narrates; (2) that which reproduces. The first is confined to jokes, plays on meaning, etc.; the second introduces devices of verbal mimicry and verbal gesture, in the form of specially devised comic articulations, word-plays based on sounds, capricious arrangements of syntax, and so on. The first creates the impression of an even flow of

[1 For a definition of *skaz*, see the introduction and the article by Chizhevsky in this collection.]

269

speech; the second often seems to be concealing an actor, so that the *skaz* here becomes a kind of play-acting, and the structure is determined not by the simple linkage of one comic episode with another, but by a system of articulated phonic gestures of various kinds.

Many of Gogol's stories, or individual sections of them, offer interesting material for an analysis of this kind of *skaz*. Structure, in Gogol, is not determined by plot; his plots are always scanty. Rather, there is no plot at all, but only some comic situation (and sometimes even that is not at all comic *in itself*), serving, as it were, merely as an impetus or pretext for the elaboration of comic devices. Thus, "The Nose" develops out of a single incident related in the form of an anecdote; *Marriage* and *The Inspector General* also grow out of a particular situation which itself does not change. *Dead Souls* is constructed by the simple accumulation of individual scenes, which are unified only by the travels of Chichikov. We know that Gogol felt cramped by the necessity of always having something resembling a plot. According to P. V. Annenkov: "He said that for any story to be successful, all the author had to do was describe a room and a street that were familiar to him."[2] In a letter to Pushkin in 1835, Gogol wrote: "Do me a favor and give me a plot of some kind, I don't care whether it's funny or not as long as it's a purely Russian story. . . . Do me a favor and give me a plot; it'll be a five-act comedy in nothing flat and—I swear—funnier than the devil!" He often asks people to send him anecdotes. For instance, he wrote Prokopovich in 1837: "Ask Jules [i.e., Annenkov] especially to write me. He has something to write about. Something funny must have happened in the office."[3]

On the other hand, Gogol was noted for his special skill in reading his own works aloud, as many of his contemporaries attest.

[2 "N. V. Gogol' v Rime letom 1841 goda," *Literaturnye vospominaniya,* Moscow, 1960, p. 77.]

[3 The letter to Pushkin was written on October 7 (o.s.), 1835, and the one to Prokopovich on January 25, 1837. Nikolay Yakovlevich Prokopovich (1810-57) was a minor poet and one of Gogol's better friends. As to why Gogol calls P. V. Annenkov "Jules," Annenkov himself has this to say: "Around 1842, when I first met Gogol, he gave nicknames to all his friends from the school at Nezhin and to their friends as well, gracing them with the names of *celebrated* French writers with whom all of Petersburg was then infatuated. There were Hugos, Alexandre Dumases, Balzacs . . . I don't know why I got the name of Jules Janin, by which I was known to the end [of Gogol's life]." ("N. V. Gogol' v Rime letom 1841 goda," *Literaturnye vospominaniya,* Moscow, 1960, p. 59.)]

Two major devices can be identified here: either a chant-like, declamatory style, or a special manner of acting things out—a mimetic *skaz*, which nonetheless never sounded like the way actors render their parts, as we know from Turgenev.[4] There is a well-known story of I. I. Panayev's about the time Gogol astonished his audience by making such an abrupt switch from ordinary conversation to acting that at first his belching and the sort of utterances appropriate to it were taken for real.[5] And as Prince D. A. Obolensky reports:

> Gogol was a master of the art of reading aloud: not only did he articulate each word distinctly, but he often varied his intonation, thereby giving his language diversity and making his listeners absorb the subtlest shadings of thought. I remember how he began in a muffled and rather sepulchral voice: "But why depict poverty, always poverty. . . . And now once again we find ourselves in the backwater, once again we have stumbled on an out-of-the-way place." After these words Gogol raised his head slightly, tossed back his hair, and went on, but now in a loud and triumphal voice: "Yet what a backwater, what an out-of-the-way place!" Following which he began the magnificent description of Tentetnikov's village [in Part 2 of *Dead Souls*], which came out, the way Gogol read it, *as if it had been written in a certain meter.* Above all I was struck by the extraordinarily harmonious quality of his language. Here I perceived what wonderful use Gogol had made of those local names for grasses and flowers that he had so painstakingly collected. *Apparently he would sometimes put in some sonorous word just for the harmonious effect.*[6]

I. I. Panayev characterized Gogol's manner of reading as follows:

> Gogol was an inimitable reader. Among today's men of letters, Ostrovsky and Pisemsky are considered the best readers of their

[4 I. S. Turgenev, "Gogol'," *Polnoe sobranie sochinenii i pisem*, XIV (*Sochineniya*), Moscow-Leningrad, 1967, 69-70.]

[5 *Literaturnye vospominaniya.* Cf. V. V. Veresayev, *Gogol' v zhizni*, Moscow-Leningrad, 1933, p. 231. Ivan Ivanovich Panayev (1812-62) was a sometime writer of fiction, but his real importance for Russian literature is as a journalist: he was one of the editors of the famous journal *The Contemporary*.]

[6 "O pervom izdanii posmertnykh sochinenii Gogolya," *Russkaya starina*, December, 1873. Dmitry Alexandrovich Obolensky (1822-61) was a high-ranking professional civil servant. The italics are Eichenbaum's.]

own works. Ostrovsky reads without any dramatic effects, with the greatest simplicity imaginable, yet he gives each character the proper shading; Pisemsky reads like an actor—he acts out his play, so to speak, in the reading. . . . In Gogol's manner of reading there was something midway between these two styles. He read more dramatically than Ostrovsky and with much greater simplicity than Pisemsky.[7]

Even when he dictated, Gogol would put on a kind of performance. P. V. Annenkov writes:

Opening his notebook before him, Nikolay Vasilievich . . . would become completely engrossed in it and would begin dictating in a measured and solemn manner, with such feeling and such expressiveness that the chapters of the first volume of *Dead Souls* took on a special coloration in my memory. It was like the calm, even flow of inspiration that usually comes from the profound contemplation of a subject. N. V. would patiently wait for me to catch up with him, and he would then go on with a new sentence in exactly the same tone of voice, suffused with concentrated feeling and thought. . . . I remember that Gogol's dictation never reached such emotional intensity as in this passage [the description of Plyushkin's garden], yet all the naturalness of his art was preserved. Gogol even got up from his chair . . . and he *accompanied his dictation with a proud and rather imperious gesture.*[8]

Such accounts indicate that the basis of a Gogolian text is *skaz*, and that it is made up of the actual elements of speech and verbalized emotions. Even more, this *skaz* has a tendency not simply to narrate, not simply to talk, but also to reproduce words with an emphasis on mimetic and articulated sounds. Sentences are

[7] *Literaturnye vospominaniya.* Cf. Veresayev, *Gogol' v zhizni,* pp. 231-232. Alexander Nikolayevich Ostrovsky (1823-86), Russia's most famous and most prolific playwright, specialized in "realistic" accounts of merchant-class life. His best-known play is *The Thunderstorm* (*Groza,* 1860).

Alexey Feofilaktovich Pisemsky (1820-1881) was an excellent writer who just missed greatness. He is best known for the novel *A Thousand Souls* (*Tysyacha dush,* 1858), and the play *A Hard Lot* (*Gor'kaya sud'bina,* 1859).]

[8] "N. V. Gogol' v Rime letom 1841 goda," *Literaturnye vospominaniya,* Moscow, 1960, p. 86. The italics are Eichenbaum's.]

devised and put together not according to the principles of logical speech alone, but more according to the principles of expressive speech, where articulated sound, mimicry, phonic gestures, etc., play a special role. Hence the phenomenon of sound-semantics in Gogol's language: the phonic "envelope" of the word, or its acoustic characteristics, take on significance quite independent of logic or of concrete meaning. Articulated sound, and its acoustic effect, assume priority as an expressive device. This is why Gogol loved surnames, given names, etc.: they allow for the play of such devices of articulated sound. Moreover, his manner of reading was often accompanied by gestures (see above), and became mimetic, as we can also see in its written form.

Reports by Gogol's contemporaries point up these same features. For instance, D. A. Obolensky writes:

> At the posthouse I found the complaint book and read out a rather amusing grievance by some gentleman or other. After hearing it, Gogol asked me: "And who do you think this gentleman is? What sort of character and special traits does he have?" "I really don't know," I replied. "Well, I'll tell you." Whereupon he began, in the most amusing and original way, to describe to me first this gentleman's physical appearance; then he told me all about his professional career, even *acting out* certain episodes from his life. I remember that I laughed like a lunatic, but he was doing all this in complete earnest. Then he told me that he had once shared lodgings with N. M. Yazykov (the poet) and that while getting ready for bed at night, they would amuse themselves by describing various characters and then would think up an appropriate name for each of them.[9]

O. N. Smirnova also has something to say about surnames in Gogol:

> He devoted an extraordinary amount of attention to the names of his characters; he looked for them everywhere; they became evocative; he found them on notices (the name of Chichikov, in Part 1 of *Dead Souls*, was found on a house—in the old days there were no numbers, just the name of the owner) and on signboards. When he was beginning the second volume of *Dead Souls*, he found the name of General Betrishchev in a book in

[9 Cf. Veresayev, *Gogol' v zhizni*, p. 409. The italics are Eichenbaum's.]

a posthouse, and he told one of his friends that at the sight of this name, the figure and gray mustache of a general appeared before him.[10]

Gogol's special attitude toward personal names and his inventiveness in this area have already been noted in the scholarly literature, e.g., in Professor I. Mandelshtam's book:

Dating from the period when Gogol was still concerned with amusing himself are, first of all, names that are obviously devised without regard for "laughter through tears" [i.e., for purely comic effect]: Pupopuz, Golopuz, Dovgochkhun, Golopupenko, Sverbyguz, Kizyakolupenko, Pereperchikha, Krutoryshchenko, Pecherytsya, Zakrutyguba, etc. Moreover, Gogol followed the same habit of devising amusing names even in later works: we see it in Yaichnitsa (*Marriage*), Neuvazhay-Koryto (*Dead Souls*), Belobryushkova and Bashmachkin ("The Overcoat"), with the latter also providing the basis for a play on words. Sometimes he deliberately chose names that actually exist: Akaky Akakievich, Trifily, Dula, Varakhasy, Pavsikakhy, Vakhtisy, etc. . . . In other cases he used names as puns. (This device has long been employed by all comic writers. Molière amuses his audiences with names like Pourceaugnac, Diafoirus, Purgon, Macroton, Desfonandrès, Villebrequin; Rabelais, to an infinitely greater extent, uses improbable combinations of sounds which provoke laughter merely because they have only a remote resemblance to existing words, e.g.: Salmiguondinoys, Trinquamelle, Trouillogan, etc.)[11]

[10] Olga Nikolayevna Smirnova (1834-93) was the daughter of Gogol's great friend Alexandra Osipovna Smirnova, and the real author of her mother's "memoirs."]

[11] I. Mandelshtam, *O kharaktere Gogolevskogo stilya*, Helsingfors, 1902, pp. 252-553. This book is interesting for its specific observations, but disorderly as far as methodology is concerned.

[Several points within the quotation require commentary.

(a) The "period when Gogol was still concerned with amusing himself" refers to Gogol's discussion of his "laughter" in "An Author's Confession." He explains the humorous element of his earlier works as follows: "I was subject to inexplicable attacks of melancholy, which were the result, perhaps, of my sickly condition. In order to amuse myself, I would think up all the funny things I possibly could." But later he saw that his "laughter" must "become more serious and serve a purpose higher than himself"

And so, plot in Gogol is of only external importance and therefore is in itself static: there is good reason why *The Inspector General* ends with a mute scene, for which everything that comes before is only a preparation, as it were. The real dynamic force and therefore the structure of Gogol's works depends on the way the *skaz* is put together, on the play of language. His characters are only petrified poses. They are dominated by the mirthful and ever-playful spirit of the artist himself, as stage-director and real hero.

Proceeding from these general principles of structure and from the material on Gogol that we have introduced, let us now try to throw some light on the primary layer in the structure of "The Overcoat." This story is especially interesting for this type of analysis, because it combines a purely comic *skaz*, containing all the devices of verbal play that are so characteristic of Gogol, with a highly emotional, declamatory style which forms, as it were, a secondary layer. This secondary layer has been taken by our critics as the primary one, and the whole complex "labyrinth of linkages" (Leo Tolstoy's expression) has been reduced to one particular idea, which has been repeated, by tradition's decree, down to the present day, even in so-called scholarly studies of Gogol.[12] Gogol might have replied to critics and scholars of this ilk in the same way Tolstoy did to the critics of *Anna Karenina*: "I congratulate them and can confidently assure them *qu'ils en savent plus long que moi.*"

("Avtorskaya ispoved'," *PSS*, VIII, 1952, 439 ff. See also the opening paragraph of Gippius's article in the present collection).

(b) The names cited by Mandelshtam are all "meaningful" ones. Pupopuz: Navel-Belly; Golopuz: Naked Belly; Dovgochkhun: Long Sneeze; Golopupenko: Naked Navel; Sverbyguz: Scratch-Arse; Kizyakolupenko: Peat-Dung Picker; Pereperchikha: Over-Pepperer; Krutoryshchenko: Abrupt Roarer; Pecherytsya: a kind of mushroom; Zakrutyguba: Curl-Lip.

(c) Yaichnitsa means "omelette"; Neuvazhay-Koryto means "don't respect the feeding-trough"; Belobryushkova is made from the words for "white" and "belly"; and Bashmachkin is made from the word for "shoe." Later on in the article, Eichenbaum discusses the play on words that arises from Bashmachkin.

(d) By "existing names" Mandelshtam means those that can actually be found in the saints' calendar, however peculiar they may sound.]

[12 By "particular idea" Eichenbaum means the "pathetic" or "humane" interpretation that has often been given to the story. For a more extensive discussion, see Chizhevsky's article in this collection.]

II

Let us first examine the most important *skaz*-devices separately, and then study the system by which they are linked.

An important function is played by puns of various kinds, especially at the beginning. They are constructed either on similarities of sound, plays on etymologies, or hidden absurdities. The first sentence of the initial draft contained a play on sound: "In the Department of *Assessments* and *Collections*—which, however, is sometimes called the Department of *Nonsenses* and *Confections*." In the second draft, a sentence was added which carried this particular play on sound even further: "Let readers not think, however, that this name could actually be found in real life—not at all. It's entirely a matter here of the etymological similarity of words. In consequence, the Department of Mining and Salt Affairs is called the Department of Whining and Salty Affairs. Sometimes a great deal enters the heads of clerks during the period between work and the whist-game." This particular pun did not go into the final version.[13]

Etymological puns are particular favorites of Gogol's, and to bring them off, he often devises special surnames. Thus, Akaky Akakievich's last name started out as Tishkevich—but that in itself did not provide any basis for punning. Then Gogol wavered between two forms—Bashmakevich (cf. Sobakevich, in *Dead Souls*), and Bashmakov. Finally he settled on the form Bashmachkin. The shift from Tishkevich to Bashmakevich was of course motivated by the desire to create something on which puns could be made; and the choice of the form Bashmachkin can be explained by Gogol's predilection for diminutive suffixes, which are characteristic of his style, as well as by the greater expressive power inherent in this particular form, in terms of articulated

[13 I have tried to suggest the flavor of the puns here, rather than making a literal translation. In Russian they read: "v departámente pódatei i sbórov, —kotoryi vprochem inogda nazyvayut departámentom pódlostei i vzdórov" (literally "The Department of Assessments and Collections—which, however, is sometimes called the Department of Basenesses and Nonsenses"); and the second group: "departáment górnykh i solyanýkh del . . . departáment gór'kikh i solénykh del" ("The Department of Mining and Salt Affairs. . . . The Department of Bitter and Salty [or Salacious] Affairs"). The italics are Eichenbaum's.]

sound (sound-imitation): it produces a kind of phonic gesture.[14] The pun created by means of this name is made more complex by comic devices which make it look completely serious:

> From the name alone it is already clear that it was derived from the word for shoe [*bashmak*]; but when, at what time, and in what manner it derived from "shoe"—of this nothing is known. His father, his grandfather, and *even his brother-in-law* (the pun is imperceptibly reduced to the absurd—a common device in Gogol), and absolutely all the Bashmachkins wore boots, merely having them resoled about three times a year.[15]

The pun seems to be destroyed by commentary of this sort— the more so since utterly irrelevant details (the soles) are introduced in passing. In point of fact, the result is a complex or, as it were, a double pun. The device of reducing something to absurdity or of making a non-logical combination of words is often met with in Gogol, but it is usually masked by strictly logical syntax and therefore creates the impression that it is unintentional—as, for example, in the description of Petrovich, who "despite being one-eyed and *having a completely pockmarked face*, was rather successful at mending the trousers and coats of clerks and all other varieties." Here the logical absurdity is further masked by a plethora of details which distract our attention. The pun is not flaunted; on the contrary, it is concealed in every possible way, and its comic effect is therefore heightened. The purely etymological pun occurs rather frequently: "misfortunes are strewn on the path of life not only of titular, but even privy, actual, court, and all other councilors, even those who *give no counsel to anyone, nor themselves take it from anyone.*"[16]

[14 The root of the name *Tishkevich* is *tikh-*, "quiet." *Sobakevich* is derived from *sobaka*, "dog." *Bashmachkin* is derived from *bashmak*, "shoe"; the *ch* in the name is a diminutive suffix, suggesting something small, weak, endearing, or helpless. When Eichenbaum says that Tishkevich "did not provide any basis for punning," he presumably means that Gogol would not have been able to come up with anything resembling the "shoe"/"sole" pun in the following paragraph.]

[15 The italics and the parenthetical comment are Eichenbaum's.]

[16 For once the puns more or less correspond in Russian and English. They are closer, to the eye, in Russian, because the root word is spelled the same in both cases: *sovétnik* (councilor)—*sovét* (counsel, or council). The italics in both quotations above are Eichenbaum's.]

These are the most prominent types of jokes and puns in "The Overcoat." Let us add another device here: the pun based on sound-effects. We have already spoken of Gogol's fondness for "meaningless" terms and names; such words "transcend" meaning and open up possibilities for a distinctive semantics of sound.[17] *Akaky Akakievich* is deliberately chosen for the sake of its sound. Significantly, the scene describing his name is accompanied by a whole little story. In the rough draft, Gogol notes specifically: "Of course, it might have been possible somehow to avoid the frequent repetition of the letter *k*, but circumstances were such that it was absolutely impossible to do so." The sound-semantics of this name is further prepared by a series of other names that are also especially expressive as sheer sound and are obviously chosen or "contrived" for just this reason.[18] In the rough draft, the selection was somewhat different:

1) Yevvul, Mokky, Yevlogy;
2) Varakhasy, Dula, Trefily;
   (Varadat, Farmufy)[19]
3) Pavsikakhy, Frumenty.

In the final version:

1) Mokky, Sossy, Khozdazat;
2) Trifily, Dula, Varakhasy;
   (Varadat, Varukh)
3) Pavsikakhy, Vakhtisy and Akaky.[20]

A comparison of these two lists shows that the second gives the impression of having been more carefully selected for the sake of

[17 Here Eichenbaum cites two words from the story "The Carriage": *pul'putik* and *monmun'ya*. Both are terms of endearment, with no dictionary meaning—a kind of baby-talk. "Transcend" in the previous sentence renders *zamunye* (*slova*), which is a reference to "trans-sense language" (*zaum'*, or *zaumnyi yazyk*), a movement in Russian Futurism aimed at creating a new poetic language by inventing words that had no dictionary equivalents and by emphasizing sheer sound.]

[18 "Contrived" is the term used by Gogol in the story: "Perhaps the reader will find the name somewhat strange and contrived."]

19 Names proposed by the mother.

[20 Even readers who know no Russian may grasp Eichenbaum's point here. The second group of names is more organized, in rhythm and sound, than the first. In "Mókky, Sóssy, Khozdazát," the sounds "o" and "a" predominate; in "Pavsikákhy, Vakhtísy i Akáky," the sound "a." Each line has three strong beats.]

articulated sound: it forms a distinctive sound-system. The comic effect of the sound of these names does not depend on their being unusual (unusualness in itself cannot be comic), but rather on the way the selection is made: its highly monotonous quality prepares the comic name of Akaky, and even more, Akakievich, which in combination—Akaky Akakievich—actually sounds like a *nickname*, which conceals a meaning dependent on sound. The comic effect is further intensified by the fact that the names preferred by the mother remain within the same general system. The result of all this is an imitation in articulated sound—a phonic gesture.[21]

Still another passage in "The Overcoat" is interesting in this respect—the one where Akaky Akakievich's appearance is being described: "And so, in a certain department there worked a certain clerk, a clerk who could not be called very remarkable— shortish in stature, rather pockmarked, with rather reddish hair, even rather near-sighted, with a smallish bald patch atop his head, with wrinkles on both cheeks and the sort of complexion that is known as hemorrhoidal." The last word is so placed that its phonic structure acquires a special emotional and expressive force, and is perceived as a comic phonic gesture, independent of the meaning. It is prepared, on the one hand, by the device of rhythmic accretion, and on the other, by the identical endings of several words, which attune the ear to catching sound-impressions (shortish-reddish-smallish); the last word—"hemorrhoidal"—therefore sounds grandiose and fantastic, quite apart from any reference to meaning.[22]

---

[21] This Gogolian device is repeated by his imitators. Cf. an early story by P. I. Melnikov-Pechersky, "On Who Yelpfidor Perfilevich Was" ("O tom, kto takoi byl El'fidor Perfilievich," 1840). Cf. the article by A. Zmorovich in *Russkii filologicheskii vestnik*, 1916, No. 1-2, p. 178 ff.

[22 The point here is difficult to put across in translation. The Russian reads: "chinovnik nel'zya skazat' chtoby ochen' zamechatel'nyi, nizen'kogo rosta, neskol'ko ryabovat, neskol'ko ryzhevat, neskol'ko dazhe na vid podslepovat, s nebol'shoi lysinoi na lbu, s morshchinami po obeim storonam shchek i tsvetom litsa chto nazyvaetsya gemoroidal'nym." The effect depends on the contrast between the pompous, foreign, and vivid "hemorrhoidal" (*gemoroidal'nym*), and the preceding adjectives, which are all garden-variety Russian and are made vague not only by the *-ovat* suffix (roughly equivalent to English "ish"), but also by the "somewhat" (*neskol'ko*) that comes before them. "Hemorrhoidal" also shatters the rhythm set up in the preceding lines. A less literal translation might read: "somewhat shortish, somewhat reddish, somewhat blindish, somewhat baldish, and with a complexion that could be called hemorrhoidal."]

Interestingly enough, this sentence was much simpler in the rough draft: "And so, in this department there worked a clerk, who was not very attractive—shortish, baldish, rather pockmarked, reddish in complexion, even rather near-sighted." In its final form, this sentence is not so much a *description* of Akaky's appearance as a *reproduction* of it by means of articulated sound. The words are chosen and placed in a certain order, not in accordance with any principle of character-delineation, but in accordance with the principle of sound-semantics. The reader's inner eye remains blank (I think nothing is more difficult than to make drawings of Gogol's heroes); all that remains of the entire sentence in one's memory is the impression of a certain order of sounds, which culminates in a resounding word virtually devoid of logical meaning yet extraordinarily expressive as sheer articulated sound—"hemorrhoidal."

Here D. A. Obolensky's observation is entirely to the point— that Gogol sometimes "would put in some sonorous word just for the harmonious effect." The sentence gives the impression of being whole and complete in itself—a system of phonic gestures which has been created by the careful choice of words. Therefore these words are virtually not perceived as logical units or as emblems of concepts: they have been broken down and reassembled according to the principle of language based on sound. This is one of the remarkable effects of Gogol's language. Some of his sentences function as phonic inscriptions,[23] so prominently do articulated sound and acoustics stand out in them. The most commonplace word is sometimes introduced in such a way that the logical or concrete meaning recedes, but the semantics of the sound stands out, and a simple term takes on the appearance of a nickname: "he came upon a policeman who, his halberd placed beside him, was shaking tobacco out of a hornlet into a calloused fist." Or: "Maybe seeing as how it's come into fashion, we'll even fasten the collar with silver-plated clasps." This represents an obvious playing with articulated sound.[24]

[23 *zvukovye nadpisi*—that is, a merging or correlation of the acoustic and the written form.]

[24 The first example does not quite come off in translation. Eichenbaum has in mind the word "halberd"—*alebardu*—which in Russian sounds foreign and grandiose, and intrudes suddenly into the "ordinary" texture of the rest of the sentence. In the second example, the sound-play of "*si*lver-*pl*ated c*la*sps" corresponds pretty well to the Russian "*la*pki *p*od a*pli*ke," although it does not suggest the "foreignness" of *aplike*, which is originally the French *appliqué*.]

There is no neutral level of language in Gogol, no logical bringing together of simple psychological or concrete concepts into ordinary sentences. A highly intensified intonation alternates with this mimetic and articulated sound and gives the sentences their shape. Gogol's works are frequently structured on this alternation. In "The Overcoat," there is a striking example of an intonational effect of this kind, a highly emotional piece of declamation:

Even during those hours when the gray St. Petersburg skies grow completely dark and when the entire population of clerks have dined and eaten their fill, each as best he can according to his salary and his own whims, when all have already rested from the scratching of pens and the bustle of the office, from seeing to their own essential occupations and those of other people, from all the tasks that restless man willingly assigns himself even beyond what is necessary, when the clerks are hastening to devote their remaining time to pleasure: some, more lively, rush off to the theater; some to the streets, there to devote their time to examining ladies' pretty little hats; some to spend an evening paying compliments to some attractive girl, the star of a little circle of clerks; some—and this happens most frequently—simply visit a fellow-clerk on the fourth or third floor, in two small rooms, with a hall or a kitchen, and with certain pretensions to fashion, with a lamp and some other little object which has cost many sacrifices of dinners and evenings out—in a word, even at that time when all the clerks are scattered about the small apartments of their friends to play a stormy game of whist, sipping tea from glasses and eating one-kopeck biscuits, and drawing the smoke out of long-stemmed pipes, and while the cards are being dealt, relating some piece of gossip which has trickled down from high society —a habit that a Russian can never resist under any circumstances, or even, when there is nothing to say, repeating the everlasting story about the commanding officer who was told that the tail on the horse of Falconet's statue had been cut off. . . ."

This enormous period, which ultimately builds the intonation up to a point of enormous tension, is resolved with unexpected simplicity: "in a word, even during the time when everyone was bent on diverting himself, Akaky Akakievich allowed himself no diversion." The result is a sense of comic disparity between the

281

intonation of the syntax, which begins in a muffled and mysterious way and builds up to a point of great tension, and the way it is resolved semantically. This impression is further heightened by the choice of prosaic words, which seem to be deliberately at variance with the texture of the syntax: pretty little hats, the attractive girl, the sipping of tea from glasses along with one-kopeck biscuits, and finally the story of Falconet's statue of Peter the Great that is thrown in as an afterthought. This contradiction or disparity acts upon the words themselves in such a way that they become strange, enigmatic, unfamiliar-sounding, striking to the ear, as if they had been dismembered or invented by Gogol for the first time.

"The Overcoat" contains another kind of declamatory style as well, which makes an unexpected intrusion into the general style that is based on word-play: the sentimental and melodramatic. This is the famous "humane" passage, which has enjoyed such celebrity in Russian literary criticism that it is no longer a secondary artistic device but has become the "idea" of the entire story. " 'Leave me alone. Why do you insult me?' And there was something strange in these words and the tone of voice in which they were uttered. Something that aroused compassion could be heard in them, so that one young man, who had been recently appointed. . . . And for a long time thereafter, the shortish figure of the little clerk with the bald-patch atop his head would appear before him, in his happiest moments. . . . In these heart-rending words, others could be heard. . . . And the poor young man would bury his face in his hands," etc. This passage does not exist in the rough drafts; it was put in later, and undoubtedly belongs to the secondary layer, whose elements of emotional declamation give greater complexity to the purely anecdotal style of the original versions.[25]

[25] Vasily Rozanov also speaks of this passage, explaining it as "the artist's sorrow at the law of his creation, the tears he sheds over the amazing picture that he does not know how to draw differently . . . and, having drawn it thus, though admiring it, he scorns and hates it" ("Kak proizoshel tip Akakiya Akakievicha," *Legenda o Velikom Inkvizitore, s prilozheniem dvukh etyudov o Gogole*, 3d ed., St. Petersburg, 1906, pp. 278-279). Or again: "And then, as if interrupting this torrent of gibes and striking the hand that is depicting it and cannot stop, there follows, as a kind of marginal comment that has been tacked on later: . . . 'but Akaky Akakievich did not answer a single word . . . ,'" etc. (p. 279). Leaving aside the question of the philosophical and psychological meaning of this passage,

Gogol gives his characters in "The Overcoat" little to say, and, as is always the case with him, their language is fashioned in a very special way. Despite individual differences, it never gives the impression of being everyday language, as it does, for instance, in Ostrovsky (there is very good reason why Gogol read his works in a different manner); it is always stylized. Akaky Akakievich's language is part of the general system of Gogolian language and its mimetic, articulated sound: it is constructed in a special way and garnished with commentary: "It must be noted that Akaky Akakievich expressed himself for the most part in prepositions, adverbs, and, last but not least, in particles of a kind that have absolutely no meaning." Petrovich's language, unlike the jerky articulation of Akaky Akakievich, is condensed, terse, solid, and acts by way of contrast. It contains no traces of everyday language: a normal colloquial intonation is inappropriate to it; it is just as "contrived" and artificial as the language of Akaky Akakievich himself. As is always the case with Gogol (cf. "Old-Fashioned Landowners," "The Two Ivans," *Dead Souls*, and the plays), these phrases stand outside time, outside the moment—they are motionless, forever so: they are a language that might be spoken by puppets.

Gogol's own language—his *skaz*—is just as contrived too. In "The Overcoat," this *skaz* is stylized as a special brand of offhand and naive chatter. "Unnecessary" details pop up in the most natural-looking way: "On her right stood the godfather, a most excellent man, Ivan Ivanovich Yeroshkin, who worked as one of the head clerks in the Senate, and the godmother, the wife of a police official and a woman of rare virtues, Arina Semyonovna Belobryushkova." Or, the *skaz* can become verbose and familiar in tone: "Of course, not much should be said about this tailor, but since it is already an established practice in stories to describe each character fully, there's nothing to be done—let's have Petrovich here too." What is comic here is that after such a pronouncement, the "characterization" of Petrovich is exhausted by the reference to his drinking on every holiday indiscriminately. The same device is repeated with regard to his wife: "Since we've now mentioned the wife, it will be necessary to say a couple of words

---

we regard it, in the given instance, only as an artistic device, and we are evaluating it from the standpoint of structure, as the intrusion of the declamatory style into the system of the comic *skaz*.

about her too; but unfortunately, very little was known about her except that Petrovich did in fact have a wife, and that she even wore a bonnet, not a kerchief; but it would seem that she could not boast of beauty; at least, only soldiers of the guard would peer beneath her bonnet when they encountered her, twitch their mustaches, and give vent to a curious sound."

This *skaz* style is especially marked in one sentence: "Just where the clerk who had invited him lived, we can't say, unfortunately; our memory has begun to play real tricks on us, and everything in Petersburg, all the houses and streets have gotten so muddled and mixed up in our head that it's extremely difficult to get anything out of it in proper order." If we add to this all the numerous expressions like "some . . . or other," "unfortunately, little is known," "nothing is known," "I don't remember," etc., then we get, as a result, the impression of a device which creates the illusion that the work as a whole is a real story, related as a fact but not known to the narrator in every small detail. He readily digresses from the basic story and tosses in incidental remarks such as: "they say that"—for example, at the beginning, when he is talking about the petition made by some police chief ("I don't remember from what town"); also about Bashmachkin's ancestry, the tail of the horse on the Falconet statue, the titular councilor who was made a director and proceeded to partition off a special room for himself which he called the "presence chamber," and so on. It is well known that the plot of "The Overcoat" derived from an "office story" about a poor clerk who lost a gun for which he had long been saving up. "The anecdote was the germ of the wonderful story 'The Overcoat,'" P. V. Annenkov writes.[26] Its original title was "The Tale of a Clerk Who Stole Overcoats," and in the rough drafts the general manner of the *skaz* is marked by an even greater stylization in imitation of careless chatter and informality: "I really don't remember his name"; "deep down he was a very kind-hearted beast," etc. In the final version, Gogol toned down devices of this sort to some extent, and embellished the story with puns and anecdotes, but he also introduced a declamatory style, thereby making the original structural layer much more complex. The result is a grotesque, in which the mimicry of laughter alternates with the mimicry of sorrow—both creating the impression of

[26 "N. V. Gogol' v Rime letom 1841 goda," *Literaturnye vospominaniya*, Moscow, 1960, p. 76. See the article by Chizhevsky, in the present collection, for an account of the anecdote.]

being a performance, with a pre-established order of gestures and intonations.

III

Let us now follow this alternation through the story with the aim of discovering the basic method by which the individual devices are linked. Beneath this linkage, or texture, lies the *skaz*, whose characteristics have been defined above. It has been shown that this *skaz* is not a narration, but instead a mimesis and a declamation; it is not a teller of tales who hides behind the printed text of "The Overcoat" but, rather, a performer, almost a comic actor. What then is the scenario for this role?

At the very beginning of the story there is a collision, a break, an abrupt change in tone. The factual introduction ("In the department of") suddenly breaks off, and instead of the epic manner of the story-teller, which might be expected to follow, there comes a tone of exaggerated irritation and sarcasm. As a result we get the impression of improvisation: the initial manner of narration immediately gives way to various digressions. Nothing has as yet been said, but there is already an anecdote, told in a casual and hurried manner ("I don't remember from which town," "of some romantic work or other"). But this is followed by what looks like a return to the tone in which the story begins: "And so, in a certain department there worked a certain clerk." However, this resumption of the epic manner is immediately interrupted by the sentence that was discussed above—one that is so contrived, so suggestive acoustically that nothing remains of the factual *skaz*. Gogol starts playing his role; and, after rounding off this whimsical and striking choice of words with one that is grandiose-sounding and virtually meaningless ("hemorrhoidal"), he ends this episode with a mimetic gesture: "Nothing can be done about it, it's all the fault of the St. Petersburg climate."

A personal tone, with all the devices of the Gogolian *skaz*, becomes embedded in the story and takes on the character of a grotesque leer or grimace. This in itself prepares the transition to the pun on the surname and the story of the birth and baptism of Akaky Akakievich. The statements of fact that round off this story ("This is the way, then, that Akaky Akakievich *came to be*. . . . And so, this is the way all this *came to be*") create the impression that the narrative form is being played with; there is good reason why they contain a mild joke, which makes them look like an awkward repetition.[27] The "torrent of gibes" flows on, and the *skaz* continues in this tone right up to the sentence, "but he did not answer a single word," where the comic *skaz* is suddenly interrupted by a sentimental and melodramatic digression, which contains the characteristic devices of the sentimentalist style. With this device, Gogol succeeds in raising "The Overcoat" from the level of a simple anecdote to that of a grotesque. The sentimental and intentionally unsophisticated content of this passage (in this respect the grotesque coincides with the melodrama) is conveyed by means of a steadily intensifying intonation, which is solemn and emotional (as indicated by the introductory "ands" and by the particular word order: "And there was something strange. . . . And for a long time thereafter . . . would appear before him. . . . And in these heart-rending words. . . . And he would bury his face in his hands . . . and many times in his life thereafter he would shudder. . ."). The result is something that resembles the device of "theatrical illusion," when the actor suddenly seems to step out of his role and begins to speak like a real person (cf., in *The Inspector General*: "What are you laughing at? You're laughing at yourselves!"; or the celebrated "It's a dreary world, my dear sirs," at the end of "The Two Ivans."

We are accustomed to taking this passage literally: an artistic device which transforms a comic story into a grotesque and prepares the "fantastic" ending is seen as a sincere intervention of "the heart." Granting that such a deception is, in Karamzin's words, a "triumph of art," granting that the reader's naiveté may be charming in itself, such naiveté in scholarship represents anything but a triumph, because it reveals just how incompetent scholarship is. Such an interpretation destroys the entire structure and the entire artistic design of "The Overcoat." Proceeding from the basic proposition that in a work of art *not a single* sentence can, in and of itself, be a mere "reflection" of the author's personal feelings, but rather is always a construct and a performance, we

[27 The "mild joke" is more obvious in Russian than in English. The equivalent of the verb "came to be" is normally used only for events, not persons. Gogol here uses it for both (not only making a "joke" but also emphasizing the facelessness of his hero): "Takim obrazom i *proizoshel* Akaky Akakievich . . . Itak, vot kakim obrazom *proizoshlo* vse eto." The effect is further heightened by the syntactic parallel: "Takim obrazom . . . kakim obrazom." The italics in the quotation are Eichenbaum's.]

cannot and have no right to see anything other than an explicit artistic device in such a passage. The customary procedure of identifying some given statement with the contents of the writer's "psychology" is false in scholarship. In this sense, the mind of the artist as a man who *experiences* various moods always remains and must remain outside the bounds of what he creates. The work of art is always something that is made, fashioned, contrived; it is not only artful but also artificial, in the best sense of the word. Therefore, *there neither is nor can there be* any place in it for the reflection of the empirical reality of the inner self. The artfulness and artificiality of Gogol's devices in this passage from "The Overcoat" come out particularly well in the way he builds the highly melodramatic cadence of the sentence, as an unsophisticated sentimental maxim that serves to reinforce the grotesque: "And the poor young man would bury his face in his hands, and many times in his life thereafter he would shudder on seeing how much inhumanity there is in man, how much brutal coarseness lies hidden in a refined and educated worldly manner, and—oh, Lord! —even in a man whom the world recognizes as being noble and honest."

The melodramatic episode is used by way of contrast with the comic *skaz*. The more skilful the word-plays in the latter, then, of course, the more emotional and stylized in the manner of unsophisticated sentimentalism must be the device which destroys the comic performance. A passage that was presented as a serious reflection would not have provided a contrast and would have been incapable of immediately imparting a grotesque quality to the entire texture. It is therefore not surprising that immediately following this episode, Gogol returns to what has gone before— first to the pseudo-factual style, and then to playful and careless chatter, with jokes such as: "Only then did he notice that he was not in the middle of a line, but rather in the middle of the street." After describing how Akaky Akakievich eats and stops only when his stomach begins to "swell up," Gogol again launches into a declamatory style, but of a somewhat different kind: "Even during those hours when. . . ." Here, in the interest of this same grotesque, a "muffled" and mysteriously serious intonation is adopted, which gradually builds up as an immensely long period, and is then resolved in an unexpectedly simple way. The type of syntax leads us to expect a balance of semantic energy between the prolonged rise ("when . . . when . . . when") and the cadence, but this does

287

not occur, as indeed the very choice of words and expressions inti-
mates. The disparity between a solemn and serious intonation and
the actual meaning of the sentence is again employed as a grotesque device. This new "deception" on the part of the comic
actor is followed naturally by a new play on words—the "councilors"—which brings the first act of "The Overcoat" to a close:
"Thus flowed on the peaceful life of a man . . . ," and so on.

The pattern established in the first part, whereby a purely
anecdotal *skaz* is interwoven with declamation of a melodramatic
and solemn kind, is in fact decisive for the entire texture of "The
Overcoat" as a grotesque. The grotesque style requires first of all
that the situation or event being described should be enclosed in a
fantastically small world of artificial experiences (such as in "Old-
Fashioned Landowners" and "The Two Ivans"), that it be completely isolated from reality at large and from the true fullness of
the inner life;[28] and, second, that this should be done not with a
didactic or satirical intent, but rather to make it possible to *play
with reality*, to break up its elements and displace them freely, so
that normal correlations and associations (psychological and
logical) will prove inoperative in this *newly* constructed world,
and any trifle can grow to colossal proportions. It is only in the
context of such a style that the faintest flicker of genuine feeling
can take on the appearance of something earth-shaking.

The thing that Gogol found of value in the story about the clerk
was precisely this fantastically limited and self-enclosed complex
of thoughts, feelings, and desires, within whose narrow confines
the artist is at liberty to exaggerate details and violate the normal
proportions of the world. "The Overcoat" is laid out along precisely these lines. The point is certainly not Akaky Akakievich's
"insignificance," or a sermon on "humaneness" toward one's lesser
brethren, but, rather, Gogol's ability, once he has isolated the
entire realm of the story from reality at large, to join together what
cannot be joined, to exaggerate what is small and diminish what is

---

[28] "I sometimes like to descend for a moment into the realm of this
*extraordinarily isolated life, where not a single desire flits beyond the
wicker fence that surrounds the small courtyard*," etc. ("Old-Fashioned
Landowners"). As early as "Ivan Fyodorovich Shponka and His Aunt,"
Gogol is using grotesque devices. Mirgorod is a fantastic and grotesque
town that is completely fenced off from the whole world. [The italics are
Eichenbaum's.]

great.[29] In a word, he is able to play with all the norms and laws of the inner life as it really is. And this is exactly how he proceeds. Akaky Akakievich's inner world (if in fact such a term is permissible here) is not insignificant (this notion has been introduced by our naive and sentimental historians of literature, who have been mesmerized by Belinsky),[30] but is fantastically limited and his very own: "In his copying he somehow *saw a variegated (!) and pleasant world of his own.* . . . Outside his copying nothing seemed to exist for him."[31]

This world has its own laws, its own proportions. According to the laws of this world, a new overcoat proves to be a grand event—and Gogol supplies a grotesque formulation: "he did partake of spiritual nourishment, for his thoughts were constantly on the eternal idea of the future overcoat."[32] And again: "It was as if he were no longer alone but were accompanied by some agreeable helpmeet who had consented to walk the road of life with him. This helpmeet was none other than the new overcoat, with its warm padding and its sturdy lining." Small details stand out, such as Petrovich's toenail, which is "thick and hard as a tortoise shell," or his snuff-box "with the portrait of some general or other on it—just which general nobody knew, because the spot where the face used to be had been poked through with a finger and then pasted over with a square piece of paper."[33]

---

[29] "But by a strange order of things, it is always insignificant causes that give rise to great events; and, on the contrary, great undertakings that end in insignificant consequences" ("Old-Fashioned Landowners").

[30 See the introduction and the article by Merezhkovsky in the present collection.]

[31] "The life of their modest owners is so quiet, so very quiet, that for a moment you are lost in forgetfulness and you think that the passions, desires, and disquieting creations of the evil spirit that trouble the world have no existence at all, and that you have seen them only in a glittering, glistening dream" ("Old-Fashioned Landowners"). [The italics and the parenthetical exclamation in the quotation are Eichenbaum's.]

[32] In the rough draft, which had not yet been developed into a grotesque, it was put in a different way: "carrying the future overcoat constantly in his thoughts."

[33] Naive people will say that this is "realism," "the workaday world," and so forth. It is useless to argue with them; but let them bear in mind that a great deal is said about the toenail and the snuff-box, but about Petrovich himself only that he drank on every holiday, and about his wife that she existed and even wore a bonnet. It is a characteristic device of grotesque

This grotesque hyperbolization unfolds, as before, against the background of the comic *skaz*, with puns, humorous words and expressions, ancedotes, etc.: "They did not buy marten because it really was too expensive; instead they selected the finest cat-fur that was to be found in the shop, cat-fur that from a distance could always be taken for marten." Or: "The exact position and function of the Important Personage remain unknown to this day. Suffice it to say that a certain Important Personage had only recently become an Important Personage, but that until then he had been an unimportant personage." Or elsewhere: "They even say that a certain titular councilor, on being made director of some small separate office, promptly partitioned off a special room for himself, called it the 'presence chamber,' and stationed lackeys with red collars and gold braid at the door, who grasped the handle and opened it for everyone who came, although there was barely enough room in the 'presence chamber' for an ordinary writing table." These are accompanied by statements "from the author"—in the same casual tone which is set at the beginning, and which seems to conceal a grimace: "But maybe he didn't even think that—after all, you can't get into *a man's heart* (there is a kind of joke here as well, if one bears in mind the way in which Akaky Akakievich is handled generally) and find out everything he may be thinking" (here the anecdote is being played with—as though it were a question of real reality).[34]

The death of Akaky Akakievich is described just as grotesquely as is his birth—with the alternation of comic and tragic details, with the sudden statement that "finally poor Akaky gave up the ghost,"[35] with the transition to sundry trifles (the enumeration of his inheritance: "a bundle of goose quills, a quire of official white paper, three pairs of socks, two or three buttons that had come off his trousers, and the 'dressing gown' that is already familiar to the reader"), and finally, with the conclusion stated in the now familiar style: "Who inherited all this, Lord only knows; I confess that the person telling this story didn't even take any interest in this matter." And then—as is by now the rule after the

---

texture to set forth minutiae in exaggerated detail while pushing into the background things that would seem to warrant greater attention.

[34 The italics and parenthetical comments are Eichenbaum's.]

35 In the general context, even this ordinary expression sounds unusual and strange, and looks almost like a play on words. This is a regular phenomenon of Gogol's language.

depiction of such a sad scene—comes a new melodramatic declamation which takes us back to the "humane" passage: "And St.
Petersburg went on without Akaky Akakievich, as if he had never
lived there at all. A creature disappeared and vanished who had
been defended by nobody, who was dear to nobody, of interest to
nobody, who never attracted the attention even of a naturalist,
who lets no opportunity slip to fix an ordinary fly on a pin and
examine it through the microscope . . . ," etc.

The ending of "The Overcoat" is an effective apotheosis of the
grotesque, something like the mute scene in *The Inspector General*.
The naive scholars who have seen the whole point of the story in
the "humane" passage stop in bewilderment before this unexpected
and unaccountable intrusion of "romanticism" into "realism."
Gogol himself has given them some encouragement: "But who
could have imagined that this was not all there was to tell about
Akaky Akakievich, that he was destined to go on living and making
his presence felt for a few days after his death, as though he were
being rewarded for a life that had gone unnoticed by anyone. But
so it happened, and our little story unexpectedly has a fantastic
ending." Actually, this ending is no more fantastic or "romantic"
than the story as a whole. On the contrary: up to now we have had
a truly grotesque fantasy, which was rendered as a playing with
reality; here the story emerges into a world of more normal concepts and events, but everything is treated as a playing with fantasy.
This is a new "deception," a device of the grotesque in reverse:
"The ghost suddenly looked around, and, coming to a stop, asked:
'What is it you want?' brandishing a fist of a size you don't see
even on living men. The policeman said 'Nothing,' and immediately
turned back. This ghost, however, was much taller and had enormous mustaches, and, turning his steps apparently toward the
Obukhov Bridge, vanished completely into the darkness."

The anecdote that is developed in the ending leads away from
the "pathetic story" with its melodramatic episodes. The purely
comic *skaz* of the beginning returns, with all its devices. Along
with the mustachioed ghost, the entire grotesque also disappears
into darkness, resolving itself in laughter. Khlestakov vanishes in
this same way in *The Inspector General*, and the mute scene takes
the audience back to the beginning of the play.

8

Dmitry Chizhevsky
(1894 –)

THE CARD-CATALOGUES also list "Dmytro Chyzhevsky" and "Dmitrij Tschiževskij," in recognition of the far-flung career of one of the most important Slavists of the twentieth century. A native of the Ukraine (whence "Chyzhevsky"), he studied mathematics, philosophy, and Slavic literatures at the Universities of St. Petersburg and Kiev. Between 1919 and 1921 he taught in various high schools in Kiev, and then continued his studies in Germany (whence "Tschiževskij"). After a spell of teaching in Prague, where he was also associated with the famous Linguistic Circle, he settled at the University of Halle. At the end of World War II, he was forced to leave his home and his priceless private library—moving first to the University of Marburg, then to Harvard (1949), and finally, in 1956, to Heidelberg, where he has been living ever since and doing more than any other individual to make West Germany one of the leading centers of Slavic studies today.

His scholarly activities continue unabated. In volume and range they are enormous: Chizhevsky is probably the most versatile and productive student of the Slavic world now living. His major interests include: folklore (especially Ukrainian), the history of philosophy (with monographs on Skovoroda and on Hegel in Russia), linguistics (especially etymology and style), German influences on Slavic cultures, and comparative Slavic literatures. He is also active as an editor of Slavic texts. His best-known books in English are: *Outline of Comparative Slavic Literatures* (1952), *On Romanticism in Slavic Literatures* (1957), and *History of Russian Literature from the Eleventh Century to the End of the Baroque* (1960).

Chizhevsky has long been an original and prolific contributor to Gogol studies. Among his articles in English are: "Gogol: Artist and Thinker," in *Annals of the Ukrainian Academy of Arts and Sciences in the U.S.*, IV, 1952, 261-278; and "The Unknown

Gogol," in *Slavonic and East European Review*, xxx, 1952, 476-493. The Russian text of the present article, under the title "O 'Shineli' Gogolya," appeared in the journal *Sovremennye zapiski* (Paris), LXVII, 1938, 172-195.

About Gogol's "Overcoat"

by Dmitry Chizhevsky

I

DOES ANYTHING more need to be written about "The Overcoat"? We have all been familiar with this story since our schooldays; if, in later life, we have happened to read books and articles on Gogol, they have told us the same old things, regardless of whether they have been the outgrowth of a "social approach," which is typical of Russian criticism and Russian literary history, or the work of the Formalists: that "The Overcoat" represents one stage in Gogol's development in the direction of realism, that its theme is the poor clerk, one of the "insulted and injured"—a theme subsequently elaborated in more than a hundred Russian stories and tales, e.g., in "Poor Folk," "A Faint Heart," and other early works by Dostoevsky, by Gogol himself in "Diary of a Madman," and by Veinberg: "He was a titular councilor and she was a general's daughter."[1]

People usually locate the main idea of "The Overcoat" in the famous "pathetic" passage which follows after Akaky Akakievich's reaction to the teasing of his fellow clerks: "Leave me alone. Why do you insult me?":

> And there was something strange in these words and the tone of voice in which they were uttered. Something that aroused compassion could be heard in them, so that one young man, who had been recently appointed and who, following the example of the others, had allowed himself to tease him, suddenly stopped as if cut to the heart, and from that moment on everything seemed to change and present itself to him in a different light. Some unseen force turned him away from his colleagues, with whom he had become acquainted because he had taken them for decent and well-bred people. And for a long time thereafter the humble little clerk with the bald patch atop his head would appear before him in his happiest moments, speak-

[1 Pyotr Isayevich Veinberg (1830-1908) was a writer of popular verse who is now all but forgotten. Chizhevsky has "a governor's daughter," but this is a mistake.]

ing the heart-rending words: "Leave me alone! Why do you insult me!" In these heart-rending words, others could be heard: "I am your brother!" And the poor young man would bury his face in his hands, and many times in his life thereafter he would shudder on seeing how much inhumanity there is in man. . . .

There is no doubt that this passage contains ideas which are fundamental for Gogol. But is it not strange that such a crucial passage should stand at the very beginning, apparently anticipating the entire subsequent development of the story and making it superfluous? For the tragic story of Akaky Akakievich only begins after this. At first glance it might be called "tragi-*comic*" instead; as fine a connoisseur of the Russian classics as Dostoevsky saw it as an expression of ridicule and scorn for a hero whose first real human emotion is directed at—an overcoat. Did not Gogol ruin the beginning by continuing it in this vein? Did he not weaken its effect? Did he not declare that Akaky Akakievich is our brother only to mock him all the more cruelly after that?

Such an odd disjuncture in the structure of the story, if nothing more, forces us to look for Gogol's meaning elsewhere than in the words "I am your brother"; for all its pathos and its Christian sentiment, this idea smacks of a truism and calls to mind Karamzin's celebrated statement that "peasant girls know how to feel too" (which we cannot read without a smile nowadays, even though we fully acknowledge it as being true).[2]

Let us try to get closer to Gogol's story through the method of close reading. This is the only proper way of reading the classics, but we have been trained out of it by the newspaper, the detective story, and other light reading, as well as by our schools, where explanations by textbooks and teachers made it unnecessary for us to think for ourselves about a work of literature (though were we, as school children, mature enough to have a true understanding of the meaning of a work of art?).

In the process of reading Gogol's story slowly and savoring it drop by drop, we shall notice many small details, many tiny and apparently trivial touches. Perhaps it is worth while beginning our analysis of "The Overcoat" with one of these "unimportant trifles." In this story, the same virtually meaningless word is repeated with

[2 The quotation comes from Karamzin's sentimental story, "Poor Liza" ("Bednaya Liza," 1792), which tells of a peasant girl who gives her love to and is betrayed by a nobleman.]

extraordinary frequency: *"even."* Within the thirty-two to forty pages that "The Overcoat" takes up in the usual editions of Gogol, this little word crops up no fewer than seventy-three times. Moreover, in some places, it is especially frequent: we run across it three, four, and even five times on a single page. Is this just accidental? Is Gogol simply repeating an unnecessary word because he once just happened to write it down? Is such a repetition simply a sign of that well-known tendency of style—inertia—which is familiar to all of us when, in our own articles or letters, we suddenly find some not very meaningful or unnecessary word or particle being repeated several times in several successive sentences?

From all we know about Gogol's method of writing, such explanations are rather improbable—in fact, simply impossible. We know that Gogol recast and reworked the texts of his compositions endlessly; he went over them word by word, making changes and alterations until he achieved the greatest possible refinement and polish. S. T. Aksakov describes two readings of a chapter from the second part of *Dead Souls* that Gogol gave in 1850. On the second occasion, the Aksakovs reacted as follows: "We were utterly astonished: the chapter seemed even better to us, and appeared to have been rewritten. To all appearances, the alterations were very minor: one little word had been deleted here, one had been added there, one was transposed to another place—and everything came out different." We might have some doubts about the judgment of a man like Aksakov, we might suspect that he could have been over-enthusiastic about Gogol as a writer, a person, and a "prophet," and could therefore have rated him too highly. (Aksakov senior, however, by no means shared his sons' unqualified enthusiasm for Gogol.)[3] But we do find sufficient evidence in Gogol's own published revisions of his works ("The Portrait," *The Inspector General, Taras Bulba*), as well as in his manuscripts. Both these sources fully confirm what Gogol said in those years— according to N. V. Berg—about his method of writing:

At first you have to jot down everything just as it comes, even though it's bad and flat—absolutely everything—and then forget about this notebook. Then, in a month or two, sometimes even longer (you'll know for yourself just when), take out what you have written and read it over again: you will see that a great

[3 S. T. Aksakov's sons were Konstantin and Ivan. See footnote 28 of Merezhkovsky's article in this collection.]

deal is not the way it should be, that there's much that's unnecessary and some things that are missing. Make your corrections and annotations in the margins—and again put the notebook away. When you come to look it over again, make new annotations in the margins, and where there is no space, take a separate piece of paper and attach it to the edge of the page. When everything is covered with revisions, go ahead and rewrite the notebook in your own hand. Here too fresh clarifications, cuts, additions, and refinements of style will appear by themselves. In between the old words you suddenly see that new words absolutely must be there, but for some reason they don't come right away. And then put the notebook away once more. Take a trip, relax, do nothing, or perhaps write something else. The time will come and the forgotten notebook will be remembered; take it up, re-read it, make your revisions in the same way; and when you have marked it all up once more, rewrite it in your own hand. In the process you will notice that as your style gains in power and your sentences take on polish and refinement, your hand will also seem to grow stronger: the letters will be set down more firmly and decisively. This process must be repeated, I think, eight times. Some people perhaps require less, but some require even more. I do it eight times. Only after the eighth rewrite—and always in my own hand—does the work take on a final artistic finish and become a pearl of creation. Further corrections and revisions will very likely spoil the whole thing: that is what artists call over-painting. Of course it is impossible and difficult to follow such rules consistently. I'm talking about the ideal. Some things you can let go sooner, of course. A man after all is a man and not a machine.[4]

It can hardly be supposed that a writer who worked *this way* would have let an unnecessary little word stand—and with such inordinate frequency—out of mere mental inertia, and in a work to which he attached such importance. Evidently "even" has some significance, "bears some function," as the Formalists say, or rather, several functions. This is always the case with Gogol: his artistic devices are multifaceted and multifunctional. What then

[4 As reported from a conversation of Gogol's by Nikolay Vasilievich Berg (1824-84), a poet and translator now remembered only for his reminiscences of Gogol (*Vospominaniya o N. V. Gogole*, 1872), from which this passage is taken. Cf. V. V. Veresayev, *Gogol' v zhizni*, Moscow-Leningrad, 1933, p. 421.

is the role of "even" in "The Overcoat"? Let us look at it a little more closely.

II

First of all, repetition of exactly the same word is characteristic—in Gogol and in other writers—of conversational speech or *skaz*, as the literary historians now call it.[5] In "The Overcoat"—and we must mark this well—the story is, to all appearances, told not by Gogol himself but by a narrator whom Gogol very deliberately keeps at a certain distance or remove from himself. Here Gogol follows the narrative technique of *Evenings on a Farm Near Dikanka* and *Mirgorod*. He uses various devices to emphasize that the story is being told by some narrator (who is not himself further characterized). For example, he uses parenthetical expressions such as: "nothing is known of that"; "I don't remember from what town"; "Akaky Akakievich was born—if my memory doesn't betray me—sometime on the night of March 22"; "it's hard to say on precisely what day"; "just where the clerk who invited him lived we can't say, unfortunately: our memory has begun to play real tricks on us"; "what exactly were the position and function of the Important Personage remains unknown to this day"; "who inherited all this [Akaky Akakievich's effects] Lord only knows—I confess that the person telling this story didn't even take any interest in the matter"; etc., etc.

Gogol employs digressions for the same purpose. For example, at the very beginning of the story—"In the department of . . ."—the narrator breaks off: "But it's better not to specify in just which department"—and twenty lines of digression follow, after which the story begins all over again: "And so, in a certain department there worked a certain clerk. . . ." In his Ukrainian stories (*Evenings on a Farm Near Dikanka*) Gogol makes use of Ukrainian words and phrases to remind the reader of the presence of the narrator who is telling the story. In "The Overcoat" and "Diary of a Madman" Gogol brings his diction as close as possible to the conversational. This is easier to do in "Diary of a Madman," where the author has the hero keep a diary. Akaky Akakievich would hardly have been capable of doing that!

But the narrator is made to resemble Akaky Akakievich in a

[5 For other discussions of *skaz*, see the introduction and the article by Eichenbaum in the present collection.]

certain way. This is done by the repetition of certain unnecessary words. For example, in place of words which modify substantives in an expressive and meaningful way, we find qualifiers which have no meaning whatsoever: "a certain" ("a certain police inspector," "a certain director," etc.); "some . . . or other" ("some attitude or other," "some town or other," etc.); "something or other"; "somehow or other"; etc. Gogol himself draws attention to his hero's way of speaking: "It must be noted that Akaky Akakievich expressed himself for the most part in prepositions, adverbs, and, last but not least, in particles of a kind that have absolutely no meaning. And if the matter was very complicated, he even had the habit of not finishing a sentence at all, so that very often, after he would begin with the words 'This really is quite, you know, but . . . ,' nothing at all would follow, and he himself would forget, thinking that he had already said everything. . . ." And even the Important Personage—the second hero of the story—"remained everlastingly in the same taciturn state, only now and then delivering himself of some monosyllabic sounds. . . . His communication with subordinates was usually marked by severity and consisted almost entirely of three phrases. . . ."

The impoverishment of the narrator's diction is therefore no accident. Obviously Gogol was unable to bring it all the way down to the level of the speech of Akaky Akakievich or of the Important Personage. If the narrator had "expressed himself . . . in prepositions, adverbs, and, last but not least, in particles of a kind that have absolutely no meaning," or if he had "remained everlastingly in the same taciturn state"—then the result would have been no story at all. However, Gogol does to some degree make his narrator's diction resemble that of his heroes. This is the purpose of the peculiar impoverishment of the language of "The Overcoat." Such impoverishment would seem to contravene the fundamental, intrinsic law of every work of art, which necessarily strives to achieve the greatest possible richness, fullness, and plenitude. But in this case, the possibilities for a richness and fullness of diction are obviously limited by the inarticulateness that is so characteristic of the narrator and the heroes.

The later development of the naturalistic style in Russian literature provides examples of such language which go far beyond the modest first steps that Gogol made. Examples from Dostoevsky are the speech patterns of Makar Devushkin, in *Poor Folk*, and of the anonymous narrator of *The Double*. On certain pages a reader who has not grasped the author's intention sometimes feels some irritation: why make narrators out of stammerers like these? But even Gogol topped himself in "The Tale of Captain Kopeykin" (*Dead Souls*): on just eight pages he has amassed such a wealth of parenthetical and often meaningless words that we can only stand in wonderment at the artistry of this inimitable master in apportioning and distributing such a variety of *skaz* elements within such a small space. Here we find "my dear sir" thirteen times; "you can just imagine" and "you can just picture" fifteen times; "you know" or "you understand" twenty-three times; "such a" twenty times; "some . . . or other" seventeen times; "to a certain extent" twelve times; "so to speak" eleven times; "relatively" or "relatively speaking" nine times, and so on. Take, for example, the following passage.

> Suddenly there's a whole world, relatively speaking, right in front of him, a certain arena of life, such a fairy-tale Scheherazade, you understand. Then suddenly there's some such, if you can just imagine, Nevsky Per-spect, or some, you know, Gorokhovoya Street there, damn it all, or some such Liteinaya there; some sort of spire is in the air there; the bridges are hanging there by some, if you can just imagine, devilish power, without, that is, touching anything at all; in a word, a Semiramis, sir, and that's that!

Or:

> He'd be walking by some such restaurant or other; the cook there, if you can just imagine, is a foreigner, a sort of French fellow with a friendly countenance, the linen on him is of the finest Holland kind, and an apron that's the equal in whiteness of, to a certain extent, snow, and he's working away at, what do you call it, "finez herbz" and cutlets with truffles, in a word, some super-duper delectation that's so tasty he'd just, that is, eat his very own self up. Or he might happen to be walking past the shops on the Milyutinskaya; there, peeping out the window, in a certain sense, is a terrific salmon, and juicy little cherries for five roubles a measure, and a whopper of a watermelon, a real stagecoach leaning right out the window, looking, so to speak, for anyone fool enough to plunk down a hundred roubles for

it—in a word, there's temptation at every step, his mouth, relatively so to speak, is watering, and he's supposed to wait.[6]

It is obvious how utterly "useless" all these verbal patterns are for presenting a specific body of material. Perhaps such examples bring out more clearly than anything else could the essential characteristics of the verbal art: as *performance* and as *craft*. This eludes the reader who approaches a work from the standpoint of content while disregarding form. Nevertheless, as we shall see, it is precisely these formal elements, precisely the nature of verbal creativity as performance and craft ("how something is made," "how it is shaped") that point up the really essential material in a work of literature.[7]

III

But the numerous "evens" in "The Overcoat" do not only perform the function we have mentioned, that of stylizing speech as *skaz*. They also bear upon the essential characteristics of Gogol's humor.

The comic element in Gogol consists of a distinctive play of oppositions, or antitheses, between something meaningful and something meaningless. These antitheses alternate, so that one particular thing—a phrase, a word, an idea—which has seemed to make sense suddenly proves to be nonsense; or, vice versa, what has seemed like nonsense proves to make good sense. Among such instances of word-play is the way in which "even" is used. "Even" introduces an intensification, a heightening: it marks a tension, an anticipation; and if no heightening follows, if the thing that is anticipated does not come off, we feel thwarted and surprised, and

[6 These passages are much funnier and less contrived-sounding in Russian. The humor depends to a large extent on the speaker's use of high-falutin phrases that are unnatural to him, and on his distortions of foreign words, such as *preshpekt* for *prospekt*, *fenzerv* for *fines herbes*, and—the masterpiece—*rassupedelikates* ("super-duper delectation"), which is a melange of Russian and French morphemes. Leskov carried this technique to perfection in his story "The Left-Handed Smith" (see footnote 13). The original version of "The Tale of Captain Kopeykin" was considered subversive by the censor and was not passed. Gogol then rewrote it, and got it through. Chizhevsky uses this second version, which is even more inventive linguistically than the first.]

[7 See the commentary on the word "performance" (*igra*) in my introduction to Eikhenbaum's article in this collection.]

Gogol has achieved a comic effect. Instead of intensification, Gogol sometimes introduces a "zero meaning" after "even" (meaningless phrases are very common in Gogol);[8] and sometimes we are surprised by a slackening instead of an intensification. Thus there is an alternation of the serious and the humorous; and if a rise in the level of diction is given special emphasis by highly emotional and rhetorical intonation, then even ordinary diction looks like nonsense: having soared too high into the realm of intense emotion, the diction suddenly breaks off and everything ends in nothing, in trivialities—exactly the opposite of what the reader was anticipating.[9]

It is in just such places that the word "even" frequently occurs. This is true in works that were written both before and after "The Overcoat." Let us take an example from *Dead Souls*. Gogol is speaking of the "enlightened nature" of the "town of X": "the others were also enlightened people: some read Karamzin, some *The Moscow News*, and some read *even* nothing at all" (chapter eight). In the same vein is the well-known statement that "the governor was an extremely kind man and at times *even* did fancy embroidery on tulle" (chapter one). Similar passages can be found earlier, in Pushkin's *Eugene Onegin*—a work whose influence on Gogol is indisputable (a fact literary historians have not bothered to note). For example, take the description of Zaretsky, Lensky's second in the duel:

> Good and simple-hearted,
> The bachelor father of a family,
> A loyal friend, a peaceful landowner,
> And *even* an honest man (VI, 4).

As if honesty were the rarest and most unusual of human qualities!

In "The Overcoat," the word "even" very often has the same function: it introduces phrases and ideas which lack the anticipated logical connection or perhaps in fact any connection at all with what precedes. Thus, "even" robs what is meaningful of its mean-

[8 The example that Chizhevsky cites here—*v pritochenii oshel'movavshis' sostoyalsya*—occurs in the second of Ivan Ivanovich's official complaints against Ivan Nikiforovich ("The Two Ivans"). It represents his ludicrous attempt to imitate the language and cadences of a legal document. It has a strong Ukrainian flavor, as do all four petitions. We might render it something like: "in addition having disgraced himself."]

[9 See also the article by Slonimsky in this collection.]

ing. And what seems meaningful is not always so: such is Gogol's artistic plan here. Some examples: "The clerk's surname was Bashmachkin. From the name alone it is already clear that it was derived from the word for shoe [*bashmak*]; but when, at what time, and in what manner it derived from 'shoe'—of this nothing is known. His father, his grandfather, and *even* his brother-in-law, and absolutely all the Bashmachkins wore boots, merely having them resoled about three times a year." After the first break in logic—the transition to the brother-in-law, who, after all, is not a blood relative of Akaky Akakievich—there follows still another break—the transition to the soles [*podmyotki*], a word that bears absolutely no resemblance to the name Bashmachkin.

Similar breaks in the logical train of thought, all introduced by "even," go along with the narrator's distinctive ideas about the relation of the weather and fate to the higher levels of the Russian "table of ranks." The St. Petersburg cold makes "the forehead ache and tears come to the eyes . . . *even* in those who occupy higher positions"; or: "Various misfortunes are strewn on the path of life not only of titular, but *even* privy, actual, court and all other councilors, *even* those who give no counsel to anyone, nor themselves take it from anyone" (here there is a double break: "councilor" certainly does not mean "one who gives counsel").[10] When the ghost begins pulling overcoats off the backs of St. Petersburgers, "a steady stream of complaints came in from every quarter, to the effect that backs and shoulders, not merely of titular but *even* of court councilors, were exposed to catching cold, as a result of being frequently stripped of their overcoats." In the same vein: "The mistress of the house [the wife of the tailor Petrovich] was frying some sort of fish and had smoked up the kitchen so much that you could not see *even* the cockroaches."

Gogol plays in this same way not only with "even," but with other words as well: "The tailor Petrovich, *despite* being one-eyed and having a completely pockmarked face, was rather successful at mending the trousers and coats of clerks and all other varieties, when he was in a sober state and had no other enterprise cooking in his head." Gogol's other works provide a good many parallels. For example, the contrast between Ivan Ivanovich and

[10 For a discussion of the Table of Ranks, see footnote 12 of Merezhkovsky's article in the present anthology. Akaky Akakievich is a titular councilor, which is Grade 9. The italics are Chizhevsky's in all the quotations in this section. Hereafter I shall omit them.]

304

Ivan Nikiforovich is topped off as follows: "Ivan Ivanovich was rather timid by nature; Ivan Nikiforovich, *on the contrary*, wore trousers with such ample pleats that if they were to be inflated, an entire farmyard with barns and outbuildings could fit in them." Or, Taras Bulba and a few friends, on their own initiative, start beating the kettledrums, which are used to call the Cossack assembly into session: "At the sound of the kettledrum, the first to run up was the drummer, a tall man with only one eye, which *nonetheless* was very bleary from sleep."

This is the technique Gogol uses to take the reader by surprise. But often—and especially in "The Overcoat"—his method is just the opposite: the reader expects something ordinary, understandable, and positive, but instead, Gogol surprises him with something bizarre, unusual, and negative. Here are some examples from "The Overcoat." The saints' calendar is being consulted for a name for the new baby (Akaky Akakievich): Mokky, Sossy, Khozdazat; then, Trifily, Dula, and Varakhasy. "What an infliction!" the mother mutters, "what strange names! I've never in my life heard the likes. I'd be willing to settle for . . ."—and after this, we expect rather ordinary names, but Gogol comes up with some startling ones: "I'd be willing to settle for Varadat or Varukh, but Trifily and Varakhasy!" Further on we read: "Making his way up the stairway to Petrovich's, which, to do it justice . . ."—the reader expects to hear something positive about the stairway, but is all the more surprised to read: "which, to do it justice, was soaked with water and strewn with slops and reeked of that ammoniac smell which, as we know, is an inseparable attribute of all the back stairs of St. Petersburg houses."

Gogol's playing with the word "even" is also part of this technique of taking the reader by surprise.

IV

But there is another reason why the word "even" is repeated so often: it is also essential to one of the key aspects of the story, and affords us a glimpse of it, if we are sufficiently attentive.

We have already talked about the way in which "even" introduces and accompanies intensification, augmentation, tension— all of which, however, Gogol takes back, thereby frustrating and at the same time surprising the reader. In this way he reveals the insignificance of the realm or segment of life that he is depicting.

305

What comes after "even" proves to be trivial and insignificant. This means that in this particular realm of life, insignificance, emptiness, "nothingness" are represented as being significant and essential. It is not so very easy to depict and understand "nothingness": philosophers from Hegel to Heidegger have had many an occasion to grapple with this problem themselves. Gogol attempts to overcome this difficulty by using "even." The substance and the goals of life prove to be insignificant, insubstantial, nonexistent.

This particular usage of "even" is also found in the passages we have already cited, where Gogol creates the impression that in the opinion of his narrator, nature, fate, and even the supernatural world (the ghost) honor the Table of Ranks, since they normally spare the bodies, the shoulders and the "path of life" of higher-ranking officials.

Gogol uses this same device to show Akaky Akakievich's most powerful and elevated feeling—passion for the new coat. His feelings are depicted in a tone of pathos, but the ways in which they manifest themselves are shallow and commonplace. Akaky Akakievich "even" laughs or smiles, he is "even" inattentive at work, "very nearly" makes a mistake in his copying, "even" notices a pretty lady. "At times a fire glowed in his eyes, and the most daring and audacious thoughts even flashed through his mind: shouldn't he really have marten-fur put on the collar?" But actually Akaky Akakievich's entire life is depicted in the same way: his enthusiasm for his work is such that "if he were given rewards commensurate with his zeal, then he might, to his astonishment, have become even a state councilor." His own desires, however, are rather more modest: "and even if the director were to be so kind as to give him a bonus of forty-five or fifty roubles instead of forty." Only his new goal in life creates something in him that resembles a personality and makes him living and breathing. "He became somehow more alive, even more strong-willed, like a person who already knows who he is and has set himself a definite goal." Out in the evening for the first time after acquiring the new overcoat, Akaky Akakievich "strolled down the street in a happy frame of mind, he very nearly even broke into a little canter all of a sudden, Heaven knows why, in pursuit of some lady. . . . However, he checked himself, and again began to walk quietly as before, surprised even himself at the sudden impulse to canter that had come from nowhere." And after the climax (and it must not be forgotten that the climax consists entirely of the loss of

306

the new overcoat), when Akaky Akakievich is fighting against death, he "finally even fell into blasphemies, and uttered the most dreadful words, so that his old landlady even crossed herself, never before having heard anything of the kind from him, and all the more horrified because these words came directly after the phrase 'Your Excellency' "—such is the highest order of protest possible for a poor clerk!

But it is not only the basic plot-line that is studded with "evens" which serve to expose the insignificance of the hero's life and experiences. The secondary characters are themselves no better: the Important Personage to whom Akaky Akakievich brings his plaint against life and fate; Akaky Akakievich's colleagues; indeed the entire milieu in which he lives—all are just the same. Even the fateful invitation to the party that Akaky Akakievich receives is not motivated by a feeling of human fellowship on the part of his co-workers. People can, of course, experience such a feeling if only for a brief moment, but not in "The Overcoat"—no! "One of the clerks, even some sort of assistant to the head clerk, probably in order to show that he was not a snob and would associate even with people inferior to him, said, 'Come to supper at my place tonight. By the way, today's my birthday. . . .' " The company that gathered there was of the best sort: hanging in the foyer were "nothing but overcoats and cloaks, among which some even had beaver collars or velvet lapels."

The characterization of the Important Personage is built entirely on the word "even," on "breaks." The Important Personage was "in every respect even a rather intelligent man," and "even he himself sensed" some of his shortcomings. The scene in which the Important Personage dresses Akaky Akakievich down is also full of "evens": "At this point he stamped his foot and raised his voice to such a pitch that even anyone else besides Akaky Akakievich would have been terrified." And when Akaky Akakievich is about to collapse in a faint, the Important Personage is "pleased that the effect exceeded even his expectations," and he is "utterly intoxicated with the thought that his words could deprive a man even of his senses." The same device is used to characterize the pangs of conscience that gnaw at the Important Personage: "He even began brooding about poor Akaky Akakievich, and the thought of him proved so troubling that a week later he made up his mind even to send a clerk to see how he was." Learning that Akaky Akakievich "had died suddenly and in a fever," the Important Personage "was even shocked, felt the reproaches of conscience, and was out of sorts all day long." On his way home from the party, the Important Personage decides to visit his friend Karolina Ivanovna, "a lady, it seems, of German extraction." The appearance of the dead man terrifies him: though he seemed resolute and robust, he "felt such terror that not without reason did he even begin to fear that he might have a fit of some sort. He even threw his overcoat off his back as fast as he could, and shouted at the driver in an unnatural voice: 'Home just as quick as you can!' The driver, on hearing the tone of voice that was usually reserved for critical moments and was then even accompanied by something more tangible . . . shot off like an arrow." This adventure makes a deep impression on the Important Personage: "he even began to say to his subordinates much less frequently: 'Do you understand who is standing before you?' "

The police, too, suffer defeat in their contest with the deceased Akaky Akakievich. Their heroism is also characterized by this same word "even": "In the police station orders were given to seize the corpse at all costs, alive or dead . . . and they very nearly even succeeded in doing so." But when the ghost is finally in the hands of the police, one of them "reached down into his boot for just a minute in order to take out a snuff-box . . . but the snuff was probably of such a brand that even a dead man could not stand it . . . ," and he sneezed so violently that "he sprayed all three in the eyes. . . . From that time on, policemen have had such a fear of dead men that they have even been afraid to apprehend the living . . ." and the "dead clerk began turning up even beyond the Kalinkin Bridge."

And so, it is through this use of "even," through constantly breaking the narrative line off into nothing that all the hollowness and emptiness of a great love—for an overcoat—is revealed, as well as the utter insignificance of the poor clerk's milieu (his colleagues, and the Important Personage who quiets his conscience in the company of a few friends of equal rank). This is also the way that even the "heroism" of policemen dissolves into utter insignificance with a pinch of foul-smelling snuff.

V

A story gains in psychological intensity when the author moves close to his hero. It is precisely in the interest of getting closer that

Gogol introduces a narrator, who takes everything seriously. The same effect is achieved in "Diary of a Madman" through the diary form, which affords the reader a glimpse into Poprishchin's soul. Dostoevsky brings it off in *Poor Folk*, by having his hero write letters. In his Ukrainian stories Gogol gets close to his heroes with amazing ease, and even merges with them through his narrators (Foma Grigorievich, in "St. John's Eve") and through his use of two levels of language: literary Russian saturated with Ukrainianisms. But there his task is made substantially easier by the intrinsic interest, in some cases, of the story line ("A Terrible Vengeance," *Taras Bulba*, "St. John's Eve," etc.) or, in other cases, by the lyrical attitude he takes toward the microcosm that he is describing ("Christmas Eve," "A May Night," "Old-Fashioned Landowners," etc.).

The task of establishing a close identity with the hero and his inner world is far more difficult in "The Overcoat." As we have already said, it is much harder to depict emptiness, insignificance, and nothingness than great and elevated things. It would have been utterly impossible to have Akaky Akakievich himself tell about his own adventures and experiences. It is really not so easy to create a type of narrator who is close to Akaky Akakievich.

Nonetheless Gogol does try to transport us into the inner world of his hero wherever he can, and to show us how Akaky Akakievich looks at life. To a large extent, Gogol shows us the angle from which Akaky Akakievich views the world by means of those everlasting "evens." "Even" indicates how many things and people there are in the world that the poor clerk looks up at from below. After all, "even," logically, points to things or objects which are higher, elevated, significant, unattainable. And as it happens, there is a great deal that lies in this higher realm as far as Akaky Akakievich and the narrator of his story are concerned: overcoats with beaver collars and velvet lapels; state councilors, court councilors and other councilors who are not subject to the operations of those laws of nature and fate that a poor clerk is. This is also the world of the other characters in the story: a new overcoat is an unusual event not only for Akaky Akakievich but for his tailor as well.

The small world or microcosm of a poor clerk is a big world for him precisely because it is filled with objects that he looks up at from below. It is just this sort of existence that Gogol wished us to understand; hence the innumerable "evens" that mark out the configuration of the hero's inner world, his spiritual posture. The small world—the big world: it is on this antithesis that the movement of the entire story depends. "The Overcoat" is built on the oscillating rhythm of contrasting experiences. Gogol transports us into Akaky Akakievich's little world; we cannot remain there, because we do not find it easy to reincarnate ourselves as Akaky Akakievich. Over and over again our own awareness that his world is a microcosm shatters any illusion that we are in a big world and are experiencing a profound tragedy which decides the matter of the hero's life and death. We move out of Akaky Akakievich's little world, but over and over again Gogol takes us back into it, to a considerable extent by means of his "evens." It is on the oscillation between the value-judgments of "little," "tiny," "insignificant" (for us, the reader) and "enormous," "great," "significant" (for Akaky Akakievich and the narrator) that the basic structure of "The Overcoat" as a work of art is built.

VI

"The Overcoat" represents one stage in the development of a theme which is so characteristic of Russian literature—that of the poor clerk. Next to "The Overcoat," the best-known stories in this genre are those of Dostoevsky which have already been mentioned here on more than one occasion: *Poor Folk*, *The Double*, "A Faint Heart," and "Mr. Prokharchin."

Of all the versions of this story (which have been numbered at around two hundred by literary historians), Gogol's is the most successful and effective. An exclusively "social viewpoint" became prevalent in the poor-clerk stories of later vintage. But even Belinsky took Gogol's story as a social protest, a protest against the situation of poor clerks.[11] However, if social protest really were at the center of the story, would Gogol not have achieved a much greater effect by drawing a portrait of an individual of depth and complexity working in a low-level job? Let us not forget that in his youth Gogol himself had to snatch time for his literary labors from sterile and inane office work.[12] Of course, a reading of Gogol's story as a moral, ethical protest ("I am your brother") is more in line with his own moralizing tendencies; but is Akaky

[11 Perhaps Chizhevsky has in mind Belinsky's "Otvet 'Moskvityaninu'" (1847): cf. *Polnoe sobranie sochinenii*, x, Moscow, 1956, 244.]
[12 See footnote 6 of Pereverzev's article in this collection.]

Akakievich a literary type who can successfully illustrate the idea of "I am your brother" to the reader? One does not, after all, have to be particularly snobbish to refuse to see a brother in Akaky Akakievich, whose life is a pitiable and ridiculous tragedy. Should not Gogol have understood that the plot of the story and the mind of Akaky Akakievich being what they are, many, very many readers have to acknowledge Akaky Akakievich not as a brother but, at most, as some very distant relative? Are not other stories about poor clerks much more effective, such as Dostoevsky's *Poor Folk*, or—to take one of the very best on this same theme— "Yakov Yakovlevich," by Gogol's biographer, P. A. Kulish?

We cannot dwell in detail here on the fact that for Gogol, the social aspect was one of the least important. The idea that every human being is our brother was axiomatic in Gogol's Christian view of life and he deemed it necessary to remind us of that at the beginning of the story. But actually, if we read even this passage carefully, without any preconceived ideas, the person who comes out as a human being, as a counterweight to the inhumanity of Akaky Akakievich's fellow clerks, is not Akaky Akakievich himself, but that same young man for whom "everything seemed to change." The theme of "The Overcoat" is much more closely associated with a problem that is central to Gogol's view of life: that of "one's own place." In its social reflex, this problem was later vulgarized into the pseudo-problem of superfluous people. (Leskov's answer to this pseudo-problem—in his story "Righteous Men," which attempts to show that there are no superfluous people—is remarkable for its ideas and for its artistry, but nobody has remarked on it.)[13] But in keeping with the analysis we have

[13 The Russian title is "Pravedniki." Nikolay Semyonovich Leskov (1831-95) is one of the masters of Russian prose fiction and is finally winning a reputation among foreign readers. His best-known works are *Cathedral Folk* (*Soboryane*, 1872), *The Enchanted Wanderer* (*Ocharovannyi strannik*, 1874), "Lady Macbeth of the Mtsensk District" ("Ledi Makbet Mtsenskogo Uezda," 1865), and "Tale of the Cross-Eyed Left-Handed Smith from Tula and of the Steel Flea" ("Skaz o tul'skom kosom Levshe i o stal'noi blokhe," 1882).

The "superfluous man" (*lishnii chelovek*) is a major character-type in nineteenth-century Russian literature. He is a sensitive and intelligent hero who is incapable of acting on his insights and convictions, and who can find no real place for himself in society. Famous examples are Pushkin's Eugene Onegin, Lermontov's Pechorin (in *A Hero of Our Time*), and Goncharov's Oblomov.]

made of "The Overcoat," we shall now approach the story's ideology from a different angle.

We happen to know the source of "The Overcoat." It was an anecdote, which Gogol heard long before he created his story. One of Gogol's friends, P. V. Annenkov, tells of the circumstances:

> On one occasion, while Gogol was present, somebody told an office story about a certain poor clerk who, by extraordinary scrimping and saving and by unrelenting and arduous extra work, saved up enough money to buy a good Lepage shotgun, for about 200 paper roubles. The first time he went out hunting on the Gulf of Finland in his small boat, with the valuable gun propped up before him in the bow, he went into a kind of trance, by his own account, and came to himself only when he glanced toward the bow and failed to see his new acquisition. The gun had been pulled into the water by a thick growth of reeds that his boat had passed through somewhere along the way; and all his efforts to find it were in vain. The clerk returned home, took to his bed, and stayed there; he came down with a fever. He was restored to life only because his fellow workers learned what had happened, took up a collection, and bought him a new gun; but from that time on, he could never recall this dreadful event without turning deathly pale. . . . Everyone laughed at the story, which was based on an actual happening, except Gogol, who bowed his head in thought after he had heard it through to the end. . . .[14]

What, then, did Gogol make out of this story? For a gun, the appurtenance of the "noble sport" of hunting, he substituted a prosaic object of basic necessity. Yet he speaks of this object in a language of passion and love, in an erotic language; and there is no doubt that he does so intentionally:

> He had even grown quite accustomed to going hungry in the evenings; but he did partake of spiritual nourishment, for his thoughts were constantly on the eternal idea of the future overcoat. From that time on, his very existence seemed to become somehow fuller, as if he had gotten married, as if some other person were present with him, as if he were no longer alone but were accompanied by some agreeable helpmeet who had con-

[14 "N. V. Gogol' v Rime letom 1841 goda," *Literaturnye vospominaniya*, Moscow, 1960, pp. 76-77.]

sented to walk the road of life with him. This helpmeet was none other than the new overcoat, with its warm padding and its sturdy lining, something that would never wear out. . . . Nevertheless, just before the end of his life he was visited by a radiant guest in the guise of an overcoat, which for a brief moment enlivened his drab existence.

The reader is apt to interpret such lines more as a mockery of the poor clerk than as an expression of real sympathy or as evidence of a feeling of brotherhood for him. But it is only in this "erotic" context that certain small details in Gogol's story become intelligible. For example, the thief does not merely strip Akaky Akakievich of his coat but, for some reason or other, says: "But this coat belongs to me!" Is not this nocturnal robber a variant of the powerful-rival type in love stories? Love for the overcoat is the only thing that is capable of arousing any erotic feelings in Akaky Akakievich. He runs after a charming lady, and studies an erotic picture in a shop window. And is not the appearance of a ghost searching for an overcoat a kind of parody of the romantic "dead lover" who rises from the grave in quest of his bride? (The first version of the story was entitled "The Tale of a Clerk Who Stole Overcoats," which in itself shows that the concluding pages are essential and central to the work, and were not simply tacked on in a spirit of mischief.) The plot of "The Overcoat" is the well-known plot of Bürger's "Leonora" and of Zhukovsky's "Ludmilla" and "Svetlana," the theme of certain stanzas in Pushkin's *Eugene Onegin* (VIII, 11, and its variant versions) and certain of his poems ("An Invocation" and others) and Lermontov's "The Dead Man's Love." It is the theme of the power of love that conquers all, a love that triumphs over death.[15]

The sensitive—and of course forgotten—literary critic, N. N. Strakhov, drew attention to the fact that Dostoevsky's *Poor Folk* is a kind of "objection" or answer to Gogol's "Overcoat." A. L. Bem has recently made a superb study of this problem.[16] The

[15 "Zaklinanie" (Pushkin); "Lyubov' mertvetsa" (Lermontov).]

[16 Nikolay Nikolayevich Strakhov (1828-96) had a varied and vigorous intellectual career, but is best remembered as a philosopher. He wrote an extensive biography of Dostoevsky, which is what Chizhevsky seems to have in mind. Adolf Ludvigovich Bem (1886-1946) was an eminent scholar and critic. Presumably Chizhevsky refers to his book *K voprosu o vliyanii Gogolya na Dostoevskogo* (*On the Question of Gogol's Influence on Dostoevsky*, Prague, 1928).

313

overcoat—an inanimate object—is, in Dostoevsky, replaced by a living human being, the girl Varenka Dobroselova; the shy and selfless love of the poor clerk Makar Devushkin is shown without any scorn or condescension, without any annihilating laughter, without the slightest trace of mockery. The honor of the poor clerk as a human being has been fully restored.

But did Dostoevsky understand what Gogol intended? He did not, any more than had Belinsky. As we have already said, both the "social aspect" and "I am your brother" are only secondary motifs in "The Overcoat." Gogol, a reader of the Church Fathers and of the *Philokalia*[17]—Gogol, who was regarded as a prophet by many of his friends, or at least as a teacher of the right way to live—this, after all, is the very same Gogol who wrote "The Overcoat." Students of Gogol (Zenkovsky, Gippius, Mikolayenko)[18] are gradually becoming aware of the fundamental role that religious problems, problems raised in the writings of the Church Fathers—the "spiritual deed," the heroic feat of "spiritual struggle"—played in the themes of Gogol's fictional work. Gogol's letters—not only *Selected Passages from Correspondence with Friends* but the actual letters (which, of course, nobody reads)— are not a fanciful and hollow exercise in preachifying, but a serious, even if unsuccessful, attempt at actively laying hold of human souls, at asserting spiritual leadership.

The psychological subtlety with which the Church Fathers worked out the problem of spiritual struggle in their writings, the amazing psychological insights of the *Philokalia*—did all this go unnoticed by Gogol? Of course not. But we do not at this point wish to offer an interpretation of "The Overcoat" that is based on

[17 The *Philokalia* is a collection of writings by the Eastern Church Fathers, which aims at "presenting a complete picture of the traditional way of Christian spirituality as it had been practiced throughout the centuries from the earliest times of Christianity." The original Greek *Philokalia* was published in 1792, the Slavonic version shortly thereafter by Paissy Velichkovsky, and the Russian version in the late nineteenth century. The Slavonic and Russian title is *Dobrotolyubie*, which is simply a calque from the Greek. An abridged version is available in English, under the title *Early Fathers from the Philokalia*, selected and translated from the Russian by E. Kadloubovsky and G.E.H. Palmer (London, 1954); the quotation above is taken from their introduction (p. 11).]

[18 Cf. V. V. Gippius, *Gogol'*, Lenigrad, 1924; V. V. Zenkovsky, *N. V. Gogol'*, Paris, n.d.; L. Mikolayenko, the chapter on Gogol in Chizhevsky's *Narysy z istoriji filosofiji na Ukrajini (Sketches of the History of Philosophy in the Ukraine)*, Prague, 1931.]

the writings of the Church Fathers. An intrinsic analysis of the story will, in itself, be enough to bring us to the problems of spiritual struggle. The purpose of our remarks has been merely to emphasize that first and foremost we should expect Gogol's fictional works to attempt to resolve complex psychological problems, not merely rehearse axioms ("I am your brother") and shopworn truisms ("even peasant girls"—that is to say, even "poor clerks"—"know how to feel too").

The theme of "The Overcoat" is the kindling of the human soul, its rebirth under the influence of love (albeit of a very special kind). It becomes evident that this can happen through contact with any object—not only with one that is grand, exalted, or important (a heroic deed, one's native land, a living human being such as a friend, a beloved woman, etc.), but also with one that is common and ordinary too. As we have seen, the hero's attitude toward the overcoat is depicted in the language of erotic love. And it is not only love for what is grand and important that can destroy a man or pull him down into a bottomless pit; so too can love for an insignificant object, once it has become the object of passion, of love.

One of the leading ideas in Gogol's fictional works is that each person has his particular fervor, his passion, his enthusiasm. It is an old theme—a theme of Horace, of the poetry of the European and Ukrainian baroque, of one of the so-called verses of the Ukrainian mystic Skovoroda, which was probably familiar to Gogol if only from Kotlyarevsky's play *Natalka Poltavka*. (This last writer was the source of some of the epigraphs to Gogol's story "The Fair at Sorochintsy," in *Evenings on a Farm Near Dikanka*.) Skovoroda was an exact contemporary of Paissy Velichkovsky (1722-94), the compiler of the Slavonic *Philokalia*, and both came from the same part of the country.[19] In one of his so-called "verses" (*virshi*, religious songs that were sung at Ukrainian fairs by blind bards in Gogol's own time, of course, just as they were even as late as the beginning of the twentieth century), Skov-

[19 Ivan Petrovich Kotlyarevsky (1769-1838) was a poet, translator, and dramatist, who is known as the founder of modern Ukrainian literature. Grigory Savvich Skovoroda (1722-94) was a philosopher of great originality, who enjoyed a considerable vogue in Russian literature of the late nineteenth and early twentieth centuries as a mystic, a proto-symbolist, and a pre-anthroposophist. Paissy Velichkovsky (1722-94) was a monk, of very strict observance, who eventually became archimandrite of a monastery in Moldavia. He made many translations from the Greek Fathers.]

oroda first has a few introductory lines, which contrast the author's "single-minded" spiritual enthusiasm ("I have only one thought in the world, and there is only one thing that will not pass from my mind. . . .") with the variegated interests and enthusiasms of the world ("every head has its mind, every heart has its love, every throat has its taste . . ."); and then he presents a motley picture of the variety of human fervors—to use Gogol's term. A certain passage in *Dead Souls* which Vasily Gippius correctly recognized as being one of those that are the most important for the ideology of the "poem,"[20] recalls the humorous bent of Gogol's fellow-Ukrainian, Skovoroda:

> Every man has his particular fervor: one man's fervor is turned toward wolfhounds; another fancies himself a great lover of music, and is wonderfully sensitive to all the profound passages; a third is an expert at dining with gusto; a fourth feels that he can play a part in life ever so slightly higher than the one allotted him; a fifth, with more modest aspirations, sleeps and dreams of promenading with some aide-de-camp, in order to show himself off before friends, acquaintances, and even strangers. (Part 1, ch. two.)

Passions, enthusiasms, fervors are here all directed at insignificant objects (except for the love of music—but that too is only an apparent love). At the beginning of "Nevsky Prospect" Gogol describes the "exhibition" that takes place every day as people stroll along the Nevsky: "One displays a smart frock-coat trimmed in the highest-quality beaver; another, a splendid Greek nose; a third, magnificent sidewhiskers; a fourth, a pair of charming eyes and a perfectly marvelous hat; a fifth, a signet ring on a stylish little finger; a sixth, a foot in a perfectly delightful little shoe. . . ." This is an exhibition of the objects of fervors; there is not the slightest suggestion of any serious interests here.

But in "The Overcoat" the hero's fervor is of a lower order than anywhere else in Gogol. Yet Akaky Akakievich does have a fervor; he displays the object of this fervor—the overcoat—to his fellow workers and rejoices that he can show himself in it "even in the evening." The intensity of his enthusiasm for the object of his

[20] V. V. Gippius, *Gogol'*, Leningrad, 1924, pp. 158-159. Gogol called his work a "poem" (*poema*), although it was written in prose. This caused considerable stir at the time, and has been a small problem in Gogol criticism ever since.]

fervor somehow places him in the ranks of Gogol's other heroes, both serious and humorous. He has something in common with Gogol's fops, accumulators, and unhappy lovers.

The fop type appears in Gogol as early as the Ukrainian stories:

In the old days the judge and the mayor were the only ones in Mirgorod who wore cloth overcoats lined with sheepskin in the winter, while all the lesser officials wore just plain sheepskin; but nowadays the assessor and the reeve have latched onto new cloth coats lined with Reshetilov astrakhan. The year before last the office clerk and the district clerk got themselves some dark blue duck at sixty kopecks a yard. The sexton had some nankeen summer trousers and a vest of striped worsted made. In short, everybody's trying to be somebody! ("Christmas Eve").

But with Akaky Akakievich, even this particular fervor is reduced to a minimum: strictly speaking, he dreams only about something that is absolutely necessary to cover his body. In saving up to get the overcoat, Akaky Akakievich sets out on the road of accumulation or acquisition, thereby becoming one of Gogol's "acquirer" types. We see different variations on this type in Gogol: from his Ukrainians (the traditional theme of the treasure hunt in "A Bewitched Place" and in "St. John's Eve"), to Chartkov (the hero of "The Portrait"), Chichikov in *Dead Souls*, and the gamblers (in the play of that name). But here too, Akaky Akakievich stands infinitely lower than all his brethren: his accumulation has a limited practical goal. Akaky Akakievich in fact perishes from love; he is a strange variant of those lovers in Gogol who end tragically—from Petro (in "St. John's Eve") and Andry (in *Taras Bulba*) to Poprishchin ("Diary of a Madman") and the hapless Piskaryov ("Nevsky Prospect"). Gogol returned to this type again and again; in fact, even Chichikov's fleeting infatuation with the governor's daughter proves fatal for him. In this company Akaky Akakievich looks like a parody, a caricature, with his ardent love, capable of overcoming death itself, his love for—an overcoat.

We will perhaps understand the meaning of this utter debasement of fervors more clearly if we turn to the letters of Gogol that date from the same period as the writing of "The Overcoat." One of the most important themes in the correspondence between 1840 and 1842 is the question of whether a person can attach his life to things of the external world. Dostoevsky asked himself the same question when he talked about "immovable ideas" (an expression that goes back to Pushkin's story "The Queen of Spades").[21] Actually, for Gogol it was not even a question: he resolved it immediately and categorically. In a letter to A. S. Danilevsky (June 20, 1843) he sets the external and the internal life in sharp contrast. It is necessary to have an "immovable anchor"; since all things in the world are doomed to destruction, man must have within him "a center on which he can lean and thereby overcome the very worst sufferings and the sorrow of life . . . forming a contrast with internal life is external life, where man, swept up by passionate enthusiasms, is pulled along by life's currents without a struggle."

The "center" of which Gogol speaks here is the "centrum securitatis" of Christian mysticism—God. In Him there is certitude and constancy. It is He who indicates man's place in the world (something that every person has); God is a "customer" for whom we all work. To lose one's link with this center means to lose one's place in the world, to lose one's goal in life (or the customer's "order"). And to surrender to the external world, to tie one's destiny to the objects of this world, also means to lose the center and at the same time to lose oneself. "External life is outside God, internal life is in God," Gogol writes. Therefore, the cognition of God (as is traditional in Christian mysticism) is self-cognition: "It is necessary to go deep within ourselves and query and discover which of the facets that lie hidden within us are useful and necessary to the world . . . for there is no unnecessary link in the world."[22]

In the "Petersburg stories"[23] Gogol depicts people who are "losing themselves," giving themselves over to the power of the external world. He himself says this of the artist Chartkov (in "The Portrait"), who perishes in pursuit of money and fame, disregarding the "order" that God has given him. The clerk Poprishchin (in "Diary of a Madman") and the artist Piskaryov (in "Nevsky Prospekt") perish from love for a woman. Akaky Akakievich perishes from "nothing." His passionate enthusiasm is directed at an insignificant, unworthy object—and he has no center on which he can lean and withstand the world, or "overcome the very worst

[21 I.e., *idées fixes*.]
[22 Letter to A. S. Danilevsky, June 20, 1843.]
[23 "Petersburg stories" is not actually a title: it is used by critics to refer to stories by Gogol that are set in St. Petersburg: "The Portrait," "The Nose," "Diary of a Madman," "Nevsky Prospect," "The Overcoat."]

sufferings and the sorrow of life." One can meet a tragic end not only from great passions, from passions that are directed at something grand, exalted, important, but also from passions that are directed at something trivial. Everything that is of this world is perishable, and any man who has built his life on it is carried away to destruction with it, regardless of whether this worldly life is something grand or—just an overcoat.

Even if we mark off a particular area of worldly life as containing objects of lawful, permissible, or perhaps simply understandable passions or fervors—passions that are directed at something "grand" or simply at something big (which Gogol does not do, as we have seen)—the example of "The Overcoat" nonetheless remains incontrovertible. Gogol probably chose such an extreme and paradoxical example just to make the point clear to us, the public, the reader. The letter to Danilevsky, from which we have quoted, tells of painful experiences, which Gogol himself takes seriously. If Gogol considers it possible to speak of losing the inner world and yielding to the external world even in an exalted context like this, then just imagine what his opinion of Akaky Akakievich must be. The world and *the Devil* ensnare man not only with things that are grand and exalted, but also with trivia; not only with ardent love for a woman, or with dreams of beatific happiness, or with mountains of gold, but also with the humdrum life, with a few sorry coins squeezed out of an already meager salary, with an overcoat. If a man becomes entangled in such trivia with all his soul, there is no salvation for him. The plot of "The Overcoat" is a unique adaptation of the Biblical parable of the widow's mite; just as a mite, a small coin, can represent a great sacrifice, so too can a trifle such as an overcoat represent a great temptation (this is an idea that comes from the *Philokalia*). Not only God, but also the Devil, evaluates such a mite accordingly.

VII

The main hero of nearly all Gogol's works, the hero whose name we encounter in nearly every work, is the Devil. There seems to be no reference to the Devil in "The Overcoat." But perhaps it only seems so. The Devil actually is mentioned several times, but all in one part of the story and always in reference to the tailor Petrovich. He is the one who refuses to mend the old "dressing gown" and puts the idea of a new coat into Akaky Akakievich's head, thereby setting the plot rolling. Perhaps Gogol is only playing with the word "devil" when he says that Petrovich's wife used to call him a one-eyed devil whenever he was drunk: "He's fortified himself with rotgut, the one-eyed devil." But Petrovich was sober when Akaky Akakievich came to see him, "and he was therefore gruff, intractable, and likely to demand the Devil only knows what price." Generally speaking, "Petrovich had a mania for suddenly demanding the Devil only knows what exorbitant price." Perhaps it is also mere chance that Petrovich possesses a snuff-box "with the portrait of some general or other on it—just which general nobody knew, because the spot where the face used to be had been poked through with a finger and then pasted over with a square piece of paper." But the only thing that Akaky Akakievich sees at the moment when the matter of a new overcoat is being decided is precisely this faceless general, and the Devil is faceless. As someone who was well read in religious literature, as a connoisseur and collector of folklore materials—popular songs and legends— Gogol of course knew about the Christian and folk tradition that the Devil is faceless. Petrovich fans the flame of passion in Akaky Akakievich's soul, stirring up the "most daring and audacious thoughts" about a new overcoat. When Akaky Akakievich visits him for the second time, Petrovich is drunk, "but nonetheless, as soon as he heard what was what, it seemed as if the Devil had nudged him. 'Impossible,' he said: 'you must order a new one. . . .' "

Gogol not only wished to present Akaky Akakievich as our "brother"; the main purpose of "The Overcoat" was to point to the danger that lurks even in trivia, even in the daily round: the danger, the destructiveness of passion, of passionate enthusiasms quite apart from the object they attach to, even if that object is only an overcoat. For Gogol, the word "even" serves as the means for emphasizing this basic idea. "Even" carries our thoughts to the heights, like an arrow, like an irrepressible thrust of passion, only to let them fall, all the more impotent, and plunge into the common ruck. Akaky Akakievich's impotent aspiration is directed at an unworthy object and is toppled from an illusory height ("even") by the Devil, who is the one responsible for providing such a prosaic yet fantastic goal for this aspiration.

And Akaky Akakievich's aspiration, his earthly love, does conquer death itself; this means, for Gogol, the utter loss of self, a loss that extends even to the life beyond the grave. By returning from the other world to the cold streets of St. Petersburg, Akaky Akakievich shows that he has not found peace beyond the grave, that he is still bound, heart and soul, to his earthly love. The illusory victory of earthly love over death is therefore really the victory of the "eternal murderer," the evil spirit, over man's soul. Gogol's story of the poor clerk is not humorous, but terrible.

VIII

We began our analysis with an obvious trifle, a linguistic detail ("even") in the texture of "The Overcoat." We have seen how important this trifle is for Gogol, as a means of stylizing the colloquial language or *skaz* of the story. We have seen that Gogol employs the same trifle as a device in the play of his humor (and it is perhaps not even necessary to repeat that humor is Gogol's special way of struggling against insignificance, against a demonic nothingness). We have seen that this same verbal detail is a means of moving closer to the hero, understanding his psychology, and conveying his particular upward-directed angle of vision. Finally, we have seen that this "detail" contributes to an understanding of the idea of work. The subsequent development of "The Overcoat" in Russian literature (Dostoevsky said that "we have all come out of 'The Overcoat' ")[24] could be traced. This would mean tracing the evolution of the *skaz*, tracing the history of the antithetical humor that is characteristic of Gogol, tracing the changes in the naturalistic techniques of characterizing the psychology of the insignificant hero, tracing the evolution of the poor-clerk plot (i.e., the way in which Gogol's profound insights into psychology were vulgarized into social commentary)—but here we shall merely mention these themes.

We should say a few words about one thing, however. It may be that our analysis—to make the point once again—emphasizes the necessity and usefulness of reading and re-reading the classics, reading with attention to the trivia and the details (what M. Gershenzon calls "close reading" and A. L. Bem calls "the method of making small observations").[25] In concentrating on the *content* of

[24 This is nowhere to be found in Dostoevsky's writings, but it has become lodged in Russian criticism.]

[25 Mikhail Osipovich Gershenzon (1869-1925) was a historian of Russian literature and culture, a translator, and a bibliophile. His best-known works are probably *Mudrost' Pushkina* (*The Wisdom of Pushkin*, 1919)

works of literature, as we have been taught to do by the schools, by literary criticism, and by the whole tradition of Russian life, we have missed a great deal, particularly in the content itself; we have missed everything there that is shaped by and tied in with *form*. There are no trivial details (what Tolstoy called "little raisins") in the form of a literary work, precisely because there are no trivial details in a performance or a craft; and a work of art is both performance and craft at one and the same time. Mountains of prejudices have risen up around the classics. In order to free ourselves from them, we must read the works as something completely new, unknown, and hitherto unread. Actually, here we may have defined the basic principle of understanding works of art properly—not only literature, but any art: approaching the works as if we were spectators or listeners who have been born anew. We must be spiritually born anew in order to gain the right—and the possibility—of access to the treasure-house of art.

---

and *Perepiska iz dvukh uglov* (*Correspondence from Two Corners*, 1921), which was written with Vyacheslav Ivanov (the author of an article in the present collection).]

9

Alexander Slonimsky
(1881-1964)

SLONIMSKY earned a modest reputation as a writer of stories for children (his younger brother, Mikhail, became one of the more important Soviet novelists and short-story writers). But he is known primarily as a critic, who wrote on nearly all periods of Russian literature, capping his career with a monograph on Pushkin (*Masterstvo Pushkina*, 1959). Undoubtedly his most famous and influential work is the small study entitled *The Technique of the Comic in Gogol* (*Tekhnika komicheskogo u Gogolya*), which was published in 1923 and is here offered in translation. I have made only minor editorial revisions of the text, and I have taken up certain problems of terminology in the notes.

The Technique of the Comic
in Gogol

by Alexander Slonimsky

Prefatory Note

MY PROBLEM here is one of theory: to throw some light on comic
devices in Gogol from the viewpoint of a theory of the comic. The
question of the origin of these devices belongs to the history of
literature and is therefore not considered here. My method is not
formalistic, as it might appear to be at first glance, but rather,
"esthetic." I examine "technique" only insofar as it has teleological
value and serves certain esthetic ends. In addition, the main emphasis is given to the semantic weight of individual devices. It is not
part of my task at present to examine Gogol's comic devices in
their aggregate or to rank them in order of importance. I am taking
only those devices which have an architectural function, that is,
those which have a broader structural and semantic significance.

Humor and the Grotesque

I

Gogol's works, in the main, are examples of the most complex
form of the comic: humor. Humor is such a distinct form that
some theoreticians, as, for example, Lipps, set it off from the
comic and contrast it with everything else falling within the
purview of the comic. The justification for doing so is the special
significance that non-comic elements acquire when they are present
in humor. As long ago as 1841, Jean-Paul Richter drew attention
to the inherently philosophical nature of humor. He regards "totality" (*Totalität*) as the essential characteristic of humor: "Humor, as the opposite of the sublime, annihilates not what is individual, but rather what is finite, by setting it in contrast with the
idea. For humor, no individual foolishness and no individual fools
exist, but only foolishness as such and a nonsensical world (*tolle
Welt*)."[1] Lipps defines humor as the manifestation of "the ele-

[1] Jean-Paul Richter, *Vorschule der Aesthetik*, Section 32 (*Jean Pauls
Werke*, Berlin, 1841, XVIII, 142).

vated" in and through the comic (*in der Komik und durch dieselbe*).[2] According to Volkelt's theory, the prerequisite for humor is "a comprehensive and detailed study of the various areas of life" (*ausgebreitetes und zusammengehendes Eingehen auf die verschiedenen Gebiete des Lebens*), a "contemplation of the world" (*Betrachten der Welt*).[3] Volkelt also puts the main emphasis on the subjective aspect of humor—the author's assertion of his individuality in manipulating images at will. He regards humor as the highest achievement of subjective comicality, which is present when the person who is manipulating comic concepts at will (i.e., the subject) adopts a contemplative attitude toward the world and attains to a higher cognition of life.[4]

The nature of Gogol's humor corresponds fully with Jean-Paul's formulation (of which Volkelt's definition is a further development). This correspondence can be explained in part by the fact that the rise of humor is intimately associated with Romanticism. Humor was the most important form taken by the comic during the Romantic age. The high point of contemplation, which is essential to Jean-Paul's definition, was reached in full measure by Gogol during the final period of his work in prose-fiction, the period when "The Overcoat" and *Dead Souls* were completed (1842). But the serious elements of his comic vision were already present as early as *Mirgorod* and *Arabesques* (both 1835). Vissarion Belinsky, writing in 1835, concluded that the characteristic feature of Gogol's art was "a comic outlook that is always overcome by a deep feeling of sadness and despondency."[5] By way of objection to S. P. Shevyryov, he asserted that "the comic is definitely not the predominant and preponderant element in Gogol."[6] Later, Shevy-

---

[2] Th. Lipps, *Komik und Humor*, Hamburg and Leipzig, 1898, p. 112.

[3] J. Volkelt, *System der Aesthetik*, II, 1910, 530.

[4] Volkelt calls "subjective" that version of the comic in which we perceive not only what is contained in comic concepts, their objective reality, but primarily the individual "free will" (*Willkur*) of the person who is manipulating them (the subject): "In linking comic concepts, the subject's free will, the freedom of his individuality, the capricious play of his independent spirit manifest themselves the most. The subjectively comical depends on the appearance of comic concepts and their linkage by means of the highly individualistic independent activity of the subjective mind." (*System der Aesthetik*, II, 449). [Slonimsky's version is a not entirely accurate paraphrase.]

[5] "O russkoi povesti i povestyakh g. Gogolya ('Arabeski' i 'Mirgorod')" [*Polnoe sobranie sochinenii*, I, Moscow, 1953, 297]. In speaking about the "comic," Belinsky obviously means the purely comic.

[6] "O kritike i literaturnykh mneniyakh Moskovskogo Nablyudatelya."

ryov himself, in writing about *Dead Souls*, pointed to the presence
of a "deep hidden sadness" in Gogol's "bright laughter." In addition, he noted the philosophical nature of this "sadness"—a
broad outlook on life, or a "totality" (for which Jean-Paul uses
the term *Totalität*). "The entire poem is studded with a multitude
of short episodes, vivid observations, profound glimpses into the
essence of life; these all give evidence of an inner inclination
toward a heartfelt pensiveness and a serious contemplation of the
life of mankind *in general* and of Russian life in particular."[7]

Gogol himself, in *Dead Souls*, offered a definition of his humor
which points up the philosophical aspect (the broad contemplation
of life) as well as the convergence of the serious and the comic:
"And for a long time to come, I am destined . . . to contemplate
the whole of life (*Totalität*) as it rushes by in all its immensity,
contemplate it through laughter which is perceptible to the world
and through tears which are invisible to it and unknown" (ch. seven).
Gogol sets his humor—"lofty enraptured laughter"—in sharp contrast to pure and "merry" comicality, which he calls "the grimacing
of a clown in a showbooth": "lofty enraptured laughter is worthy
of taking its place beside a lofty lyrical impulse, and a vast gulf
separates it from the grimacing of a clown in a showbooth" (*Dead
Souls*, ch. seven). The same contrast is made in "Leaving the Theater" (1842): "not the light laughter which provides people with empty diversion and amusement, but the laughter which wings up out of
man's bright nature, which gives depth to an object. . . ." Also, in
"The Denouement of *The Inspector General*" (1846): "Not the
frivolous laughter with which one man mocks another in society
and which is engendered by the sloth and emptiness of idle time,
but laughter that is engendered by a love of man." Finally, in "An
Author's Confession" (1847), Gogol draws a definite dividing-line
between his early works, in which the predominant element is
"merriment," and later ones, in which the serious nature of humor
is already evident. He defines the "merry" comicality of his early
period as purposeless, i.e., as pure and unadulterated: "In order
to amuse myself . . . I would invent characters and personalities
in my head and would mentally place them in the most comical
situations, without the slightest concern as to why this was so,

[*Polnoe sobranie sochinenii*, II, Moscow, 1953, 137. This is an extensive
reply to various articles by S. P. Shevyryov, the leading critic of *The
Moscow Observer* (*Moskovskii Nablyudatel'*).]

[7] *Moskvityanin*, 1842, Part II, p. 348, 352.

what it was for and what use it was to anyone." The second period is characterized by "totality," by a broad grasp of life, and, at the same time, by an intensification of the comic element: "If you must laugh, then it is better to have a good hearty laugh at something that is really worthy of general derision." Gogol dates the beginning of this new kind of laughter from *The Inspector General*: its kind of comicality, as he puts it, created "a staggering effect." And this effect is associated with an intensification of the purely comic element: "Through the laughter, which had never before come out with such intensity in my work, the reader detected a note of sadness. . . . After *The Inspector General*, I felt, more than ever before, the need to create a full-bodied work, which would contain something more than things that ought to be laughed at."[8]

Humor, as a form of the comic, requires above all that the comic and the serious be fused. The serious functions in a humorous way only when it arises out of comic situations—not apart from the comic, but through it (*durch die Komik*, in Lipps's formulation). The first work of Russian literature that approximated humor, in this sense, was Denis Fonvizin's play *The Minor* (1782). Humor lent this work a special power and raised it above the general level of eighteenth-century comedies. Fonvizin is therefore remembered as the only truly comic writer of that time. When Gogol appeared on the scene, Pushkin compared him with Fonvizin first of all: "How astonished we were at seeing a Russian book that made us laugh—we who have not laughed since Fonvizin's time."[9]

The serious element in *The Minor* develops out of several comic lines.[10] The basic one consists of Prostakova's efforts to

[8 The references to the quotations other than from *Dead Souls* in this paragraph are, in order: "Teatral'nyi raz"ezd posle predstavleniya novoi komedii," *PSS*, v, 1949, 169; "Razvyazka Revizora," *PSS*, IV, 1951, 132; "Avtorskaya ispoved'," *PSS*, VIII, 1952, 440. The parenthetical *Totalität* is Slonimsky's.]

9 *Sovremennik*, 1836, No. 1 [This is a review of the second edition of Gogol's *Evenings on a Farm Near Dikanka*. Denis Ivanovich Fonvizin (1745-92) was the leading playwright of eighteenth-century Russia. He wrote two satirical comedies, *The Brigadier* (*Brigadir*, publ. 1786), a satire on the Francophilism rampant in Russia, and *The Minor* (*Nedorosl'*, 1782), a satire on the low cultural level of the Russian provincial gentry.]

[10 "Line" renders *dvizhenie*, literally, "movement." It might also be translated as "thread." Sometimes in Slonimsky's article it *does* mean "movement," and is then translated as such.]

327

marry off her son, Mitrofanushka, to Sofia. These efforts take various forms: at first, Prostakova attempts to achieve her purpose by flattering Sofia and Starodum; then she tries to demonstrate her son's brilliant achievements in learning; finally she arranges to have Sofia abducted. A series of comic scenes are strung along this basic framework: the lesson-scene and the fight between Mitrofanushka's tutors (Act III), the examination-scene (Act IV), etc. A secondary line develops in connection with the primary one: the rivalry between the uncle and the nephew (Skotinin and Mitrofan). From this comes a fresh series of comic scenes: the confrontation between Skotinin and Mitrofan, when they face each other "with bulging eyes" (Act II), Prostakova's fight with Skotinin (Act III), etc. The failure of Prostakova's efforts takes a serious turn—i.e., a series of comic lines results in a serious effect. There is virtually nothing comic in Act V. Mitrofan's rudeness to his mother—"Lay off, mother! What a pest!"—is not perceived comically by the audience; it creates a feeling of indignation. Prostakova, a conventionally flat comic character, becomes psychologically more rounded and more complex because of the motif of genuine despair. Her language, which has been highly comic throughout, now becomes natural and emotional, and is calculated to play upon the sympathy of the audience: "I'm finished, done for! My power is gone! I can't show my face anywhere, I'm so ashamed! I have no son!" That Prostakova's situation is pitiable, not comic, is emphasized by the attitude of the "virtuous" characters—by the help Sofia offers when Prostakova faints, by Pravdin's indignant remark to Mitrofan: "Scoundrel! Who are you to insult your mother?" And the moral that is drawn by Starodum in his final speech has a starkly tragic ring to it: "These are the well-deserved fruits of evil ways!" The serious tone of the climax develops wholly out of the comic lines that come before; in other words, we see here a case of the close interaction of the comic and the serious.

Act V of *The Inspector General* shows the same sort of transition from the comic to the serious. Here too the serious tone of the ending depends on comic lines. The play is built on the mayor's comic efforts to deceive the inspector general. The failure of these efforts at the very moment when they appear to have met with success is what creates the "staggering effect" of which Gogol speaks in "An Author's Confession."[11] It is the very magnitude of

[11 "Avtorskaya ispoved'," *PSS*, viii, 1952, 440.]

this sudden change that sets a tragic stamp on the ending. The mayor is no longer the flat and unsophisticated comic character that he was; he becomes more complex because of normal human emotions, which evoke sympathy on the part of the audience. His language, which has been highly comic, is now tinged with pathos. His concluding monologue reveals the subjective side of humor—a contemplation of events in their totality, an awareness of their general significance. He adopts, as it were, the point of view of the author, who manipulates his characters at will and creates a comedy from them: "Some quill-driver, some scribbler will turn up and stick you in a comedy . . . and everyone will grin and clap their hands. What are you laughing at? You're laughing at yourselves!" The mayor's monologue prepares us for the final words of the play, which are spoken by the gendarme and are the only serious words uttered in the comedy: "The inspector general who has been sent from St. Petersburg by imperial command," etc. This suddenly serious note creates a starkly tragic impression: it has the ring of a moral sentence being passed, like the concluding words of Starodum in Fonvizin's play. At this point, the comic line comes to an end, and the mute scene, to which Gogol attached so much importance, is a graphic representation of this sudden cessation.

There is more room for the subjective aspect of humor in works of prose-fiction, where the author can speak directly in his own voice, evaluating events, showing their general significance, and revealing his attitude toward the world. Here the serious and the comic are linked in two ways. On the one hand, the transition from the comic to the serious is indicated by breaks in the tone of the author's voice, by a rapid shift of his point of view, by a different attitude toward what he is depicting. On the other hand, events and characters become serious in themselves. And there is an interaction here: a change in the author's attitude and tone depends on a change in the nature of events and characters. We see the combination of both aspects of humor—the subjective and the objective—in "The Tale of How Ivan Ivanovich Quarrelled with Ivan Nikiforovich" (1835).

The basic line of the story consists of the comic efforts made by Ivan Ivanovich in defense of his honor, which is besmirched when Ivan Nikiforovich calls him a gander. A whole series of comic episodes[12] is connected with this: the attack Ivan Ivanovich

[12 "Episode" renders the Russian *khod*—literally, a "move." Often it suggests calculation or artifice (it is, for instance, the term used for a

makes on Ivan Nikiforovich's goose-pen at night; the recourse to
legal action by both heroes; the brown pig's running off with the
document containing Ivan Nikiforovich's complaint; everyone's
efforts to bring the two men together again. The story continues
to widen in scope because the entire town participates in the events.
The comic climax (the failure of the general efforts to reconcile the
two Ivans) comes, as it does in *The Inspector General*, at the
moment when success seems to have been achieved.

As it turns out, the cause of the climax is that same "gander"
which set the comic line moving in the first place. But when the
quarrel flares up for the second time, the impression it creates is
no longer merely comic. The growing sense of anticipation just
before the climax gives the comic characters a serious side. There
is even a certain solemnity about the remarks of the guests at the
party: "Tell us honestly, now: what did you quarrel about? Wasn't
it over a trifle? Don't you feel ashamed in the eyes of others and
of God?" There is something in the words Ivan Nikiforovich addresses to his adversary which inspires a sympathy that is almost
moving: "To tell you, in all friendship, Ivan Ivanovich . . . ,"
and in the gesture he makes: "while saying this, Ivan Nikiforovich
touched his finger to the button of Ivan Ivanovich's coat, which
gave evidence of his complete good will." Ivan Nikiforovich's
repetition of the word "gander" so enrages Ivan Ivanovich that
the episode ceases to be purely comic. The jocular tone is still
sustained in the narrative, but it now contains a serious element:
"He cast a glance at Ivan Nikiforovich—and what a glance! . . .
The guests understood the meaning of this glance, and made haste
to separate them. . . . He ran out in a dreadful fury." This prepares us for the transition to the serious ending, where the comic
element in the two Ivans completely disappears. Correspondingly,
the narrator's bantering tone, which has been sustained from the
very beginning, now undergoes a radical change. The tone of the
story becomes pensive and sad. The point of view has been shifted,
as it were: up to now, the narrator has been on the same level
with what he is depicting; he has viewed everything through the
eyes of an average citizen of Mirgorod. At the end, however, he
suddenly contemplates things from a higher vantage point, from
which everything that was once funny proves to be sad. This is
the transition from the amusing to the sad, of which Gogol speaks

"move" in chess). So, "line" (*dvizhenie*) stands for the long line of a
literary work, which is made up of several "episodes" (*khody*).]

330

in "An Author's Confession": "What I had been laughing at became sad." And finally, the element of totality, which is characteristic of humor, comes out clearly in the concluding sentence: "It's a dreary *world*, my dear sirs!"[13]

II

The linkage between comic and the serious is brought about in a different way in "Old-Fashioned Landowners" (1835) and in "The Overcoat" (1842). Here there is nothing comic about the plots themselves. As far as plot is concerned, "The Overcoat" is just as much a sentimental story—a "piteous tale"—as is "Old Fashioned Landowners," but it does have a stronger comic coloration. In both stories, the comic effect is created by individual comic episodes, which give a comic coloration to events and characters. Such, for example, are the circumlocutions with which Afanasy Ivanovich endeavors to divert attention from his appetite, and also the little jokes he makes ("Old-Fashioned Landowners"). Such are the discussions between Akaky Akakievich and the tailor Petrovich about the overcoat, and the scene between Akaky and the Important Personage. In both stories, the climax—the disappearance of the cat, the theft of the overcoat—is not in itself comic. Therefore, the transition from the comic to the serious does not coincide with the climax (as it does in *The Inspector General* and in "The Two Ivans"); the comic and the serious alternate throughout both stories.

In the main, these alternations depend on a shift of the angle of vision onto what is being depicted—i.e., they occur in the subjective world of the narrator. In "Old-Fashioned Landowners," the narrative voice maintains a sentimental tone throughout, but with a light tinge of amiable ridicule. At the same time, the comic element in the characters is gentle and restrained. For example, the comic impression created by the conversations between Afanasy Ivanovich and Pulkheria Ivanovna is softened by the love and tenderness the two feel toward one another, and this prepares us for the ending, where the serious strain becomes predominant. Taken as a whole, this story is, in Pushkin's apt characterization, an "amusing and touching idyll which makes us laugh through

[13 "Avtorskaya ispoved'," *PSS*, VIII, 1952, 441. The italics are Slonimsky's.]

tears of sadness and tender emotion."[14] As far as narrative devices are concerned, "Old-Fashioned Landowners" does not move beyond the tradition established by Karamzin. There is a lyrical descriptive monologue at the beginning: "I am very fond of the modest life of those solitary owners . . . ," just as there is at the beginning of Karamzin's "Poor Liza": "Perhaps no one who lives in Moscow knows this city as well as I. . . ." Both stories are framed by a scene of desolation, which contrasts with the prosperity of an earlier time; at the beginning of Gogol's story, we see "a deserted dwelling" and "tumble-down huts," and at the end "tumble-down houses," drunken peasants, and a profligate heir. Karamzin's story begins with Liza's "empty cottage" and concludes with the same picture of desolation: "the cottage is empty." The predominant tone is one of nostalgia, with elegiac digressions. There are exclamations and interjections characteristic of the sentimental style. In Gogol: "To this day I cannot forget two old people of a past age who—alas!—are no longer among the living; but my heart to this day is still filled with pity, and my feelings are touched in a strange way! . . . It is sad! I feel sad already. . . . Good old woman! . . . Good old people!" Karamzin has: "Ah, I love those things that touch my heart and make me shed tears of tender sorrow," etc.

The comic element in the characters of "The Overcoat" is intensified until it becomes grotesque. Correspondingly, the diction of the narrator is also marked by sharp contrasts: a highly comic tone unexpectedly opens up a serious side to things, a lofty flight of emotion and ideas comes to an abrupt end in a comic anticlimax. The angle of vision is constantly being shifted onto what is being depicted. In *The Inspector General* and "The Two Ivans," the transition from the comic to the serious is the net result of all the comic lines that run throughout both works; but in "The Overcoat" it is brought off within the confines of an individual comic episode. At the beginning, Akaky Akakievich's insignificance is comically exposed—in a "torrent of gibes," as Vasily Rozanov put it—but with just a glimmer of serious feeling: "The child was christened, during which he set up such a cry and made such a face as if he had a presentiment that he would be a titular coun-

---

[14] *Sovremennik*, No. 1, 1836. [Review of second edition of *Evenings on a Farm Near Dikanka*.]

cilor."[15] The ethical position of the narrator, which is above mere "chaffing," is established straightway: "As for rank, he . . . was what people call a permanent titular councilor, at whom, as we know, various writers who have the praiseworthy habit of attacking those who can't bite back have jeered and gibed to their hearts' content." And the "office humor" of the young clerks who make fun of Akaky Akakievich becomes in itself an object of ridicule for the narrator: "The young clerks laughed and jeered at him with all the resources of their office humor." All this serves as a preparation for the serious resolution of this particular comic episode. The narrator imperceptibly reduces Akaky Akakievich to a position in which he is no longer funny but merely pitiable (the scene where the other clerks scatter pieces of paper on his head). And then the tone of the narration turns sentimental: "But Akaky Akakievich did not utter one word in reply." And finally, in the reflections that a certain young man makes on Akaky Akakievich's moving words ("Leave me alone! Why do you insult me?"), the moral idea of the story comes out, i.e., the high point of contemplation from which the author laughs at the world:

> And for a long time thereafter, the shortish figure of the little clerk with the bald-patch atop his head would appear before him, in his happiest moments, speaking the heart-rending words: "Leave me alone! Why do you insult me?" In these heart-rending words, others could be heard: "I am your brother!" And the poor young man would bury his face in his hands, and many times in his life thereafter he would shudder on seeing how much inhumanity there is in man (here is the shift to "totality"), how much brutal coarseness lies hidden in a refined and educated worldly manner, and—oh, Lord!—even in a man whom the *world* (again, a generalization) recognizes as being noble and honest.[16]

[15 V. Rozanov, "Kak proizoshel tip Akakiya Akakievicha," *Legenda o Velikom Inkvizitore F. M. Dostoevskogo, s prilozheniem dvukh etyudov o Gogole*, 2nd ed., St. Petersburg, 1906, p. 279.]

16 [The italics and the parenthetical comments are Slonimsky's.]

Boris Eichenbaum regards this whole passage as a "sentimental and melodramatic digression" which is necessary only to interrupt the comic *skaz* and which therefore has no literal meaning [cf. the article "How Gogol's 'Overcoat' Is Made," in this collection]. However, this "digression" does include an account of Akaky Akakievich's patient attitude when he is being badgered by the young clerks, and does record his own words ("Leave me alone!") with an indication of the tone in which they are

The story as a whole recapitulates this movement from the comic to the serious. The opening comic episode, with its serious resolution, serves as a kind of blueprint for the development of the plot as such (the account of the loss of the overcoat). The comic account of Akaky Akakievich's efforts to outwit Petrovich and get him to mend the old overcoat takes a serious turn when these efforts end in failure. There are serious touches throughout this entire comic episode. "Akaky Akakievich's heart sank. 'Why is it impossible, Petrovich?' he asked in the pleading voice of a child. . . . Poor Akaky Akakievich gave a cry . . . he went out utterly annihilated . . . he seemed to be wandering in a dream. . . . His spirits sank utterly . . . ," etc. A new comic episode then begins: the making of the overcoat. The serious note in the narrative voice gradually grows in intensity and swells into pathos in the discourse on how Akaky's life is filled with dreams of the future overcoat. At the same time, this process is punctuated by sudden comic anticlimaxes. The note of pathos makes a comic contrast with the trivial subject-matter. The contrast is eliminated by a sudden drop into anticlimax; yet the sentence retains its original serious intent. Such sentences as: "He did partake of spiritual nourishment, for his thoughts were constantly on the eternal idea of the future overcoat," take on a double meaning, as it were: they are both comic and serious. Comic because there is a disparity between the lofty concept of an eternal idea and that of an overcoat. (The beginning of the sentence—"his thoughts

---

uttered—i.e., it is a part of the plot. As we have seen, this is not in fact a "digression" at all, but the culmination of an entire comic episode, an organic part of the story. As regards a "literal" interpretation (which Eichenbaum finds irrelevant): if this means that the passage is read with a feeling of compassion, then the "naive people" whom Eichenbaum chides are not so very wrong; the entire episode is calculated to create just such a sentimental effect. Of course, nobody has a right to ascribe the emotions expressed here to Gogol personally; but we can see in them, without being naive, the high-point of contemplation on which the "author" (the one in the story, not the real one) wishes to place the reader. Eichenbaum's study (which is general is extremely interesting) is itself not entirely free of subjectivity in some instances. For example, he denies that the word "hemorrhoidal" (which describes the color of Akaky Akakievich's face) has any significance as an image in its own right; instead, he calls it "devoid of logical meaning" merely because it is "resounding" and comes at the end of a long sentence. Likewise, he has doubts about the "concrete meaning" of such "resounding" words or archaic expressions such as "halberd," "silver-plated clasps," etc.

were constantly on the eternal idea"—leads us to anticipate something important.) Serious because up to this point in the story, the issue of the overcoat has already assumed considerable importance for Akaky Akakievich, and its juxtaposition with the eternal idea has to some extent been prepared. Further on, this theme develops into a long sentence which takes an even more precipitous plunge into anticlimax: "From that time on, his very existence seemed to become somehow fuller, as if he had gotten married, as if some other person were present with him, as if he were no longer alone but were accompanied by some agreeable helpmeet who had consented to walk the road of life with him. . . ." Then comes an unexpected anticlimax, which does not, however, destroy the seriousness of what has just come before: "This helpmeet was none other than the new overcoat, with its warm padding and its sturdy lining, something that would never wear out." And then comes an abrupt anticlimax which is unambiguously comic: "At times a fire glowed in his eyes, and the most daring and audacious thoughts even flashed through his mind: shouldn't he really have marten-fur put on the collar?"

As in *The Inspector General*, the climax occurs at the moment of apparent success, right after "the triumphal day" when Akaky Akakievich has at last acquired the new overcoat. But now there is no doubt about its being a disastrous and touching event, as is emphasized by the description of how the other characters felt. "The account of the theft of the overcoat—despite the fact that there were clerks who even then made it a point to laugh at Akaky Akakievich—did nonetheless move many people." The final comic episode develops—the search for the overcoat—and the plot as such comes to an end with the tragic death of Akaky Akakievich. The fantastic ending, like the beginning, unfolds entirely in the subjective world of the narrative voice. By manipulating the comic elements at will, the narrator gives the events a general significance, bringing in the entire city and having the Important Personage feel remorse. Yet despite its intense comicality (the "playing" with the supernatural, which conceals the realistic intent), the ending does not destroy the "touching" effect of the plot itself. Thus, the entire story takes on a double meaning, as it were. In the stories produced by the so-called natural school, which derived from Gogol's "Overcoat," this "touching" element is almost entirely divorced from the comic.[17]

[[17] "The natural school" is the term used to designate a group of minor

335

In *Dead Souls*, the serious element is confined almost exclusively to the narrative voice: the "lyrical digressions," as it were, stand apart from and in contrast to the plot, which is comic. Gogol's contemporaries also noticed this fact. The narrative voice moves in two directions: upward (highly emotional) and downward (intensely comic). The shifts from one to the other are not determined exclusively by changes in the plot, as they are in "The Overcoat"; rather, they have their own inner, subjective motivation. The playful free spirit of the artist is always in control as he makes comic connections between events at will. And he moves higher and higher, as events develop and proceed toward a climax (general confusion with regard to the dead souls and the governor's daughter). In his first digression (on Korobochka, in chapter three), the narrator himself indicates the subjective factor that motivates the shift from the comic to the serious, from "merriment" to "sadness."

But why spend so much time on Korobochka? Whether it's Korobochka or Manilov, with their well-ordered or disordered households—let us pass them by! For other things in this world are wondrously arranged: merriment can turn into sadness in the twinkling of an eye, if only you stare too long at it, and then Lord only knows what notions may pop into your head. . . . But let them pass, let them pass! Why talk about this? But why, then, at unreflective, happy, carefree moments, does another wondrous current sweep unexpectedly by all of itself? Laughter has not quite left the face when it has already turned into something different among the very same people, and the face is already illuminated by a different light. . . .

And then comes an abrupt shift to comic narrative: " 'And here's the carriage, here's the carriage,' cried Chichikov." The comic "annihilation" of the characters is not brought off in the plot, but rather, in the subjective world of the narrator: their narrow natures are contrasted with the fullness of life, which contains a higher meaning that is revealed to the contemplating mind of the narrator. This moment of evaluation is noted by the author

writers in the 1840's who concentrated on the lower classes and injected a strong "humane" (sometimes sentimental) element into their descriptions. At the time, Gogol's "Overcoat" was widely regarded as the starting-point for this school. Belinsky is responsible for popularizing the term. See also Chizhevsky's article in this collection, for a fuller discussion.]

himself at the beginning of chapter seven: "Different is the destiny of the writer who has dared to bring out . . . all that lies deep within the cold, fragmented, workaday characters with whom our earthly path, often bitter and dreary, teems." This fragmentedness is precisely what Jean-Paul, in his definition of humor, means by the finite (*das Endliche*). *Dead Souls* serves, as it were, as a happy instance of Jean-Paul's Romantic formulation: showing "the finite by contrasting it with the idea" (*durch den Kontrast mit der Idee*)."

The cognitive significance and emotional power of the lyrical digressions increase as the comic line itself develops, as Chichikov's comic "rounds" draw a greater and greater number of comic characters into the plot. The first digression occurs in chapter three, when Korobochka's place "on the endless ladder of human perfectibility" is defined. After Chichikov has made all his rounds (cf. the beginning of chapter seven: "Happy is the traveler . . ."), the narrator contemplates, as a whole, the comic figures he has created ("all the terrible, overwhelming morass of trivialities in which our lives are mired"); then comes the celebrated formula of laughter through tears, and for the first time, there is an indication of the majestic course the "poem" is to take in the future. The narrative voice swells into the exalted rhetoric of a sermon; it becomes not only intensely emotional but markedly solemn: it takes on the characteristics not of a sentimental but a "high" style (even including Church Slavonicisms):[18] "And as yet far distant is that time when, in another surge, an awesome storm of inspiration will rise from a head invested with sacred horror and refulgence, and when, trembling and abashed, men will harken to the majestic thunder of other words. . . ." The intense note of pathos, which at times approaches a "high" style (especially in chapter nine: "but people have streamed past it in pitch darkness"), remains predominant in the digressions, right up to the "troika" passage at the very end. In the final chapters (ten and eleven), the author's attitude toward the world is fully revealed: it is that "serious contemplation of the life of mankind in general and of Russian life in particular" of which Shevyryov spoke.[19]

[18 Church Slavonic was the first Eastern Slavic literary language, introduced in the tenth century along with Christianity. It remains a strong element in modern Russian, and often is used for "high" or more abstract effects. The passage quoted by Slonimsky is full of Church Slavonicisms.]

19 With regard to *Dead Souls*, S. P. Shevyryov notes also that the artist

The swings from the serious to the comic that occur in the subjective world of the narrator are paralleled by a shift to the serious in the story-line itself. The tremendous commotion stirred up by the dead souls, and the resultant death of the public prosecutor, cast a tragic pall on the events. Thus, the comic development of the "poem" is resolved in a serious way. Taken as a whole, the "poem" follows a course that is characteristic of humor—from the "merriment" to "sadness" and "solemnity."[20]

III

In Gogol, as we have seen, the fusion of the serious and the comic is brought about either within the narrative voice (as subjectively motivated discontinuities of tone), or within the plot, along with a comic climax (as a serious resolution of a comic episode). The result is a general movement from "merriment" to "sadness" within the structure of the work as a whole. But this "structural" movement is in turn composed of more or less large-scale movements which are comic in the narrow sense of the word, that is, which take the reverse direction and resolve themselves in laughter. As a result, therefore, we have the sense of two opposing directions: one rising into intense pathos, the other breaking off abruptly into comic anticlimax. Each is essential to the other; each conditions the other: the higher and more impassioned the rise, the steeper is the line of descent and the more sudden its breaks. Gogol himself was aware of the precipitant nature of this anticlimax:

---

is independent of the comic scene he is depicting—i.e., he notes the subjective side of humor in Gogol: "The lower, coarser, and more material the world of objects depicted by the poet, then the loftier, freer, fuller, and more self-contained must be his creative spirit; in other words, the lower the objective world depicted by him, the higher, more detached, more free of this world must his subjective personality be" (*Moskvityanin*, 1842, Part IV, No. 8, p. 347).

[20] Mention is made of this feature of humor in Shevyryov's article on *Dead Souls*: "Look at the whirlwind that precedes the onset of a storm: at first it wafts by, light and low, it sweeps up dust and sundry rubbish from the ground; feathers, leaves, and scraps of paper fly up and whirl about; and soon the whole air is filled with its capricious whirling. . . . At first it is light and harmless, but hidden within it are the tears of nature and a terrible storm. Gogol's comic humor is exactly the same" (*Moskvityanin*, 1842, No. 8, p. 356).

And as yet far distant is that time when, in another surge, an awesome storm of inspiration will rise from a head invested with sacred horror and refulgence, and when, trembling and abashed, men will harken to the majestic thunder of other words. . . . But on with the journey, on with the journey! Away with the wrinkle that has furrowed the brow and the dismal gloom that has overcast the face. Let us plunge suddenly and all at once into all the noiseless crackle and tinkle of life . . . (*Dead Souls*).

Such sharp contrasts, together with highly distorted comic figures, give Gogol's humor a grotesque quality. In Volkelt's definition, the comic grotesque combines a bold upward movement with a sudden comic anticlimax:

The free, powerful, bold, perhaps audacious impulse that runs through the grotesque creates the impression of an upward movement into the sublime, the extraordinary, and the grand. But the powerful movement quickly becomes a comic anticlimax on a grand scale. The majestic upward movement of the line proves to be only a stage that is essential to its sudden collapse. And these sudden breaks bear witness to the collapse of some vast pretension. They reveal two things: insofar as they contain a feeling of powerful movement, they create the impression that they conceal some special value. At the same time, the fact that the movement is broken points to the comic disintegration of the presumed value.[21]

Volkelt also points out that the broad scope of humor pulls it in the direction of the grotesque:

Whoever sees the world as being full of false grandeur, whoever notices empty glitter, frivolous vanity, false pretensions, and puffed-up conceit everywhere, and wishes to expose these false

[21] Volkelt, *System der Aesthetik*, II, 413-414. V. V. Rozanov was the first to characterize Gogol's work as a comic grotesque, without using this particular term, however. He was quite right in pointing to two lines in Gogol: "an intense and nonobjective lyricism which soars to the heights," and "irony directed at everything that lies below." But he did not place sufficient emphasis on their interdependence ("Pushkin i Gogol'," *Legenda o Velikom Inkvizitore F. M. Dostoevskogo, s prilozheniem dvukh etyudov o Gogole*, St. Petersburg, 1906, p. 255).

values by means of humor—he will be naturally attracted to grotesque distortion.[22]

Gogol's concern with the grotesque developed along with his moral and religious preoccupations. The grotesque reaches its fullest expression, its high point, in "The Overcoat" and in *Dead Souls*, i.e., in the works dating from his Roman period, when his mystical tendencies assumed their full and final form. Later on, the element of pathos stifled the comic element; the result was the disintegration of the grotesque. This dated approximately from 1842, when the first version of the second volume of *Dead Souls* was completed (Gogol destroyed it about 1843). Until 1842, an ever-increasing intensification of the comic element in Gogol's writings is evident. Thereafter, the opposite can be observed: he excludes everything humorous that does not have an immediately satirical or didactic significance.[23] In "An Author's Confession"

[22] *System* . . . , II, 416.

[23] In the last surviving version of the second part of *Dead Souls* (1848), Gogol eliminated many comic passages that were fully worked out. Here, for example, is the beginning of ch. three in an early version:

"There's no great wisdom required here," said Petrushka [Chichikov has just called him a blockhead; they are talking about which direction to take], looking out of the corner of his eye, "except that after we get to the bottom of the hill we go straight, there's nothing more to it than that."

"Are you sure you haven't had a sip of anything except rotgut? Are you sure you're not three sheets to the wind now too?" [Chichikov asks.]

Seeing the tack that things were taking, Petrushka merely gave a sniff. He had been about to say that he hadn't even touched a drop, but he felt somehow ashamed. . . .

Selifan flicked the whip lightly over the sloping flanks of the horses, and directed his words at Petrushka: "Listen, they say Koshkaryov, the master, has dressed his peasants up like Germans; you can't recognize them from a distance—they go strutting around like cranes, like Germans. And the women don't just stick a kerchief or headdress on, they wear a German-like hood, you know the way the German women wear hoods— it's called a hood—you know, a hood, a German-like hood."

"And what if he dressed you up like a German in a hood!" said Petrushka, gibing at Selifan and smirking. But the face this smirk created! There wasn't the slightest resemblance to a smirk; it was just as if a person had caught cold in the nose and tried to sneeze but couldn't, and simply remained in the state of a man intending to sneeze.

Chichikov glanced up at his face, wanting to know what was going on there, and said: "A handsome fellow indeed! And yet he imagines he's good-looking!"

In the later version, the entire comic dialogue between Selifan and

(1847), he dismissed the "merriment" of his first works as "stupidity":

> this is the origin of my first works, which made some people laugh in as carefree and spontaneous a manner as they did me, while they made other people wonder how such stupidities could ever enter the head of an intelligent person.[24]

Gogol's attitude toward his own humor, as seen in the sermonizing passages in "The Overcoat" and *Dead Souls,* to some extent affected the way his contemporaries read him. Little by little, all attention came to be focused upon the "serious" side of his work, on the "heartfelt tears" that were "unseen" and "unknown" by the world. At the same time, the counterbalancing side—"laughter perceptible to the world"—was disregarded. In the 1840's, Gogol was recognized as the leader of the "natural school" and was interpreted as a "realistic" writer. And Gogol himself, caught up in the general political ferment of the time, became convinced that his real purpose was to serve the state. In writing Part 2 of *Dead Souls* (which was meant to be "more intelligent than the first part"), he therefore strove to avoid comic oversimplification in drawing his characters and tried instead to give them a lifelike, "realistic" fullness and richness. Thus, the comic figure of Chichikov was now made more complex with motifs of suffering and repentance, and therefore ceased to be comic.[25] In keeping with

---

Petrushka, and the comically burlesque gestures (Petrushka's smirk) disappear; the language loses its characteristic grotesqueness ("What was going on *there?*") and becomes smoother and more standard. Instead, a complacent remark by Chichikov is inserted, for satirical purposes. This whole section is reduced to the following:

> "There's no great wisdom needed here!" said Petrushka, turning halfway around and looking out of the corner of his eye, "except that after we get to the bottom of the hill we go straight on, there's nothing more to it than that."
> "And you haven't had a sip of anything except rotgut [said Chichikov] . . . A handsome fellow, really handsome! Why, you might say that you've astonished all Europe with your good looks!" Having said this, Chichikov stroked his chin and thought: "Indeed, what a difference there is between an enlightened citizen and the coarse physiognomy of a servant!"

[24 "Avtorskaya ispoved'," *PSS,* VIII, 1952, 439.]

25 Chichikov's comic remark in Part 1—"What indeed have I not suffered, I am like some barque tossed by the angry waves" (ch. two)—has a completely serious and pathetic ring in Part 2 (the scene with Murazov): " 'What has my whole life been, then? A savage struggle, a vessel tossed by the waves. And to suddenly lose everything I've earned, Afanasy Vasilie-

the new direction that *Dead Souls* was to take, Gogol intended to rework the first part in a "realistic" vein (i.e., to make the motivations more complex). The outline that he made emphasizes the ideological aspect of humor: "The whole town, with the whole whirlwind of gossip, a prototype of the slothfulness of the life of *all mankind* . . . how can the slothfulness of the town be expanded into a prototype of *universal slothfulness*?" (what Jean-Paul calls the *tolle Welt*).[26]

The view of Gogol as a "realist" has long distorted the way people have read him, and has created irreconcilable contradictions. Because the serious element in his humor has been studied in isolation from the comic devices, the significance of these devices has not been understood. How, for example, can Kalenik's "hop-tra-la" that interrupts the lyrical description of the Ukrainian night ("A May Night") be classified under the rubric of "tears"? It is interesting to note that Professor I. Mandelshtam, though proceeding from traditional ideas about Gogol, was nonetheless compelled, in studying the details of Gogol's style, to conclude that Gogol's humor does not always serve lofty purposes. He had to recognize (at least as far as the early works are concerned) that "Gogol's language stimulates laughter only for laughter's sake." From the standpoint of "realism," this kind of comicality strikes Professor Mandelshtam as being fortuitous, unnecessary, and inartistic. "This is a kind of grimacing or clowning. Actually, one can see nothing in common between it and the artistic depiction of truth."[27]

On the other hand, the authorial "digressions" and Gogol's own personal views (his mysticism and conservatism) were also considered to be incompatible with the supposed "realism" and "social significance" of his works. N. A. Kotlyarevsky hit on this particular contradiction in his well-known book on Gogol. This respected scholar points to the unfavorable conditions in which Gogol lived while in Rome (from 1836 to 1842). Estheticism intensified by the atmosphere of Italy; a tendency toward religious enthusiasm fanned by living in the very center of Roman Catholicism;

---

vich, everything I've acquired through such struggle. . . .' He did not finish speaking, and began to sob loudly . . . and fell back into the chair . . . ," etc.

[26 "(Zametki) k l-oi chasti [Mertvykh dush]," *PSS*, VI, 1951, 692. The italics and the parenthetical remark are Slonimsky's.]

[27] *O kharaktere gogolevskogo stilya*, Helsingfors, 1902, p. 243.

removal from Russia; a growing self-importance—all this, he thinks, must have had a harmful effect on the "talent of a humorist and a painter of manners and mores." However, it was precisely during this period that "The Overcoat," *Dead Souls*, and *Marriage* were written, and that new versions were made of *The Inspector General*, "The Portrait," and *Taras Bulba*. In other words, it was during this period that all of Gogol's most important work (even from the "social" point of view) was created. Kotlyarevsky is compelled, willy-nilly, to resort to mere verbiage in order to extricate himself from this difficulty: "but just before his final collapse, this creative talent gathered all his powers and triumphed over the attitudes and thoughts that were inimical to him as an artist."[28]

The destruction of the legend of Gogol's "realism" began with Vasily Rozanov. In evaluating Gogol from just this old "realistic" point of view, he was struck by the "lifelessness" and "stiffness" of the characters. Echoing Rozanov, Valery Bryusov tried to show that Gogol's portrayals were caricatures, "monstrous exaggerations," "improbable."[29] These strangely divergent points of view— the fact that exactly the same phenomena could be interpreted as both realistic and improbable—can be explained, first of all, by the haziness of the very notion of realism, and, second of all, by the fact that neither interpretation took account of the conditions of the comic art.

In any self-contained comic episode (i.e., in narrative and dramatic works)the comicality depends on an oversimplification of motivation and on a certain arbitrariness in the way events are linked, i.e., on a distortion of normal perception.[30] The term "realism" refers to the greater or lesser degree of correspondence between impressions received from a work of art and from reality. And this correspondence (in the case of narrative and dramatic works) can exist when the motivation for actions and events suggests—in fullness, complexity, and *irrationality*—the endless in-

---

[28] *N. V. Gogol'*, 4th ed., Petrograd, 1915, p. 356.

[[29] V. Rozanov, "Pushkin i Gogol'," *Legenda o Velikom Inkvizitore* pp. 259-262; V. Bryusov, "Burnt to Ashes," as translated in the present collection.]

[30] In this regard, cf. Volkelt: "In the realm of the comic, full play is given to the caprice of chance, the unexpected, the improbable. The predominance or irrational chance is significant in that a fillip, as it were, is hereby given to a rationally symmetrical world-structure, to a strictly logical chain of events. A wavering, mocking sheen is cast upon the entire lawful order of things" (*System der Aesthetik*, II, 482). [Slonimsky paraphrases the original.]

terlacing of motifs that occurs in real actions and events. The perception of a work of art with a complex motivation involves an element of empathy, which is incompatible with the purely contemplative state of mind required for the perception of a comic work. In the latter, this detached state of mind is achieved primarily through an oversimplification of motivation.[31]

Extreme comicality is at the same time an extreme distortion of life, a removal from its complexity and fullness. Let us grant that it is improbable that an experienced person like the mayor should so readily believe that Khlestakov is the inspector general, or that Kochkaryov should want to drive Podkolyosin to the church immediately after he has proposed to the girl (*Marriage*), or that the officials, who are past masters at tricky deals of every sort, should be unable to figure out the scheme involving the dead souls. It is equally improbable that Molière's Monsieur Jourdain should give his daughter's hand to her beloved, who is dis-

---

[31] Bergson regards mechanical inelasticity and automatism in the structure of comedy (i.e., an oversimplification of motivation) as the fullest expression of that "mechanization of the living" which is fundamental to his theory of laughter. At first glance, it appears that Bergson's theory is diametrically opposed to German theories of the comic. Bergson's method is objective: he proceeds from the way in which comic objects are grouped. The German theorists work by analyzing comic perception: their method is strictly psychological. But in the end Bergson's formulation coincides with the conclusions reached by the German estheticians. Both distinguish two elements in the comic. For Bergson, these are the living and the mechanical; for Volkelt, the serious and the unserious. According to Volkelt, comic perception operates when the comic object, which claims to have serious significance, reveals its emptiness, in consequence of which the initial serious perception (*Ernstnehmen*) becomes unserious (*Nichternstnehmen*). The equivalent process for Bergson occurs when mechanical inelasticity is revealed in an object which appears to be living. Essential to the comic, for both Bergson and Volkelt, is the exposure of an empty pretense. The deficiency of Bergson's theory is its imprecise definition of the basic concepts of "mechanical" and "living." They are used sometimes in the literal sense (where physical comicality is meant), and sometimes metaphorically (the inelasticity of thought and speech). In addition, Bergson's theory applies only to phenomena which are of a vivid and objective comic nature. Therefore, the only thing that is of unquestionable value for Bergson is the way in which the structural devices of comedy are grouped. (Cf. Bergson, *Le rire*; Volkelt, *Aesthetik*, II, 350-360.) [I borrow the English versions of the terms "mechanical inelasticity" and "automatism" (of which Slonimsky's Russian versions are poor equivalents) from *Comedy: An Essay on Comedy*, by George Meredith; *Laughter*, by Henri Bergson, ed. and with an introduction by Wylie Sypher, New York, 1956, esp. pp. 61-74.]

guised as a Turk, or that the miser Géronte (in *Les fourberies de Scapin*), who trembles over every last *sou*, should hand over 500 *ecus* to Scapin without checking his story of the abduction of Scapin's son on a Turkish galley. Improbability is the tireless companion of the comic. The vaudeville, which is the purest comic genre, is wholly constructed on improbable motivations. The stronger the comic element, the more radical is the violation of the natural and complex relationships of phenomena. Therefore, Gogol is improbable not because he is a fantast or a mystic, but simply because of the grotesquely exaggerated nature of his comic vision.

Comic Alogism

I

The most striking form of the comic grotesque in Gogol's works is nonsense. It is largely on nonsense that the general impression of improbability depends. Nonsense not only lies at the heart of the individual comic episodes but shapes the comic line as a whole, and ultimately creates an entire nonsensical world (*tolle Welt*). This point has already been made by Shevyryov in his article on *Dead Souls*: "It is as if a demon of confusion and stupidity soars over the entire town and pulls everyone together into a whole; here—in the words of Jean-Paul—there is no one fool in particular and no one stupidity in particular, but a whole *nonsensical world* that is embodied in an entire town."[32]

Unreality, improbability, impossibility—this was the impression that *The Inspector General* made on a majority of Gogol's contemporaries. Faddey Bulgarin, for example, reacted as follows: "He has built his play not on resemblances or verisimilitude, but on improbability or *unreality* . . .this scene [between the mayor and Khlestakov] does not contain even the slightest hint of truth to life . . . it's just like being on the Sandwich Islands in the days of Captain Cook."[33] According to P. V. Annenkov, the general impression, after the first performance of *The Inspector General*, was: "This is an impossibility, a slander, and a farce."[34]

[32] *Moskvityanin*, 1842, Part IV, No. 8, p. 351.

[33] *Severnaya pchela*, 1836, No. 97, Thursday, April 30, pp. 386-388.

[[34] "N. V. Gogol' v Rime letom 1841 goda," *Literaturnye vospominaniya*, Moscow, 1960, pp. 81-82.]

The sense of fantasy, improbability, and strangeness is emphasized by Gogol himself in his works, with words like "strange," "unreal," "implausible," "incongruous," "rubbish," etc. "On March 25th there occurred in St. Petersburg an unusually strange incident"—this is the lofty tone (designating the rising, i.e., pathosladen line of the grotesque)[35] in which "The Nose" begins. The theme of strangeness is developed in detail in the ending: "Only now do we see that there is much that's implausible. . . . But what is strangest, what is most incomprehensible of all . . . well, where after all do absurd things not exist?" And in the middle of the story: "He had absolutely no idea what to think of such a strange incident . . . all signs point to an unreal incident. . . . But what is there that's absurd about this business? . . . This world is full of utter nonsense; sometimes there isn't the slightest truth to life."

The same sort of thing can be found in other works as well. For example, in *Dead Souls*: "But come now, this is absurd! This makes absolutely no sense! It is impossible . . . readers will accuse the author of writing nonsense. . . . It turns out that it's all a lot of hot air, nonsense, rubbish, balderdash. It's simply the Devil only knows what!" *Marriage* is even subtitled: "An utterly incredible incident."

This same general impression is reinforced by the commentaries that Gogol himself made on his own works. "Hovering before my mind's eye was a comedy whose name was *muddle*" ("An Author's Confession"). The sense of universal muddle—which grew to grandiose proportions and became overwhelming—also represented Gogol's personal attitude toward the world. "The overwhelming muddle of our times fills everyone with terrible anguish."[36]

The comedy of nonsense, which has an architectural function in Gogol's works, is created by means of a basic comic device which may be most conveniently called *comic alogism*. This device consists of the comic destruction of logical and causal connections. It runs through the entire system of Gogol's work; it comes out in the

[35 The term is *liniya groteska*. The rather simple point that Slonimsky makes rather too elaborately in the following paragraphs is that the grotesque depends on the tension created between the sublime (or tragic or pathetic)—the "rising line"—and the ridiculous—the "falling line."]

[36 Letter to A. O. Smirnova, November 24, 1846. For the quotation earlier in the paragraph, cf. "Avtorskaya ispoved'," *PSS*, viii, 1952, 452. The italics are Slonimsky's.]

language of the characters and the narrator, in the way the dialogue is constructed, and in the motivations given for actions and events. Finally, it develops into the grotesque spectacle of an "overwhelming muddle" which is both funny and terrifying at the same time.[37]

The most extreme version of this device is the *comicality of absurd deductions*. The mayor announces that an inspector general is on the way. Ammos Fyodorovich hits upon the reason for such an "extraordinary" event: "Russia wants to go to war." The postmaster in turn also ventures an hypothesis, or "misses the target completely," as the mayor promptly observes: "What do I think? There'll be war with the Turks." The mayor is unhappy with a certain assessor, who smells "as if he's just come out of a distillery." Here too Ammos Fyodorovich has an explanation: "No, there's no way of getting rid of that now: he says his nurse bumped him against something when he was a baby and ever since then he's smelled slightly of vodka." Zhevakin, in *Marriage*, offers the following explanation for his visit: "I too saw an announcement of something in the newspapers. Well, I thought to myself, I'll go. The weather looked good, grass was everywhere along the road." This explanation surprises nobody: it is completely in the order of things in Gogol's world. In reply, the only question that Arina Panteleymonovna asks is: "And what is your name, sir?"

Chichikov is buying up dead souls. For the Lady Agreeable in All Respects, this can only mean that he is planning to abduct the governor's daughter. In Manilov's daydream, also in *Dead Souls*, friendship with Chichikov seems reason enough for receiving the rank of general: "Then [he imagined that] he and Chichikov arrived in fine carriages at some social gathering, where they charmed everyone with their agreeable ways, and the Emperor, it seemed, on learning of such a fine friendship as theirs, bestowed upon both of them the rank of general." The same sort of logic holds in Shponka's dream: "Then he was suddenly hopping on one leg, and his aunt, looking at him, said with a dignified air: 'Yes, you must hop, because you are now a married man.'" This is

---

[37] Prof. Mandelshtam points out the "device, introduced by Gogol, of juxtaposing statements that have no logical connection," and he indicates the importance of this device in Gogol's humor: "This method best defines Gogol's humorous style . . . he handles it with extraordinary ease" (*O kharaktere Gogolevskogo stilya*, Helsingfors, 1902). A number of examples of comic alogism are cited in Mandelshtam's book, but in no systematic order (e.g., pp. 273, 277, 279, 282, etc.).

the earliest instance of alogism in Gogol ("Ivan Fyodorovich Shponka and His Aunt," 1832). Such mental chaos reaches its height in Proprishchin's delirium ("Diary of a Madman"): "It's all ambition, and ambition because there's a little blister under the tongue, and in it a little worm the size of a pinhead, and it's all the doing of a certain barber who lives in Gorokhovaya Street." "Apothecaries write letters, but only after wetting their tongues with vinegar, because otherwise their faces would break out all in a rash."[38] Sometimes the comic effect depends not on the absurdity of a statement, but on the naive seriousness of the objection that is raised against it. "Of course Alexander the Great is a hero," says the mayor, "but why break up the chairs? It's a drain on the budget" (as if the heroism of Alexander the Great could really be an argument in favor of breaking chairs).[39]

To heighten the effect of the absurd deduction, Gogol employs the device of prolongation or retardation. The news of the inspector general's arrival throws everyone into a state of bewildered curiosity. "What do you mean, an inspector general? What do you mean, an inspector general?" The comic tension is increased by the news that he is traveling incognito and, what is more, with secret instructions ("Good Lord! With secret instructions too!"), and by the mayor's mysterious dream about rats "of a huge size": "They came up, sniffed, and went away." The officials seek an explanation for this unusual event: "Yes, it's such an unusual

[38 This last sentence is found only in a draft-variant of the text. The final version reads only as: "letters are written by apothecaries. . . ." Cf. *PSS*, III, 1938, 569.]

[39 The mayor is telling Luka Lukich, the superintendent of schools, about the local history teacher. "He's a smart one, that's for sure, and he's picked up a tremendous amount of information, but he explains things with such enthusiasm that he forgets himself. Once I was listening to him: while he was talking about the Assyrians and the Babylonians—well, that was all right; but as soon as he got to Alexander the Great—well, I can't tell you what happened to him. I thought there was a fire. I swear, he ran from behind the desk and banged a chair on the floor as hard as he could. Of course Alexander the Great is a hero, but why break up the chairs? It's a drain on the budget" (Act I, Scene 1).]

Cf. this with Burdyuk's naively serious reply, in Gogol's dramatic fragment *The Lawsuit* (*Tyazhba*): "But that's no name—Obmokni. Why are they talking nonsense: the dead woman's name was Yevdokia, and not Obmokni." [Obmokni is not a name in Russian: it is the imperative form of the verb *obmoknut'*, meaning "get wet, get damp." What makes the remark plausible, and funny, is the similarity in sound between the two words: ob*mók*ni/Yev*dók*ia.]

situation, most unusual. There's something behind it." The rising line of the grotesque—the expectation that something dreadful and important is about to happen—reaches a high-point—everything is so mysterious and peculiar—and is abruptly broken off in a comic anticlimax: Ammos Fyodorovich's theory that Russia wants to go to war. The effect of this unexpected conclusion is even greater because Ammos Fyodorovich speaks with great effort, as if he were racking his brains: "This is what it means: Russia—yes—Russia wants to go to war, and the ministry, you see, has sent an official to find out whether there's any treason afoot here."[40]

The effect of the ingenious conclusion suggested by the Lady Agreeable in All Respects, concerning Chichikov's intention of abducting the governor's daughter, is prepared by the same kind of retarding device. " 'Listen now, and I'll tell you just what these dead souls are'—and her visitor, on hearing these words, became all ears . . . she began to resemble a piece of fluff that would float into the air at the slightest puff. Thus a Russian nobleman, a lover of dogs and a hunting enthusiast (a long sentence then follows:

[40] Interestingly enough, these retardations—"this," "yes," "you see"—appear only in the 1842 [and final] text of the play. In the earlier versions (1836 and 1841), Ammos Fyodorovich's language flows along smoothly: "This means that Russia wants to go to war, and the ministry has dispatched an official specifically to find out whether there's treason afoot anywhere." Thus, up to 1842, Gogol was working for an intensification of comic effects.

The effort expended by Ammos Fyodorovich here is analogous to the "effort" that accompanies the striking of Korobochka's clock, in *Dead Souls*: "His hostess's words were interrupted by a hissing sound, so strange that the visitor was startled: it sounded as if the entire room were filled with snakes; but, raising his eyes, he felt reassured, for he perceived that the clock on the wall had conceived a desire to strike. The hissing was immediately followed by a wheezing, and finally, summoning up all its strength, the clock struck two, with a sound as if someone had hit a broken pot with a stick, after which the pendulum again proceeded to tick calmly from right to left." Ammos Fyodorovich's manner of speaking is described in similar terms in Gogol's instructions to the actors: "He speaks in a bass voice, with a prolonged drawl, wheezing and snorting beforehand, like an old-fashioned clock which hisses before it strikes." The passage on Korobochka's clock is a repetition, in miniature, of the cumulative tension that is built up in the opening scene of *The Inspector General*: at first there is the anticipation of something significant—a "strange hissing"; "the visitor was startled"; "was filled with snakes" (the rising line of the grotesque); then comes the high point of the tension: "it gathered up all its strength," and finally, the comic anticlimax: "a broken pot with a stick." The rise and fall of the sentence coincides here with the rise and fall of the line of the grotesque.

Gogol purposely lets the flow of language build up great tension so that the comic anticlimax will be that much more perceptible). . . . 'Dead souls,' intoned the Lady Agreeable in All Respects— 'What? What?' said her guest, all aquiver—'Dead souls . . .'—'Oh, do tell me, I beg of you!' " Here maximum tension is reached, and then the anticlimax suddenly occurs: " 'It's something that's simply been invented as a cover-up, and the whole point is this (cf. Ammos Fyodorovich's 'This is what it means') : he wants to abduct the governor's daughter.' " The effect of the anticlimax is underscored by the impression that this revelation produces on the Simply Agreeable Lady: on hearing this extraordinary verdict, she "sat rooted to her chair, and turned pale as death."[41]

Related to this is the *comicality of disconnectedness*: combinations of unrelated sentences, and unexpected discontinuities of theme. Khlestakov's statement, "I have an extraordinary lightness of thought," indicates the nature of this particular device. Poprishchin's moving appeal—"Oh, mother! Have pity on your sick child!"—is unexpectedly interrupted by a buffoonish apostrophe to the reader: "And do you know that the Dey of Algiers has a lump right under his nose?" ("Diary of a Madman"). In "An Official's Morning," Alexander Ivanovich says: " 'Hm,' His Excellency said, 'this is an official, and moreover . . . (raises his

---

[41] The preliminary sketches for this scene contain neither the preparation of the effect nor the absurd juxtaposition of dead souls and the abduction of the governor's daughter. Here the Lady's surmise is linked with Chichikov's supposed attempt to "do violence to" Korobochka, so that the transition to the theme of the governor's daughter becomes natural. "No, no, Anna Grigorievna! I know the real reason; it's not to do violence to Korobochka—that's just a cover-up. The real object (here is the logical transition) is the governor's daughter!" In the next draft, the theme of dead souls is added, and this introduces an element of the absurd: "Believe me, Sofia Ivanovna, the dead souls and Korobochka—that's all deliberate, just a cover-up; his real purpose is to abduct the governor's daughter. . . ." In the final version, Korobochka disappears, and there remains only the absurd juxtaposition of dead souls and the governor's daughter; the device of growing anticipation is introduced. In the final version, the effect of growing anticipation is strengthened: the Lady Agreeable in All Respects begins her explanation three times ("Now listen and I'll tell you what these dead souls are"—"dead souls"—"dead souls"); and the replies of her visitor are added ("What, what?" "Oh, do tell me, I beg of you!"); and the solemn tone of the long paragraph about the hunter is heightened. The comic anticlimax is all the more resounding. This demonstrates how Gogol worked at strengthening comic effects. [The parenthetical comments in the passages quoted, both in the main text and in the footnotes, are Slonimsky's.]

350

eyes). Your ceilings are rather well decorated: was this done at your expense or the landlord's?' " In the conversation between Khlestakov and Rastakovsky, the former says: "Suddenly a friend of mine—a guardsman, from a cavalry regiment—comes to him and says. . . . But listen, couldn't you lend me a bit of money?" The comic effect of the sudden transition is underscored by Rastakovsky's confusion: "Who was asking whom for money? Was the official asking the guardsman or the guardsman the official?"[42] Ivan Fyodorovich Shponka's aunt writes to him: "In anticipation of the genuine pleasure of seeing you, I remain your ever-loving aunt, Vasilisa Tsupchevska. One of the turnips in our garden has grown in a wonderful way: it looks more like a potato than a turnip." The comic quality of this unexpected postscript is emphasized by the parallel structure of Shponka's reply: "I have been unable to carry out your commission with regard to the wheat-seed; there is none in all the Mogilyov Province. As for the pigs here, they are mostly fed on brewers' grain with a little beer added after it has gone flat." The same sort of epistolary comedy can be seen in the letter written to the mayor by Andrey Ivanovich Chmykha, in *The Inspector General*: "I advise you to take precautions, for he can arrive at any time, if indeed he has not already done so and is living somewhere incognito. Yesterday I—oh, here he starts going into family matters: my cousin, Anna Kirillovna, visited us with her husband; Ivan Kirillovich has gotten very fat and is constantly playing the violin."[43] Ivan Kirillovich and his violin, which he is constantly playing, are evidently stuck in just for the sake of the comic incongruity.

A consequence of this lack of logic and relevance is that images and utterances are brought together in completely unexpected and meaningless combinations. Hence, the *comicality of arbitrary associations*. In reply to the question about the peasant in Sicily—whether he ploughs the land or not—Zhevakin deems it necessary, quite out of the blue, to report on the taking of snuff, to wit, that in Sicily "everyone not only sniffs it but even tucks it away in their mouths" and that "transportation is also very cheap" (*Marriage*). In "The Nose," the policeman, in talking about his nearsightedness, throws in the remark that his mother-in-law, "that is, my wife's mother, can't see anything either." Then, politely re-

[42 In *The Inspector General*. Actually, of course, Khlestakov is asking Rastakovsky for money.]

[43 Here the mayor is reading the letter aloud to the assembled officials.]

fusing a cup of tea—"I would consider it a great pleasure, but I just can't: when I leave here I've got to stop in at the penitentiary" —he goes right on to add: "The cost of everything has gone up tremendously." (Here the comicality of disconnectedness is complicated by the veiled hint for a bribe that is contained in the remark about the high cost of things.) Then he unexpectedly moves on to details of family life: "Living in my house are my mother-in-law, that is, my wife's mother, and my children; the older one in particular shows great promise, he's a very bright lad, but there is absolutely no money for his education."

The babblers in Gogol are comical because they lose the thread of logic, wander off the track, and get bogged down in a mass of parenthetical details that clutter up their talk. The result is a situation in which speech flows on by association and is not governed by logic and relevance. Comedy of the *à propos des bottes* type (i.e., without rhyme or reason) can first be seen in "A May Night" (*Evenings on a Farm Near Dikanka*): here the village headman, whatever the topic of conversation, always "knew how to bring it around to how he had once been the driver for the Tsaritsa and had sat on the box of the royal carriage." (The comic alogicality is complicated here by his comic vanity.) Gogol's characterization of the way Chichikov's servants, Petrushka and Selifan, carry on conversations, makes a direct reference to this comic device:

> This class of people has a very odd custom. If you ask them a direct question about something, they can never remember; but if you ask them about something else, right away they come up with the answer to the first question and give it to you in far greater detail than you could possibly want.

Bobchinsky's account of the inspector general bristles with parenthetical motifs—a cask for French vodka, a booth where meat pies are sold, a rumbling in the stomach of Pyotr Ivanovich, and his whistling tooth. He even manages to stick in a whole little story about the wife of Vlas the innkeeper, who has had a baby three weeks earlier: "He's such a lively little boy, he'll be an innkeeper, just like his father." Bobchinsky also has a specific ulterior motive in mind—the desire to prolong his triumph of being the first to see the inspector general, and to prepare the effect that will be created by the unexpected news.

Fyokla's garrulousness, in *Marriage*, lacks any ulterior motive:

it is pure alogism. She starts with the bride-to-be, then moves on to the merchant who rented out a garden-plot on the Vyborg Side—"and he's such a sober merchant, he doesn't touch a drop of any strong drink, and he has three sons"—and here she gets stuck on these sons and finally wanders off the track altogether: "He's already married two of them off, but the third, he says, is still too young, let him stay in the shop—then it'll be easier to run the business; I'm already old, he says, so let my son stay in the shop, so that business will move along smoother."[44] In "The Two Ivans," the mayor, Pyotr Fyodorovich, has a very logical answer to Ivan Ivanovich's remark that "the pig is a creature of God": "It is known to all the world that you are a learned man, that you know the sciences and various other subjects"—but then he drifts off: "Of course, I haven't studied any sciences; I began to learn to write only when I was thirty. After all, I rose from the ranks, as you know. Yes, in 1801 I served in the 4th Company of the 42nd Chasseurs Regiment as a lieutenant. Our company commander was, if you permit me to say so, Captain Yeremeyev."[45]

II

Figuring prominently among the devices of language in Gogol is the *comicality of awkward speech*. It is expressed in the comic displacement of semantic categories in the structure of the sentence: a disparity between syntax and semantics, and irrelevant word-usage. Thus, comic alogism is also present in the structure of Gogol's language.

Feeble exertions of thought and clumsy turns of speech provide an inexhaustible source of comic effects for Gogol. His works are a virtual treasury of linguistic monstrosities:

1) "I confess to you in all sincerity, I did not expect at all, and all the more with regard to the unjust reproaches on your part" (Podtochina's letter, "The Nose").

[44] Cf. Selifan's repetitions: "a German-like hood, you know the way the German women wear hoods—it's called a hood—you know, a hood, a German-like hood" [see footnote 23].

[45] The comicality of Molière's garrulous pedants (in *Monsieur de Pourceaugnac, Le mariage forcé, Le malade imaginaire*) depends not on the absence of logic, but on the profusion and verbosity of their talk. The same can be said of Cervantes's *The Windbags* (*Los habladores*) and Khmelnitsky's *The Big Talker* (*Govorun*).

2) "In consequence of said petition of mine, which from me, Ivan Nikiforovich, son of Dovgochkhun, nobleman, was to be to the purpose of, in connection with Ivan Ivanovich, son of Pererepenko, nobleman, to which the very district court of Mirgorod expressed its connivance. And said insolent arbitrariness on the part of the brown pig, being kept in secret and already having come to notice from other people" ("The Two Ivans").

3) "I hasten to inform you, my dear, that my position was very difficult, but, trusting in divine mercy, especially for two pickled cucumbers and a half-portion of caviar, 1 rouble 25 kopecks" (the mayor's letter, *The Inspector General*).

The comic effect created by Ivan Fyodorovich Shponka and Akaky Akakievich depends entirely on the difficulty they have with words, on their inarticulateness, which contrasts with the mindless garrulity of Bobchinsky and Fyokla. In all four cases, however, the comic effect comes from muddled thinking. Shponka, "ungenerous with words," is "sincerely gratified" when he succeeds in constructing a "long and difficult" sentence like the following: "That is, I have had occasion to note what far-off countries there are in the world." Akaky Akakievich expresses himself mostly in pronouns and particles: "Actually, this matter is such a . . . I really didn't think it would come out, errr. . . ." Even the more lively and talkative of Gogol's heroes run into trouble when they have to express something that lies beyond their usual mental horizons: "What sort of gun?" Ivan Ivanovich asks the servant-woman, but he himself evidently does not know just what he wishes to hear in reply ("The Two Ivans"). Likewise, Yaichnitsa (*Marriage*) hesitates as he tries to express his curiosity about Sicily in clearer terms: "You said—a peasant. What sort of peasant? What's he like? Is he exactly like a Russian peasant—broad in the shoulders and ploughing the soil, or not?" And this nonsensical question receives an equally absurd reply: "If it was mine, then maybe I'd know what it's made of, but it belongs to the master . . . and as concerns snuff-taking, not only do they sniff it, but they even tuck it away in their mouths." Manilov expresses his thoughts about selling dead souls with great strain and effort:

I'm not saying it because I have any critical reproach to make of you. But permit me to state, will not this undertaking, or, to express it even more, so to say, this negotiation—will not this negotiation be incompatible with the civil regulations and the future plans of Russia? (*Dead Souls.*)

The comicality of fruitless efforts is emphasized here by a gesture (as in Korobochka's case too): while Manilov is speaking, he wears "such a profound expression as has perhaps never before been seen on a human face." The same sort of painful effort can be seen in Ammos Fyodorovich (*The Inspector General*), in Korobochka, in her clock, in Ivan Fyodorovich Shponka. The only thing the latter can squeeze out of himself, in a *tête-à-tête* with the girl from the neighboring estate, is: "There are a lot of flies in summer, miss." The conversation between Podkolyosin and Agafia Tikhonovna represents a further development of this scene. But here opinions are exchanged on all of five topics; boating, flowers, church, promenading at Yekaterinhof, and the braveness of the Russian people; and the comic effect of great effort is emphasized by a gesture (tapping the fingers on the table) and by pauses, which set each new topic off from the preceding one (*Marriage*).

The nonsensical and incoherent language of Gogol's heroes is embedded in a context of ironic devices within the language of the author-narrator. The most important of these is a characteristically Gogolian play on meaning. It consists of a disparity between grammar and semantics. For example: the comparison between Ivan Ivanovich and Ivan Nikiforovich is built on syntactic parallels. Ivan Ivanovich is lean and tall, Ivan Nikiforovich is somewhat shorter and is running to fat, etc. And when we have been thoroughly lulled in this cradle of logic, suddenly: "Ivan Ivanovich was of a rather timid nature; Ivan Nikiforovich, on the contrary, wore trousers with such ample pleats. . . ." The violation of the logical structure of speech strikes us all the more forcefully in that the grammatical form of the adversative clause not only remains intact, but is pointed up even more by the phrase "on the contrary." In *Dead Souls*: "The others were also educated people: some read Karamzin, some *The Moscow News*, and some even read nothing at all." Here the syntax grows in intensity (some—some—some even) and moves in just the opposite direction to the meaning, which diminishes in intensity (Karamzin—*The Moscow News*—nothing). The rising and falling lines of the grotesque cross, as it were.

Here the comic effect depends on the displacement of semantic categories; the grammatical skeleton of the sentence seems to have been taken from another semantic context (to make a "verbal mask"),[46] or else some expression seems to have intruded unexpectedly from a different category of meaning and carried the idea onto another semantic level:

1) "What a stupid woman!" thought Ivan Ivanovich [as he watched her hanging things out on the clothesline]; "the next thing you know she'll pull out Ivan Nikiforovich himself to air." And so it was: five minutes or so later, the nankeen trousers of Ivan Nikiforovich swung up [onto the line].

(The transition "and so it was" leads us to expect that Ivan Nikiforovich himself, and not his trousers, will actually swing up.)

2) His father, and his grandfather, and even his brother-in-law, and absolutely all the Bashmachkins wore boots, merely having them resoled about three times a year ("The Overcoat").

(The subordinate clause refers to another semantic category; it is as if the main clause had made the point that the Bashmachkins rarely got new boots.)

3) Only then did he notice that he was not in the middle of a line [of copying] but rather in the middle of the street ("The Overcoat").

(*Rather* prepares us to expect the juxtaposition of like objects.)

4) Petrovich, despite being one-eyed (first semantic category) and having a completely pockmarked face (second category) was rather successful (third category) at mending the trousers and coats of clerks and all other varieties (fourth category) ("The Overcoat").

(Here the word "one-eyed" has pulled the word "pockmarked" after it; such a condition would certainly not make it difficult for Petrovich to mend any kind of coat.)

III

Gogol also makes use of comic alogism in *constructing dialogue*. Here the comic effect depends on a break in logic between a re-

[46] The term "verbal mask" (in a different context) is used by Yu. N. Tynyanov, *Dostoevskii i Gogol'*, Opoyaz, 1921, p. 21.

mark and the rejoinder. Sometimes this break is motivated by deafness. Then we have a case of the familiar comic dialogue of the "conversation-of-the-deaf" type. Such, for example, is the conversation between Zhevakin and Yaichnitsa, in *Marriage*:

"Ivan Pavlovich Yaichnitsa, serving as an executive clerk."

"Yes, I've had a bite to eat too. I know there's a long way yet to travel, and the weather is rather cold. I've had a bit of herring and onion."

Then comes the explanation.

"I think you've misunderstood. That's my name—Yaichnitsa."

"Oh, pardon me! I'm a bit hard of hearing. I really thought you'd said you had an omelette to eat."[47]

Basically, the scene between the mayor and Khlestakov, in *The Inspector General*, is a "conversation of the deaf" of just this type. Each says his own piece, without understanding or listening to the other. But here the disparity between the speeches is motivated by "mutual misunderstanding":

Mayor: It is my duty as chief magistrate of this town to take measures to ensure that visitors and all persons of gentle birth should feel no inconvenience.

Khlestakov: But what's to be done? . . . It's not my fault. . . . I'll certainly pay. . . . They'll send me money from home.

After this, it becomes the mayor's turn to play the "deaf man":

Khlestakov: The beef they serve me is as hard as a log, and the soup—the Devil knows what he [the innkeeper] spat into it. I should have thrown it out the window. . . . Why should I. . . . That's a fine idea, indeed!

Mayor: Pardon me, it's really not my fault. The beef is always good in my market. It's brought in by merchants from

[47] The conversation between Prince Tugoukhovsky and the old countess, in Griboyedov's play *Woe from Wit*, can serve as a striking example of a comic dialogue "of the deaf" (Act III, Scene 20). ["Tugoukhovsky" is a name manufactured from the Russian expression for "hard of hearing." In the dialogue from *Marriage*, the "misunderstanding" takes the form it does because Yaichnitsa means, literally, "omelette"; it is a very odd name in Russian too.]

Kholmogory, who are sober people and of exemplary conduct.[48]

Then again there is a misunderstanding on Khlestakov's part:

Mayor: I have a wife and small children . . . don't ruin me.
Khlestakov: No, I won't go! What next? What business is it of mine? Just because you have a wife and children I'm supposed to go to jail, that's just fine.

And farther on:

Mayor: As regards the sergeant's widow, who I am supposed to have flogged, that's just slander, I swear it. It's something my enemies invented; they're the sort of people who wouldn't mind murdering me.
Khlestakov: What of it? They're no concern of mine. . . . But I don't see why you're talking about enemies or some sergeant's widow. A sergeant's wife is an entirely different matter, but don't you dare try and give me a flogging.[49]

[48] Cf. Fyokla and her account of the merchant from the Vyborg Side (*Marriage*): "and he's such a sober merchant too—he doesn't touch a drop of anything strong." Similar to this is Krylov's statement, in his fable "The Musicians" ("Muzykanty"): "They're not awfully good musicians./ But then, they don't touch a drop of anything strong" ("Oni nemnozhechko derut, zato uzh v rot khmel'nogo ne berut"). [Ivan Andreyevich Krylov (ca. 1769-1844), is Russia's most important writer of fables.]

[49] The comic dialogue of the "mutual-misunderstanding" type is a traditional device of the comedy which goes back as far as the folk theater. Cf., in Shakespeare's *Twelfth Night*, the dialogue between Olivia and Malvolio (Act III, Scene 4); in Molière, the dialogue between Harpagon and Cléante (*L'Avare*, Act IV, Scene 5) and between Sganarelle, on the one hand, and Valère and Lucas on the other (*Le médecin malgré lui*, Act I, Scene 6). This sort of dialogue is cultivated by the vaudeville in particular—e.g., in P. A. Karatygin's *Wives on Loan* (*Zaemnye zheny*), between Darmoyedov and Ognivkin (Scene 12) and *The Wife and the Umbrella, or the Tuner Untuned* (*Zhena i zontik, ili rasstroennyi nastroishchik*), between Pedal and Fricassee (Scene 5). Similar dialogues can be found in novels as well—e.g., in Dickens's *Pickwick Papers* (between Pickwick and Mistress Bardle). However, the distinguishing feature of Gogol's dialogue is, in the first place, that it is structured as a quarrel and, in the second place, that the disparity between exchanges is more pronounced. As a result, the comic effect of alogism stands out in greater relief. [Pavel Andreyevich Karatygin (1805-1879) was an actor and a prolific writer of melodramatic vaudevilles, largely borrowed and adapted from French and German originals. He was very hostile toward Gogol and toward the natural school generally.]

Dialogues constructed on misunderstandings enable the characters to make remarks that depend on word-plays. These give the dialogues greater pungency and at times constitute the basic comic situation. Plays on words may have some specific motivation (i.e., it may be premeditated), or may be unintentional. Premeditation can be seen in the case of Sobakevich (*Dead Souls*), when he is singing the praises of his dead serfs. Chichikov tries to stem the flow of words by saying: "But this is a dream." Sobakevich retorts: "Oh, no, it's no dream! I'll tell you the sort of man Mikheyev was, you won't find people like that any more: he was such a giant of a man that he wouldn't fit into this room. No, it's no dream! He had far more strength in his shoulders than any horse. I'd like to know where you'd find a dream like this anywhere else!" (This deliberate substitution of one idea for another is motivated by Sobakevich's desire to jack up the price on dead souls.) There is also calculation involved when Petukh, in reply to Chichikov's apologetic "I'm ashamed, it's such an unexpected mistake," says: "It's no mistake, no mistake. First you try to see what kind of dinner it is, and then you say whether it's a mistake or not."

The confusion which marks Korobochka's replies to Chichikov is completely ingenuous. She is bewildered by his offer to purchase her dead souls: "Do you perhaps want to dig them up out of the ground?" Chichikov has to explain the sense in which the purchase should be understood. Of the same order is Yankel's misunderstanding of Taras Bulba's question: "So it turns out that in your opinion he has sold his country and his faith?" Yankel takes this literally: "I'm not saying he sold anything: I'm only saying he went over to the enemy."[50]

The disappearance of Kovalyov's nose provides the basis for a number of rejoinders that are built on plays with words. To Kovalyov's assertion that "you are my own nose," the nose makes the following objection: "There can be no close relationship between us. Judging by the buttons on your uniform, you must be working in another department." And Kovalyov

[50] Interestingly enough, Yankel's comic reply appears only in the 1842 version. In the 1835 version, this dialogue went as follows:
"That he sold the Christian faith and the fatherland!"
"Perhaps it is so."
Thus, it was precisely during his Roman period (1836-42) that Gogol was heightening the comic element in his work.

writes Podtochina: "Rest assured that the incident of my nose is fully known, as is that fact that you are the chief participant in this affair." She replies: "You again mention your nose. If you mean by this that I wanted to leave you with your nose, that is, to make a formal refusal. . . ."

In addition to discontinuity in dialogue, Gogol uses another comic technique: the lack of logical development in arguments between two characters. (The equivalent of this in the language of individual characters—Shponka and Akaky Akakievich—is difficulty in speaking.) Inert logic can be seen in the very hollowness of the arguments that are advanced, in the perplexed reiteration of the questions, and in the repetitiveness of the rejoinders. Thus, for example, in "The Two Ivans," Ivan Nikiforovich asks the same question, wording it differently, while Ivan Ivanovich simply goes on repeating his original proposal:

"Who has ever heard of anyone exchanging a gun for two sacks of oats?"

"But you've forgotten, Ivan Nikiforovich, that I'm giving you a pig besides."

(Ivan Nikiforovich seems unable to grasp Ivan Ivanovich's proposition all at once: there is something he cannot quite put his finger on.)

"What! Two sacks of oats and a pig in exchange for a gun?"
"What do you mean, isn't it enough?"
"For a gun?"
"Certainly, for a gun."
"Two sacks for a gun?"

(The repeated questions have the cumulative effect of evoking visual images: goggling eyes, etc.; cf. Korobochka's gaping mouth.)

"Two sacks—not empty ones, but full of oats; and have you forgotten the pig?"

(Ivan Ivanovich picks up Ivan Nikiforovich's words: this is the comic technique on which the argument is built.)

Finally, abuse takes the place of argumentation: "Go kiss your pig, or if that doesn't appeal to you, go kiss the Devil himself!"—and the argument, after getting thoroughly bogged down, starts moving again.

Then comes a discussion of the relative merits of a gun and a pig. The same ploy is repeated: neither of the two characters can open up the topic by introducing new arguments, and both mark time helplessly. Ivan Nikiforovich has only one argument—that a pig is "the Devil only knows what."

> "I don't know how you can say that, Ivan Ivanovich. What do I need a pig for? Perhaps to make a funeral-feast for the Devil?"
>
> "Again! You can't seem to get along without the Devil!"
>
> "How can you, Ivan Ivanovich, give in exchange for a gun the Devil only knows what—a pig!"
>
> "But why is it the Devil only knows what, Ivan Nikiforovich?"
>
> "What do you mean? You should give it a little thought yourself. Here you have a gun, something that's familiar to everyone (this is his attempt to find something resembling an argument), but the Devil only knows what that is—a pig!"
>
> "What did you notice about the pig that's not good?"
>
> "What do you really take me for? That I and a pig. . . ."[51]

Instead of arguments, the two Ivans resort to parenthetical verbal devices such as invocations of the Devil, appeals to reasonableness ("you should give it a little thought yourself") and definitions that lack substance ("something that's familiar to everyone," "the Devil only knows what that is"). Here words serve to mask the emptiness of logic.

The scene between Kochkaryov and Podkolyosin, in *Marriage*, illustrates the same comicality of inert logic. Here too one speaker's remarks are cast in the form of mindless repetitions of the same question, which indicate that the discussion cannot be developed by any fresh arguments:

> "What [says Podkolyosin], have you lost your mind? Get married today?"
>
> "Why not?"
>
> "Get married today?"
>
> "But after all, you yourself have given your word."

Then comes a reversal of roles: it is Kochkaryov's turn to express surprise (the verbal form of this is a question or exclamation):

> "A month!"

[51 The parenthetical remark is Slonimsky's.]

"Yes, of course."
"But have you lost your mind?"

And then the roles reverse again:

"Listen, Ivan Kuzmich [says Kochkaryov], don't be stubborn, my friend, get married now."
"What in heaven's name are you saying, friend? What do you mean 'now'?"

With Zhevakin (*Marriage*), as with Ivan Nikiforovich, the repetition of the same questions has such expressive force that it virtually turns into a gesture:

"Now what sort of figure do you cut, confidentially speaking? Like a chicken's leg."
"A chicken's?"
"Of course. What do you look like?"
"But how do you mean: like a chicken's leg?"
"Why, simply, a chicken's."

At last he gets the point:

"It seems to me, however, that this is a personal remark."

Korobochka is absolutely incapable of grasping what Chichikov is saying to her.

"Do let me have them, Nastasia Petrovna!"
"Have who, sir?"
"Why, all those who've died."
"But how am I to let you have them?"
"It's really very easy. Or perhaps you'll sell them. I'll give you money for them."
"Why, what do you mean? I honestly don't understand. Do you perhaps want to dig them up out of the ground?"

The comic nature of Korobochka's obstinacy is emphasized by a general observation on the part of the narrator: "Many a highly respected man, even a servant of the state, in fact proves to be a perfect Korobochka. Once he's got something lodged in his head, there's absolutely no way of getting it out. No matter how many arguments, clear as day, you may put forth, they all bounce off him like a rubber ball from a wall." The argument with Korobochka is just this sort of ball game. She goes on repeating the same thing: "But after all, they're dead . . . I just don't know; after all, I've never sold any dead people before. . . . The only thing that makes it hard for me is that they're already dead. . . . Well, there's only one thing stopping me, and that's the fact that they're dead. . . . Really, I just can't figure out what I'm to do; I'd better sell you some hemp instead. . . . I swear, it's such an odd piece of merchandise, I've never heard the likes of it." And when she tries to come up with something like an argument to back up her indecision, the result is so very odd that she herself gapes in astonishment (the comic alogism is reinforced by a gesture): " 'Well, maybe they'll be of some use around the place . . . ,' the old woman replied, but she did not finish speaking: she opened her mouth and looked at him almost in fear, waiting to see what he would say to this."

In reply to the innkeeper's demand for payment, Khlestakov can come up with only one objection: "I could waste away to nothing. I'm terribly hungry, I am saying this in all seriousness."

> "I think [says the waiter] that he [the innkeeper] wanted to go and complain to the mayor today."
>
> "But why [says Khlestakov] should he complain? Judge for yourself, my friend, why? After all, I need to eat. Otherwise I could waste away to nothing. I'm terribly hungry, I am saying this in all seriousness."
>
> "Yes, sir. He said: 'I can't give him any dinner until he's paid me for what he's already eaten.' That was his answer."
>
> "But you reason with him, persuade him."
>
> "But what am I to say to him?"
>
> "You explain to him in all seriousness that I need to eat. . . . He thinks that just because a peasant like himself can go a whole day without eating, other people can do the same. That's ridiculous!"

"Judge for yourself," "reason, persuade," "explain in all seriousness"—these all indicate a blockage of the thought-process, a verbal patch that has been stuck over a hole in logic, an urgent desire to convince when there are no proofs.

Kochkaryov, in *Marriage*, uses the same method of trying to convince: "Listen, judge for yourself (cf. Khlestakov, above). . . . Look at it through the eyes of a reasonable man. . . . No, I see that it's necessary to talk seriously with you; I will speak frankly, like a father to a son. . . . Now take a look, a close look at yourself—the way, for instance, you're looking at me now (the comic attempts to produce something very convincing). What are you now? Just a log; you have no importance (again an attempt to come up with something). Go and take a look in the mirror (his exertions build up to the point where they become a gesture): what do you see there? A stupid face, nothing more."

The arguments advanced by Kochkaryov on Podkolyosin's behalf (in the scene with Agafia Tikhonovna) form a structural parallel with Ivan Nikiforovich's assertions as to the superior qualities of the gun: "Just judge, just compare (cf. Ivan Nikiforovich: "You should give it a little thought yourself"): this is Ivan Kuzmich, after all is said and done, and not some plain ordinary Ivan Pavlovich, Nikanor Ivanovich—the Devil only knows what ("but the Devil only knows what that is—a pig!").[52]

[52] A vicious circle of exchanges, with restatements and repeated questions —but without the absurd argumentation—is a device that plays an important role in Molière (*Les fourberies de Scapin, Le malade imaginaire, L'Avare*). Cf., e.g., Argante and Scapin (*Les fourberies de Scapin*, Act I, Scene 4):

"Cela m'aurait donné plus de facilité à rompre ce mariage."
"Rompre ce mariage?"
"Oui."
"Vous ne le romprez point."
"Non . . . C'est une chose dont il ne demeura pas d'accord."
"Il n'en demeura pas d'accord?"
"Non."
"Mon fils?"
"Votre fils. . . ."
"Il le fera, ou je le déshériterai."
"Vous?"
"Moi. . . ."
"Vous ne le déshériterez point."
"Je ne le déshériterai point?"
"Non."
"Non?"
"Non."
"Hoy! voici qui est plaisant! Je ne déshériterai pas mon fils?"
"Non, vous dis-je."
"Qui m'en empêchera?"
"Vous-même."
"Moi?"
"Oui. Vous n'aurez pas ce coeur-là."
"Je l'aurai."

The same sort of thing, involving word-for-word repetitions, is found in

IV

Comic alogism is also present in the structure of Gogol's works—in the way actions and events are motivated. An oversimplified motivation and a certain arbitrariness in the way one incident is linked with another are, in general, characteristic of comic structure. But in Gogol, there are comic constructs in which all motiva-

---

Le malade imaginaire, in the scene between Argan and Toinette (Act I, Scene 5):

"Elle le fera, ou je la mettrai dans un couvent."
"Vous?"
"Moi. . . ."
"Vous ne la mettrez point dans un couvent."
"Je ne la mettrai point dans un couvent?"
"Non."
"Non?"
"Non."
"Ouais! voici qui est plaisant. Je ne mettrai pas ma fille dans un couvent, si je veux?"
"Non, vous dis-je."
"Qui m'en empêchera?"
"Vous-même."
"Moi?"
"Oui. Vous n'aurez pas ce coeur-là."
"Je l'aurai."

Here there is one difference between Molière and Gogol: Molière's repetitions have a specific motivation—vexation (Argante, Argan, Géronte), cunning (Scapin, Toinette), stubbornness (Harpagon's "Sans dot!"), whereas in Gogol, the comic effect depends entirely on muddle-headedness and the lack of logical arguments. This can be seen from the way the exchanges are worded: in Molière the language is smooth, in Gogol it is choppy and hesitant.

The device of repetition is also present, in more schematic form, in Gogol's play *The Gamblers:*

"Yes, but man is a part of society."
"He is, but not entirely."
"Yes, entirely."
"No, not entirely."
"Yes, entirely."
"No, not entirely."
"Yes, entirely."
"Don't argue, my friend, you're wrong."
"No, I'll prove it. It's an obligation . . . it . . . it . . . it . . . it's a duty!"
"Oh, your tongue's run away with you."

tion and causality are deliberately missing. In such cases, causality lies in the lack of causality, and motivation lies in the absence of motivation. Causal sequence has no foundation: it hangs in the air. Gogol points up this structural device in *Dead Souls*: "There's absolutely no logic to dead souls. How can dead souls be bought? . . . But what then is the reason for the dead souls? There's no reason at all."[53]

Why does Ivan Ivanovich try to get the gun? In the atmosphere of utter vacuousness, where the eating of a melon counts as an event ("this melon was eaten on such-and-such a day"), a gun, which floats into the field of vision purely by accident, attracts attention as something new and unknown. ("But what does this mean? I've never seen a gun at Ivan Nikiforovich's before.") And, since it encounters no resistance from any other motif in the story, it mushrooms to the proportions of an irresistible urge, which determines the entire course of subsequent events. Why does Ivan Nikiforovich stubbornly refuse to give up the gun? He can offer absolutely no reason. "You don't need it," Ivan Ivanovich says. "What do you mean, I don't need it?" replies Ivan Nikiforovich. "Suppose I have occasion to shoot? It's an essential thing." Ivan Ivanovich asks: "But what is it essential for?" And the other replies: "What do you mean, what is it essential for? What if robbers break into the house?" We have here an unmotivated insistence, on the one hand, and an unmotivated bullheadedness on the other.

This pattern is repeated in *Marriage*, by Kochkaryov and Podkolyosin. Kochkaryov's idea of getting Podkolyosin married off pops up "suddenly": "see how everything suddenly . . ." (cf. Khlestakov: "I do everything suddenly"); it is just as arbitrary and unmotivated as is Ivan Ivanovich's desire to get the gun. And when it does occur to Kochkaryov to wonder just why he is taking such great pains with Podkolyosin, there is only one answer: "Just try and ask a person sometime why he does something!"[54]

[53] On the predominance of chance, of "lack of motivation" in the world of the comic, cf. Volkelt, *System der Aesthetik*, II, 482.

[54] Interestingly enough, the first drafts of *Marriage* do hint at a specific and natural motivation for Kochkaryov's efforts: "Look, you didn't find one like that for me, did you? And do you think I'll ever let you arrange the marriage without me? Why, you might play such a trick on him and marry him off to such a horror that it would make your flesh creep." In the final version (1842), Kochkaryov's project is completely unmotivated.

Podkolyosin comes up with only one argument to motivate his obstinacy: that he feels "strange." "What's stopping you?" asks Kochkaryov. "Nothing's stopping me. It's just strange. . . ." "What's strange?" "Of course it's strange. I've always gone along being unmarried, and now suddenly I'm to be married."[55] As a result, we have the same situation that prevails in the story of the two Ivans: mindless insistence and mindless resistance. The comic fabric of *Marriage* is made up of Podkolyosin's vacillations, which are like the swaying movements of a tumble-up doll. The harder Kochkaryov pushes at him, the more vigorous the movements he makes in return. And once this tumble-up doll is pushed onto his back and the restraining hand removed, he springs back up so energetically that he even flies out the window.[56]

An absence of motivation and intelligibility lies at the very heart of *The Inspector General* as well. How is it that an old-timer in government service like the mayor could believe that Khlestakov is an inspector general? The only grounds for it are provided by Bobchinsky's profound observation: "He's the one! He doesn't pay out any money and he doesn't leave. Who else could it be but him? And his order for horses is made out for Saratov."[57]

[55] Cf. Ivan Fyodorovich Shponka: "What do you mean, a wife! . . . I've never been married before." In certain respects, Shponka is a prototype of Podkolyosin (but lacks his passive resistance). *Marriage* develops the comic themes that are adumbrated in "Shponka" (the conversation with the potential fiancée, fear of the wife).

[56] Podkolyosin springs back six times. At first there are slight hesitations. Podkolyosin gives in: "Well, to tell you the truth, I like it when a pretty woman sits down next to me." But when Kochkaryov begins to paint a picture of the wedding dinner, Podkolyosin suddenly gets frightened: "Oh, no, I haven't fully agreed yet!" In the same scene, when he is already dressed, he suddenly sits down (the retreating movement is signalled by a gesture): "You know what—you go by yourself." At the end of Act I, influenced by the opinions the other suitors have expressed, he makes a new retreating movement: "I admit I don't care for her." Then, in Act II, he tries to put a brake on Kochkaryov's hasty actions: "What, have you lost your mind? Get married today?" Finally, just before the definite proposal, he says: "What in heaven's name are you saying?" And the final and strangest retreat is accompanied by an appropriately energetic gesture— leaping out the window. The change occurs very abruptly, in the middle of the monologue, after the enraptured disquisition on the "bliss" of family life: "Still, you can say what you like, but it's somehow frightening."

[57] In the earlier versions there is a semblance of a rational, specific motivation. In 1836: "And why would he be living here, when his order for

Motivation of a natural and specific kind is almost totally lacking in Gogol. In the enterprise undertaken by Chichikov, the most "motivated" of all Gogol's heroes, there is more pure art than deliberate swindling.[58] Chichikov's mercenary motive undergoes no development, gradually recedes from view, and remains important only as a framework for the narrative. The failure of the play *The Gamblers* can be explained by the fact that Uteshitelny and company have a specific motive in mind: to deceive Ikharev.[59]

V

The device of the absurd runs throughout all Gogol's work. It permeates his language, determines the interrelationship of remark and reply in the dialogues, lies at the heart of the development of the comic action, and ultimately destroys logical and causal connections. "It is as if some demon had crumbled the whole

---

horses is made out to Saratov?" (The meaning of "Saratov" is clearer here than in the final text.) It is even more intelligible in the rough drafts: "But why is he living here, then, when he's on his way to Lord knows where—to Yekaterinoslav Province? Why doesn't he go, then? . . . Well, even supposing there's nothing to the fact that he's not moving on—let's suppose he's just an ordinary person, but why then doesn't he pay his bills?" It is only in 1842 that the speculations of Bobchinsky and Dobchinsky become absurd [in the lines quoted in the text of Slonimsky's article]. In the 1836 version, Khlestakov's "powers of observation," which motivate Bobchinsky's error, are described in greater detail: "He's so observant: he looked everything over, *in all the corners, and even* took a look into our plates" (the words in my italics are omitted in the 1842 version). In reworking the play, Gogol systematically strengthened the comic effect of the absurd. Bulgarin called attention to the alogical nature of the conclusions drawn by Bobchinsky and Dobchinsky: "He takes everything on credit, he pays for nothing, *therefore* (Bulgarin's emphasis) he must be that very same official they are expecting from St. Petersburg." (*Severnaya pchela*, No. 97, 1836.)

[58] An ordinary reader who comes fresh to *Dead Souls* will be keenly aware of the comic aspect of the book, but will be hard put to answer the question: what exactly is the nature of Chichikov's enterprise? This shows that Chichikov's scheme is not the motivating force of the book.

[59] In keeping with the play's design, the comic effect should develop out of the conscious purposes of a comic character—as it does, for example, with Scapin, Silvestre, Toinette, and other rogue-types in Molière, whereas in *The Gamblers*, it is the roles played out before Ikharev that are funny (the young Glov's hussar mannerisms, Zamukhryshkin's bribe-taking), and not the intentions of the rogues. Several of the characters who play roles even remain shadowy figures to the audience (old Glov and Zamukhryshkin).

world into many different pieces and had jumbled all these pieces together without any sense or purpose" ("Nevsky Prospect").

The atmosphere is one of "fog," in which Gogol's heroes wander about in confusion, bump into one another, argue without any mutual understanding, and suddenly come to a dead stop, "staring like sheep" (the officials in *Dead Souls*), or stand agape, like Korobochka, in fear and astonishment. "Fog" is a common word in Gogol. It emphasizes the device of a break in the logic of ideas or events. "It's as though a fog of some sort had blinded us, as though the Devil had confounded us!" (Ammos Fyodorovich, in *The Inspector General*). "To blow a blinding fog into each other's eyes. . . ." (*Dead Souls*). In "The Nose," "fog" indicates logical breaks between the three parts of the story, which otherwise cannot be brought together into a unified whole.[60]

In Gogol's world, there is no truth or untruth, no probability or improbability: people believe *quia absurdum.* "Good heavens, what are you saying! It can't be him!" But as soon as they hear the shattering observation—"his order for horses is made out for Saratov"—the officials are immediately convinced that the inspector general has arrived, just as the Simply Agreeable Lady, in *Dead Souls*, is immediately convinced that the governor's daughter is going to be abducted. And when the "fog" dispels, they themselves cannot understand what has happened to them. The mayor says: "It really is true that if God wants to punish you, He takes away your reason first of all. Really, what was there in that featherbrain the least like an inspector general? Nothing!" Zemlyanika says: "How this could possibly have happened I can't for the life of me explain. It's as though a fog of some sort had blinded us, as though the Devil had confounded us!"

The officials in *Dead Souls* get just as hopelessly entangled in the net of the absurd fiction concocted by the two ladies. They propose this and suppose that, they even intend to call a legislative meeting—and they simply cannot fathom what has happened to them:

There's absolutely no logic to dead souls. How can dead souls be bought? . . . And what does the governor's daughter have to do with all this? If he really did want to abduct her, then why buy dead souls? And if he was buying up dead souls, then why

[60] This has been studied by V. V. Vinogradov, "Syuzhet i kompozitsiya povesti Gogolya 'Nos,'" *Nachala*, No. 1, 1921.

would he want to abduct the governor's daughter? . . . What
sort of nonsense, actually, had been spread around town? What
are things coming to when you scarcely have time to turn
around and a story like that is already being put out—if only
there were some sense to the whole thing. . . . But what then is
the reason for the dead souls? There's no reason at all. It turns
out that it's just a lot of hot air, nonsense, rubbish, balderdash!
It's simply the Devil only knows what!

The second volume of *Dead Souls* concludes with the same sort of
turmoil:

> Scandals and intrigues and everything else were so mixed up
> and entangled with Chichikov's case and with the dead souls
> that there was absolutely no way of determining which of these
> matters was the most nonsensical.

And then the line of the grotesque soars majestically upwards, in
a rhythmic, flowing and solemn diction:

> What twisted, remote, narrow, impenetrable wandering roads
> have been chosen by mankind in its efforts to reach eternal truth,
> whereas the straight road has stretched completely open before
> them, like the road leading to a magnificent structure designated
> as a tsar's palace! Illuminated by the sun and brightly lit all night
> long, it is broader and more luxuriant than all other roads. But
> people have streamed past it in pitch darkness. And how often
> have they already been shown the way by wisdom coming down
> from the heavens, and yet they have nonetheless contrived to
> step back and lose their way, and yet they have contrived, in
> broad daylight, to wander anew into impenetrable, out-of-the-
> way places, and yet they have again contrived to veil each
> other's eyes in a blinding fog. . . .

In this "blinding fog," perceptions become sharper, exaggerated,
distorted, and fantastically grotesque:

> Everything before him was shrouded in a sort of fog. The side-
> walk rushed past beneath him, the carriages with their trotting
> horses seemed to stand still, the bridge stretched out and broke
> in the center of its arch, the houses were upside down, the
> watchman's booth reeled toward him, and the sentry's halberd,
> and the gilt letters of the signboard and the scissors painted on

it, all seemed to flash directly on his eyelashes ("Nevsky Prospect").

The interrelationships of objects change. A "Tula pin in the shape of a bronze pistol" (the opening of *Dead Souls*) moves into the foreground. "A peasant woman wearing a red kerchief" and "two shop assistants" are shuffled together with "grapeshot" and "bitter almonds" ("The Carriage"):

> small shops; in them you can always see a string of bagels, a peasant woman wearing a red kerchief, forty pounds of soap, several pounds of bitter almonds, grapeshot, some cotton material, and two shop assistants who spend all their time playing quoits by the door.

Objects lose their sharp outlines and become blurry: "Long shadows flicker over the walls and the pavement and nearly touch the Police Bridge with their heads" ("Nevsky Prospect"). "The square looked like a terrible desert"; "The ghost, however, was much taller and had enormous mustaches" ("The Overcoat"). And finally, when all the commotion about Chichikov has reached its height, there comes a shift into the realm of the fantastic and the terrible, like the gigantic dead men who rise from their graves in "A Terrible Vengeance": "in the drawing rooms someone tall, very tall, began to appear, with his arm in a sling, someone taller than anyone had ever seen before."

In this strange world it is also understandable that a horse can have a blue or pink coat; that a sergeant's widow should have given herself a flogging; that dead people might be "of some use" around the place; that Vasily Fyodorov (despite his purely Russian name) could be a "foreigner" (and even directly "from Paris and London"); that Kovalyov's nose, which on March 25 was found in Ivan Yakovlevich's bread, should, on April 7 (the dates are deliberately given so that the whole story cannot be attributed to delirium), turn up in its proper place, as if nothing had happened; and that a brown pig should carry off Ivan Nikiforovich's petition, at Ivan Ivanovich's instigation.

Khlestakov's rambling is a poem in itself, which overwhelms his listeners with its grandiosity. Khlestakov's fantasy soars *excelsior*, higher and higher, and a miraculous world is created—a microcosm of the Gogolian world—where everything is fantastic and

371

SLONIMSKY

incongruous, where "messengers, messengers rush about on their rounds, 35,000 messengers alone!" A dreadful nightmare takes shape: "The director went off—no one knew where. Naturally, people began to talk" (as they do about Chichikov). The line of the grotesque moves boldly upward—and abruptly breaks off into the comic burlesque of drunkenness ("he almost falls to the floor"; he shouts, "smoked cod, smoked cod!").[61]

The grotesque line, which moves through the center of the work, is accompanied by secondary lines, which repeat, in miniature, the movement of the basic line. Little worlds—small-scale models of the Gogolian world as a whole—take shape within the works. Such is Khlestakov's "poem," or the story, told by the Simply Agreeable Lady, of Chichikov's nocturnal visit to Korobochka:

> "Just imagine him appearing dressed from head to foot in the manner of Rinaldo Rinaldini. . . . No, he says, they're not dead, it's my business, he says, to know whether they're dead or not; they're not dead, not dead, he shouts, not dead! In a word, he kicked up a frightful row; the whole village came running, the children were crying, everyone was shouting, nobody understood anyone else (exactly like the confusion that ends *Dead Souls* or the commotion that is stirred up in the city by Kovalyov's nose)—well, it was simply *horreur, horreur, horreur!*"[62]

The usual structure of a Gogolian work can be described by a specific formula: some line arises in a void (the gun, Kochkaryov's project, the disappearance of the nose, the "unexpected news" of an inspector general, the stolen overcoat, the governor's daughter); it undergoes very rapid development, without intersecting any other motifs, and becomes a "whirlwind of misunderstandings," which makes up the rising line of the grotesque.[63] It entangles

[61] Interestingly enough, Khlestakov's grotesque flight of fantasy was added only in the 1842 version of *The Inspector General*. Here the watermelon costing 700 roubles, the soup brought from Paris, etc., appear for the first time. In the 1836 version, everything is much more simple and natural: there are only fifteen messengers, the director has gone off to the country for a perfectly natural reason (illness), etc.

[62 The parenthetical remark is Slonimsky's.]

[63] Gogol indicates this phase in his "Notes" on Part I of *Dead Souls*, where he speaks of a "whirlwind of gossip" ["(Zametki) k 1-oi chasti," *PSS*, VI, 1951, 692]. In "An Author's Confession," speaking about *Selected Passages from Correspondence with Friends*, he uses an expression that could well apply to his own method of structuring a work: "a whirlwind of misunderstandings" ["Avtorskaya ispoved'," *PSS*, VIII, 1952, 438].

372

everyone in a comic round-dance (the general efforts to reconcile the two Ivans, the confusion in *The Inspector General* and *Dead Souls*, the commotion over Kovalyov's nose and over the search for the stolen overcoat; the dismissal of the suitors in *Marriage*)— with one person or a couple in the middle (Khlestakov, Chichikov, Ivan Ivanovich-Ivan Nikiforovich, Kochkaryov-Podkolyosin); it grows to gigantic proportions and takes on a menancing and fantastic coloration ("there appeared someone tall, very tall. . . .").

In *The Inspector General* and in *Dead Souls*, the vehicle of this line, the source of the "whirlwind," is the central character, who appears out of space and disappears back into space. The jingling of harness-bells is heard at the end of both works ("Now the bells will jingle for the entire journey": Khlestakov; "the bells set up a marvelous jingling": Chichikov.) The motif of the journey and the carriage in *Dead Souls*, the "bird-troika" that ends Part 1, the journey at the end of "The Two Ivans"—all this is an imagistic expression of the rapid, rising, pathos-laden line of the grotesque.

10

Leon Stilman

(1902 –)

LEON STILMAN left his native St. Petersburg a year after the Revolution, settled in Paris, and practiced law there for two decades. In 1941, he moved to the United States, and embarked on what was to prove a distinguished academic career, first at Cornell and then at Columbia, where he earned the Ph.D., rose to a full professorship, and became chairman of the Department of Slavic Languages. He has produced several successful textbooks and has written on Karamzin, Pushkin, Goncharov, Tolstoy, and, most extensively, Gogol. Recently retired from Columbia, he now divides his time between New York and Paris.

The article "Men, Women and Matchmakers" ("Nevesty, zhenikhi i svakhi") appeared in the literary journal *Vozdushnye puti*, No. 4, New York, 1965, pp. 198-211; "The 'All-Seeing Eye' in Gogol" (" 'Vsevidyashchee oko' u Gogolya") appeared in *Vozdushnye puti* No. 5, 1967, pp. 279-292. Some changes have been made in the translated versions, in consultation with Professor Stilman.

The "All-Seeing Eye" in Gogol

by Leon Stilman

THEMES connected with vision, with seeing, occupy an important place in Gogol's writings. They appear in many variants. Let us note two of them. One is that of the magic, lethal power of a glance, or the fear of being seen. The other is that of vision which encompasses very large, "boundless" spaces and resembles the vision of an all-seeing divinity; this expanded vision sometimes takes the form of viewing things from a height, a tower, or a very tall building.

The role of vision in Gogol's art—in particular, the magic power of a glance—has been pointed out, among others, by I. D. Yermakov, a member of the now extinct species of Russian Freudians. His interesting though by no means always convincing book *Sketches for an Analysis of the Art of N. V. Gogol* appeared in 1923, during that strange period when the Soviet State Publishing House was putting out a series entitled "The Psychological and Psychoanalytical Library."[1] But the motif of expanded vision, of the "all-seeing eye" seems to have escaped the attention of scholars so far.

The first of the two motifs mentioned above—that of the lethal glance, of terror at being seen—plays an especially prominent part in the account of the death of the heroes of two of Gogol's stories—the seminary student ("Philosopher") Khoma Brut, in "Viy," and the artist Chartkov, in "The Portrait."

In "Viy," Khoma is in the church, reading prayers over the coffin of the "young lass" (actually the witch); and he wards off "diabolical powers" by uttering incantations and by tracing a magic circle around himself. The third and fateful night arrives: demons and monsters fill the church, but neither they nor the witch, who rises from her coffin, can step across the "mysterious circle" drawn by Khoma. Then, at the witch's behest, Viy is brought in: he is the "chief of the gnomes," with "long eyelids that reach right down to the ground." He is led up to Khoma, and then the following occurs:

[1 See Yermakov's article on "The Nose" in this collection; it is one chapter of the book referred to by Stilman.]

376

"Raise my eyelids. I cannot see!" said Viy, in a voice that seemed to come from the depths of the earth—and the whole swarm of creatures rushed to raise his eyelids. "Don't look!" an inner voice whispered to the Philosopher. But he could not resist, and he looked.

"There he is!" shouted Viy, and pointed an iron finger at him. And all, the whole swarm of creatures, hurled themselves on the Philosopher. He fell lifeless to the ground, and his soul fled from his body in terror.

Thus, Khoma dies from fear the moment Viy sees him. And Viy sees him when Khoma himself looks, unable to resist and heedless of the inner voice. Khoma is betrayed by his own glance, so that "not to look" here means "to be invisible": you must not look at something horrible; the temptation is great, but you must not yield to it; if you do look, then you yourself will be seen, and there is no salvation for you.

In a note to the title of the story, Gogol explains that "Viy is a colossal creation of the folk imagination. This is the name that the Little Russians use to refer to the chief of the gnomes, whose eyelids reach right down to the ground. . . ." However, Viy is unknown in Ukrainian folklore; so, in fact, are gnomes, who in all likelihood migrated into Gogol's story from Grimms' fairy tales. Viy therefore is a creation not of the imagination of "the folk" but rather of Gogol himself. And the word "Viy" was most likely derived by Gogol from the Ukrainian viya, meaning "eyelash."[2] In any event, the long eyelids of the "chief of the (Grimm brothers'!) gnomes, and his name, which serves as the title of the story, are both associated with a glance, with eyes, with vision.

In "The Portrait" the artist Chartkov has committed a crime against art by buying up and destroying the work of other artists. The evil that takes possession of him issues from the dreadful eyes that glare from the portrait of the mysterious money-lender. And at the end of the first part there is the following description of Chartkov's delirious visions, as he lies dying:

He began to be haunted by the long-forgotten, living eyes of the strange portrait, and then his frenzy was terrible. All the people standing around his bed looked to him like horrible portraits.

[2] In the commentary to "Viy" in *PSS*, ii, 742, it is stated that the Ukrainian word *viy* means "eyelid." This is incorrect: "eyelid" in Ukrainian is *povika*, and the word *viy* simply does not exist.

The portrait doubled and quadrupled before his eyes; all the walls seemed to be hung with portraits that fastened their motionless, living eyes on him. Terrible portraits looked down from the ceiling and up from the floor, the room opened up and expanded endlessly to provide more space for these staring eyes.

"The Portrait" is very close in structure to the somewhat earlier story "A Terrible Vengeance." In "The Portrait," after the death of the hero, the narrator is introduced in part two. He is the son of the artist-turned-monk who painted the mysterious portrait. Similarly, in "A Terrible Vengeance," after the death of the sorcerer, an "old bandore-player" is introduced in the final chapter, and he sings a song "about a happening of old." Both the son of the artist and the bandore-player, in their narrative epilogues, present a *Vorgeschichte* of the events described in the text, and provide a clue to the mysterious happenings which tell the story of a curse. In "The Portrait," this curse is embodied in the portrait of the money-lender, a variant of The Wandering Jew; in "A Terrible Vengeance," it is in the sorcerer, the last in the line of the Cossack Petro who murdered his sworn brother Ivan (the Cain motif). As a result of this curse, the sorcerer—a "sinner without parallel"—himself perpetrates many monstrous crimes.

Ivan, who has been "murdered" by his brother in the days of King Stefan (i.e., Stefan Batory),[3] carries on a kind of semi-earthly existence, wandering through the Carpathian Mountains as a gigantic knight in shining armor. His soul will find peace only when vengeance is visited upon the last in the line of his murderer.

Chapter fourteen of "A Terrible Vengeance" begins with a description of the following event:

An extraordinary miracle occurred outside Kiev. All the nobles and hetmans came together to marvel at this miracle: suddenly one could see far away, to the very ends of the earth. Far off the blue glimmer of the Dnieper estuary was visible; beyond it spread the Black Sea. Men who had travelled recognized the Crimea too, rising like a mountain out of the sea, and the marshy Sivash. To the left the Galician land could be seen.

[3 Stefan Batory, King of Poland (1576-86). At the time, Poland was in union with Lithuania, and controlled much of the Ukraine. Batory organized the Zaporozhian (Dnieper River) Cossacks as a kind of militia. See footnote 3 of Pereverzev's article in this collection.]

"And what's that there?" the assembled people inquired of the elders, pointing at gray and white crests that shimmered far off in the sky and looked more like clouds than anything else.

"Those are the Carpathian Mountains!" said the old men. "There are some among them that the snow never leaves; and the clouds cling to them and spend the night there."

Then a new marvel appeared; the clouds slipped off the very highest peak, and atop it, in full knightly regalia, appeared a man on horseback with his eyes closed; and he could be seen just as distinctly as if he had been standing nearby.

The sorcerer, who is standing in the crowd, recognizes the knight as the one destined to punish him for his sin and tries to hide. He gallops on his horse through that immense space, which is now being watched by hundreds of eyes and which offers no hiding-place. He loses his sense of direction, and, after a mad gallop, his horse carries him to the Carpathians and to Krivan, the highest peak—and there awaiting him is the "motionless horseman," the knight in armor, the Cossack Ivan, who was long ago murdered by an ancestor of the sorcerer. He sees that the horseman "stirred and suddenly opened his eyes; he caught sight of the sorcerer galloping toward him and began to laugh. His wild laughter echoed through the mountains like a thunder-clap." The horseman seizes the sorcerer with his mighty hand; the "terrible vengeance" is carried out.

In all three works, then, to be seen means to be doomed. In all three works the death of the hero comes in retribution for an act that has been committed; the instrument of this retribution is a person who is "dead" but who carries on a sort of supernatural existence somewhere between life and death.

In "Viy" and "The Portrait," the death of the hero represents a victory for demonic or satanic powers; in "A Terrible Vengeance" it is a sinner—a murderer and incestuous father—who perishes, and the vengeance is taken with God's consent—although the consent is given somewhat reluctantly, according to the old bandore-player's account. The motif of the doom-dealing glance is common to all three works we have examined; but in "A Terrible Vengeance" still another motif appears: that of expanded vision. An immense stretch becomes visible to all; people can see the whole earth from the Black Sea to the Carpathians. Vengeance is to be exacted in accordance with God's will; and vision—which resembles the all-seeing eye of God—becomes a miraculous gift that is given to all for a certain period of time.

Expanded vision—the miracle that is described at the beginning of chapter fourteen of "A Terrible Vengeance"—is a free motif in this particular story, in the sense that it is not tied to the development of the narrative-line, and is not organic to the structure of the work. It seems to emerge from a store of images and ideas lodged within the author himself.

The idea of expanded vision as a special gift that he possesses or needs is found repeatedly in Gogol, particularly in his statements about *Dead Souls*, as well as in the text of the novel itself. Gogol conceives of it as looking from a height (a tower), i.e., downward, or else—and this is a peculiar equivalent of height—as taking in vast expanses from a great distance, "from the beautiful far-away."

Characteristically, the images of the tower or the tall structure are used for the most part as a means of parodying Gogol's own ideas of what we have chosen to call the "all-seeing eye."

In the earliest known reference to *Dead Souls*—a letter to Pushkin dated October 7 (o.s.), 1835—Gogol speaks of great scope and of a wide field of vision. He informs Pushkin that he has "begun writing *Dead Souls*," and that "the plot has expanded into a very long novel which I think will be very funny," and that he wants "to show all of Russia in this novel, if only from one angle."

In June 1836, Gogol went abroad. Writing from Paris in November of that year, he tells Zhukovsky that *Dead Souls* "is flowing along swiftly" and that he has the impression that "all of Orthodox Russia" is before his eyes. He then goes on to say:

> I'm even amused when I think that I'm writing *Dead Souls* in Paris. Another Leviathan has gotten under way. A holy quiver runs through me in anticipation when I think of it; from it I perceive something . . . I shall savor divine moments . . . but . . . now I am completely engrossed in *Dead Souls*. My creation is enormously vast, and it will not seen come to an end. . . . Someone invisible is writing before me with a mighty staff (November 12, 1836).

In letters that were written about the time he went abroad, Gogol associated his departure from Russia with the unfavorable reception accorded *The Inspector General*. Later, however, in "An

Author's Confession" (written in 1847), he gave another explanation, which linked his departure with the writing of *Dead Souls*. It was specifically his work on this book which made a "removal from Russia" essential:

> being among others and more or less acting along with them, you see only those people who are close by you, you do not see the whole crowd and mass, your eye cannot take in everything all at once. I began to think of a way I could extricate myself from others and place myself at some point from which I could see the whole mass of people, and not just those close by me—a way in which I could, as it were, remove myself from the present and in some way turn it into the past for myself. My precarious state of health, together with small unpleasantnesses, which I could now tolerate easily but which at that time I had not yet learned to tolerate, forced me to move to foreign climes.

It is highly likely that this explanation occurred to Gogol *post facto*, that it was just these "small unpleasantnesses" (the hostile reactions to *The Inspector General*) which prompted him to go abroad. The trustworthiness and sincerity of the explanation are, in this instance, of small importance. What is important is the idea itself—of "taking in everything all at once," of "placing [himself] at some point from which [he] could see the mass as a whole."

Similar ideas are expressed in *Dead Souls* itself. It was conceived as a comic novel (Gogol wrote Pushkin that "I think it will be very funny"), but as Gogol continued working on it, the lyrical and rhetorical strain grew stronger and stronger. A didactic, prophetic and messianic current, ever more powerful, flowed into the fundamentally comic stream of the novel. The famous lyrical digression at the beginning of chapter seven ends as follows:

> And for a long time to come, I am destined by a wondrous power to walk hand in hand with my strange heroes, to contemplate the whole of life as it rushes by in all its immensity, contemplate it through laughter perceptible to the world and through tears invisible to it and unknown!

The business of laughter and tears, which has been endlessly quoted, goes back, we must assume, to Pushkin. He recalled that when Gogol's *Mirgorod* appeared, "everyone eagerly read the story

'Old-Fashioned Landowners,' this amusing and touching idyll which makes us laugh through tears of sadness and tender emotion."[4] But particularly important in this passage from *Dead Souls* are the two phrases following "contemplate." These words can be compared with the idea expressed in "An Author's Confession," to the effect that the writer had to remove himself from his subject, leave Russia, and "place [himself] at some point from which [he] could see the mass as a whole."

In the last chapter of Part 1 of *Dead Souls*, after Chichikov's hasty departure from the provincial town of X, there is a lyrical digression which contains something reminiscent of the miracle in "A Terrible Vengeance": things can be "seen" over an enormous distance. But here, this miraculous power of sight is granted only to the author: "Russia! Russia! I behold thee, from my wonderful and beautiful far-away do I behold thee. . . ." And at the very end of the book, this power of sight becomes a vision, and Russia, in a somewhat unexpected metaphor, is transformed into a troika which "cannot be overtaken," and before which other peoples "stand aside."

But earlier, one finds a somewhat different image of Russia, as seen "from the beautiful far-away": "Exposed and empty and flat is everything in thee, thy low-lying towns like dots, like specks, are barely perceptible amidst the plains. . . ." These words create the impression that one is looking not so much from a distance as from a great height. On the other hand, in the strange dialectic of "An Author's Confession," distance seems to replace height. Gogol starts out by saying: "I began to think of a way I could . . . place myself at some point from which I could see the whole mass . . . ," and this naturally suggests the idea of elevation, albeit metaphorically; but then height is somehow replaced by distance, and it turns out that the solution to the problem lies in going abroad.

The motif of surveying great expanses from a height, from a tower or a tall building, appears several times in Gogol. The first mention of a tower seems to occur in the article entitled "On the Architecture of the Present Day," which was written at the end of 1833 or the beginning of 1834, and was included in *Arabesques*:

Huge, colossal towers are essential in a city, quite apart from the importance of their function for Christian churches. Besides adding a vista and ornament to the city, they are necessary to

[4 Review of second edition of *Evenings on a Farm Near Dikanka, Sovremennik*, No. 1, 1836.]

give the city distinctive features, to serve as a beacon which points the way to every traveler, not letting him lose his way. The need for them is even greater in capital cities, for observing the environs. In our country they are usually limited to a height from which just the city itself can be seen. But in a capital city it is essential to see at least 150 versts [about 100 miles] in all directions; and for this you need perhaps only one or two extra stories and everything changes. As you ascend, the horizon opens out in extraordinary proportion. The capital gains a substantial advantage by being able to survey the provinces and foresee everything in advance; a building takes on grandeur by virtue of having become somewhat higher than the ordinary; the artist gains, being more disposed to inspiration by the colossal size of a building, and feeling a stronger creative tension within himself.

What is curious in this passage is the attempt to convince, to persuade; curious too is the combination of fantasy and hyperbole with the pseudo-efficiency, the pseudo-practicality which are generally characteristic of Gogol's writings when he gives advice— whether to his mother, in letters from "the beautiful far-away" to his home village of Vasilievka, or to his compatriots as a whole, in *Selected Passages from Correspondence with Friends*—advice which can rarely be followed, but which is detailed, concrete, and insistent to the point of being rather importunate. Of the towers which are "essential" in cities, Gogol writes that they can serve as an ornament, as landmarks, as a source of inspiration for the artist, and as a means of surveying the surrounding areas. And the capital must see "at least 150 versts in all directions"—a minimum of 150 versts. Characteristic here is the concern for the interests of the state: by "capital" Gogol obviously means the authority of the state, the imperial government which is situated in the capital. And it is essential for the government to have a colossal watch-tower in order to keep an eye on the environs and thereby to "foresee everything in advance" which, by the way, is an odd idea, where removal in space somehow merges with removal to future time.

The motif of an unusually tall building from which great distances can be seen is found in *Dead Souls*, at the end of chapter two, in the "meditations" of Manilov. After Chichikov's departure, he sinks into a pensive but somewhat bewildered state of mind:

Manilov stood on the front steps for a long time, his eyes following the receding carriage; and when it had completely disappeared from sight, he continued standing there smoking his
pipe. At last he went indoors, sat down on a chair, and abandoned himself to meditation, his heart rejoicing that he had
afforded his guest some slight gratification. Then his thoughts
drifted imperceptibly to other matters and finally wandered off
heaven knows where. He thought about the felicity of a life
devoted to friendship, about how delightful it would be to live
with his friend on the bank of some river, and then in his mind
a bridge began to span this river, then an enormous house with
a belvedere so lofty that you could see even Moscow from it,
and there, in the evening, you could drink tea in the open air
and discourse on pleasant topics of one kind or another. Then
he and Chichikov arrived in fine carriages at some social gathering, where they charmed everyone with their agreeable ways,
and the Emperor, it seemed, on learning of such a fine friendship
as theirs, bestowed upon both of them the rank of general, and
what he thought about after that heaven only knows—he himself could no longer make any sense out of it.

Curiously enough, in the earlier, so-called second edition of
Dead Souls, an even broader vista opened out from the "enormous
house": "then a huge house with such a lofty belvedere that from
there you could see even St. Petersburg and Moscow at one and the
same time."[5] This "St. Petersburg and Moscow at one and the same
time" calls to mind the miracle in "A Terrible Vengeance," when
the Crimea and the Black Sea became visible all at once, along
with Galicia, and then the Carpathian Mountains. In working
on this version, Gogol evidently deemed it necessary to tone down
the element of fantasy somewhat. The final version reads "even
Moscow." Thus, the miraculous and supernatural element was
removed; only the hyperbolic remained.

"An enormous house with a belvedere" is not the only architectural fantasy entertained by Manilov. In the middle of chapter
two we read:

Sometimes, standing on the porch and looking down at the yard
and the pond, he would talk about how nice it would be if you

[5 The so-called second edition (in manuscript) dates from 1840-41. The
first published edition of the work dates from 1842.]

could suddenly run an underground passage from the house, or build a stone bridge over the pond which would have shops on both sides, with merchants selling wares that the peasants needed.

And among those of Manilov's dreams that have come true is the arbor in his garden, "with a low green cupola, blue wooden pillars, and the inscription: 'Temple for Solitary Meditation.'" This "temple" echoes the sentimental projects undertaken by Gogol's father, who built arbors and grottoes in Vasilievka, the family estate, and attached names, such as "The Valley of Rest," to various spots there. But the enormous house that rises up in Manilov's imagination reflects—parodically—the architectural fantasies of Gogol himself—in particular, the fantasy of "huge, colossal towers" in the article "On the Architecture of the Present Day."

It is worth noting that the motif of the state, of power, is present in Manilov's fantasy too: he not only moves up to the top of an enormous house with a lofty belvedere, but also moves up in the hierarchy of the civil service, being promoted to general by the Emperor personally, along with his friend Chichikov.

Let us cite one more passage, this time from "Leaving the Theater." Among the rapidly shifting scenes and the fragments of conversation exchanged by members of the audience as they come out of the theater, there is one entitled "Conversation in a Group Standing off to One Side." It begins as follows:

First Gentleman: They say that something similar happened to the author himself—that he was put in jail in some town or other for not paying his debts.

A Gentleman in Another Part of the Group (chiming in): No, it wasn't a jail, it was a tower. People driving past saw it. They say it was something really unusual. Imagine: the poet in a high, high tower, mountains all around, a delightful location, and from it he is reciting his verses. Wouldn't you say this is a trait peculiar to a writer?

A Positively Disposed Gentleman: The author must be an intelligent man.

A Negatively Disposed Gentleman: No, not at all. I know that he had a government job, and they all but kicked him out, he didn't know how to write a petition.

At this point a "mere babbler" enters the conversation. He knows that the author has a "ready head" but that he could not get a job for a long time; but then "from being just a copy-clerk he shot up to run the department."[6]

What is the meaning of this story of the author and the tower? Is it merely a joke, an instance of irresponsible gossip? Possibly: a little later on, mention is made of "impromptus" and of the fact that a person "blurts out" something and the next day he himself cannot remember just what it is he thought up. Of course, the "poet in a high, high tower" is an example of just such an "impromptu" or invention. But whose invention is it? After all, the "gentleman" himself and his "impromptu" about the tower were both invented by Gogol, as were Manilov and his reverie. This in turn calls to mind another invention of Gogol's—the miracle of expanded vision in "A Terrible Vengeance." And finally, the dreams of "huge, colossal towers" in the article on architecture are those of the author himself, who is not concealing himself behind any fictional characters here.

The tower, it seems to us, signifies two things. First, and metaphorically, it signifies the ability to survey vast expanses, the sort of vision that resembles the all-seeing eye of the Divinity—in essence, that is to say, knowledge which comes close to divine, or, more precisely, to prophetic knowledge or omniscience. (For example: "And for a long time to come, I am destined by a wondrous power to . . . contemplate the whole of life as it rushes by in all its immensity"; also the idea, in the article on architecture, that a sufficiently high tower would enable one to observe the provinces and "foresee everything in advance.") In the second place, the tower—for the observer atop it—signifies an elevated and dominating position, one that rises above the mass of ordinary mankind, the crowd of "existers."[7] Both these meanings—all-seeing or all-knowing, and the predominance over the mob that is associated with distance from it (symbolically it is expressed vertically, as an upward distancing, but in actuality, it was a horizontal distancing, as expressed in Gogol's going abroad)—were undoubtedly present in Gogol's conscious mind and ran throughout his life.

At the age of eighteen, as he was nearing the end of his school years at Nezhin, Gogol shared his plans for the future with those

[6 "Teatral'nyi raz"ezd posle predstavleniya novoi komedii," *PSS*, v, 1949, 165.]

[7 See footnote 9 of Pereverzev's article in this collection.]

who were close to him. For example, on March 24, 1827 (o.s.), he wrote his mother:

> I am testing my powers for the initiation of an important and noble task: for the benefit of the fatherland, for the happiness of its citizens, for the good of the life of my fellow man; and, though heretofore indecisive and unsure of myself (and justifiably so), I am blazing in a fire of proud self-awareness, and my soul sees this divine angel [i.e., his father, who had died some two years earlier], firmly, inflexibly and unceasingly indicating the goal of my avid quest. . . . In a year I shall enter the service of the state.

Gogol also wrote about his "lofty propects" to P. P. Kosyarovsky, his cousin once removed, on October 3 (o.s.) of the same year. He informed him that he had chosen a career in the Ministry of Justice: "only here can I be a boon, only here will I be truly useful to mankind." But in addition to an "unquenchable zeal" to do something for the good of the state, "alarming thoughts" are expressed in the letter too: what if nothing comes of the "lofty projects," what if "obscurity shrouds them in its gloomy cloud?" And also, in the same letter: "A cold sweat broke out on my brow at the thought that perhaps it would be my fate to perish in dust, not having marked my name with a single beautiful deed."

Ideas like these—though expressed somewhat less melodramatically—can also be found in letters to G. I. Vysotsky, Gogol's old classmate from the school at Nezhin, who by then had moved to St. Petersburg. But here another theme can be heard too (as, for instance, in a letter of June 26 [o.s.], 1827), that of scorn for those ordinary mortals whose well-being Gogol has been intending to serve:

> How painful it is to be lowered into the tomb of silence together with creatures of low obscurity! You know all our existers, all those who inhabit Nezhin. They have crushed the lofty purpose of mankind with the crust of their earthliness, their paltry self-satisfaction.

In contemplating a career in the Ministry of Justice, Gogol very likely had in mind the example of D. P. Troshchinsky, the "benefactor" of the family and a distant relative of his mother's, a very rich and powerful man who had made a brilliant career in the government service: he had been Minister of Justice, and was now

living out his days on his magnificent estate not far from Vasilievka. It should be added that he was a man known for great probity
and independence of character.

It is obvious, in any event, that young Gogol had in mind a
successful career in the government, one which would enable him
to "mark his name" and not "perish in dust." In his mind, then,
dreams of service to mankind mingled with dreams of power, of a
lofty calling, of distancing himself from the "existers," rising above
them, above their "earthliness" and their "paltry self-satisfaction."

Gogol's career in the government service in St. Petersburg did
not last long and was not very successful.[8] But he did succeed in
another field: by the time he went abroad, in 1836, he had become
a famous writer. Later on he explained that he had to go so that
he could "place [himself] at some point from which [he] could
see the whole mass of people and not just those close by"—the
whole mass, "the whole of life as it rushes by in all its immensity."
But what he saw was Chichikov, Manilov, Sobakevich, Korobochka, Plyushkin, Nozdryov, Petrushka and Selifan, Ivan Antonovich's "pitcher-snout," his own immortal "existers" and also the
flat Russian plain that flowed on toward Chichikov's carriage.[9]

It was in "An Author's Confession" that Gogol wrote about
placing himself at some point from which he could see the "whole
mass." There too he said that by fulfilling his duty as a writer, he
would "at the same time be rendering service to the state, as if he
were actually in the state service." In this way, he brought about
synthesis of service to art and service to the state; in this way he
found a justification for distancing himself from the "existers."
Poet and civil servant, prophet and teacher—all were united in
one person. "The poet in a high, high tower, mountains all around,
a delightful location": the location really was delightful. It was
Italy, with its "bold wonders of nature crowned with bold works of
art"; and from this "beautiful far-away," this tower, the poet saw
distant Russia—much more distant than 150 versts.

But as the years went by, this gift of all-encompassing vision
began to fade, it would seem; the poet's sight grew dim. In private
correspondence and in the preface to the second edition of *Dead
Souls* (1846), Gogol called on his compatriots to send him information about Russian life, observations, excerpts from diaries. It
was becoming more and more difficult to contemplate "the whole

[8 See footnote 6 of Pereverzev's article in this collection.]
[9 All are characters in *Dead Souls*.]

of life as it rushes by in all its immensity." The tragic denouement of his novel (which in all probability he never did finish) was drawing near: the second burning of the second volume of *Dead Souls*, which occurred just before his death.[10]

[[10] There were two versions of Part 2 of *Dead Souls*, dating from 1842-45 and 1848-51, respectively. Gogol worked long and hard at it, but burned both versions in discouragement. What survives are the first four chapters, and fragments of the conclusion.]

Men, Women, and Matchmakers

Notes on a Recurrent Motif in Gogol

by Leon Stilman

A NUMBER of recurrent motifs can be traced through Gogol's writings. In some works they are obvious, inasmuch as they form part of the basic story-line. In others, they may be concealed or disguised; they become apparent when individual works are compared, and they reveal the inner or "latent" themes of these works.

One such motif can be seen most clearly in the play *Marriage,* where it carries the main burden of the plot. The characters in this comedy, or this "utterly improbable incident in two acts," as it is subtitled, are: Podkolyosin and other "suitors"; Kochkaryov and Agafia Tikhonovna, who is a merchant's daughter; and finally her aunt. The rivalry among the suitors, however essential to the action of the comedy, may nonetheless be regarded as an interpolated or secondary motif. The basic plot amounts to the following: Podkolyosin is thinking about getting married, but he is incapable of taking the decisive step. He is being pushed in that direction by the matchmaker, Fyokla Ivanovna, and even more insistently by Kochkaryov. Agafia Tikhonovna is agreeable to getting married. She is identified as a bride-to-be in the list of dramatis personae, just as Fyokla Ivanovna is identified as a matchmaker and Yaichnitsa as an executive clerk. Thanks to Kochkaryov's intercession, Podkolyosin wins out over the other suitors (the interpolated motif); and, yielding to the matchmaker's coaxing and to Kochkaryov's prodding as well as to his own dreams of the bliss of conjugal life, he resolves at last to take the fateful step. Moreover, after kissing Agafia Tikhonovna, again at Kochkaryov's urging (Act II, Scene 19), Podkolyosin demands that "the wedding should take place right away, right away without fail." When Agafia Tikhonovna observes that "this is perhaps very soon," Podkolyosin protests even more impatiently: "I don't want to hear another word about it! I want it to be even sooner; I want the wedding to take place this very instant." There is nonetheless a certain delay, for the bride-to-be has to put on her wedding dress. And at this point, when Podkolyosin is left alone for a few minutes

(Scene 21), the consuming fire of love is quenched, his thoughts of impending bliss grow pale, and he "even feels a vague sense of terror." But, he reasons, "it's absolutely impossible to back out . . . it's even impossible to leave." However, it does still prove possible to leave: the window is open, and, seeing that "it's not too high, there's only the basement and it's a very low one," Podkolyosin, "saying 'Lord help me!' hops out into the street."

This particular theme or pattern—a reluctant man, a passively consenting woman (a bride-to-be), and a third person (two persons in *Marriage*: the matchmaker and Kochkaryov) who pushes the man to take a "decisive step"—can be traced, in various configurations, through several of Gogol's works.

In the story "Ivan Fyodorovich Shponka and His Aunt" (1832), the aunt, Vasilisa Kashporovna, takes her nephew's future in hand on the grounds that he is, in her words, "still just a child."[1] In fact, Ivan Fyodorovich is "pushing forty" (the aunt is about fifty). She decides that it is time he got married, and she starts looking for a wife:

> "Listen, Ivan Fyodorovich! I want to have a serious talk with you. You're going on thirty-eight, Lord be praised. You have a good rank in the service. It's time to give some thought to having children as well! You certainly must have a wife. . . ."
>
> "What do you mean, auntie!" cried Ivan Fyodorovich in alarm. "What do you mean, a wife! Oh, no, for heaven's sake, auntie . . . . You make me feel dreadfully ashamed. . . . I've never been married before . . . I wouldn't know what to do with her!"

By way of comparison, see the scene between Maria Petrovna, "a lady of mature years," and her son Misha, in the rough draft of Gogol's unfinished play published under the title of "Fragment":

> *Maria Petrovna*: Now I want to have a talk with you about something else that's also very important. Listen, I want to find you a wife.
> *Misha*: But look, I'm not yet, you know. . . .
> *M.P.*: What not yet?
> *M.*: How shall I put it? I don't yet feel an inclination.

---

[1] This phrase is in Ukrainian in Gogol's text. It creates an amusing ambiguity for a Russian reader: the Ukrainian word for "child" or "infant"—*dytyna*—closely resembles the Russian word *detina*, meaning a "burly" or "husky" fellow.

391

On learning from his aunt that he must certainly get married, Ivan Fyodorovich stands "as if thunderstruck . . . getting married! This seemed so strange and peculiar to him that he could not think about it without feeling terrified. Living with a wife! . . . unimaginable! He would never be alone in his room; instead, there must always be two of them everywhere! . . . . Perspiration broke out on his face the more deeply he meditated on this situation."

Two people—the matchmaker and Kochkaryov—bring pressure to bear on Podkolyosin (who, like Shponka, "even feels a vague sense of terror"). Shponka is completely under his aunt's thumb. In *Marriage*, a comedy of manners about matchmaking, the active participation of a matchmaker is natural and even obligatory. But a matchmaker by herself could not bring the same degree of pressure—almost force—to bear on Podkolyosin that Kochkaryov can. If Podkolyosin had had to deal with just the matchmaker, he would simply have kept dragging his feet and putting off a decision, and the central dramatic or comic situation could not have arisen. Therefore, it was necessary to "strengthen" the matchmaker, by giving her an ally in the person of Kochkaryov, who is capable of imposing his will on the balking candidate for marriage.

In "Ivan Fyodorovich Shponka," the roles of the matchmaker and of Kochakaryov are combined in the aunt. And appropriately enough, she embodies both feminine and masculine characteristics, with the latter predominating. Her physical appearance is described as follows:

> She was of almost gigantic stature, and her girth and strength were fully in proportion. It seemed as though nature had made an unforgivable error in condemning her to wear a dark-brown dress with little frills on weekdays, and a red cashmere shawl on Easter Sunday and her birthday, when a dragoon's mustaches and top boots would have suited her better than anything else.

The aunt is thus a woman of markedly mannish appearance. Her feminine characteristics are minimal, amounting apparently to nothing more than wearing a gown and a cashmere shawl, both of which are attributed to "an error of nature" (which would seem to be easily correctable). We are also told that she had never been courted by anybody, because "all men felt a certain timidity in her presence and never had the courage to make her a proposal."

Shponka is terrified when his domineering aunt announces that he must get married. This motif of terror—terror in the face of the unknown and the incomprehensible—is developed in Shponka's dream. He dreams that he is running and running, and can barely take another step when suddenly he feels someone seize him by the ear. This proves to be his wife. Then the wife appears to him in the form of a creature with a goose's face; then he sees another wife, and another; these wives, these creatures with goose-faces, multiply, and he sees them everywhere he looks. He again tries to run, and finds wives in his hat, his pocket, and his ear. His aunt also appears in the dream, and she turns into a belfry: "He moved toward her, but his aunt was no longer an aunt, but a belfry. And he felt someone pulling him up the belfry with a rope. 'Who is it pulling me?' Ivan Fyodorovich asked plaintively. 'It is me, your wife, I am pulling you because you are a bell.' " In this vision of Shponka as a bell and the aunt as a belfry, there occurs, on the level of fantasy, the identification of the aunt (who is trying to pair off Shponka and the neighbor's daughter) with the bride-to-be or the wife herself—the object of the pairing off. Finally, toward the end of the dream (and of the story), the wife appears to Shponka as "some sort of woolen material . . . the most fashionable material," which a shopkeeper "measures and cuts off."

In *Marriage*, Podkolyosin saves himself by taking flight, by "hopping" out the window "into the street." In the story of Shponka, the flight of the suitor is transferred into the realm of the fantastic. The next morning he consults the fortunetelling book, but can find no interpretation of his dream there.

In this particular work, Gogol employs the structural device of the unfinished story. There is an introductory section in which we are told that the story had been written down in a notebook, but that the pages containing the second half had been used to bake meat patties on and were lost. In *Marriage*, the bridegroom-to-be makes good his escape off stage: after he jumps out the window, we hear (but do not see) his conversation with the cabbie, and then "the rattle of a droshky driving off." In "Shponka," the narrative itself disappears, with this "disappearance" also taking place "off-stage," as it were—in the introductory remarks. Here the narrator is the one who, so to speak, jumps out the window: it is not the prospective bride, the matchmaker, and Kochkaryov who are left empty-handed, but the reader.

393

In "The Nose," Podtochina, the widow of an army officer, wants to marry her daughter off to the hero, Platon Kuzmich Kovalyov. Gogol says of him:

He himself liked to dangle after her [the daughter], but he shied away from a final outcome.[2] When, however, the widow came right out and told him that she wanted to marry her daughter off to him, he presented his compliments and gently steered away, saying that he was still young, that he had another five years to serve so as to be exactly forty-two years old.

If, after five years, Kovalyov reaches the age of "exactly" forty-two, then obviously he is thirty-seven when the events described in the story take place—that is to say, just the same age as that "child" Ivan Fyodorovich Shponka. In referring to his "youth," Kovalyov seems to be anticipating a second coming-of-age: forty-two ("exactly") is, after all, twice twenty-one.

Apart from age, it would seem that Kovalyov has nothing in common with the timid and weak-willed Shponka. In his letter, Shponka thanks his aunt for sending on the cotton socks; his orderly has "darned the socks four times so they've gotten very tight." Kovalyov, on the other hand, is concerned above all with "giving himself greater distinction and importance"; every day he strolls along the Nevsky Prospect, showing off his magnificent side-whiskers, the immaculate starched collar of his shirt-front, and the many cornelian seals hanging from his watch-chain. He also notices the "comely lasses," likes to "dangle after" Podtochina's daughter, and is "not averse" to getting married, though only "in the event that his fiancée happens to have a fortune of 200,000 roubles."

Let us note that Podkolyosin—if not Shponka—is also keenly aware of his own worth and often makes reference to his rank of

---

[2] "Final outcome" renders *razdelka*. This word does not exist in the Russian language, nor is it a Ukrainianism, as are some of Gogol's other odd usages. It is not particularly suggestive or expressive, as coined words usually are. Rather, it is meaningless: the rendition as "final outcome" is suggested by the context. Curiously enough, *razdelka* is the result of a revision; in an earlier draft, Gogol had written *otdelka*. This word does have a meaning, but it is meaningless in this particular context. It signifies the final stage of a piece of work—finishing, polishing, adding ornamental details. Gogol's avoidance of a meaningful word to describe the outcome of a courtship is highly significant. This outcome was for him something "unnamable"—whence the *otdelka-razdelka* gibberish. It may be said that Gogol's verbal dodge is akin to Podkolyosin's fenestral exit in *The Marriage*.

court councilor.[3] He has his tail-coat cut from the finest cloth, albeit black: he is "of the opinion that black tails are somehow more dignified." And as far as "comely lasses" are concerned, Podkolyosin is anything but indifferent to feminine charms, as is obvious, for example, from the following remarks he addresses to Kochkaryov: "Ah, the deuce with it, just think of the pretty little hands there are. They're just as white as milk, my friend." And a little further on: "And to tell you the truth, I do like it when a pretty girl sits down beside me." Shponka, when left alone with "the fair-haired young lady"—Maria Grigorievna, the neighbor's daughter—"sat on his chair as if it were pins and needles, blushed, and cast down his eyes," vainly trying to strike up a conversation. This is shyness and embarrassment, but not indifference or lack of interest. And later, though frightened out of his wits by his aunt's announcement that he must marry, Shponka nonetheless does admit to himself that "Maria Grigorievna is quite a good-looking young lady." All three heroes retreat before what in "The Nose" is called the "final outcome": the indecisive Podkolyosin "hops into the street"; the terrified Shponka tries to escape by running away in his dream; and Kovalyov, the self-assured fop, "steers away" with a reference to his "youth."

It is the imminence of this final outcome that throws fear into Podkolyosin and Shponka—fear of the unknown and the incomprehensible. Kovalyov feels no such fear: he "steers away" rather calmly. However, at the very beginning of the story, he suffers a misfortune that utterly defies explanation: his nose disappears. Is there any connection between this event and the theme of matchmaking and "resolution"? In other words, is it possible to find a thematic link between "The Nose," on the one hand, and *Marriage* and "Ivan Fyodorovich Shponka" on the other?

In his efforts to restore the errant nose to its normal place, Kovalyov seeks the help of the authorities, the daily press, and medical science. He tries to fit this strange happening into some pattern of cause and effect, some accepted order of things, and then exert an influence on the extraordinary circumstances to which he has fallen victim. All his efforts lead to nothing: there is no causal or logical pattern. The whole point is, after all, that the nose vanished for no reason whatsoever—"it just did"—and it returns to its proper place for no reason whatsoever—"it just

[3 For a discussion of the Table of Ranks, see footnote 12 of the article by Merezhkovsky in this collection.]

does"—without Kovalyov's having exerted the slightest influence on the course of events.

In casting about for an explanation of what has happened, Kovalyov hits on the possibility of witchcraft and the supernatural. Here, however, he violates the logic of the story, the logic of that special world in which the author wills him to act and exist. Of course, what has happened to him is supernatural; but it is supernatural precisely because it lies outside cause and effect.

Kovalyov's surmise about witchcraft does, however, deserve special attention because it establishes a link between the plots of "The Nose," *Marriage*, and "Ivan Fyodorovich Shponka," a link between the theme of matchmaking and marriage and the theme of a danger that threatens the "suitor."

The idea of witchcraft comes to Kovalyov in connection with Podtochina's efforts to marry off her daughter. He thinks that since he has "evaded a resolution" of the matter, she has "made up her mind to ruin him, probably out of revenge, and for that purpose has hired some old women skilled in witchcraft." This conjecture prompts him to write Podtochina a letter: it is obvious to him that the loss of his nose is "the result of the sorceries" of Podtochina or of the witches she has employed. "Rest assured," he says, "that you will gain nothing by acting in such a manner, and that you will certainly not force me to marry your daughter." He ends the letter by threatening to call in the law if his nose is not immediately returned to its proper place.

Podtochina's reply convinces Kovalyov that she is innocent. He thinks better of his suspicions. Yet, as has already been indicated, his conjecture does create an obvious thematic link between the three works under consideration. Podtochina joins the ranks of the other matchmakers—Fyokla Ivanovna, Kochkaryov, and the aunt, Vasilisa Kashporovna. They are all endowed with unusual power over the reluctant suitor. In *Marriage*, this power is given to Kochkaryov, who acts in concert with the matchmaker; in "Ivan Fyodorovich Shponka," it is the mannish aunt who keeps her nephew completely under her thumb; in "The Nose," Kovalyov's imagination endows the prospective bride's mother with magic power which she uses either to "ruin him" out of spite, or to make him marry her daughter. In terms of plot-structure, the suitors in *Marriage* and "Ivan Fyodorovich Shponka" are afraid of something they have never experienced, a danger which they do not understand and of whose existence they are not even sure. In "The

Nose," an incomprehensible and inexplicable misfortune has already befallen the hero. The sequence of events here is therefore different; but the analogy among the elements of the three plots is evident.

This analogy can be extended to two other works of Gogol's, "Viy" and "Nevsky Prospect." Here the image of the matchmaker and that of the bride-to-be (we are not using these words literally now, of course) are combined in a single character. But this character actually separates out into two. In "Viy," the separation occurs in the realm of the supernatural: the witch-matchmaker turns into the witch-bride-to-be. In "Nevsky Prospect," it occurs in the mind of the hero.

Khoma Brut, the hero of "Viy," stops for the night at the house of a certain old woman (a "gran'ma"), who offers him an empty sheep pen. During the night, gran'ma comes into the pen, and walks "straight toward him with outstretched arms." Khoma, in fear and revulsion, tries to get away from her; but the power of her "gleaming eyes" robs him of the ability to move his arms and legs and to utter a sound. The old woman leaps on his back, and his legs, moving against his will, bear him and the witch over the ground in a fantastic gallop. The sensations experienced by Khoma during this gallop or flight are remarkable: "He felt a kind of languorous, unpleasant, yet delectable sensation," and somewhat later: "He felt a fiendishly delectable sensation, a kind of piercing, languorously terrifying delight." Below him, fantastic and even seductive scenes come into his field of vision, as, for example, a water-nymph in the river: "and now she turned on her back, and the outline of her cloud-like breasts, matt-white like unglazed porcelain, shimmered translucent from the sun in their white and tenderly resilient roundness."

"Viy," of course, is far removed from a comedy of manners such as *Marriage*. Let us recall, however—making the necessary allowance precisely for the difference in literary genres—Podkolyosin's remarks about "hands as white as milk," about the pleasure he feels "when a pretty girl sits down" beside him, about "bliss such as is to be found only in fairy-tales, which simply can't be expressed." This is, of course, eroticism, as is the agitation he feels after he kisses Agafia and demands that the wedding take place right away; but it is an eroticism of vision, of touch, and of anticipation. While he gallops along above the ground, Khoma Brut enjoys the spectacle of the water-nymph, and experiences certain vague sensations: unpleasant yet delectable, fiendishly delectable, languorously terrifying.

Khoma Brut admires the water-nymph while he is in the witch's power. But finally he succeeds in throwing her off his back and climbing onto hers. They gallop on, though no longer through the air. At length, Khoma snatches up a piece of wood and begins beating the old woman with it. She turns into a beautiful young girl "with luxuriant tresses all tousled, with eyelashes as long as arrows. She lay senseless, her bare white arms flung to the sides, and she moaned, with tear-filled eyes uplifted." Let us recall that Khoma keeps his wits about him even while the old woman is on his back: he remembers various incantations and uses them to free himself from her. And even after that, he does not flee, but, as if revelling in his victory, he leaps on her back himself and then beats her. But when the repulsive old woman turns into a beautiful young girl lying helpless on the ground at his feet, then Khoma "began to tremble, like a leaf on a tree . . . a strange agitation and timidity which he had never before experienced took possession of him, and he began to run at full clip."

As the reader recalls, Khoma does not succeed in escaping the witch after all. It turns out in the course of the story that she is the daughter of a Cossack captain; just before her death, she expresses the desire that Khoma Brut should be the one to read the prayers for the dying over her. When Khoma sees her, she is already dead. Gogol writes that "she was lying in the coffin as if she were still alive"; actually, her death was, so to speak, only relative, for eventually she does rise from her coffin. The description of her extraordinary beauty mentions eyelashes which fall upon "cheeks that were flushed from the heat of hidden desires"; and her lips, in a none too successful metaphor, are called "rubies that were ready to break into a laugh." The witch's beauty (Khoma recognizes her) fills him with terror, and he dies of terror when he looks into the eyes of Viy, who has been led into the church by the demons and monsters that are already there.

In "Viy," as has already been indicated, there is no complete division between the two female figures, that is, between the matchmaker who dominates the "suitor," and the willing but passive bride-to-be. A magical equation of two images takes place: that of the old woman who coerces the will of the man (for the purpose of matchmaking, and, ultimately, of destroying him), and that of the young woman (the object of the "matchmaking"). Here the matchmaker and the bride-to-be are one image, woman in her two manifestations, from whom the man attempts to escape.

In the episode involving the artist Piskaryov in "Nevsky Prospect," the doubling of the female image occurs in the realm not of magic, but of psychology: the "ideal image" arises in Piskaryov's mind as a substitute for the real image, that of the prostitute. This occurs the moment Piskaryov notices the young woman on the Nevsky Prospect: to his eyes, she is the "Bianca of Perugino."

"Shy, retiring, but carrying in his heart sparks of feeling that were ready to burst into flame at an opportune moment," Piskaryov hurries along the Nevsky Prospect after the "Bianca of Perugino," the "object of his pursuit, who had made such a powerful impression on him." Further on, mention is made of "the beautiful young woman who had bewitched him." And as Piskaryov, "trembling all over," hurries along in pursuit of the goal, he in many respects resembles Khoma Brut during the fantastic gallop with the witch on his back. "His breath caught in his chest, he began to quiver all inside, all his feelings were aflame, and everything before him was shrouded in a sort of fog." Or, somewhat later: "The beating of his heart, the irresistible violence and agitation of all his feelings drove him on. . . ." Significant (although not entirely justified by the circumstances) is the very swiftness of his movements, which virtually turn into flying: "He darted over the light traces of the lovely feet, making an effort to moderate the swiftness of his own steps, which flew along in time with the beating of his heart." Or: "The sidewalk rushed past beneath him, the carriages with their trotting horses seemed to stand still." And then: "He saw the beautiful stranger fly up the stairs" and "he flew up the stairs."

Piskaryov finds that he has blundered into a den of sin, where the "real image" is revealed: the girl "gave a meaningful smile, looking him straight in the eye. But this smile brimmed with a sort of pitiable brazenness." Here the woman is offering herself, without the aid of a matchmaker; the man is being invited to participate in a "final outcome." Piskaryov shudders at the sight of her smile, and "instead of taking advantage of such graciousness, instead of rejoicing at such an opportunity, which anyone else in his position would undoubtedly have done, he picked up his heels like a wild goat and rushed headlong out into the street."

Piskaryov cannot bear the thought of depravity, the desecration of "everything pure and holy," the profanation of woman ("the

399

crowning glory of creation") and her beauty, which "blends only with chastity and purity in our thoughts." Like Gogol himself (as, for example, in the essay entitled "Woman," in *Arabesques*), Piskaryov idolizes feminine beauty, thereby making woman (the incarnation of idolized beauty) inviolate. At least, this is the explanation, perhaps not an entirely convincing one, given for his confusion and for his precipitate exit from the house.

As he "flies" up the stairs in pursuit of the beautiful stranger, Piskaryov is described as follows: "His knees trembled; his feelings and thoughts were aflame; joy pierced his heart, with unbearable sharpness, like a bolt of lightning. No, this was no dream! Lord, what happiness in one instant! What a wonderful life in two minutes!" Then mention is made of "ineffable bliss." Podkolyosin also speaks of bliss; he is likewise seared by the flame of love, which is quickly extinguished, and he likewise experiences "a wonderful life in two minutes." And, for all the dissimilarity between Piskaryov, the poor artist, the romantic hero, and Podkolyosin, the very prosaic court councilor, it is nonetheless difficult to avoid setting the two side by side—the one who hops out into the street just before the outcome, and the other, who rushes out into the street like a wild goat. Let us also remember the feelings of ecstasy that Khoma Brut experiences during his mad gallop; the "indefinable feeling of agitation and shyness" which comes over him at the sight of the beautiful young girl, and his panic-stricken flight from her.

The ideal image created by Piskaryov (the "Bianca of Perugino") crumbles when the beautiful girl, refusing to be the object of idolization and adoring contemplation, offers herself, offers an "outcome." She proves to be a matchmaker (or a witch) and a bride-to-be all in one. Piskaryov resurrects the ideal image in his dreams by detaching it from actuality. Let us note one passage from the first dream, in which Piskaryov sees the mysterious beauty at a splendid ball. She sits down next to him: "her hand (oh, Divine Creator, what a superb hand!) dropped on her knee and rested upon her filmy gown . . . and its delicate lilac hue set off the dazzling whiteness of this lovely hand even more (let us recall Piskaryov's remark about "pretty little hands" that are "just like milk"). Just to touch it, and nothing more! No other desires—they would all be insolent."

With the help of opium, Piskaryov does summon up the beautiful vision several times more, in various manifestations, and this

400

vision brings him keen pleasure, but it is a chaste and purely visual pleasure. These nocturnal visions gain a greater and ever more destructive power over him. On one occasion he attempts to heal the terrible "discord between dream and actuality" by trying to change actuality; once more he makes his way to the brothel, in hopes of persuading the girl who has "bewitched" him to share a modest life of toil with him. This attempt ends in failure: it proves impossible to transport terrible actuality into the world of his dream of a chaste and immaculate love and Piskaryov does away with himself. Thus, he becomes the victim of a tragic paradox: he flees from the object of his passion precisely because it is available to him, and such availability strikes him as sacrilegious. Running away, however, does not save him. He is overtaken by the "sorceries" of woman, as is the hero of "Viy." Piskaryov's chaste passion leads him to madness and suicide.

These observations could very likely provide material for a psychological interpretation of Gogol. It is possible that the complex, often enigmatic language of recurrent motifs, images, and situations was the language of Gogol's subconscious. However, we have been interested not in the hidden, subconscious sources of a theme and its variations, but rather in the ways it is consciously employed for artistic purposes. In other words, these notes are concerned primarily with the description and study of particular plot-situations, which vary from work to work according to such factors as: structure; the presence or absence of an element of the fantastic or supernatural; the presence or predominance of an element of the comic; the genre of the work (dramatic or narrative), and so on.

Rather than offer definitive conclusions, we shall turn to still another recurrent motif in Gogol, one which is particularly characteristic of his endings.

In the ending of Part 1 of *Dead Souls*, the carriage in which Chichikov is making his hasty exit from the provincial town of X becomes a "bird-troika"; and this troika, in a rather unexpected metaphor, turns into Russia: she is sweeping along, in some unspecified direction, and "other peoples and nations, eyeing her askance, stand aside and make way for her." Thus, the hero of the "poem," along with his servant Petrushka and his coachman Selifan, make their exit to the jingling of the troika-bell and the song of the teamster; and with them goes the author, the lyrical "I," who has been accompanying Chichikov on his travels.

In the last entry in his diary, Poprishchin, the hero of "Diary of a Madman," cries out: "Give me a troika with steeds swift as a whirlwind! Driver, to your seat! Ring out, little bells! Soar upward, my steeds, and carry me out of this world!" After this comes the vision of a speeding troika, the appeal to "mother" ("Have pity on your poor son!"), and finally the celebrated lump under the nose of the King of France, who was changed to the Dey of Algiers to placate the censors.

The ending of "The Two Ivans" consists of a departure, this time of the narrator himself. It is set in a minor key: there is no troika or jingling bell here. "The scraggy horses, known in Mirgorod as 'couriers' set off, making an unpleasant sound as their hooves sank into the gray sea of mud. The rain poured down in buckets onto the Jew who was sitting on the driver's seat, with a piece of sacking pulled over him." Poprishchin had cried: "Carry me out of this world!" The "Two Ivans" ends with an exclamation by the narrator: "It's a dreary world, my dear sirs!"

In *Marriage*, neither speeding troikas (real or imaginary) nor even sorry Mirgorod nags could be "shown" on the stage, for obvious technical reasons. However, at the end of Scene 21 of the last act, the voice of Podkolyosin, who has just jumped out the window into the street, is heard off stage: "Hey, cabbie!" This is followed by a brief dialogue:

Cabbie's voice: Where to?
Podkolyosin's voice: Kanavka, by the Semyonovsky Bridge.
Cabbie: Ten kopecks, and that's a fair price.
Podkolyosin: All right! Get going! (The rattle of a droshky driving off is heard.)

Act IV of *The Inspector General* also ends with an off-stage dialogue—the farewells that are being exchanged with the departing Khlestakov. At the very end of the dialogue, the "driver's voice" is heard: "Giddyap, my beauties! (The bells jingle. The curtain falls.)" The hero and his servant Osip do not appear on stage again: while the denouement is taking place on stage, they are being carried off by "the best troika, the express," which Osip has ordered in advance.

Khlestakov is not of course running away from matchmaking, but rather from a resolution of an entirely different sort which poses a threat to him. Let us note, nonetheless, that his engagement to Maria Antonovna, the mayor's daughter, takes place just before his departure. Khlestakov, always the improviser, proposes because Maria Antonovna finds him on his knees in front of her mother, Anna Andreyevna; Khlestakov is in that position because just a moment before, the mother had found him on his knees before her daughter. But once he is on his knees before Anna Andreyevna, he proceeds to ask for her hand, brushing aside her objection that she is "in a manner of speaking . . . married." And then, when the daughter appears once more, Khlestakov gets out of a sticky situation by asking for *her* hand. The mother promptly gives her consent, and presses her husband, the mayor, to bestow his blessing quickly. In the next scene, Osip announces that the horses are ready. The "beauties" save Khlestakov from resolutions of any kind. They bear him off into the distance, to the sound of jingling bells, while the other characters in the play, who have been made utter fools of (or rather, who have made fools of themselves), stand petrified, in the celebrated mute scene.

Selected Bibliography
of Works on Gogol in English

(For a much more extensive listing up to the mid-1960's, including works in German and French, see *Letters of Nikolai Gogol*, selected and edited by Carl R. Proffer, Ann Arbor, 1967, pp. 237-243.)

Čiževskij, D. (Chizhevsky). "Gogol: Artist and Thinker," *Annals of the Ukrainian Academy of Arts and Sciences in the USA*, II, No. 2 (4) (1952), 261-276.

————. "The Unknown Gogol," *Slavonic and East European Review*, XXX (1952), 476-493.

Debreczeny, Paul. *Nikolay Gogol and His Contemporary Critics. Transactions of the American Philosophical Society*, New Series, Vol. 56, Part 3 (April, 1966).

Driessen, F. *Gogol as a Short Story-Writer: A Study of His Technique of Composition.* The Hague: Slavistic Printings and Reprintings, 57, 1965.

Erlich, Victor. *Gogol.* New Haven and London, 1969.

Gogol, Nikolay. *The Collected Tales and Plays of Nikolai Gogol*, edited and with an introduction and notes by Leonard J. Kent. New York: The Modern Library, 1969.

————. *Dead Souls*, translated and with foreword by Bernard Guilbert Guerney. Rev. ed. New York: The Modern Library, 1965.

————. *Selected Passages from Correspondence With Friends*, translated by Jesse Zeldin. Nashville, 1968.

Magarshack, David. *Gogol.* London, 1957.

McLean, Hugh. "Gogol and the Whirling Telescope," in *Russia: Essays in History and Literature*, ed. L. H. Legters. Seattle, 1972, pp. 79-99.

————. "Gogol's Retreat From Love: Towards an Interpretation of *Mirgorod*," *American Contributions to the Fourth International Congress of Slavists.* The Hague, 1958, pp. 225-245.

Nabokov, Vladimir. *Nikolai Gogol.* New York, 1961.

Rahv, Philip, "Gogol as a Modern Instance," *Image and Idea.* New York, 1958, pp. 203-209.

Setchkarev, Vsevolod. *Gogol—His Life and Works.* New York, 1965.

Stilman, Leon. "Gogol's Overcoat, Thematic Pattern and Origins," *American Slavic and East European Review*, XI, No. 1 (1952), 138-148.

Todd, William Mills, "Gogol's Epistolary Writing," *Columbia Essays in International Affairs*, v, *The Dean's Papers, 1969*, New York, 1970, 51-76.

Troyat, Henri. *Divided Soul: The Life of Gogol.* New York, 1973.

Wilson, Edmund. "Gogol: the Demon in the Overgrown Garden," *The Nation,* CLXXV (December, 1952), 520-524.

Index of Names

(The number in italics refers to the page on which an annotation occurs.)

Index of Titles of Gogol's Works

Library of Congress Cataloging in Publication Data

Maguire, Robert A.   1930-   comp.
  Gogol from the twentieth century.

  Bibliography: p.
  1. Gogol', Nikolaĭ Vasil'evich, 1809-1852—Criticism and interpretation—
Addresses, essays, lectures.
  I. Title.
PG3335.Z8M18   891.7'8'309   73-16750
  ISBN 0-691-06268-4 (hardcover edn.)

  ISBN 0-691-01326-8 (paperback edn.)